MINIATURE HORSES

THEIR CARE, BREEDING AND COAT COLORS

BARBARA NAVIAUX

Raintree Publications
Fort Bragg, California

This book is dedicated to my four inspirational sons:
Robert Keith, David Bruce, William James and Jeffrey
Steven; and to my eight grandchildren: Ryan, Jordan,
Rebecca, Marina, Nikki, John, Steven and Jacob. Their
unconditional love and faith in me, and my adoration for
them have been the driving force of my adult life.

❧

For information contact:
        Raintree Publications
        P.O. Box 1338
        Fort Bragg, California 95437
        Phone (707) 964-4380 Fax (707) 964-1868
        raintree@mcn.org

Although all reasonable care has been taken in the preparation of this book, neither the author, publisher, contributors or editors can accept any liability for any consequences arising from the use thereof or from the information contained herein.

Library of Congress Catalog Card Number: 98-87725
ISBN: 0-9635964-1-1

Printed in Hong Kong

Foreword

Breeders and owners of miniature horses will consider themselves fortunate to have discovered this comprehensive and authoritative book. Wide-ranging in content, from historical material about breed origins to information on the multiple registry foundations, coat color genetics, nutrition, health care, training and showing, this book will become a standard reference work on managing the breeding and care of these special horses. Barbara Naviaux has experience not only with breeding miniature horses but also with other domestic species (Persian cats) and with large horses (Arabians). Given her medical background, she recognizes the importance of accuracy and use of appropriate reference sources, and therefore much of the information included here is valuable for horse owners and breeders in general, not just for those specializing in miniatures.

At the time of our first contact, the author was chair of the Genetics Committee for the American Miniature Horse Association. She asked my help in promoting the application of genetic principles in the breeding of Miniature Horses. Two of her particular concerns were accurate coat color identification on registration papers and acknowledgment by breeders of debilitating dwarfism problems in some miniature horses.

Historically, the numerous incorrect color identifications by owners and by the registry were probably due to a combination of factors, including lack of understanding of genetics and the high incidence of the silver color-dilution gene, whose effects were not even provided as a color choice on the registration application form until quite recently. It is no surprise that coat color examples are thoroughly documented in this book. While the array of color gene variants is restricted in most horse breeds, probably all the known variants occur in miniature horses. The color genetics section is well worth studying by any horse breeder, particularly for the excellent examples of the silver combinations, extremely frequent in miniature horses and less familiar in larger horses.

The author is a firm proponent of the concept that miniature horses must be physiologically and physically strong, without the debilitating consequences that accompany some forms of dwarfism. To help breeders recognize the undesirable phenotypes, she has provided photographs in this book showing clear examples of dwarfism traits. Unfortunately, lack of definition of the dwarfing genes in miniature horses means that owners currently have no tools with which to make informed decisions about the selection of breeding pairs other than the phenotypic evidence of dwarfism traits. The author recognizes the need to encourage the funding of research in miniature horses so that owners may eventually have the tools to breed genetically healthy horses. Given the current progress in molecular genetics research, including a fast-emerging map of the horse genome, perhaps in the near future the dedication of the author and others to this issue will result in genetic tests that allow breeders to select horses without the genes that produce offspring with debilitating dwarfism characteristics.

Ann T. Bowling, Ph.D.

Bowling is the Executive Associate Director in charge of genetic marker testing (blood typing and DNA testing) of horses at the Veterinary Genetics Laboratory, University of California, Davis. An internationally recognized genetics authority and an active member of the International Society of Animal Genetics, Dr. Bowling is also the Genetics Consultant for Equine Practice: The Journal of Equine Medicine and Surgery for the Practitioner.

Technical Editor	Joanne Abramson
Copy Editor	Annette Gooch
Cover and Interior Design	Hauck and Associates
Illustrators	Marsha Mello
	Barbara Naviaux
Photo Editors	Joanne Abramson
	Barbara Naviaux

Photography

Front Cover:
Pam Olsen PRO PHOTO (top)
   Little King's Buckaroo Bonsai
Nikki Vartikian (left)
   HNF's Quapau
Lisa Davis (middle)
   Haley Davis with *LTD's Red Cloud*
Marjorie Vliet (right)
   Thunderhead's Stardust with *Deer Haven Sparkle*

Back Cover:
Randy Cressall (top)
   Julie Cressall with *Kays Calico* and *West Coasts Sudden Reignbow*
Pam Olsen PRO PHOTO (left)
   Kristin Rasmussen with *FWF Blue Boy's Delft Blue*
Gail Boatman-Eads (right)
   Lance Eads with *MWF Muchos Best Kept Secret*
Harriet Rubins (bottom)
   Haligonian Halation

Interior Photography

Joanne Abramson
Dixie Baker
Devin Baldwin PRO PHOTO
Cheryl Berner
Gail Boatman-Eads
Jim Børtvedt
Ann Bowling
Jack Burchill
Wade Burns
Lisa Davis
Betty Epplin
Joan Flaby
LiLa Foucher Equestrian Photographers
Caroline Fyffe Photography
Susan Hopmans
Lynn Ingles
J Bar D Studios, Inc.
Marsha Kenley
Locke Photography
Jane Macon
Gail Malmberg
L.V. Millon

K. C. Montgomery
Barbara Naviaux
Pam Olsen PRO PHOTO
Photo by FRANK
Julia Ramos
Cloe Rehdantz
Peter J. Replinger
Nancy Rivenburgh
Harriett Rubins
Ronald Scheuring
Kim Sterchi
Mona Stone
Vern Trembly
Nancy Turner
Amy Toner Photography
Nikki Vartikian
Marjorie Vliet
Shari Washburn
Sandy Wesner
Pete West
Works of M'Art

Preface

The goals and dreams we envision for ourselves in life are almost always overshadowed by the inspirational and enlightening process that precedes their attainment. Such is the case with the planning, creation and completion of *Miniature Horses: Their Care, Breeding and Coat Colors*. As each chapter's contents were researched, written, technically verified, and repeatedly edited, it became apparent that much of the information presented had previously been unavailable to miniature horse breeders and other professionals.

This book was written primarily about American Miniature Horses; however, every attempt has been made to make the contents useful to a broad readership of horse owners and breeders worldwide and to make the scientific and medical information accessible to readers who do not have technical backgrounds. This book was written to have international application and includes metric equivalents where appropriate. I hope the readers will find this book as pleasurable to read as it was for me to write.

Acknowledgments

The author is deeply indebted to Ann T. Bowling, Ph.D., whose friendship and willingness to share knowledge have been the basis for several chapters in this work.

The author also wishes to acknowledge Leon B. Blair, Ph.D., whose selfless affection for the miniature horse breed and whose friendship, knowledge, and ethical guidance made this book possible. Now deceased, Dr. Blair founded the American Miniature Horse Association. During his lifetime Blair was never adequately credited for the many important accomplishments on behalf of the miniature horse breed for which he was solely responsible. Without his involvement and expertise, the miniature horse industry would not be what it is today. Rest in peace, Leon.

Appreciation is also due the many photographers, both professional and amateur, who have contributed to this work. Without their beautiful photographs, as well as their enthusiasm and timely cooperation, this book would not have been possible.

The positive influence resulting from my close friendship and long association with Nancy Rivenburgh cannot be overlooked. Since we first worked together on the 1988 AMHA Standard of Perfection Committee, Nancy has been my benevolent mentor and advisor. She has taught me the importance of patience, tolerance, diplomacy and quietude. We have shared our most recently acquired scientific information over the years. Without her encouragement and support, the writing of this book would have never begun.

The professional artistry of scientific illustrator Marsha Mello could not have been rendered more perfectly, nor with more expertise. Her talented contributions to this book have been very much appreciated.

Finally, the author is deeply indebted to publisher, technical editor and inspirational friend Joanne Abramson for her tireless efforts in overseeing, editing, contributing to and producing this book. Without her editing assistance, vision, firm convictions and ambition, this book could never have been completed. I will always be grateful for the unending hours of insightful assistance she has contributed.

Barbara Naviaux
August 1998

Contents

Foreword iii
Preface v
Acknowledgments v

PART ONE: INTRODUCTION

Chapter 1: Origins 1
    What is a Miniature Horse? 1
    Origins of Miniature Horses 2
    History of American Miniature Horses 4

Chapter 2: A History of the American Registries 12
    The Pre-Registry Years 12
    American Miniature Horse Registry, 1971 12
    American Miniature Horse Association, 1978 . 15
    Other Registries, Past and Present 17

PART TWO: GETTING STARTED

Chapter 3: Purchasing Basics 19
    Researching the Breed and Breeders 19
    Intended Use and Price Variations 21
    Breeding Farms 26
    Pre-Purchase Examinations 27
    Written Contracts of Sale 29
    Why Two Different Registries? 29
    Training the Newly Purchased Young Horse . . 30
    Understanding Equine Terminology
        and Usage Conventions 30

Chapter 4: Conformation 32
    Breed Type: Matching Form With Function . . 32
    Standards of Perfection: AMHA and AMHR . . . 35
    Conformation Ideals 38
    Show Disqualifications 42

PART THREE: CARE

Chapter 5: Housing and General Management . 46
    Minimal Housing Requirements 46
    Shelters, Fencing and Pastures 47
    Stallion, Mare and Foal Facilities 51
    Methods of Handling and Restraint 53

Chapter 6: Nutrition and Malnutrition 55
    Water: Quality, Quantity, Availability
        and Temperature 58
    Energy 60
    Fiber 61
    Protein 61
    Vitamins 62
    Minerals 62
    Signs and Correction of Malnutrition 63
    Show Conditioning 63
    Consequences of Obesity 64

Chapter 7: The Normal Miniature Horse 65
    Vital Signs 65
    First Aid Kit 68
    Understanding Laboratory Tests 70
    Veterinary Terminology: Roots, Prefixes
        and Suffixes 73

Chapter 8: Preventative Health Care 75
    Observing Body Weight 75
    Internal Parasite Control 79
    External Parasite Control 85
    Hoof Care and Trimming 90
    Dental Care 93
    Grooming 97
    Mare Smegma 100
    Stress and Contentment 100
    Geriatrics 103

Chapter 9: Diseases 106
    Importance of Isolation 106
    Infectious Diseases of the Equine
        Respiratory Complex 107
    Non-Respiratory Infectious Diseases 108
    Vaccinations 110
    Noninfectious Diseases and Their Prevention 111
    Poisonous Plants 117
    Snake Bites 118
    Injuries and Lameness 119

PART FOUR: BREEDING

Chapter 10: Reproduction *121*
    Mares 122
    Foaling 126
    Post-Foaling 134
    Foals 6 to 18 Months: The Critical Period . . . 136
    Teasing and Breeding Record Charts 138
    Demands of Pregnancy and Lactation 140
    Stallions 140
    Breeding Ethics and Goals 141
    Co-Ownership or Leasing Opportunities 142

Chapter 11: Genetics *144*
    Basic Genetic Terminology 144
    Inbreeding and Hybrid Vigor Balances 150
    DNA Testing and Blood Typing 153
    Congenital Anomalies 154
    Dwarfism Gene Research 160

PART FIVE: COAT COLORS

Chapter 12: Coat Colors and Patterns *165*
    Tests Available for Identifying
        Color Genotypes 166
    Paint or Pinto 170
    Tobiano, Overo or Tovero 170
    Bay Pinto or Tri-Color Pinto 173
    Silver Dapple, (Dapple) Gray or Silver White 174
    Gray or Roan 177
    Roan or Grulla 178
    Buckskin, Palomino, Cremello or White 178
    Cremello or Dun 180
    Sorrel, Chestnut or Red 180
    Black, Bay, Chestnut or Sorrel 181
    Appaloosa or Pintaloosa 181
    Progress in Coat Color Genetics 184

PART SIX: MARKETING AND SHOWING

Chapter 13: Marketing *217*
    Ethics 218
    Keeping Accurate Records 219
    Advertising 224
    Sales Contracts and Agreements 225
    Clientele Support After Sale 225
    Shipping and Transporting 225

Chapter 14: Shows and Show Rules *228*
    What to Expect at the First Show
        as an Observer 228
    What to Expect at the First Show
        as an Exhibitor 230
    Halter Classes or Performance Classes 233
    Judging Conventions 239

Sources 241
Literature Cited 242
Index of Horses' Names 246
Index 248
About the Author 264

CHAPTER 1

Origins

THE GENERAL IMPRESSION OF A MINIATURE should be that of an unusually small, yet sound and well-balanced horse. A good miniature exhibits strength, agility and alertness, and the disposition is eager, willing to please and friendly. The conformation, head and legs of a good miniature horse should be as free of faults as those of any of the larger-sized breeds of horses and ponies.

What is a Miniature Horse?

Miniature horses come in nearly every mane, tail and body color known to the horse world, with all colors, eye colors and/or marking patterns being equally acceptable at the shows and for breeding. All horses registered with the American Miniature Horse Association (AMHA) must measure 34 inches (86 cm) and under as adults. In the American Miniature Horse Registry (AMHR), however, Division A miniatures must be 34 inches (86 cm) and under, and Division B miniatures must be over 34 inches (86 cm), up to and including 38 inches (97 cm). Both registries' height measurements reflect the vertical distance from the base of the last hairs on the mane to the ground. Miniatures must meet the Standards of Perfection (see Chapter 4), which have been carefully researched and written to provide specific guidelines for breeding show-type animals.

These hardy little animals can withstand extremely cold winter weather if they are well nourished and in good condition. Only minimal shelter is necessary when they are allowed to grow their full winter coats. Often a herd of miniatures will purposely stand out in the rain or snow, even when shelter is readily available. Although miniature horses are shown in their natural-length coats throughout Europe, they are usually body clipped for showing in the United States. When clipped, they must be kept stalled and blanketed during cold weather.

There is no more economical horse to keep. To calculate the cost of keeping a miniature, divide the cost of keeping a 1,000-pound (450-kg) horse by about 4. Hay, grain, size and type of pasture or corral, worming products, hoof trimming (shoes are not permitted at the shows), mineral salt blocks and minimal fencing and shelters each cost about one quarter of the amount required for a full-sized horse.

Miniatures are shown throughout the world in breed and performance classes (see Chapter 14). Breed (halter) classes include those divided by ages, sexes, heights and colors. These classes are judged by choosing the animals that best fit the Standard of Perfection in overall quality, conformation and show condition. Performance events include such classes as pleasure driving, roadster, hunter, jumper, obstacle in hand and harness, fine harness and costume. Many types of driving classes, as well as various classes for amateurs and youth, are especially popular at the shows. Miniatures are also used in two-, four-, and six-horse hitches, and are exhibited worldwide in hundreds of parades, county and state fairs and in other special events such as Canada's famous Calgary Stampede. Often, driving groups organize and enjoy the camaraderie of getting together with fellow miniature horse owners for pleasure drives in the country.

Many of the larger miniatures are also trained as gentle and reliable small children's riding ponies. A loving and malleable disposition, as well as very specific training, must always be primary considerations in selecting or developing a child's equine companion and mount. Miniature horses, like horses or ponies of any breed, must be chosen carefully if they are to be in the constant company of a small child. It is important that the child be schooled in horsemanship, equitation and the basics of gentle handling. Without supervision, horses and ponies can develop bad habits when being handled by poorly schooled children, who may have limited regard for kindness to animals. The responsibilities, involvement and excitement of miniature horse ownership, proper care, training and showing provide an engaging solution to some of the problems often encountered with raising young children and teenagers.

Many persons who are unable or unwilling to own full-sized horses, particularly the elderly and the physically challenged, have found the miniature horse to be an ideal substitute. When there is already a love of horses and horse activities, the miniature horse can become an exciting alternative to larger, more powerful equids.

Miniatures are an excellent outlet for people who work in stressful jobs and a practical choice for children who wish to learn about and be around horses. They also can be a rewarding business investment. Well-planned matings, which take into account the qualities of both prospective parents, can yield outstanding foals of show quality that may have an even higher value than either their sire or their dam.

A mare's pregnancy averages approximately 11 months, but shorter and longer gestation periods of as few as 10 months and as many as 12 months are not uncommon in miniatures (Marcella 1992). Although it seems a long wait, the arrival of a 16- to 22-inch (41- to 56-cm) foal is an unforgettable event. Miniature horse mares are almost always excellent mothers and take the feeding, care and education of their foals very seriously.

Intelligent, affectionate, easy to train and easy to care for, miniatures may be enjoyed by young or old, by experienced horsemen or by novices, and even by the physically or mentally challenged. They are very long-lived, often into their 30s, and many are still siring or producing foals into their late 20s. Miniature equidae have been captivating horse lovers worldwide for more than 300 years.

Origins of Miniature Horses

A multitude of colorful myths abounds concerning the origins of American Miniature Horses. Most of these myths originated in an effort to establish the midget pony as a separate breed, unlike and unrelated to other pony breeds. In the United States, midget ponies were not called *miniature horses* until after the formation of the AMHR registry in 1971. It was hoped that this designation would create a unique appeal for miniature horses, which might then generate higher prices than those being obtained for registered and **grade** (unregistered)

Shetland Ponies during the 1960s, 70s, and 80s. Some of these myths referred to miniature horses exclusively having been bred down from full-sized horses. Others referred to them as having been purposefully bred by European royalty, but as a separate breed from small Shetland Ponies, which, at that time, were often less than 38 inches (97 cm) at the top of the withers. Other myths contended that miniatures were the result of natural Darwinian selection for small size, when a small group of horses was trapped within a boxed-in canyon for many generations. The facts, however, have been substantiated by several historical researchers, including Leon B. Blair, Ph.D., official historian of AMHA (Blair 1989). Blair, who founded AMHA in 1978, was the author of AMHR's first Standard of Perfection in 1974.

There is evidence that very small ponies existed as early as 600 A.D. A Celtic stone carving from before the Norse invasions (c. 800 A.D.) clearly depicts unusually small equids of the European Shetland type (Duggan 1972). However, the earliest known written references to midget ponies are two articles published in *Gentlemen's Magazine*, London, England, in 1765 (Blair 1989). One article reports the arrival in England from Bengal of a tiny black stallion measuring only 30 inches (76 cm). The second article reads as follows:

> Captain Tinker in his Majesty's ship 'Medway,' has lately brought from the East Indies, a little mare only two feet four inches [71 cm] high. This little prodigy is four years old and as neatly made as a deer, and perhaps is the greatest curiosity of her kind in the universe. The Captain has landed at Portsmouth, and the mare was brought to the governor's house in a gentleman's lap in a post-chaise and shown to H.R.H. the Duke of Gloucester, who happened to be there at the time on his tour through England.

Each of these little horses was probably imported as a novelty, which lends some substance to the theory that miniature-sized equids were then being bred as playthings for the royalty and landed gentry of Europe. Given the miniatures' diminutive size and very rare occurrence prior to the 19th century, this could well be true, but that speculation has never been historically documented. One author refers to "records which occasionally tell of European royalty having one or two midget ponies for palace children to play with" (Griffen 1966), but investigative historians have been unable to locate or substantiate any of these written records.

At least two paintings produced during the 1800s depict small ponies being ridden by very small children dressed in royal clothing. There is one painting of a prince of Spain, who appears to be about 5 years old, mounted on a very small pony doing a **levade**, a dressage term describing a particular type of controlled and sustained rearing onto the hind legs (Krienke 1987). Another painting of the 1800s, viewed by the author in 1995, suggests that the pony being ridden by the royally dressed youngster is about 34 inches (86 cm) in height. The pony is only slightly taller than the collie running at its side.

Shetland Ponies

Prior to the late 1800s, the earliest island-bred native Shetland Ponies rarely grew taller at the withers than 42 inches (107 cm). Their long, thick manes, tails and coats protected them from the harsh oceanic climates while their small size, compact conformation and extreme hardiness enabled them to survive and reproduce with limited sources of food and shelter. Even today, there is a distinct difference between the native island type of Shetland Pony and the Classic (American type) Shetland Pony, with the latter often being taller, more refined and of smaller bone. The American Shetland Pony Club (ASPC) sets the maximum height for American Shetland Ponies of any of the three types allowed for registry (Classic, Modern, and American Show Pony) at 46 inches (117 cm). However, the maximum height allowed for Shetlands registered in England through the Shetland Pony Stud Book Society is still only 42 inches (107 cm).

Although there were no Shetland Pony registries until the late 1800s and no Standard of Perfection for the breed, the native Shetland Pony had been bred for many years on the 550-square-mile (880-km) area of the various Shetland Islands. Noted for harsh weather and limited forage, the Shetland Isles are in the North Atlantic ocean, about 105 miles (168 km) northeast of Scotland. In the early 1800s, Shetlands Ponies were small, extremely hardy, strong, and heavy set, used primarily as small draft animals and as children's pets. Only a few were then being shipped out (on small sailing vessels) to other countries. However, a radical change occurred in 1847 when an Act of Parliament was passed, prohibiting children from working in the coal mines. Children had been employed for pulling coal tubs along the seams, many of which were too low to allow even a child to stand upright. Almost immediately there was a great demand from mine owners for the smallest of Shetland Ponies and a corresponding sales explosion. In the 1850s a mature, stout, short-statured pony would command a very substantial price, even by today's standards, and more than 500 of the smallest (usually stallions and geldings) were shipped annually from the Shetland Isles, for use in European coal mines (Boomhower 1990).

One British mine owner who realized the importance of pedigree documentation and improvement of the Shetland breed was the Marquis of Londonderry. In 1890 he founded the oldest of the British native pony societies and, with other mine owners, was largely responsible for the formation of the British registry as well as for the printing of its first Shetland Pony stud book in 1891.

History of American Miniature Horses

News of the European small pony boom traveled rapidly to the United States. In July of 1888, a short article in an Iowa newspaper read as follows:

> Eli Elliott came in Saturday night all the way from the Shetland Islands and brought with him pretty much all of the merchantable ponies the islands contained, 140 frisky, lively little rascals, among them, 'Yum Yum', a pony just 31 inches [79 cm] high and full grown.

This article described the last of three sizable importations made by Eli Elliott, a United States trader of cattle and horses, from the Shetland Islands (Bedell 1959). Many of the ponies Elliot imported were subsequently registered with the ASPC, which in 1888 had begun registering Shetland Ponies, with the purpose of guarding the purity of the stock and maintaining reliable records of pedigrees and transfers. The ASPC was one of the very first equine registries established in the United States: Volume I of the ASPC Stud Book, published in 1893, contained 72 individuals, while Volume I of the (American) Arabian Horse Club Stud Book, published in 1908, contained only 76 individuals. With the printed records of this earliest of Shetland stud books, it is well documented that many registered Shetlands were as small as 28 inches (71 cm), and 36 of the 72 entries were registered as being under 38 inches (97 cm) in height (at the top of the withers).

Also well documented in these early records is the prevalence of silver dapple coloration in the Shetland (Castle & Smith 1953; Castle 1960) and, much later, in the miniature horse (Naviaux 1991, 1995). Castle's original article was entitled "Silver Dapple, A Unique Color Variety Among Shetland Ponies," published in *The Journal of Heredity*. The beautiful silver dapple patterns and colors occur only rarely in other breeds of American horses and ponies.

Elliott wrote an impressive "Historical Sketch," which appeared in Volume I of the ASPC Stud Book, published in 1893. He and his family had come to Iowa in 1855, and in the early 1880s he traveled over much of the western United States, buying and selling cattle and horses. Elliott's ponies were primarily of small size. He once wrote, "As long as I can get them straight in the legs and round in the body they cannot be too small." Eli Elliott died in 1917 after spending his life breeding the smallest of Shetland Ponies (Bedell 1959).

In the late 1800s, when many other small equids were being imported from Europe and the Shetland Isles, there were several additional well-documented occurrences of 30-inch (76-cm) and smaller animals being among them. The American Shetland breeders' habit of maintaining correct pedigrees and recording accurate heights of their smallest registered animals was becoming widespread and well documented by published records within the ASPC Stud Books.

Two other early pioneers credited with the purposeful development of miniatures in the United States were Moorman Field (often misspelled "Norman Fields") and Smith McCoy. Moorman Field, who bred and raised miniatures for 53 years, supplied Virginia coal mines with most of their 30-inch (76-cm) and under midget ponies. Tiny draft animals such as these were still being used in Appalachian coal mines as late as 1950 (Bedell 1959).

Beginning in the early 1930s, Field began forming a breeding herd of miniatures by importing the smallest of Shetland **pit ponies** (ponies used in mine pits) from Europe. He also purchased 20 of the smallest mares offered at a 1947 pony sale held in Orange, Virginia. All of the 120 ponies consigned to this sale had originally been imported from Holland by a Canadian enthusiast named Stewart (Pauley 1980).

An advertisement for "Marks' Palomino Pony Farm," which appeared in the April 1957 issue of the *ASPC Journal*, is similar to a few other Shetland breeders' advertisements of the 1950s. At that time, Mr. Marks of Winchester, Virginia, was the owner of *My Golden Toy*, a registered Shetland appearing on the cover of that same issue. Marks offered 10 ponies for sale, all sired by *My Golden Toy*, and his advertisement states: "Anyone wishing to breed quality ponies of the miniature type should latch on to one of these as they are perfect all over, the type you do not see every day. All of these foals should mature at 35 to 38 inches [89 to 97 cm]." *My Golden Toy*, later sold to Gene Hash of Petaluma, California, was the sire of many small Shetlands under 36 inches (91 cm) during the early 1960s.

By the early 1960s many farms were specializing in the raising of miniature-type Shetland ponies (Cabell Self 1964). Prior to 1964, Margaret Cabell Self personally visited a large breeding farm of miniatures in Roanoke, Virginia. She does not specify the owner's name, but offers the following description:

We saw a sign, 'Ponies for Sale,' outside a rather ramshackle-looking barn. It was not a very good day to look at ponies, being drizzly and gray, but we went in anyway, expecting to be shown perhaps a dozen animals. To our surprise this barn housed several hundred ponies of the miniature type. None were over 36 inches [91 cm] high at the withers and many were under. They looked like little fairy horses; their tails dragged the ground and their manes were so soft and silky and full that often only the very tips of the ears were visible. Unfortunately, though their small size makes them enchanting, these very small ponies are really only proportioned for the child under five or six. They are very strong, however, and do make excellent driving ponies.

Moorman Field's farm consisted of 600 acres of beautiful, rolling, lush green pastures in the foothills of the Blue Ridge Mountains. At one time there were said to be 900 full-sized horses and ponies grazing together there, of which 50 were the smallest of miniatures. In 1964, Moorman Field and his son, Tom, still had about 50 miniatures in their breeding herd. One of their mares, nicknamed "Fast Mare," had a live foal every year until she was 35 years old; 80% of her foals were fillies. She never received any medication during her entire life and did not die until she was 41 years of age. After Moorman's death in 1967, Tom Field continued raising the little horses for several years, but by 1980 he had retained only two, a mare and a stallion (Pauley 1980, Blair 1989).

Meanwhile, Smith McCoy was in the process of developing the largest herd of midget ponies in the United States, with very few over 32 inches (81 cm) tall. McCoy was a prolific writer and as a result, his activities in the industry were more easily followed than those of his predecessors and peers. His written confrontations with the Falabella family in Argentina over some of their claims became well known and widely publicized (McCoy 1963). In a 1963 article, McCoy wrote:

> I'm afraid I don't agree with the man in Argentina about his 20 inch [51 cm] ponies. I believe they are at least 31 inches [79 cm], not 20 inches [51 cm]. If anyone can show me a full grown, 20 inch [51 cm] pony that is not a dwarf and I can't buy that pony, I'll gladly donate $100. to their favorite charity! I believe I am the only person in the United States, or in the world perhaps, raising ponies under 32 inches [81 cm] exclusively.

McCoy traveled over the entire United States searching for the smallest of Shetland Ponies and was able to purchase a dozen or so that met his requirements of being less than 33 inches (84 cm) at the top of the withers. From these few ponies, by breeding the smallest back to the smallest, and with considerable inbreeding, he was able to increase his herd to well over 200. Many far-sighted and enthusiastic early miniature breeders obtained their first foundation stock from the Smith McCoy final dispersal sale (Pauley 1981).

Prior to McCoy's last sale of 1967, an exotic zoo animal importer and exporter named Alton Freeman purchased 40 head of the McCoy herd. Freeman sold a large number of his acquisitions to zoos and individuals in other countries. A few were retained, however, and his home-bred 30-inch (76-cm) stallion *Freeman's Star* is recorded as being the "legendary sire of the first registered American Miniature Horse" (Iron Gate Farm 1985).

A Midget Pony Sale

SATURDAY, SEPTEMBER 16, 1967 -- 2 O'CLOCK

Tazewell County Livestock Market, TAZEWELL, VIRGINIA

Located on Route 19-460, 18 Miles Southwest of BLUEFIELD, W. VA.   THERE ARE PLENTY OF MOTELS AND HOTELS

The kind of a Sale that's never been held before, anywhere in the World

I'LL HAVE THE SMALLEST PONY IN THE WORLD FOR YOU TO SEE

I am selling 80 out of the herd of the world's smallest midget ponies. The largest pony in this sale will be under 34" tall, down to 28½"; full-grown, over three years old. The big majority of them will be under 32" tall, full-grown. Many will have a foal with them. Around ten good breeding stallions will be sold. The colors are red, black, dapple, and spotted. I have around 100 of these midget ponies, after twelve years of careful breeding. I also have a large general store, with only fifteen acres for the ponies; and don't have the time it takes to sell one at a time. I have only sold these ponies in eight different states and three foreign countries. So, you can see, you have the whole world to work.

For Further Information, Write

SMITH McCOY

Box 68, Roderfield, W. Va. 24881

If anyone can bring a pony to the sale, as little and as good (not a dwarf) he gets $100 Free

Whether you want to buy or not, come and see the world's smallest pony with good conformation.

TERMS — CASH AT THE TIME OF SALE F. O. B. TAZEWELL, VA.

No ponies or horses will be sold, at the sale, inside or out, except McCoys midgets!

Figure 1.1 A copy of the poster advertising Smith McCoy's final dispersal sale of 1967.

Because herd records and reliable pedigrees had not been maintained by most miniature breeders prior to 1971, accurate documentation of their ancestry was both elusive and rare. Many breeders seemed to prefer the more interesting myths that prevailed at the time and chose to drop from their recorded pedigrees many registered Shetland Ponies known by them to have appeared in the ancestry. The literature was saturated with accounts of miniature horses being rescued from a remote canyon and anecdotal references concerning the miniature horse's descent from only full-sized horse breeds.

Figure 1.2 *Reproduction of early postcards featuring the "Little Wild Horses from Grand Canyon." Note the short length of the manes and tails, which indicates that the horses were very young foals less than 2 months of age, not mature animals.*

Up until 1971, heavy demands and high prices dictated that emphasis on small size would prevail, with little regard for conformation and accuracy of pedigree. For this reason, early breeders often encountered dwarfism characteristics in their tiniest stock (see Chapters 4 and 11). Maintaining predictable gene pools, without excessive inbreeding, is dependent upon meticulous herd records. The necessity for a means of recording and registering miniatures in the United States was quickly evident.

When the AMHR registry was first established in 1971, many of the first recorded miniature horses were registered with unknown backgrounds when, in fact, their ancestry sometimes could have been easily traced by the breeders and owners of record. Of the 209 miniature horses registered in the first AMHR Stud Book of 1972, only 60 were listed as having any known parentage, but 14 of those 60 were recorded as being sired by registered Shetlands. Well-known stallions such as *Gold Melody Boy, My Golden Toy, C-Jo's Topper, Charro of Arenosa* and *Rowdy* are excellent examples of Shetlands that became important foundation sires of the miniature horse breed (Roberts 1960). Originally, both the AMHR and AMHA (later formed in 1978) were open registries for any horse measuring 34 inches (86 cm) or under, and known parentage was not a requirement for registration.

By May of 1998 there were 87,000 miniature horses registered with AMHA and 86,000 registered with AMHR. Breeding, showing and owning miniature horses has become a fascinating and lucrative hobby for horse lovers in every country.

Falabellas

In 1962, Julio Cesar Falabella, whose ranch was near Buenos Aires, Argentina, sold some midget ponies to President Kennedy's family, an event that brought instant fame to the Falabella Ranch's colorful and attractive little horses. The Falabella strain of miniatures was originally started in 1868 by Julio's great-grandfather, Patrick Newell. When Newell died, he passed on the herd and his breeding methods to his son-in-law, Juan Falabella. Juan added European Shetland blood and, with considerable inbreeding, was able to gain consistently small size within the herd (Griffen 1966). Juan's son, Emilio Falabella, later passed the herd on to his son, Julio Cesar Falabella. In 1980, when Julio Cesar passed away, both the herd and ranches were divided between his second wife, Maria Luisa, and his daughter, Maria Angelica.

Today, Maria Angelica Falabella resides in the United States, although she maintains a breeding herd of approximately 200 animals in Argentina. She also maintains a 100% pure Falabella herd of about 70 animals in Roebuck, South Carolina. When new blood is desired, she obtains individuals from her herd in Argentina and does not include any miniatures of non-Falabella lineage (M.A. Falabella pers. comm. 1997).

Although the earliest Falabella ranch owners did not keep records, it has been verified by investigative historians that the main stock used to reduce size was Shetland (Griffen 1966; Blair 1989). However, many of the little horses are vividly marked with appaloosa spots, which could not have been inherited from Shetland Ponies, as the pattern does not occur in that breed. For this reason, it is possible that the Criollo and the short-legged Petizo, both Argentinean ponies, as well as other native stock, contributed to some of the original herd's breeding animals (Brady 1969).

Also in the early 1960s, the Regina Winery of Edwina, California, imported some stock from the Falabella family herd in Argentina. Some of these horses were later acquired by a few California miniature breeders. Probably the best known of the Regina Winery's importation of miniatures was the appaloosa stallion *Chianti* (purchased by Dixie Blasingame) and the solid brown mare *Regina* (purchased by Ron and Sami Scheuring).

Jack Burchill

Figure 1.3 *100% Falabella (imported from Argentina) black appaloosa stallion, now hardshipped into AMHA as* Grosshills Comofin. *Breeder: Angelica Falabella. Owner: Jack Burchill.*

Prior to the mid 1960s, the exclusive distributor of Falabellas in the United States, Canada, Mexico, Central America and the West Indies was the Falabella Miniature Horse Farms, Inc., Scarborough-on-Hudson, New York. Prices at that time ranged from $1,500 for a gelding to $2,000 for a mare and $3,000 for a stallion. Famous persons acquiring the miniatures with the help of this agency included David Sarnoff (president of NBC) and actors Yul Brynner, who had two Falabellas in Switzerland and Helmut Dantine (Griffen 1966). Many Falabella-bred miniatures have since been imported from Argentina, and there are a few breeders who now specialize in Falabella stock.

Falabellas are not a separate breed of miniature horse but were developed in Argentina at about the same time that miniature horses were being developed in the United States and other countries (McCoy 1963, Griffen 1966). Falabellas were widely publicized, however, because of their acquisition by various United States celebrities. Most miniature horses currently registered and being shown with the AMHA and AMHR have no Falabella-bred ancestors. Since the closure of both North American registries, Falabella-bred miniatures cannot be registered with the AMHA or the AMHR unless they are hardshipped into those registries. Under the hardship clauses, the written records of their known pedigrees are lost on the registration certificates and must be privately maintained by the breeder.

Although Falabellas have been an important part of the history of miniature horses in the United States, it is unfortunate that some writers and editors of general horse encyclopedias have considered them the *only* history. More than 150,000 miniatures are registered in the United States, and the national shows boast entries of more than 1,000 registered miniatures each year, very few of which are Falabella bred. It is inaccurate that some encyclopedias refer only to the "Falabella" in their indexes and text rather than the American Miniature Horse breed (Edwards 1993; McBane 1997). No reference to "miniature horse" may be found in the index of *Horses: The Visual Guide to Over 100 Horse Breeds from Around the World*, which is considered to be a comprehensive listing of the world's breeds of horses (Edwards 1993). Listed under "Ponies," the section on miniatures reads as if American Miniature Horses were all descended from Falabellas. Also using "Falabella" as a synonym for "miniature horse" is the *U. C. Davis School of Veterinary Medicine Book of Horses* (Siegal 1996). Although "miniature horse" may be found in the index of this volume, most of the text refers only to the "Falabella" and makes no reference to the more than 15,000 American-bred miniatures now registered each year in the United States.

CHAPTER 2

A History of the American Registries

B EGINNING IN THE 1950s, while miniature horses were still being called midget ponies, many breeders began realizing the importance of keeping accurate pedigrees and in carefully planning matings. Simply breeding the smallest to the smallest did not always result in quality animals that stayed within the desired height limits. Although market values of the smallest miniatures remained high, most breeders were becoming increasingly aware that improvements in conformation, refinement and type would be required in the near future. Such improvements would necessitate more accurate breeding farm records to increase the predictability of certain matings.

The Pre-Registry Years

Prior to the 1940s, little was known about horse genetics and even less had been researched and published by professionals. For example, the first scientific paper on equine coat color genetics was not published until the late 1940s (Castle 1948). By the late 1960s miniatures were being bred in several different herds within the United States, and some breeders were beginning to make discoveries (that had not yet been observed in the scientific community) about the intricacies of miniature horse genetics. In addition to those already being bred in North America, miniatures were continuing to be imported in the early 1970s in large numbers from such countries as Argentina, England, Holland and Belgium. Without a miniature horse registry to document pedigrees, establish a Standard of Perfection and sponsor shows with licensed judges, the breeders were working at a great disadvantage. Furthermore, buyers of the expensive little horses were beginning to demand better documentation of their animals' backgrounds.

American Miniature Horse Registry, 1971

In March of 1971, the foundation was established for what was to become the American Miniature Horse Registry (AMHR). Executive Secretary Burt Zuege, President Robert Huston and Director George Hart of the American Shetland Pony Club (ASPC) met with a small group of dedicated breeders to discuss the feasibility of starting a midget pony/miniature horse registry. Included in that original group were Bill Ferguson, Alton Freeman, Allen Goforth, Billie Howell, Russell Jackson, Ray Lee, Delmer Moody and Earl "Bud" Soat (Blair 1989). In 1997, Soat still held an active position on the AMHA Board of Directors.

Essentially the same group (minus Hart and Howell) met again in August of 1971 to formulate rules and regulations for the registry. During that month, AMHR became the first registry in the United States for American Miniature Horses. It was agreed that the AMHR was to be owned and administrated by the ASPC, but miniature breeders were to have input through a standing American Miniature Horse Committee. ASPC Director George Hart was to provide representation for the miniature breeders on the ASPC Board, and the ASPC *Pony Journal* was to begin including news and advertisements about miniatures, in addition to Shetland Ponies.

Miniatures 34 inches (86 cm) and under were first approved and, after lengthy debate, the original committee members changed the method of measurement to the "last hairs of the mane." This method was a compromise between those who wished the measurement to be made at the top of the withers and those who felt it should be made in the middle of the back. The final decision to set the height at 34 inches (86 cm) also was a compromise, with other choices ranging from under 32 inches (81 cm) to over 36 inches (91 cm). At that time, no other requirements for registry were included.

It was not until much later that efforts were made to begin writing a basic Standard of Perfection (see Chapter 4). In 1974, Dr. Leon B. Blair chaired the committee that wrote the first Standard of Perfection for AMHR, which was later used as a basic standard by several other associations as they formed. Slight revisions to the AMHR Standard of Perfection were made at the 1994 annual meeting and it has remained unchanged since that time.

Most of the founding group's members had 34-inch (86-cm) and under miniatures that they wished to register immediately. To determine which horse was to be #001, as well as the animals' subsequent order in the Stud Book, each of the horses' names was placed in a hat and drawn out (C. Rehdantz pers. comm.1997). The first name drawn was *Mini Pony Tony*. Thus, the first American Miniature Horse registered became Russell Jackson's mature stallion, *Mini Pony Tony*, 29 inches (74 cm), registration #001P. The letter "P" designates a 3-year-old, or older, mature animal that is being permanently (rather than temporarily) registered. Registered in January of 1972, this little horse was purchased later that year by Delmer Moody for $10,000. According to an advertisement that appeared in *Miniature Horse World* magazine (Iron Gate Farm 1985), *Mini Pony Tony* was sired by *Freeman's Star*, a 30-inch (76-cm) strawberry roan stallion, originally registered as #058 to Alton V. Freeman. By 1985, *Freeman's Star* was owned by Iron Gate Farm in Bristol, Wisconsin, and his stud fee was advertised at $3,500. According to the AMHR Stud Book, however, *Mini Pony Tony* had an unknown sire and dam, as did all but one of the horses registered until #055 *Hobby Horse Hill's Tiny Tim*, sired by *Tiny Tim* (who had been registered with known parentage as #015. Following the "Tiny Tims," no known parentage was listed on any animal until #067 and #068. Both of these were mares (mother and daughter) bred and owned by Audrey M. Barrett of Victoria, Texas, and both were listed as being sired by two different registered Shetland Ponies. From the beginning, Audrey Barrett's miniatures were always registered with their correct Shetland heritage clearly specified. Since the death of Audrey Barrett, Cheryl Wilson (1995) has continued with the Audrey Barrett (Arenosa line) ponies and now breeds, advertises and sells them honestly as "Miniature Shetlands."

By the end of 1972, there were 209 miniature horses registered with the AMHR. Of these, 149 were registered with unknown sires and dams. Owners and ranch names registering animals in 1972 included many that may be of interest to historians. Listed in chronological order (of their horses' registered numbers), they were Russell Jackson (Mini), Indiana;

Delmer Moody (Del's), Missouri; C. M. and Lucy Bond (Bond Miniature Horse Farm), Georgia; C. H. Stetler (Lil' Ponderosa), Tennessee; Ray and Ruby Lee (Shady Acres Pony Farm), Kentucky; Capt. Alwin R. Brown (Hobbyhorse), Texas; Jean Hatch (Tinkerville), Connecticut; Rick Rader (Hobby Horse Hill), Tennessee; Alton V. Freeman (Freeman's), North Carolina; Gerald Spirek, Illinois; Faith Taylor (Snow Fire), California; H. H. Hess, Iowa; P. A. Madaris, Indiana; Audrey M. Barrett (Arenosa), Texas; James K. Murphy (Hilltops), Iowa; Billy M. Howell ("Moto"), Tennessee; Joel R. Bridges (Komokos), Florida; John F. Dedear (Dedear's), Missouri; Betty A. Lavelock, Missouri; Charles and Marguerite Coxe (Just), Oregon; L. C. Mitchell, Australia; Dick Cornellier (Montana Mini Horses), Montana; Robert I. Kinsel, Jr., Texas; and Rayford Ely, California.

By the end of 1973, another 662 animals had been added to the registry, bringing the total number of AMHR-registered miniatures to 871, as is documented by the AMHR Stud Books of 1972 and 1973. On December 31, 1973, the registry was officially closed to any horses whose sire and dam were not registered with AMHR. With only 871 miniatures in the registry, many members felt that the closure was premature. The miniature horse gene pool was dangerously small and excessive inbreeding was undoubtedly encouraged by this controversial action. Unfortunately, the AMHR membership was not allowed to vote on this matter. In AMHR, decision-making rests primarily with the ASPC Board; very few decisions are actually made by the AMHR miniature horse breeding membership. Even today, miniature horse breeders cannot hold positions on the ASPC/AMHR Board unless they also breed Shetland Ponies. Active breeding of registered Shetland Ponies for at least 5 years is a requirement for becoming a voting Board of Directors member, and breeders of only miniature horses are not eligible for any office, even though more than 90% of the ASPC/AMHR registry is financially supported by the miniature horse industry.

The ASPC/AMHR Board, after realizing their error and enduring the formation of several other competitive registries (in direct opposition to the closure of AMHR and to the ASPC's apparent lack of interest in miniature horse breed promotion), decided to re-open the AMHR registry in 1982. Horses with unknown background were again allowed into the registry, provided their heights were 34 inches (86 cm) or under.

In 1986, a momentous decision was made by the Board of Directors that would forever change the course of miniature horse breeding. The AMHR registry requirements were expanded to include a division for horses up through 38 inches (97 cm). All AMHR shows, including the Nationals, would now include classes for both Division A (34 inches [86 cm] and under) and Division B (over 34 inches [86 cm]), up to and including 38 inches (97 cm) American Miniature Horses. The first Division B horse to be registered was Jean Hatch's 37.5-inch (95 cm) chestnut stallion, *Tinkerville Hobby* (Hatch & Parnell 1996).

The registry was again closed December 31, 1994. Since that date, all miniature horses are required to have an AMHR-registered sire and dam in order to obtain AMHR papers. There is a hardship clause, however, that makes it possible to register an animal with unknown background. The horse must be officially measured by an AMHR-licensed steward and verified to be within the specified height limits. There are substantial hardship fees. However, AMHA-registered horses are also accepted for AMHR registration (subject to submission of the required paperwork and fees) and do not require a hardship fee.

There were more than 900 animals at the 1997 American Miniature Horse Registry's

National Show held in Columbia, Missouri, and currently there are more than 86,000 AMHR-registered American Miniature Horses (D. Diemer pers. comm. 1998).

American Miniature Horse Association, 1978

On July 26, 1978, the American Miniature Horse Association (AMHA) was chartered with Leon B. Blair, who had chaired the committee that in 1974 developed the first AMHR Standard of Perfection, as president. The incorporators were Blair, Michelle Jones (Blair's daughter), Charles F. Palmer and Beverly Thompson, with the sizable initial funding solely provided by Blair (E. Blair pers. comm. 1997). An organizational meeting of the new association was called for October 14, 1978, with 28 charter members in attendance. They ratified bylaws and elected Charles Palmer as the new president. Blair became executive vice president and chief administrative officer and was assisted by the registrar, Glyndean LaPlante. The association also adopted a Standard of Perfection largely based on that written earlier by the 1974 AMHR Standard of Perfection committee.

Figure 2.1 *Leon B. Blair, holding* Sligo Nikki, *one of his Sligo farm-bred foals. Now deceased, Blair was the founding president of the AMHA and editor of AMHA's first* Miniature Horse World *magazines from 1981 to 1984. He was appointed the AMHA Official Historian in 1988, the 10th anniversary of the registry. Blair's miniature horse measuring device, the Sligo Stick, is still considered by many to be the most reliable, durable and affordable.*

Almost concurrently with the organizational activity in the Midwest and Southwest that resulted in AMHA, breeders in California, under the leadership of Rayford Ely and James Hill, organized the International Miniature Horse Registry (IMHR). Although the first organizational meetings were held in 1976, IMHR was not chartered until October 4, 1978. Earlier discussions in July 1978 by the principals of both AMHA and IMHR about joining efforts in a single organization were not productive because of differences in the basic concept of governance, whether by the members (as proposed by AMHA) or by a small directorate (as proposed by IMHR). However, efforts to merge the AMHA and IMHR continued, and the occurrence of that merger is discussed later in this chapter.

AMHA registered its first horse, Dixie Blasingame's *Shadow Oaks Paul Bunyan*, on November 16, 1978. The horse had already been registered in IMHR, so he was given AMHA number TR I 00001B. The "TR I" designated that the horse was being transferred from IMHR. Anticipating that many horses already registered with AMHR and IMHR would transfer to the new association and in order to keep the same name and registry numbers, AMHA used #3000 as the first new number, providing room for almost 2,000 horses already known to be registered with AMHR and IMHR. In the spring of 1979 (and again in 1983) AMHA offered to purchase AMHR from the American Shetland Pony Club, but each time its offers of $10,000 were rejected (Blair 1989).

Blair edited the initial *Miniature Horse World* magazines, the first of which was published in January 1981. The early AMHA *Worlds* were 5.5 by 8.5 inches (14 by 22 cm), predominantly in black and white, but each of the quarterly issues was filled with educational articles, interesting news and many advertisements from breeders. AMHA membership participation was enthusiastic and supportive, even though IMHR's magazine, *The Miniature Horse Journal*, had been being published quarterly since the spring of 1979. Additionally, the American Shetland Pony Club was continuing to publish their *Pony Journal,* which was supposed to include all of the news and advertisements concerning AMHR-registered miniature horses. All three magazines were the same size and all were published at least quarterly. They were of comparable quality, but the *Pony Journal* continued to be devoted primarily to Shetland Ponies.

Blair continued as editor of the AMHA *World* until February/March 1984, when Barbara Ashby (formerly associate editor) became the new editor. In February 1985, the format was changed to an 8.25- by 10.75-inch (21- by 27- cm) size, with the addition of more color and more than 120 pages. However, the front cover carried the title *Miniature Horse World, the Official Publication of the International American Miniature Horse Association* and the issue was labeled Vol. 1, No. 1. Because the previous issue of the *World* had been dated January 1985 and was labeled Vol. 5, No. 1, many AMHA members became incensed that 17 prior issues of the official AMHA magazine had been disregarded, and that all of Blair's efforts as the previous editor had been effectively eliminated from the registry's history. Although the correct volume numbers were never restored, the word *International* was dropped in August/September of 1985 and the *World* magazine was again the *Official Publication of the American Miniature Horse Association.*

The AMHA officially closed their registry on December 31, 1987, and all horses registered since that time are required to have AMHA-registered sires and dams. However, a hardship clause is in place that allows horses with unspecified backgrounds, and that also meet the 34-inch (86-cm) and under height requirement, to be registered for a substantial fee. The animal in question is required to be officially measured by a regional director or at an AMHA-approved show, and DNA or blood typing of the individual also is required.

AMHA's first Rules and Regulations Handbook and first Stud Book, Volume I, were both published in 1988. The latter included 28,000 horses, along with their pedigrees, heights and breeders. Volumes II through VII of the Stud Books were printed in 1990. Now accessible via the Internet, on CD-ROMs and in book form, the Stud Books include every horse registered in AMHA since its first entry in 1978.

After a year's research and development by the Standard of Perfection Committee, the AMHA standard was expanded and revised in 1988, and the revisions were approved by the membership at the 1988 annual meeting. Chaired by the author, the committee included Verna King, Nancy Rivenburgh and the standard's original author, Blair.

Late in 1989, the author proposed the formation of an AMHA Genetics Committee at the annual meeting. Board approval was gained almost immediately and the author became the chairman for three years of AMHA's first Genetics Committee. The committee was initially responsible for research and education covering the subjects of blood typing/DNA, coat color inheritance and identification, and dwarfism. The 1989–1992 Genetics Committee was ultimately responsible for many major changes within the registry, such as the acceptance of Dr. Ann Bowling's blood typing and DNA programs (Abramson 1997) for miniatures (University of California, Davis), Bowling's on-going research project on dwarfism and the important addition of "silver dapple" as a coat color to the AMHA registration applications.

The AMHA has witnessed substantial growth and vastly improved solidarity since those early years. There are currently more than 87,000 horses registered with the AMHA and more than 900 miniatures competed at the 1997 AMHA National Show, held in Lexington, Virginia.

Other Registries, Past and Present

By 1985, there were a total of eight United States miniature horse registries: the Shetland Pony Club's American Miniature Horse Registry (AMHR), founded in 1971; a Falabella Registry in Pennsylvania, 1974; the International Miniature Horse Registry (IMHR), 1976; the American Miniature Horse Association (AMHA), 1978; the World Wide Miniature Horse Registry, 1983; the Equuleus Miniature Horse Registry (Equuleus), 1983; the Miniature Show Horse Registry, 1983; and the International American Miniature Horse Association (IAMHA), 1985 (Nystrom 1984; Blair 1989). At the time there was considerable controversy concerning which of these might survive or would possibly merge. A few of these registries still exist, but the AMHR and AMHA currently control at least 90% of the registrations, shows, magazine subscriptions and membership activity.

Each of these registries was formed for specific reasons and each had most of their members concentrated in specific areas such as California, Texas, Florida and the Midwest. However, all of the registries had members and supporters nationwide. Not trusting which registries might survive, many breeders became members of multiple associations, subscribed to and advertised in multiple magazines and had double-, triple- and even quadruple-registered miniature horses. The expense to the industry was enormous, both in dollars as well as in the loss of members who became disenchanted with all of the conflicting information. Political power struggles, personality conflicts and internal squabbles caused many to lose sight of the great need for accurate pedigrees, breed improvement and well-run, high-quality shows, and for the breed's international acceptance by judges and breeders within other equine registries.

Equuleus and IMHR both merged with AMHA in 1986 and many horses registered in AMHA still carry their original numbers from those associations, even though they are now valid AMHA-registered animals. D. J. and Marilyn Nystrom were editors and publishers of the *Equuleus* quarterly magazines from January 1983 until February 1985, when Nystrom Lithocraft Corporation became the publisher of the new IAMHA's *Miniature Horse World* magazine. Marilyn Nystrom and her corporation have continued to publish and produce AMHA's *Miniature Horse World* since that time.

During the 1990s, more registries were formed, including the Classic Miniature Horse Registry, in Alabama; the International Miniature Horse Trotters and Pacers, in Texas; the World Class Miniature Horse Registry, in Virginia; the Universal Miniature Horse Registry, in Texas; and Gold Seal Miniature Horse Registry Corporation, in West Virginia.

Although the championship miniature horses of today bear little resemblance to the small equidae from which they descended, it is imperative that miniature owners remain vigilant in their quest for individuals that meet the Standard of Perfection. Registries have come and gone, but the heart of the industry has always been the morally responsible individual breeders whose efforts are aimed at improvement in the quality of miniatures being raised at their own particular farms. Those breeders have always put high-quality horses and professional ethics far above personal financial gain. It is hoped that accurate pedigrees and genetically knowledgeable breeders will continue to write the history of miniature horses in future years.

CHAPTER 3

Purchasing Basics

B ECAUSE OF THEIR SMALL SIZE, their calm nature, economical care, and the ease with which they may be trained. miniatures have become one of the most popular among the many new breeds of horses having recently formed registries. Historically an old breed but with no official registries in the United States until 1971, the miniature horse has been rapidly increasing in popularity each year since its registries were first begun. Miniature horses currently rank number 5 in the list of top 10 United States breeds of horses. According to the yearly registration volumes of each of these recognized breeds, miniatures (more than 15,000 miniature horses are registered each year) are exceeded in number only by Quarter Horses, Paint Horses, Thoroughbreds and Arabians/Half Arabians (Thorson & Snyder 1998). Owning miniature horses for pets or for breeding, showing and pleasure driving has become a fascinating hobby, as well as a profitable business, for thousands of horse enthusiasts worldwide (see Chapter 1).

In considering the purchase of a miniature horse, some research is necessary in order to make an informed decision. Just as purchasing a new car requires comparative investigation, miniatures (and other horses) should never be purchased without similar inquiry into price, size, conformation and other considerations. Those who are not familiar with larger-sized horses must learn as much as possible about equines in general before the purchase of their first miniature horse. Even if experienced with another breed of horse, it is important to become acquainted with miniatures, specifically, as the breed has many unique characteristics.

Researching the Breed and Breeders

Prospective buyers should begin their research with a subscription to at least one miniature horse magazine. The two largest and most colorful are published by the two largest registries, the American Miniature Horse Association (AMHA) and the American Miniature Horse Registry (AMHR) (see Sources). Listings and advertisements in these publications should enable the prospective buyer to locate at least a few nearby horse farms and clubs. AMHA publishes an annual membership directory that is cross-referenced by state and country and sent to all AMHA members without charge. Contacting one or two local listings can provide information about a particular ranch and their horses; about local miniature horse clubs and their membership opportunities, newsletters, and stallion directories; about coming events, shows and meetings; and about miniature horses in general. It is useful to visit as many ranches and shows as possible before making a purchase, comparing prices, pedigrees, sizes, health, condition, disposition and quality. Most important is to study the AMHA and AMHR Standards of Perfection (see Chapter 4).

The best time to visit ranches is during the summer and early fall, when horses are in their natural summer coats. During winter, miniature horses' long, protective coats cause even refined animals to look short-legged and stocky. As a result, horses with desirable features such as long, slim necks and beautiful heads are difficult to identify. The miniature's conformation becomes invisible, as do body condition and weight, when the winter coat is

Figure 3.1 Samis Kassanova *in winter coat. Dressed as a Christmas "angel," this 6-year-old stallion shows the blockier appearance and lighter color to be expected of miniatures in their winter coats. Breeder: Ron and Sami Scheuring. Owner: Larry and Gail Malmberg.*

Figure 3.2 Samis Kassanova *in summer coat. Note the much darker color and more refined appearance. Breeder: Ron and Sami Scheuring. Owner: Larry and Gail Malmberg.*

at its fullest (see Figures 3.1 and 3.2). In the summer, animals are more easily evaluated for correct conformation, head and legs, and for healthy body condition. Body-clipped miniatures, being blanketed and kept in stalls during the winter, look as if they are a different breed of horse. Many novices have paid excessively high prices for such animals, believing that they were far superior to the pastured horses they had recently seen in full winter coats.

Becoming active in a miniature horse club results in establishing new friendships and learning in the most pleasant way possible. Most clubs ask only that prospective new members have an interest in the breed but do not require ownership of a miniature horse. Most provide newsletters and annual stallion directories; free copies often may be obtained without joining the club. These publications provide new enthusiasts with valuable information about the club's shows, meetings and other activities, as well as the phone numbers of many contacts for ranch visits and further educational opportunities.

Books and videos specific to miniature horses are valuable teaching aids, and are available through advertisements placed in the miniature horse magazines. Large-sized horse care and training videos are available at most feed and tack stores for rental or purchase. Additionally, mail-order book and video catalogs specializing in equine topics or in miniature horses, specifically, are excellent resources. The Internet is another valuable source of miniature horse information. Most magazines and newsletters now publish the e-mail addresses of many breeders and owners who are interested in corresponding with other miniature horse enthusiasts.

Throughout the pre-purchase educational process it is imperative to develop an ability to analyze and compare information to confirm its validity. Often, material published about full-sized horses cannot be applied to miniatures. Professionally written articles on infertility of mares or on colic, for example, cannot entirely be applied to miniature horses because of the hazards of rectal palpation. E-mail and verbal information, as well as published articles in magazines, newsletters, books, videos and the Internet, should be assimilated with appropriate scrutiny but should always be an important part of the pre-purchase learning process.

Intended Use and Price Variations

While gathering information, it is essential to decide what the intended use of the new miniature horse will be. Will it be a companion and a pet, used for breeding, trained for driving or exhibited at shows, fairs, or parades? Will it be enjoyed by a first-time owner, an experienced horseman, a child, an elderly couple, or a person in a wheelchair? Will it be an adult, a foal, a stallion, **gelding** (castrated male), or mare? The prices for animals in each of these categories vary widely, and in many cases price dictates the type of miniature that may be considered for purchase. A high price does not guarantee show or breeding quality, however, and a low price does not necessarily mean that a miniature has anything wrong with it.

Young Horses

It is difficult to resist a well-cared for and affectionate miniature horse foal. Like a puppy, a young horse is much more appealing than a full-grown animal, and there is a decided sentimental value placed upon starting with a weanling miniature. Because miniature foals are so small and easy to handle, and because they are usually less expensive than older horses, they often are an economical and rewarding choice as a first purchase.

Pam Olsen / PRO PHOTO

Figure 3.3 *Weanling foal,* FWF Blue Boy's Delft Blue, *being exhibited by 2-year-old Kristin Rasmussen. Miniature horses and children make ideal companions, and even the youngest child can handle a well-trained miniature. Breeder: Flying W Farms. Owner: Tom and Donita Rasmussen.*

A foal's ultimate mature size is sometimes difficult to predict, but the breeder will often make price concessions on individual foals that appear as if they might grow taller than a certain height. Some of these foals may have exquisite conformation and type, as well as the finest of bloodlines, so are often an excellent investment for the first-time buyer. Viewing both of the parents and possibly some siblings can be helpful in determining the ultimate height of a weanling (see Chapter 13). Some miniatures that appear to be tall as foals, getting their growth early, never go oversize as adults. Occasionally, a horse that is oversize at maturity may result from two very small parents, and it is fairly common for a tiny foal to result from the mating of two taller adults, even if neither of them has a small background. It is important to know the requirements of each registry in regard to mature heights allowed. All AMHA-registered horses must mature at 34 inches (86 cm) or under, while all AMHR-registered horses must mature at 38 inches (97 cm) or under.

Effective training, proper nutrition (see Chapter 6), and rigorous parasite control (see Chapter 8) are essential for any miniature going through the weanling to 3-year-old stage, and the neophyte owner should be spending a great deal of time learning about these challenging subjects while raising any newly purchased foal. If the foal has been imprinted and lovingly handled by its breeder, the new buyer's training duties will be greatly simplified. However, some foals have been raised entirely by their dams (in a large pasture with other mares and foals) without ever being handled by a human, except for worming and hoof trimming. These youngsters will be fearful of being handled by humans and can recall only being forcefully caught and subjected to unpleasant procedures (worming and hoof trimming under restraint). Gentle handling and extreme patience must be exercised at all times in order to gain their confidence and willing cooperation.

Geldings

The least expensive miniature horse available is usually a weanling colt to be gelded. Breeders need only one high-quality stallion to service many mares, so most colts are gelded or sold to be gelded. Miniatures are generally gelded between the ages of 9 months and 2 years by an equine veterinarian. Even if they are of superior bloodlines, they are usually priced very reasonably. Only the highest-quality animals, with impeccable movement, conformation and breed type, should be retained for future breeding stallions. It is essential to the stable future of most horse breeds, including miniatures, that at least 75% of the colts be gelded.

Geldings are often superior for pets because, unlike stallions, they are not interested in breeding and, unlike mares, they do not have estrus cycles. They sometimes become bonded to their owners as much as to other horses. Without the interference of breeding activity, geldings are usually more easily trained than stallions and mares, and are often more reliable with small children. If their conformation is suitable, they usually make wonderful driving horses and can be a pleasure for driving everything from sleighs in the winter months to pleasure carts on scenic trail drives, harness racing and to winning their roadster and other types of driving classes at the shows. The nutritional requirements of geldings are lower because they are never stressed by pregnancy, lactation or breeding.

Peter J. Replinger

Figure 3.4 *A well-trained driving gelding,* Pegasus Desperado *enjoys the attention of children. Breeder: Dale Arden Rogalski. Owner: Yneke Delorie.*

After extensive training, the gelding's value increases dramatically, particularly if it has been shown successfully. A well-trained gelding can provide its owner with many hours of use and enjoyment, and any extra investment in training will invariably be appreciated by the first-time buyer.

Mares

Because several mares may be kept together as pasture companions and because there is an irresistible attraction for the possible production of a foal or two, mares are usually the most often sought as a first-time purchase. Mares are usually more expensive, particularly if they are proven producers. Three-in-one packages are sometimes available, with the mare already bred back for her foal to be expected in the following year, and a nursing foal at her side. Any mare that is being sold as pregnant should be verified by ultrasound or blood test. An owner's statement that the mare has been exposed to a stallion (either by pasture breeding or by hand breeding) is not a guarantee that she is in foal, unless stated in the sales contract. The mare's status in this regard should be mutually agreed upon between the buyer and the seller, and her price should be adjusted accordingly. It is important to obtain a written production record on any mare being purchased for breeding purposes. If not available from the current owner, such information may be accessed by referring to stud books, which are available from the registries or via the AMHA web site on the Internet. The ownership of a producing mare can result in one of life's most exciting adventures: the miraculous birth of a tiny, beautiful, healthy miniature horse foal (see Chapter 10).

Mares that are not pregnant or that have never produced a foal may often be purchased very reasonably. For the buyer who wants to own such mares because of qualities other than producing foals, they are often as easily trained and affectionate as geldings.

Stallions

Only experienced horse persons should consider keeping a mature stallion. Children under age 12 are not allowed to show stallions, and their behavior can be extremely unpredictable, especially when not well trained. Even well-trained stallions may injure their handlers unintentionally, if suddenly confronted with another stallion or with a mare in heat. Small children should never be left alone with a mature stallion. Even though miniature horse stallions are usually affectionate and easily trained, their daily care and housing often requires separation from other horses. The stress and frustration created by keeping any miniature horse by itself, particularly a stallion, can sometimes develop into a serious behavior and health problem (see Chapter 8).

Stallions often make flashier and more animated driving horses, and if the owner is experienced, such animals make exceptional show horses in both halter and performance classes. Stallions of acceptable quality for herd sire breeding purposes are difficult to find at reasonable prices. Since only one stallion is needed to service many mares, the most economical choice when starting a breeding farm is to select one outstanding stallion and several mares to be bred to him.

A common mistake made in the miniature horse industry is the new owner who purchases a weanling colt (because of his very reasonable price) and who later fails to geld him. The colt may have begun developing problems such as biting or rearing, and the owner frequently becomes discouraged by the colt's aggressive behavior. Once gelded, such colts take about 6 months to lose the testosterone in their systems. If they are not allowed to develop any irreversible and unwanted bad habits, after that period has elapsed, they are much more receptive to training and handling by novices.

Devin Baldwin / PRO PHOTO

Figure 3.5 *Bill Gee and his 23-month-old son B. J. Gee enjoy their miniature horse,* AR Sampson's Domingo Royale, *in a Lead Line class. Taller miniatures with gentle temperaments that have been well trained can make ideal riding mounts for small children. Breeder: James W. Bingham. Owner: Bill and Kelli Gee.*

Older Miniatures

Many older but still beautiful, well-trained geldings and older, gentle mares who may no longer be fertile producers are available at very reasonable prices. Older geldings and mares are often well accustomed to lots of handling and are sometimes excellent and reliable trail driving horses. Older mares also can be dedicated "baby-sitters" for newly weaned foals or comforting pasture companions for stallions who must otherwise live alone. Older, experienced broodmares are invaluable when training young stallions to develop "breeding manners." They will not usually tolerate the biting, chasing and mounting attempts of a young and inconsiderate stallion.

Pet Quality

Some miniatures are suitable as potential show and breeding animals; others are not. Pet-type individuals usually are priced very reasonably because of excessive height (over 34 inches [86 cm] in AMHA or over 38 inches [97 cm] in AMHR) or because of conformation faults. Neither of these types of miniatures should be shown in conformation classes nor used for breeding, since they do not meet the Standards of Perfection, but they often make wonderful pets and performance horses. If the new miniature owner has limited finances and does not plan to show or breed, animals in this category are sometimes the wisest choice for a first purchase.

Occasionally breeders sell their smallest animals, some with dwarfism characteristics, for very low prices, and as pets only. Sometimes represented on television and at the smaller county fairs as "miniature horses," tiny animals with multiple dwarfism characteristics can have unpredictable and expensive health problems, as well as shortened life spans (see Chapters 4 and 11). They are rarely a wise investment and their acquisition should be avoided by first-time buyers.

Show Quality or Breeders

If cost is not a factor, the possibilities are limited only by the intended use, production record, and the conformation, height, show record, color or pedigree desired. Top show-quality breeding animals, with conformation meeting the Standard of Perfection, are usually the most expensive. Young stallions, having already sired many exceptional get, are usually more expensive, as are young mares who have been consistently producing show-quality foals on a yearly basis.

With the help and guidance of professional grooms, trainers and handlers, it is possible to present miniatures at their absolute best when being shown or offered at a public sale. The highest of prices is often commanded when horses are viewed in these highly professionalized situations. Conversely, an ungroomed miniature, in its winter coat, may easily be a beautiful and refined horse in disguise. It is usually difficult to assess the show or breeding potential of such an animal (see Figures 3.1 and 3.2). Heavy winter coats may also disguise various faults of conformation, as well as poor body condition and accurate coat color. Purchasing a miniature horse in winter coat can be difficult, even for experienced breeders and owners.

Breeding Farms

Many large breeders own, show and breed 50 to 100 (or more) miniature horses. Some specialize in certain bloodlines and are well known for the quality of animals they have consistently produced on their farms and ranches; some of their horses may have even won national championships. Their advertisements usually may be found within the AMHA *World* or the AMHR *Journal* magazines. Visiting one of these large farms can give the prospective buyer a wide selection of horses and prices to compare.

When visiting local ranches, a selection of large, mid-sized and a few smaller farms should be chosen. There are many mid-sized farms that do not advertise extensively but that still offer a good selection of horses for sale with desirable type and bloodlines. Both large and mid-sized farms offer the prospective buyer the advantage of being able to view many offspring from a particular stallion or mare. Some of their horses may have been shown successfully.

The small breeder owning only a few miniatures usually cannot afford expensive advertising, professional trainers, and frequent or distant shows. Both their initial investments and their daily expenses are considerably less than those of the larger breeders. For these reasons, many small breeders may not expect as much money when selling their horses. The blood-lines, health and quality of these animals may still be exceptional, however, and should be a consideration for all buyers. Spending a large sum of money on the first purchase is not necessary, and smaller breeders with only a few horses for sale may offer entrance into the fun of miniature horse ownership at a reasonable price.

Figure 3.6 *Even seniors can enjoy training a miniature horse foal. The authors' parents, Captain and Mrs. Madett N. Engs, both in their middle 80s, enjoy the trusting companionship of the 6-week-old foal* Rodabi-J Elfin Echo *during her first halter breaking session. Breeder/owner: Barbara Naviaux.*

Pre-Purchase Examinations

Many miniatures are purchased without professional pre-purchase examinations, but the option of hiring a veterinarian to evaluate an animal is an important consideration. The American Association of Equine Practitioners (AAEP) has developed a standard pre-purchase examination form. Although the AAEP form is generally too extensive for use in the miniature horse industry, it can be used as an excellent guideline for examining veterinarians asked to provide a health certificate for miniature horses. The examination necessary with the AAEP form stresses soundness, as most pre-purchase examinations are performed on pleasure horses to be used as riding animals. An equine veterinarian is bound by ethics to not give an opinion as to the suitability of a horse to its prospective buyer. This is a relative judgment best agreed upon between the parties involved and before engaging the veterinarian in a pre-purchase examination. An equine veterinarian will usually avoid such subjective terms as "sound," "unsound," "good buy" or "too expensive." In the United States, if the animal being sold is to be shipped out of the state, a Coggins test may be required. Health certificate and Coggins test regulations vary between the states, as well as internationally. The specific requirements for each area may be ascertained by contacting the local department of agriculture agency, although most equine veterinarians have access to this information as well. The veterinarian will provide a written report of the entire examination and should be willing to discuss any aspect of the findings with either the seller or the buyer.

When attending sales and auctions, it is often possible to obtain a veterinarian to examine an animal prior to its going into the sale ring. Stallions over age 3 should be checked for two descended testicles. **Cryptorchidism** refers to the failure of one or both testes to descend into the scrotum. Cryptorchids over 3 years of age are disqualified for showing and should not be used for breeding. The miniature's mouth should be examined (horses with underbites and overbites cannot be shown unless they are geldings). Mares being represented as pregnant should have been tested by an equine veterinarian with either a sonogram or a blood test for pregnancy. From those test results, the veterinarian's estimated length of gestation may also be compared with that stated on the seller's stallion report. Conformation, head and legs (see Chapter 4) should meet the Standard of Perfection if the horse is to be used for showing in conformation or for breeding. Registration papers should be current and the veterinarian should verify that the age, color, and markings of the animal being sold correspond with those stated on the registration certificate.

Because foals from birth to 4 months often have an insignificant systolic heart murmur (Rose & Hodgson 1993), the purchase of a weanling or suckling foal should not be postponed strictly on the basis of hearing a "heart murmur." The cause, significance, and possible presence of this widely defined cardiac occurrence have been described in depth by several highly qualified equine veterinary cardiologists (Physick-Sheard in Pratt 1991). Some equine veterinarians can provide cardiac advice during a pre-purchase exam.

It is advisable to bring a measuring stick to an auction or sale, and horses being considered should be measured while still in their stalls. The accurate height may have significance pertaining to registry requirements, or buyers may be looking for a horse of a particular height. Examples might include an animal that is wanted for showing in the 32-inch (81-cm) and under pleasure driving classes, the 28-inch (71-cm) and under halter classes, or any 34- to 38-inch (86- to 97-cm) (AMHR only) division.

If looking for a particular color, the prospective buyer should remember that clipped miniatures often appear different in color from what they will be in their naturally shed-out summer coats. Appaloosa and pinto skin patterns will still be visible, but many of the solid colors will lose their brilliance and intensity when body clipped. Dark make-up applied to the face and around the eyes, lower legs, mane and tail may overly accentuate point colors and eye size beyond a particular miniature's genetic endowment. Some horses may have been bathed with color-enhancing shampoos and some flaxen manes and tails may have been bleached white.

Both AMHA and AMHR provide transfer-of-ownership forms to their members. Heights must be agreed upon between seller and buyer and, in AMHA, this requires the signature of both parties. If there is any question about the registration papers, the buyer should pay only a deposit until papers are actually provided. Neither AMHA or AMHR foals may be registered without both of the horse's parents being registered. AMHA-registered horses are accepted for registration in AMHR, but the reverse is not true. AMHR-registered horses cannot be registered in AMHA without AMHA parentage. Each registry has hardship clauses, but this is an expensive option (see Chapter 2).

Written Contracts of Sale

It is sometimes important to obtain a written contract of sale. This is especially true if the miniature is to be paid for over time, or if both parties require any special terms, such as height guarantee, a live foal guarantee or a co-ownership. A contract of sale protects both the buyer and the seller. When large sums of money are involved, sales contracts are a necessity (see Chapter 13). If both parties are agreeable, however, a simple bill of sale or a sales receipt may suffice for less expensive animals. Such a receipt, if included with the registration papers and a signed transfer of ownership form, may be all that both parties require.

Why Two Different Registries?

The two main registries are AMHA and AMHR (see Chapter 2). Their height requirements differ, but their show rules and standards of perfection are similar, and many miniature horse judges are accredited in both associations. AMHA-registered miniatures must be no taller than 34 inches (86 cm) and AMHR-registered miniatures must be no taller than 38 inches (97 cm). When being shown and registered in AMHR, there are two heights: Division A (for miniatures 34 inches [86 cm] and under) and Division B (for horses over 34 inches [86 cm], up to and including 38 inches [97 cm]). Miniature horse measurements are always made at the last hairs of the mane on the withers, not at the top of the withers, as is the standard for measuring all other breeds of horses and ponies. Their heights are referred to in inches or centimeters, never in hands. Currently, each registry has 900 to 1,000 miniature horses competing at their annual national shows, and local club-sponsored shows for both AMHA and AMHR occur regularly in almost every state during the show season.

Each registry has different executive officers, boards of directors and office staffs, but each has similar regulations and fees for the multiple services they provide. Many breeders **double-register** (register each horse in both AMHA and AMHR) all of their 34-inch (86-cm) and under stock. This is a wise investment that enables all of the double-registered horses to compete in the shows of both registries. The foals of double-registered horses may be registered with either association; should any foals grow larger than 34 inches (86 cm) as mature animals, their AMHR registration remains valid, even though their owners will have to relinquish their AMHA papers. AMHA horses must be 5 years of age to be registered permanently, while AMHR horses are considered permanent at 3 years of age. For show purposes, however, both are considered mature animals on January 1 of their 3rd year.

The existence of these two large and successful registries (each with more than 86,000 currently registered miniature horses) serves to regulate and maintain a healthy influence and competitive balance within the American Miniature Horse industry. Their cooperation with each other, as well as with other miniature horse registries worldwide, is essential in this computerized age of global communication and subsequent ease of importation and exportation.

Training the Newly Purchased Young Horse

Because wild, frightened, untrained weanlings, yearlings and 2-year-olds will usually be the least expensive miniatures available to a first-time buyer, it is important to acquire some basic information about training. Harsh training methods should never be used on miniature horses and this is especially true for young foals. Many modern trainers abhor the old "break their spirit" methods of training horses. For example, Dorrance's (1995) "resistance free" and Roberts' (1996) "join-up" training methods are ideal for miniatures of all ages but are especially helpful for frightened miniature foals that have not been previously handled and for youngsters that start to develop bad habits such as biting, kicking or being difficult to catch.

Dorrance's training tips can be summarized as follows:

- Pet your horse.
- Stop giving commands to your horse as soon as he makes the smallest gesture toward fulfilling your request. Allow your horse to move forward freely, preferably on a loose rein (loose longe line or no longe line) when possible.

Dorrance, now in his late 80s, continues to give training clinics on a regular basis. In his book, *True Unity: Willing Communication Between Horse and Human*, he states, "Everything I have learned about training, I have learned from the horse" (Dorrance 1995).

Using a similar philosophy, Roberts, born in 1935, has trained horses all of his life and has become known as a "horse whisperer." Kindness, tempered with a full understanding of and respect for each horse's body communication with the human who is training it, is the basis of Roberts' popular training method, called *join-up*. His philosophy is that each horse should be gently convinced, using communication established through mutually understood body language, to join up with its human trainer and friend in a cooperative effort, and never as a result of force, inflicted pain, or confrontation.

Understanding Equine Terminology and Usage Conventions

Nothing reveals a novice horseman more quickly than improper usage of terminology. There are hundreds of common equine-specific words and usage conventions (Leland 1996a). Because this terminology is unique to the horse industry, many of the words are defined inaccurately in standard dictionaries of the English language. Some improprieties involve the incorrect usage of a word or phrase, while others involve incorrect spelling. The most common conventions are presented in Table 3.1.

Table 3.1 Some Examples of Equine Terminology

Correct Spelling or Usage	Incorrect Spelling or Usage
Foal (noun): baby horse of either sex before becoming a yearling on January 1	Not a "colt," if female
Foal (verb): to deliver a foal	
Foaled: "foaled" 2/4/90 (on a particular date)	Not "born," not "folded"
Filly: a young female, from birth to the age of producing her first foal	
Colt: a young male, before castration, from birth to the age of siring his first foal	Never "stud colt"
Gelding: any castrated male horse of any age	
Yearling: Foals become yearlings on January 1 of the year after their birth; even if foaled on December 31, they become yearlings on January 1 (the next day).	
Stud: a breeding farm	Never use "stud" to describe "stallion"
Stud fee: a breeding farm's fee for breeding to a particular stallion	
Stud service: a breeding farm provides stud services when allowing mares to be bred.	
Live Foal Guaranteed: abbreviated LFG	
Offspring: living product of any given mating	
Out of: offspring "out of " a given mare	Never "out of" a stallion
Produced by: offspring "produced by" a given mare	Never "produced by" a stallion
Produce of dam: a show classification made up of two horses that are out of the same mare	
Sired by: offspring "sired by" a given stallion	Never "out of" or "produced by" a stallion
Get: a stallion's progeny or offspring	Never refers to a mare's "offspring"
Get of Sire: a show classification made up of three horses that are all sired by the same stallion	
Palomino: yellow or gold, with white mane and tail	Not "palamino"
Conformation: basic body construction	Not "confirmation"
Longe line or lunge line: a long line used to exercise horses	Not "lounge"
Lead: to "lead" a horse (present tense)	Not to be used for past tense
Led: The horse was "led." (past tense)	Not spelled "lead"
Poll: the area between the ears when the neck is horizontal at the point of flexion of head and neck	Not spelled "pole"

CHAPTER 4

Conformation

ORE THAN 50 MILLION YEARS AGO, primitive horses began their evolution into the genus *Equus*, which first appeared in North America about 1 million years ago. The Darwinian evolution of equids was marked by their becoming larger and more streamlined and by the gradual loss of multiple toes. By means of connected land masses, equids soon migrated to Asia, Europe, Africa and South America (Hawcroft 1983). The development of the new single toe as a hoof gave these earliest of modern equines agility, sure-footedness and speed, enabling them to travel much further from water. The equid form had successfully evolved to meet its most important function, an ability to outrun predators. Over these many years of evolution, survival as a species has been ensured by the horse's attributes of speed and endurance.

Breed Type: Matching Form With Function

Because the present-day horse varies in size from the tiniest miniature of 28 inches (71 cm) or less (under 7 hands) to the largest of breeds, which can reach more than 72 inches (183 cm) (18 hands or more), it is apparent that size alone cannot be used to differentiate members of the species *Equus caballus*. Mature height, however, is one means by which some breeds may more easily be identified (e.g., Shetland Ponies, Welsh Ponies or Clydesdales) and is of crucial importance to miniature horse breeders. The danger lies in forgetting that the miniature horse has other specific characteristics, all of which must be met when breeding and showing animals. Height alone should never be the sole criterion for purchasing a miniature horse. Conformation, proper movement and accurate pedigrees are also important. Top-winning horses at the shows must conform to the Standard of Perfection, which necessitates that the miniature horse's form must match its function. The term *breed type* is often used to summarize this concept.

An individual **breed** is a group or race of animals, related by descent, with distinctive characteristics that are not commonly possessed by other individuals or groups of the same species and that are sufficiently fixed to be uniformly transmitted. Breeds have been developed by man and require his restraining influence to prevent mixture with other races and the consequent loss of distinctive characteristics. Examples of some breeds that are recognizable because of their unique characteristics include the Arabian (dish face, high tail set), the Bashkir (curly coat), the Tennessee Walking Horse (running walk), the Shire (sometimes weighing over a ton), the Hackney (high, floating action), and the Pony of the Americas (POA, with appaloosa coloration and short stature). Such distinctive characteristics or features of a breed determine its economic and aesthetic importance as well as its interest to the many different types of owners. The more closely an individual resembles its particular breed standard, the more highly valued it becomes. The American Miniature Horse Standards of Perfection (both AMHA and AMHR) have been carefully designed to be used as the ultimate guidelines in the planning of breeding programs and for show horse qualifications. Miniature horses that do not meet the Standards of Perfection can still be sold or purchased as pet quality. All prospective buyers of miniature horses should be familiar with the stated standards for the miniature horse breed.

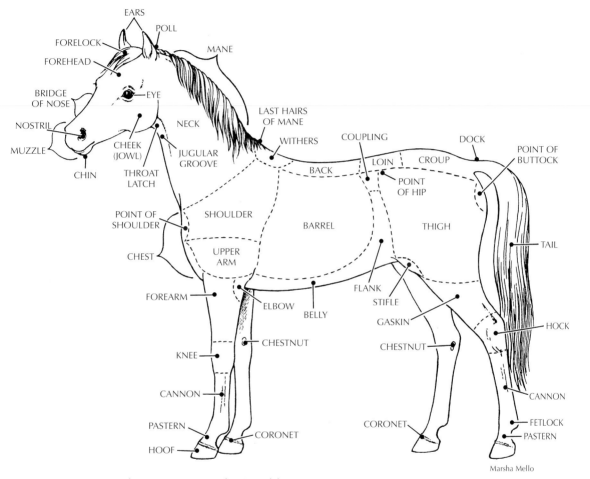

Marsha Mello

Figure 4.1 *Anatomical Points of the Horse*

With the preceding definition of a breed in mind, miniature horse breeders must focus upon the breed characteristics, other than height, that are most desirable. With height alone as the criterion, there is the danger of breeding animals for disproportionately short legs. Fortunately, breeding programs that concentrate upon short-legged, large-headed, thick-bodied individuals (for the exclusive sake of short stature) are becoming less common. Within such gene pools, the refined type currently sought after is rarely achieved.

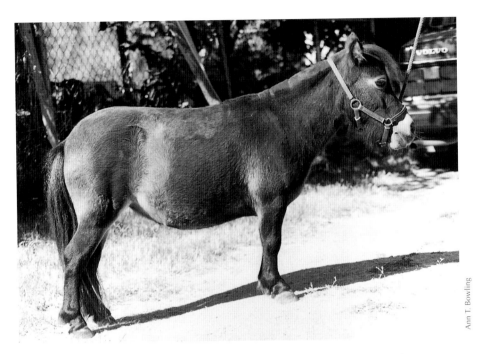

Ann T. Bowling

Figure 4.2 *A 27-inch (69-cm) mature miniature horse mare, illustrating typical conformation faults often seen in the smallest animals. These faults include a very long body, legs shorter than girth depth, steep croup, poorly angulated shoulder, large head (longer than length of neck) and thick muzzle. The mare fits into a rectangle, rather than a square, and is approximately one and a half times longer in body length than she is tall.*

Most light horse breeds, including miniatures, share similar ideal proportional and conformational requirements. An attractive horse of any breed must be pleasing to the eye and athletically sound, exhibiting obvious quality in its points of conformation, its gaits and its glowing condition. *Its form must fit its function* (Shively 1991). Show-quality miniatures must always be carefully selected and developed according to their intended uses: for example, taller, more refined horses with excellent movement for driving classes; shorter, pretty-headed, yet still correctly conformed animals for breeding classes; and brilliantly colored or patterned, meticulously groomed animals for the color classes. However, prior to the 1980s, miniature horses rarely met these ideals and were often the target of much ridicule among American Horse Show Association (AHSA)-accredited judges, as well as other full-sized horse and pony breeders. The exceptional genetic quality, refinement, conditioning, training and presentation of the miniature horse national winners during the late 1990s began changing the views of formerly critical judges. Breeders have accomplished these improvements by simply paying attention to winners at the shows and to the Standard of Perfection. Rarely breeding for short stature alone, they now select for breed type in their herds. Furthermore, the most successful breeders are scrutinizing top show winners in some of the larger equine breeds to more accurately visualize their goal of a perfect miniature horse.

Many judges of miniature horses do not breed or show miniatures themselves. As a consequence, these officials sometimes lack awareness of the vast improvements in miniature horse breed type that have taken place during the last few years. High-quality individuals now abound, and many championship miniatures may be best described as correct in conformation and gait, refined, elegant and professionally presented. Judges who typically are more familiar with the Standards of Perfection for the various large horse breeds should thoroughly study the AMHA and AMHR registries' Standards of Perfection before judging miniature horse shows.

Figure 4.3 *This miniature horse stallion,* Harris Polka Dot, *illustrates the type of natural (genetically endowed) action best suited for a potential driving horse. Note the well-angulated shoulder, the natural set of the neck and head, the long muscular croup, the high tail carriage and the well-lifted hocks and knees. Breeder: D. L. Rawlinson. Owner: Jim Curry and Barbara Naviaux.*

Standards of Perfection

Both conformation and gait need to be included in any accurate equine evaluation (Kainer & McCracken 1994). The basic conformation features affecting action must therefore be thoroughly understood. Form and function (the relationship of body parts to performance ability) are not yet well understood by many miniature horse breeders. Fortunately, however, the Standards of Perfection were written with both form and function in mind.

If miniature horse breeders are to continue their quest for top show winners, as well as for increased acceptance by judges of other breeds, they must use the Standard of Perfection as a guide for their breeding programs. In addition, the development of a discriminating eye for pleasingly proportionate conformation and breed type is essential. Form as it relates to function should be fully understood and utilized by breeders. The knowledge of proper miniature horse conformation and action is a necessary prerequisite for winning at the shows.

American Miniature Horse Association Standard of Perfection (AMHA 1998)

General Impression	A small, sound, well-balanced horse, possessing the correct conformation characteristics required of most breeds; refinement and femininity in the mare, boldness and masculinity in the stallion. The general impression should be one of symmetry, strength, agility and alertness. Since the breed objective is the smallest possible perfect horse, preference in judging shall be given to the smaller horse, other characteristics being approximately equal.
Size	Must measure not more than 34 inches (86 cm) at the base of the last hairs of the mane.
Head	In proper proportion to length of neck and body. Broad forehead with large prominent eyes, set wide apart. Comparatively short distance between eyes and muzzle. Profile straight or slightly concave below the eyes. Large nostrils. Clean, refined muzzle. Even bite.
Ears	Medium in size. Pointed. Carried alertly, with tips curving slightly inward.
Throat Latch	Clean and well defined, allowing ample flexion at the poll.
Neck	Flexible, lengthy, in proportion to body and type and blending smoothly into the withers.
Shoulder	Long, sloping and well-angulated, allowing a free-swinging stride and alert head/neck carriage. Well muscled forearm.
Body	Well muscled, with ample bone and substance. Balanced and well proportioned. Short back and loins in relation to length of underline. Smooth and generally level top-line. Deep girth and flank. Trim barrel.
Hindquarters	Long, well muscled hip, thigh and gaskin. Highest point of croup to be same height as withers. Tail set neither excessively high or low, but smoothly rounding off rump.
Legs	Set straight and parallel when viewed from front or back. Straight, true and squarely set, when viewed from the side, with hooves pointing directly ahead. Pasterns sloping about 45° and blending smoothly, with no change of angle, from the hooves to the ground. Hooves to be round and compact, trimmed as short as practical for an unshod horse. Smooth, fluid gait in motion.
Color	Any color or marking pattern, and any eye color, is equally acceptable. The hair should be lustrous and silky.

Show Disqualifications

Inheritable deformity	Any unsoundness or inheritable deformity. If in doubt, the show judge may request the opinion of the show veterinarian. Non-disfiguring blemishes not associated with unsoundness, or injuries which are temporary, should not be penalized unless they impair the general appearance and/or action of the horse.
Cryptorchidism in senior stallions*	All senior stallions are required to present a Certificate of Veterinary Inspection for Cryptorchidism to show management prior to entering an AMHA-approved show.
Height	No horse shall exceed 34 inches (86 cm) in height. Weanlings must not exceed 30 inches (76 cm) in height. Yearlings must not exceed 32 inches (81 cm) in height. Two-year-olds must not exceed 33 inches (84 cm) in height.

*Cryptorchidism in senior stallions refers to stallions 3 years of age or older, with one or both testicles undescended. Undescended testicles will not be checked for or penalized in horses under 3 years of age.

Marsha Mello

Figure 4.4 *Correctly proportioned miniature horse. Note that this miniature fits into a square, rather than a rectangle. Its forelegs are much longer than its girth depth, and its head is much shorter than the length of its neck from poll to withers.*

American Miniature Horse Registry Standard of Perfection (AMHR 1997)	
General Impression	A small, sound, well-balanced horse which gives the impression of strength, agility and alertness. The disposition should be eager and friendly, not skittish.
Size	The American Miniature Horse must measure not more than 34 inches (86 cm) at the base of the last hair on the mane for Division A, and not more than 38 inches (97 cm) for a Division B. Since the breed objective is the smallest possible perfect horse, preference in judging shall be given to the smallest, all other factors being equal. In no case shall a smaller horse be placed over a larger horse with better conformation. Priority in judging shall be in this order: 1) Soundness. 2) Balance, and conformity to the Standard of Perfection. 3) Size.
Head	In proportion to the body; neither excessively long or short. The eyes should be large, alert and prominent with no discrimination in color. The ears, open toward the front and carried erect. The teeth should show no signs of parrot mouth or undershot.
Neck	Strong and muscular, proportionate to body and the type of horse represented.
Body	Well-muscled, with good bone and substance, well sprung ribs, level topline, as nearly as possible of equal height in withers and rump, fore and hindquarters well angulated, so that the horse in movement shows a smooth gait.
Legs	Straight, clean, and sound.
Hooves	Round and compact, trimmed as short as practical for an unshod horse, and in good condition.
Color	Any color, eye color and/or marking pattern is equally acceptable.
Throat-Latch	Clean and well defined, allowing ample flexion at the poll.
Shoulder	Long, sloping and well-angulated, allowing a free swinging stride and alert head/neck carriage. Well muscled forearm.
Hindquarters	Long, well-muscled hip, thigh and gaskin. Highest point of croup to be same height as withers. Tail set neither excessively high or low, but smoothly rounding off rump.
Disqualifications	
	Height in excess of 34 inches (86 cm) for Division A, and 38 inches (97 cm) for Division B Miniatures. Dwarfism, blindness, unsoundness and cryptorchidism in aged stallions.

Pam Olsen / PRO PHOTO

Figure 4.5 *Typical Clydesdale gelding, showing size comparison with the miniature horse foal* Bended Knee Moqui Warrior. *Note the length of leg on both horses, which is greater than the depth of their girth measurements. Also note the small heads, which are shorter than their neck lengths. Draft horse-type does not mean short legs, with a long, thick body. Breeder of foal: Wayne and Marsha Kenley. Owner of foal: Kay Benson.*

Conformation Ideals

These Standards of Perfection, for both AMHA and AMHR, reflect the fact that most light horse breeds share similar ideals and are differentiated only by their specific breed standards, colors and height constraints. These generalized ideals include the following:

Body	Side view girth depth should be less than foreleg length. Girth circumference should be equal to or greater than mid-belly circumference (except in pregnant mares). Contrary to common opinion, potbellies (hay or grass bellies) are almost always caused by a protein deficiency, not by feeding too much hay or grass (see Chapter 6). Total body length from front of chest to back of hip should be equal to or less than height at withers. Even draft horse- or Quarter Horse-type miniature horses should not resemble basset hounds in shortness of leg, or length and thickness of body (compare Figures 4.2 and 4.4).
Chest	Broad and deep for maximum lung capacity and endurance. The term *refined* should never be equated with a lack of chest width and development.
Hindquarters and croup	Sloping or nearly horizontal, according to function of breed, but generally long and muscular. The hindquarters form the driving power needed for fast escapes. Short, poorly muscled hips or goose rumps with extremely low tail sets are not desirable in any breed.
Legs	Positioned for a square, solid stance. Forelegs, seen from the front, are parallel and straight, with feet set about a hoof's breadth apart. Hind legs, viewed from behind, are straight and perpendicular to the body. Bones are flat, not rounded. Tendons large and well defined. No puffiness or enlargement of the joints. Leg conformation faults in all breeds include bending forward, backward or sideways at the knees, hocks or any other leg joints.

Pasterns	The front of the pastern should form a straight line with the front of the hoof when viewed from the side in standing position. This line should form an angle with the ground of no more than 55° and no less than 45°. Ample flexibility in the pastern area is required for a lengthy stride and maximum speed.
Hooves	Rounded, with no cracks or rings. Well-developed frog to serve as a cushioning mechanism. Wide at the heel, for healthy and even growth of the hooves and for stability in traveling over uneven terrain. Because miniatures are rarely shod, the quality, correctness and condition of their properly maintained hooves are of crucial importance (see Chapter 8). Club feet (resulting in an overly steep hoof/pastern angle and excessive heel growth) are a serious problem in the miniature horse breed. They require regular farrier attention (see Chapter 11).
Shoulders	Sloping at an angle of about 45° (the angle of the scapula in reference to the ground). Not straight or steep. Good angulation of the shoulder is essential for providing springiness, length of stride and resistance to shock. The shoulder angle should be approximately the same as the pastern and hoof angle.
Neck	Clean-cut and refined at the throat-latch and well set into the shoulders with no sudden changes in the overall smoothness of line from poll to withers. Ewe necks (overly short and thick necks) and/or a lack of ability to flex at the poll are serious faults in any breed of horse.
Head	Proportioned for balance, larger on a short neck (draft horse), smaller on a long neck (Arabian). In either case, the head should never be greater in length than the length of the neck from the poll to the withers. Bone structure well defined. Forehead broad and flat with profile straight or slightly dished. Roman noses are characteristic of a few breeds but are not considered desirable in miniatures.
Teeth	Incisors must meet evenly. Undershot jaws (bulldog mouth or monkey bite) or overshot jaws (parrot mouth) are serious faults. Attempts at corrective orthodontistry for miniature horse undershot jaws cannot disguise the highly placed nostrils that always accompany this genetic defect. Undershot jaws are usually considered to be a dwarfism characteristic (see Chapter 11). Because incisor malocclusions are often associated with molar malocclusions, mastication of food, as well as digestion and nutrient assimilation, may be severely compromised in affected animals.
Eyes	Prominent, wide set, expressive of a good disposition. The eyes must have clear vision straight ahead but also to both sides and to the rear simultaneously (an essential for flight from predators). Unlike many other full-sized breeds of horses, miniatures may have eyes of any color or mixture of colors.
Ears	Alertly carried and finely cut. Set wide, parallel to each other and slightly forward of the poll. Various ear positions and activity are an indication of a horse's moods and are an easily understood means of communication with other horses as well as with humans. Floppy, non-attentive and non-expressive ears indicate a lack of overall quality or poor health.
Skin and haircoat	Indicators of health and good condition. The unclipped haircoat should be lustrous, fine, thick and vigorous, with a natural sheen in summer and a full, velvety plush in winter. More easily observed on a clipped horse, the underlying layers of skin should be thin, supple and smooth with no dandruff, thickened areas, wrinkling or obvious skin lesions.
Coat color and eye color	Registered miniature horses may be of any mane, tail and body color, or combination of colors, and any eye color. Bright markings and variety are both encouraged and bred for within the miniature horse breed, even those coat colors, patterns and combinations not acceptable within full-sized equine breeds. Some horse registries (such as Palomino, Paint, Pinto and Appaloosa) are necessarily restricted to certain colors and patterns. However, judges are expected to follow the American Miniature Horse Standard of Perfection when judging the color classes at miniature horse shows. Miniatures are not to be judged by the often more familiar color standards of other breeds.

Figure 4.6 *A 3-day-old heavyset miniature horse foal, 17 inches (43 cm) at birth and now mature at 26 inches (66 cm). This foal exhibits heavier bone and less refined conformation than is generally acceptable for shows. All breeds of horses become heavier set in adulthood, requiring that show-type foals appear very leggy when born. Breeder/owner: Barbara Naviaux.*

Figure 4.7 *A properly conformed miniature horse foal,* Rodabi-J Celestial Seasonings, *at 7 days; 17 inches (43 cm) at birth. Note the long slim neck, narrow girth, long fine-boned legs and tiny head in proportion to the body. Breeder/owner: Barbara Naviaux.*

Figure 4.8 *A 1-month-old miniature horse foal, 24 inches (61 cm) at birth and now mature at 36 inches (91 cm). This foal,* Rodabi-J Velvet Viking, *illustrates the appearance of an Arabian-type head. The head is quite small in proportion to the body, and the muzzle is very refined. The eyes are large, placed wide apart and almost halfway down the face towards the nostrils. Bulging foreheads, accompanied by extremely dished faces with thick muzzles, are not Arabian-type heads and are often found in combination with other dwarfism characteristics. Breeder: Barbara Naviaux. Owner: Kay Peterson.*

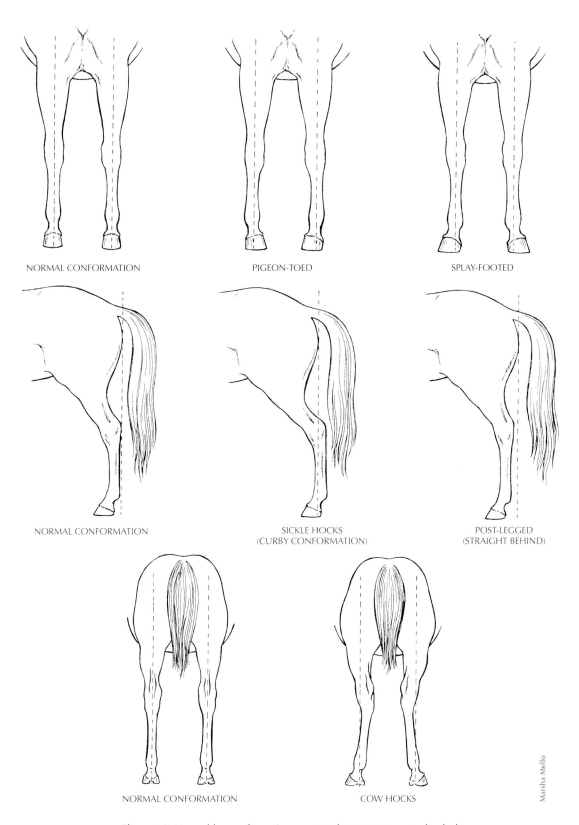

NORMAL CONFORMATION

PIGEON-TOED

SPLAY-FOOTED

NORMAL CONFORMATION

SICKLE HOCKS
(CURBY CONFORMATION)

POST-LEGGED
(STRAIGHT BEHIND)

NORMAL CONFORMATION

COW HOCKS

Marsha Mello

Figure 4.9 *Normal leg conformation compared to some common leg faults.*

Show Disqualifications

Height Restrictions

There are well-enforced height restrictions at each of the AMHA- and AMHR-approved shows, and miniature horses must be carefully measured by the licensed official or show steward present. Permanent measurement cards may be issued for the entire year on mature stock, which exempts such animals from remeasurement at each show. As specified in the Standard of Perfection, all AMHA horses must measure 34 inches (86 cm) or under, and all AMHR horses must measure either 34 inches (86 cm) and under (Division A miniatures) or over 34 inches (86 cm), up to and including 38 inches (97 cm) (Division B miniatures). Horses will be disqualified if they do not meet these criteria. The measurement is taken vertically from the last hairs of the mane to the ground, and the horse must be standing squarely and quietly on a firm level surface, with its head and neck in a normally elevated position. With the animal's head down, the withers are forced up and the measurement will be erroneously elevated. Borderline horses may return for two additional measurements if there is any dispute between the measuring official and the owner.

In addition to the maximum limits placed upon height for entry at a show, there are also height requirements within each age group and for certain other classes, such as 32-inch (81-cm) and under pleasure driving class. Each of the registries maintains and publishes an excellent rule book that is available to all members. Persons who are seriously interested in showing should always have a copy of these rule books available and should have read and studied all of the height requirements (as well as the other show rules) before entering their horses in any AMHA- or AMHR-approved show. In addition to the measurements required at shows, accurate measurements of new and growing foals, as well as any horses being sold, are essential.

For many years, the most accurate measuring device has been the Sligo Stick, originally manufactured and designed by Leon B. Blair. His first working model of the Sligo Stick cost more than $2,000 to produce because of the extensive amount of research and development involved. Sturdily constructed of heavy aluminum with a small level and currently costing less than $100, the Sligo Stick is still available to the general public (see Sources). There are other sticks being manufactured and marketed, but for the average miniature horse owner, the Sligo Stick remains the standard of choice. It is easy to use, accurate, durable and reasonably priced. The maximum height recordable with a Sligo Stick is 36 inches (91 cm).

Other measurement devices are now being used, particularly for the Nationals and for the taller Division B miniatures and Shetlands. Because the AMHR National Area Shows now require classes for American Show Ponies, Classic Shetlands and Modern Shetlands (in addition to both sizes of miniature horses), devices used at these shows must include measurements up to 46 inches (117 cm), the maximum height allowable for any Shetland. There is also a much more expensive H-shaped measurement device (with a level across the top) that has been used by AMHA officials and is available through the central AMHA office. At least two measurement officials are required for accurate measurement with this stick.

Visible Unsoundness and Injuries

Recent injuries that would be obvious to a judge or that are causing the animal pain (corneal ulcer or lameness, for example) should preclude that horse from being shown for the day in its classes. The AMHA standard states that "non-disfiguring blemishes not associated with unsoundness, or injuries which are temporary, should not be penalized unless they impair the general appearance and/or action of the horse." The AMHR standard states only that "unsoundness" is one of the grounds for disqualification. From a humanitarian stand-point, animals that are suffering from obvious injuries should not be shown. If such animals are shown, judges cannot be expected to give an award unless there are no other horses in the class. Even then, judges would be justified to withhold a win.

It is not uncommon for owners and trainers to file down the heels of animals that have measured slightly oversize on the first measurement. Without great care and expertise, how-ever, this process often results in lameness. Astute judges who follow the guidelines specified in the rule book may penalize or disqualify such an entry without further explanation.

Regardless of the type of blemish, injury, or unsoundness, if the judge is in any doubt concerning the cause, severity, or age of an injury or if the judge wishes a professional opinion concerning the degree of disfigurement or lameness involved, the show veterinarian may be summoned for consultation.

Dwarfism Characteristics

The word *dwarfism* is not written in the AMHA Standard of Perfection, but it is well covered by inference. Most dwarfism characteristics fall into the inheritable deformity cat-egory that is considered grounds for disqualification at any show. The AMHR Standard of Perfection addresses the issue more directly. It simply states that dwarfism is an adequate reason for disqualification at any AMHR-approved show.

One of the most commonly observed characteristics of dwarfism is a bad bite. Under-shot jaws, in particular, have been shown to be one characteristic of brachycephalic dwarfism in both cattle and humans, and have been scientifically documented in small equids as well (Hermans 1970). Both the AMHR and AMHA Standards of Perfection specify that miniature horses should have even bites. This means that bites are checked at the shows and animals must not be affected by either **overshot jaws** (overbites, or parrot mouths) or **undershot jaws** (underbites, monkey bites, or bulldog mouths) (see Figure 8.7). The rules state that overbites or underbites that exceed one-half the thickness of a tooth are considered grounds for disqualification at any show. Geldings are exempt from being checked for bites because they are not potential breeding animals.

In 1988, the Chairman of the AMHA Genetics Committee compiled a dwarfism charac-teristic outline that has since been used as a basic guide for breeders and veterinarians who wish to more accurately identify affected animals (Naviaux 1988). Noting the characteristics described in this outline, AMHA refuses registration on animals that appear to exhibit the varied and more disabling characteristics of diastrophic dwarfism (see Chapter 11).

Dwarfism occurs in all species of mammals; more than 200 types of dwarfism charac-teristics have been scientifically documented in humans alone (McKusick 1984). It is reason-able to assume that similar numbers and types occur in other species. Because of limited research funds, dwarfism has yet to be scientifically well documented in horses. With hu-mans, as well as with several other species, various causes of dwarfism characteristics have been shown to be inherited both dominantly (some as mutations) and recessively, but most characteristics that occur in miniature horses appear to be recessively inherited. This means that foals with dwarfism characteristics often occur unexpectedly as the result of breeding two horses that are normal in both appearance and height. Furthermore, it means that if two dwarfs are bred together, the resulting foal also will be a dwarf. Fortunately, fertility is often compromised in miniatures with severe characteristics of dwarfism. It is noteworthy that the old practice of breeding two dwarfs with one another (in an effort to get even smaller horses) is becoming less common as breeders become more educated on this subject.

Figure 4.10 *A 1- week-old miniature horse foal exhibiting several dwarfism characteristics. Both the sire and dam were normal in appearance and of normal size for a miniature horse (30 inches [76 cm] and 33 inches [84 cm]). The visible characteristics include brachycephaly (bulbous forehead, undershot jaw and highly placed nostrils), achondroplasia (resulting in extremely shortened legs that will not grow in length as foal ages), severe cow hocks (probably caused by an extra fibula), very short and twisted gaskins, enlarged head, and an abnormally shortened neck that cannot be elevated. The foal died at age 6 months of undetermined causes (probably due to previously unobserved and dwarfism-related internal congenital anomalies) as did a full brother (also a dwarf) from the previous year.*

Cryptorchidism

Cryptorchidism in senior stallions is grounds for disqualification in both AMHR and AMHA and refers to stallions 3 years of age or older, with one or both testicles undescended. Undescended testicles will not be checked for or penalized in miniature horses under 3 years of age. In AMHR, the animal must be personally checked (either visually or manually) by the show judge in attendance at the time of judging. However, in AMHA a form specifying that the animal has both testicles descended must be signed by the stallion's regular veterinarian. This form must be submitted with the entry forms and other paperwork, should the stallion be entered at any AMHA-approved show.

Cryptorchidism is generally assumed to be an inheritable trait, but because of its nature, it is difficult to pass on. If both testicles are retained, the heat of the body kills all viable spermatozoa and even though the stallion appears to function normally during copulation, he will be sterile. If only one testicle is retained, however, the stallion's descended testicle will produce viable sperm. All cryptorchid or **monorchid** (only one testicle descended) miniature horses that attain the age of 3 years or older should be gelded. If the veterinarian cannot locate the undescended testicles by superficial palpation, abdominal surgery becomes necessary and the cost of surgery is increased accordingly.

Over a period of nearly 20 years the author has observed that many miniature horses retain their testicles longer than is acceptable within the large horse breeds. Colts are usually born with both testicles fully descended, but within a week or so they cannot be easily palpated. Most individuals' testicles will then remain undescended until the colt is 7 or 8 months of age. However, it is common for miniatures to still have not dropped their testicles until the spring of their 2nd year. If the colt is of great value as a future breeding animal, both the owner and the attending veterinarian should avoid a premature diagnosis of cryptorchidism.

Bilateral cryptorchids should never be shown as geldings, but it would be difficult for any judge or other official to determine that a specific horse was a cryptorchid and not a surgically altered gelding. However, all normal stallion behaviors will continue to be exhibited in a bilateral cryptorchid, including unexpected erections in the show ring.

CHAPTER 5

Housing and General Management

ALL MINIATURE HORSE FACILITIES should have in common two primary characteristics: being both safe and comfortable for all of the horses, as well as for their human caretakers. Without constant attention to both of these important factors, an otherwise attractive facility may fall short of its intended purpose (Hill 1990). Whether one owns a single miniature, a few show horses or a large herd of breeding animals, a safe and comfortable environment should always be the first consideration. Such an environment is never overcrowded and allows each animal ample opportunity for hazard-free exercise, an essential requirement for the prevention of colic and other ailments (see Chapter 9). The comfort and safety of the farm owners can be assured by efficient pre-planning and design. The ranch layout, as well as the horses themselves, must be conveniently located, rapidly accessible, simple to keep clean, easy to continually observe on a 24-hour basis, and aesthetically pleasing to the eye.

Minimal Housing Requirements

For the homeowner who has become interested in the ownership of a miniature horse, it is possible that few modifications will be necessary to get started. A single miniature requires only a large backyard and a very small shed for shelter. Feed and tack may be stored in a garage or carport. Manure removal can be accomplished by beginning a well-managed compost pile that is used to fertilize and improve the owner's garden and landscape. The area required for the comfortable and safe maintenance of a single miniature horse can easily be contained on a large city lot, provided the neighbors do not object and the city ordinances do not prohibit such activities. Recreational exercise for both horse and owner can be generated by training the miniature to drive about the neighborhood or by hauling it in a trailer for longer drives in the country with friends.

Few miniature horse enthusiasts are satisfied with the acquisition of just one horse. More often, the purchase of a few more becomes inevitable, and the housing and space requirements must be adapted to meet the changing parameters. If the miniature horse owner has become seriously interested, it is quite possible that the breeding of a mare or two will be the next item on the agenda. Soon, the purchase of a larger facility with more acreage may become increasingly important, especially for miniature owners who become interested in showing or otherwise exhibiting their horses.

Shelters, Fencing and Pastures

When purchasing acreage for the purpose of keeping miniatures, the layout of the established buildings (if any) is not nearly as important as is the location, size and topographical layout of the land itself. The geographical location, general plot plan, and type of buildings other than the home, as well as the age, quality and size of the home itself, determine the price of an established facility. Rarely is it possible to purchase a farm that has previously been used for miniature horses. Because most horse properties have been set up and designed with full-sized horses in mind, it is imperative that additional funds be set aside for the many improvements that will be necessary. The barns, fences and pastures already in place for full-sized horses will usually require major modifications in order to make them safe and comfortable for miniature horses, and the cost for such alterations can be considerable.

Barns designed for full-sized horses, particularly the stalls, require a few modifications. Miniature horses kept in stalls should have at least one unobstructed view to the outside and to other horses. At least one low window or Dutch door should be added to each full-sized horse stall (see Figure 5.1). A miniature kept in a stall by itself, with no visual access to the outside world, endures a great deal of stress and loneliness. Such conditions can ultimately result in decreased disease resistance and the possible development of behavioral abnormalities or vices (see Chapter 8).

Figure 5.1 *Miniature horse box stall with a large, well-protected view to the outside and excellent cross ventilation. Constructed and owned by Gordon and Pam Gooby, Goose Downs Miniatures.*

Adequate ventilation of both the barn and the individual stalls is imperative. Although low, cold drafts should be avoided, cross ventilation is necessary (see Figure 5.1). This is especially true for heated barns in cold winter climates. Mold spores contained within the airborne dust of poorly ventilated stalls are known to cause chronic obstructive pulmonary

Figure 5.2 *An arena enclosed with attractive rigid PVC fencing. Lute's Komo Dandy, being driven by Meghan Cavanaugh. Breeder: Carl and Dwain Hackworth. Owner: Meghan Cavanaugh.*

disease (COPD, or "heaves") (see Chapter 9). Older horses with COPD have usually had prolonged exposure to an enclosed barn environment where there is poor ventilation (Rose & Hodgson 1993). Exposure to dusty or moldy hay and bedding over long periods of time and within poorly ventilated box stalls exacerbates all respiratory problems, including bronchitis and periodic coughing, as well as COPD. Cigarette smoke is known to be the primary cause of COPD, emphysema, and lung cancer in humans, but the probable importance of second-hand smoke in COPD of horses has yet to be investigated.

When remodeling full-sized horse barns, feed mangers and automatic watering must be lowered to accommodate the shortest horses making use of them. Automatic watering mechanisms must be protected from the miniature horse, who will repeatedly flood its stall by playing with the float. The interior surface of each stall should be examined for sharp corners, protruding nails, loose boards, holes, splinters, and any other potentially hazardous conditions. Barn walls can be dangerous to miniatures should any hole develop that might be large enough to get a hoof or a head through. Some stalled miniatures will chew and paw at any hole, whether in metal or wood, in an attempt to enlarge it and thereby gain access to the outside world and companionship with other horses.

Feeders intended for full-size horses may have widely spaced bars that can easily trap a miniature's head. Metal barrel-type feeders with bars spaced wider at the top than at the bottom are particularly dangerous. A miniature that places its head through the bars at the top may lower its head into the more narrowly spaced bar area. Upon realizing that it cannot remove its head, the horse can become alarmed, jerking back on the barrel and turning it upside down. A miniature trapped in such a manner will be unable to disengage itself from the large metal feeder hanging from the horse's neck and repeatedly colliding with its forelegs. If the entrapment is not discovered immediately by the owner, serious lacerations, massive head swelling, broken forelegs, and other potentially fatal injuries can occur.

Both new installations of safe, conveniently located, attractive fences for miniatures and modification, expansion and repair of already established fence lines can be surprisingly expensive. Miniatures are easily able to crawl under or slither through fences or gates that would not ordinarily be challenged by full-sized horses. They are very bold and curious animals, easily bored and always looking for greener pastures. Rarely are they intimidated by hazards such as the possible entanglement of their legs in a loosely woven wire fence or entrapment within a dangerous patch of blackberry bushes. Miniatures are also able to teach themselves to ascend or descend long stairways, open gate latches and barn doors, untie loosely tied knots, and slip their halters off by rubbing against the fence they are tied to. These clever personality characteristics, although charming, must always be considered when constructing facilities that are both safe and comfortable for miniature horses. Field wire (*never barb wire*), board, metal pipe, and rigid polyvinyl chloride (PVC) can be effectively and safely utilized for miniature horse-fencing. Each material has its advantages and its disadvantages (see Table 5.1) (Harper 1992).

Table 5.1 *Advantages and Disadvantages of Fencing Materials Commonly Used for Miniature Horses*

Material	Advantages	Disadvantages	Yrs Useful Life	Comments
Wood	Attractive, strong, easily seen by horses.	Expensive. Readily chewed. High maintenance if painted, chewed or splintered.	15–20	Place boards on inside of fence line. Treat posts with wood preservative.
Wire mesh or field wire (sheep wire)	Low cost. Keeps foals in, children and dogs out. Easily installed.	Leaning, scratching, and rubbing causes sagging and breakage. Not highly visible; may catch hooves.	5–15	Metal T-posts (no post holes). 39 in. (99 cm) height recommended.
Non-climb horse wire (welded)	Keeps foals in and children out. Attractive, very safe.	Expensive. Some sagging from rubbing.	15–20	Low maintenance. Metal T-posts (no post holes).
Chain link, professionally installed	Attractive, very strong, easily seen. Keeps foals in, dogs and children out.	Very expensive. Horses may catch hooves at bottom, if no pipe. Sags if pushed upon.	20–25	36 in. (91 cm) height recommended with pipe posts and pipe at top and bottom edges.
Metal pipe	Attractive. Portable panels and gates can be moved. Maintenance free. Highly visible.	Very expensive. Foals can go through.	20–30	Must be custom made for minis (bars lower down, closer together and decreased in height).
Rigid PVC or other white plastic post and rail systems.	Extremely attractive "estate" appearance. Maintenance free, no chewing, no splintering.	Extremely expensive. Dogs, children, and foals can go through spaces.	20–30	Must be custom designed for minis (spaces between rails decreased).
High-tensile wire (smooth, 8–10 strands).	Inexpensive. Fewer posts needed. Little maintenance.	Poor visibility. Possible foot, leg and head entanglements.	20–30	Breaking strength of 1,500 lb (675 kg) makes escape from entanglements impossible without cutting wire.
Electric fence				*Temporary installations only. In general, not suitable for miniature horses.*
Barb wire				*Should not be used for miniature horses.*

The strength of various types of wire is determined by the gauge size; the higher the number, the smaller the diameter of the wire. Fence wire gauges are identical to needle-size gauges. For example, a 21-gauge needle (for injections) is the same diameter as a 21-gauge fence wire. Some fence wires, although very economical, are too small a gauge for containing miniatures. These lightweight fences will sag, buckle and break individual strands of wire when used by the horses for scratching and rubbing out winter hair.

Pasture areas should provide shade during the summer months and shelter from rain, snow, and, especially, wind during harsh winter weather. Miniature horses grow thicker winter coats than do full-sized horses and seem to enjoy standing outside during rain or snow storms. However, they should always be provided with adequate windbreaks and shelters during weather extremes and should be allowed free access to these shelters. This is especially important for older animals, for foals, and for horses that may not be in good health or adequate body condition. Although large trees and rock outcroppings can provide valuable shade or protection during inclement weather, a three-sided shed with roof should be provided in each pasture. Such a shed is the most economical means of providing both summer shade and winter shelter to pastured miniatures (see Figure 5.3).

Figure 5.3 *An economical three-sided shed for miniature horses. The solid back side has been placed against the prevailing winds and weather. Constructed and owned by Barbara Naviaux.*

Miniatures should be pastured with other horses of similar ages, body conditions and temperaments. Their close contact with one another when standing under the protection of a preferred resting site should result in congenial, non-aggressive behavior. Aggressive intimidation of any individual may cause injuries, as well as failure to thrive because of inadequate access to feed and shelter.

Whenever possible, shelters, fencing and pastures for miniature horses should be created or modified to continually provide the following:

■ Safety for both the horses and their caretakers

■ Comfort, including convenient access to feed, water, salt and shelter

- Efficiency of design and convenience of location
- Economy, combined with long life and low maintenance requirements
- Ease of manure removal and disposal
- Pleasing aesthetics

Stallion, Mare and Foal Facilities

Stallion Facilities

On many miniature horse farms, several stallions are pastured together (with appropriate shelter) during the winter months, when they are not being used for breeding. For this system to be successful, it is best for these pastures to be located out of sight of any mares or other horses. Sharp-angled pasture fencing corners should be avoided, as should any other conditions that might enable one stallion to corner, trap and kick another. Barns and pastures must be free of any projections or debris, and the fences should have excellent visibility for all of the enclosed stallions, when their perimeters are being viewed from a distance.

During the breeding season, active stallions should have either pasture access to a small band of mares or individual stalls with large attached paddocks for exercise. Some breeders and trainers keep stallions stalled almost continually, with no voluntary exercise or socialization opportunities. Although this confinement is usually augmented with training, and/or exercise on the hot walker, such inactivity and isolation are probably the primary cause of the illness and disposition problems seen in some stallions.

Because stallions are prone to more chewing, pawing and other destructive behavior than are mares and geldings, their stalls and fences should be appropriately fortified to psychologically encourage good behavior, rather than bad. Miniatures do not seem to realize (or accept) that they are much smaller than full-sized horses. If miniatures are pastured or housed near larger breeds, whether stallions or mares, serious injuries may occur over or through fences and stall doors. Miniature stallions will not hesitate to fight a 15-hand (152-cm) stallion and will eagerly attempt to breed a 15-hand (152-cm) mare. Either of these actions can result in death to an aggressive miniature. Double fences, placed about 12 feet (3.6 m) apart, should separate each stallion's pastures and paddocks.

Mare Facilities

Pregnant mares are best left in pastured groups until they are almost due. It is wise to start checking their udders at least one month before their calculated due dates, or at about $9\frac{1}{2}$ months' gestation. Any mares with rapidly developing udders should be brought into a more protected environment to facilitate frequent observations of their pre-delivery status.

The ideal broodmare and foaling barn should have multiple uses. For example, one "island" type of design features two rows of box stalls, back to back, completely surrounded by a runway with perimeter fencing or walls and a covered overhang (Ensminger 1990). This arrangement results in the creation of an "indoor" exercise and training arena area into which the expectant mares (or mares with foals) may also be turned out for free exercise and socialization.

Foaling stalls for miniature horses should be large (at least 10 by 10 ft [3 by 3 m]), well ventilated, and free of any hazards such as splintered walls or metal projections (see Chapter

10). Easily opened stall doors, with ineffectual latches, should be replaced. Hay and grain storage rooms should be securely locked. Pregnant and nursing miniature mares have insatiable appetites and will gorge on grains or green pasture grasses, if allowed access.

It is ideal if at least one foaling stall is adjacent to a small room to be used by the breeder or other foaling attendant at night. These quarters can be as simple as a remodeled box stall but should be fully enclosed and well insulated, with several electrical outlets for heat, light, television, etc. An eye-level window of clear sheet vinyl (glass is dangerous for miniatures) between these quarters and the foaling stall facilitates viewing of the mare throughout the night. If the mare is fitted with a foaling alert system or the barn has a closed-circuit television, these types of quarters permit monitoring of the mare's activities and are very desirable. More elaborate facilities might include a toilet, running water, and apartment-size stove and refrigerator. The farm's first aid kit (see Chapter 7), a maternity drug and equipment inventory, as well as record-keeping and office supplies, can all be stored here. A telephone and fire extinguisher are invaluable.

Weanling and Yearling Facilities

The primary considerations when housing weanlings or yearlings are that each individual maintain a well-nourished and parasite-free body condition, and that each individual become accustomed to gentle attention and handling by humans. Young horses that are handled only when being wormed, having their feet trimmed, or being given injections become fearful and distrustful of any human contact. Miniature horse youngsters that are imprinted at birth and are frequently handled become attached to their human caretakers, often following their owners around for attention, brushing, snacks or "scratching where it feels good." To such foals the tasks of halter breaking, worming, hoof trimming and veterinary care become relaxed, everyday events. They are happier, healthier, more active foals, before and after weaning, and are highly marketable within the industry.

The quantity, quality and protein content of feeds for weanlings and yearlings are crucial to their growth and normal physical and psychological development (see Chapters 6 and 8). If overcrowded or if living with overweight or overly aggressive pasture companions, miniature horse weanlings and yearlings are unable to obtain adequate protein, calories and other nutrients. Additionally, because they should have their hooves trimmed and be wormed more frequently than mature stock, their separation from older animals is advisable. When stalls are utilized for weanlings and yearlings, it is best to stall two animals of equal sizes, weights, ages and dispositions together for company. The high-quality, high-protein legume hay portion of their ration may then be offered on a free-choice basis. Lack of exercise, inadequate water and nutrition, parasitism and overcrowding are the four basic causes of illness in miniature horses. The management and confinement practices for all young stock should be continuously evaluated. Fresh air and exercise are invaluable to weanlings and yearlings, causing the natural stimulation of endorphin production, and thus contributing to their sense of well being. Healthy appetites and optimal condition are a direct result of this type of management.

Methods of Handling and Restraint

When miniature horses are handled frequently and are well trained, most procedures require only mild restraint. For general grooming, bathing, body clipping and worming, a nylon halter and rope should suffice. The main purpose of equine restraint techniques is to ensure the safety of both the horse and its handler. Because miniatures are so small, the methods used for their restraint need not be as severe nor as frequently employed as those customarily used in the management of full-sized horses. Hoof trimming, clipping of the head and lower legs, loading into a trailer, injections, and many veterinary procedures may require additional training but should all be tolerated without additional forms of restraint by the properly trained miniature horse.

Should it become necessary to perform any painful medical procedures on a miniature (such as suturing a wound or extracting a tooth) there are many equine restraint techniques that may be employed. However, pain and anxiety in miniature horses may easily be alleviated by various tranquilizing and anesthetizing drugs, a factor that has caused many of the old physical restraint methods to become virtually obsolete. Since most horses are accustomed to being handled and approached from the left side, the assisting handler during such procedures should always stand very close to the horse and at the left side of the neck, never directly in front of the horse. This avoids injury to the handler by any possible rearing or striking, should the horse object to a painful procedure or to having a physical restraint applied, such as a **twitch** (a chain, smooth metal or digital means of restraint that is placed around the extended upper lip and twisted to hold it in place). The least amount of restraint needed to safely accomplish the procedure should be used.

The various methods of physical restraint that can be applied in miniature horse management include the following:

- Grasping and twisting a fold of the skin on the neck.
- Various types of twitches, which are applied to the upper lip and twisted. The mildest form is a hand twitch, which is excellent for miniature horse restraint. A medium-intensity form is the humane (firm metal) twitch, which can be used by a single person with attachment of the handle ends to the halter. The most severe form is a chain twitch with a hand-held wooden handle.
- Blindfolding or covering one of the eyes with the assistant's hand.
- Picking up one foot and holding it while a procedure is being performed on the opposing leg or other foot.
- Use of a chain (usually called a stallion chain), which is run through the halter rings, up over the top of the nose, and attached to the horse's lead rope. The chain should be kept loose until correction is needed; then a short, sharp jerk is applied, followed by a full release of all tension on chain and lead.
- A stallion chain may also be applied under the top lip and back around through the halter rings, in order to cause chain pressure on the upper gums. (The tension and release technique is the same as described for the preceding method of restraint).
- Single and full **sidelines** can be constructed with wide cotton ropes, which are

knotted and tied in around the neck, chest or girth and that lead to one or both hind legs at the pasterns. Sidelines must be tied and applied by a person familiar with these methods. They are used either to immobilize a single hind leg or to throw a horse to the ground for procedures such as castration.

- With one person at the rear and one person at the head, firmly but gently side-pressing a combative horse into a wall or fence.
- Tying with a strong halter and rope, with the rope run back in a loop behind the rump or around the girth. The loop should be tied in such a manner as to pull tightly on the rump or girth whenever the horse attempts to pull back on the halter.
- Breeding stocks, modified cattle squeezes, or narrow tie stalls.
- Front leg hobbles or breeding hobbles of various varieties.

As a basic acclimation and training measure, weanlings and yearlings should be handled daily but not necessarily haltered or otherwise trained. At least once weekly, however, they should be haltered, led about for a few minutes and tied. Each of their feet should be picked up and tapped with a rock or cleaned out with a hoof pick, their genitals should be handled, their ears should each be gently rubbed inside, and their mouths and lips should be opened, examined and handled. Pushing or pulling the tongue into a position between the molars ensures that full-mouth inspections will never result in the accidental biting of the examiner's hand. This weekly training session need not last longer than 15 minutes but will usually result in a foal that is accepting of any new procedure that may become necessary. The better trained and more relaxed the miniature horse is, the fewer the problems that will arise should adequate restraint be required for any difficult or painful procedures. All restraints should be applied with the aim of ensuring maximum levels of comfort and safety to both horse and handler and should never be applied or utilized in anger or frustration.

CHAPTER 6

Nutrition and Malnutrition

ALTHOUGH MUCH HAS BEEN PUBLISHED on the subject of equine nutrition, it has all pertained to the study of full-sized horses' needs and requirements. Specific recommendations for miniature horses, many of which vary from those for full-sized horses, have not yet been researched or published by professionals in the field of equine nutrition.

Miniature horses have unique problems related to nutrition and feeding program management, few of which can be directly attributed to their small size and less active nature. Statistically significant blood studies have verified that miniature horses tend to have fewer red blood cells and lower hemoglobin levels than do full-sized horses (they are slightly anemic), and they often exhibit hypothyroidism (have decreasing activity levels) (Harvey, Hambright, & Rowe 1984). They grow much thicker and longer winter coats than those grown by taller horses. Hair is composed of more than 90% protein, which implies that the protein requirements of miniatures during the fall and winter might be higher that those of any taller and slicker-coated breed. Their sometimes overcrowded and less efficient teeth require regular care and observation by a professional to ensure that their food is consumed and assimilated normally (see Chapter 8).

Because the majority of miniature horses are enjoyed as pets or breeding animals, the physical and nutritional demands of training and performance (the primary focus of nutritional research on riding horses) are considered less important than those for full-sized horses. During the 1900s, much progress has been made in the feeding of chickens, beef cattle and other meat animals, but only limited progress has occurred in the feeding of pleasure horses. Little scientific research regarding the nutritional management and feeding of miniature horses has been initiated. These studies require funding for research grants, which must be provided by concerned registries or individuals.

Equine nutritionists use terms that may be unfamiliar to non-scientists, yet the basic principles of good nutrition are not complicated. The digestive tract includes the entire tube that begins at the mouth and ends at the anus (see Figure 6.1).

The most important terms used by equine nutritionists are total digestible nutrients (TDN), digestible energy (DE), crude protein, and calcium/phosphorous ratio (Ca:P). TDN is computed by using a complicated formula involving protein, fat, carbohydrates, fiber and other factors. Although it is slowly being replaced by more accurate energy-evaluation systems, the TDN system remains the standard (Ensminger 1990). When analyzing a horse's diet, the importance of providing ample bulk (long-stemmed roughage) should be considered in addition to the TDN evaluation. Factors such as healthy intestinal peristalsis and sufficient chewing activity (to maintain tooth health and decrease boredom) are dependent upon an ample supply of roughage. The general condition and age of the individual or the many stress factors that can alter both consumption

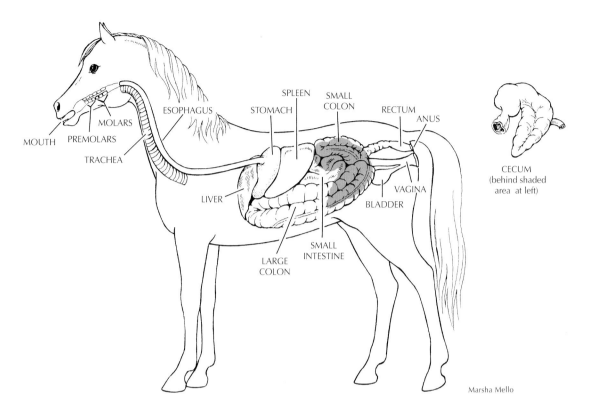

Figure 6.1 *The digestive tract of a normal miniature horse. Horses are classified as non-ruminant herbivores. Following mastication (chewing), swallowing and initial processing of food, the large intestine is able to efficiently ferment fiber-rich plant materials. The large intestine includes the cecum, large colon, small colon and rectum.*

and assimilation of foodstuffs may require alterations of recommended diets to meet a particular horse's more specific needs.

Crude protein requirements vary widely in the miniature horse, from as low as 10% in mature, non-producing animals to as high as 20% in newly weaned and thin 6- to 12-month-old foals. Proteins are composed of various assortments of the 23 known amino acids, a few of which are synthesized within the horse's cecum. Many amino acids, including lysine, one of the most important, must be provided in the horse's daily ration. The rapidly growing foal's ration must be significantly increased in protein content and requires corresponding increases (and delicate balancing) of vitamin A, vitamin D and mineral intake to prevent skeletal abnormalities. Excess protein is either converted to energy or is harmlessly excreted as nitrogen in the urine. There is no such entity as "protein poisoning" in equine nutrition, and diets that are excessively high in protein do not cause kidney damage or any other deleterious effects in normal horses (J. L. Naviaux 1985; Ensminger 1990).

Growth, lactation and reproduction require the greatest and most critical protein levels. In the cases of young, growing foals and late-term pregnant or lactating mares, additional protein, calories, vitamins and minerals must be provided in amounts greater than the maintenance requirements. Fertility and libido of the breeding stallion are also dependent upon a nutritional plane greater than the usual levels. The protein requirements are the lowest for mature animals not being used for any phase of reproduction and having a body condition score (BCS) of

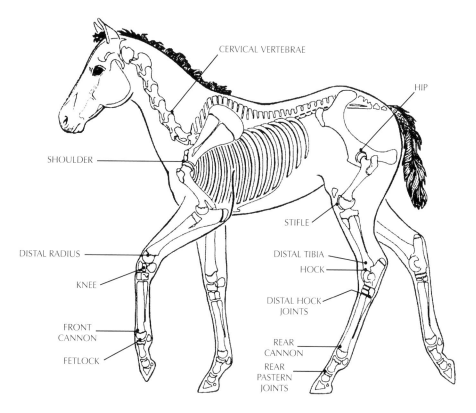

Figure 6.2 *Foal Growth.*
List of Manifestations of Developmental Orthopedic Diseases by Frequency of Sites:
Osteochondrosis—Stifle, Hock, Shoulder, Cervical vertebrae, Fetlock, Hip, Knee.
Epiphysitis—Distal radius, Front cannon, Rear cannon, Distal tibia.
Common Sites of Juvenile Arthritis: Distal hock joints, Rear pastern joints.

A critical time period: From birth to one year, the average foal will increase its body weight six to seven times, building bone and muscle at an extremely rapid rate. To support this growth, young horses have increased vitamin, mineral, protein and energy needs. A lack or imbalance of proper nutrients can damage body tissues, prevent bones from hardening properly and lead to bone abnormalities and skeletal breakdown. Often, this damage is not correctable. To complicate matters, a foal's stomach is very small and they can be picky eaters.

Problems with hay and pasture: Hay and pasture vary considerably and can be inconsistent in nutrient value. Of particular concern is a deficit, excess or imbalance of calcium, phosphorus, copper, zinc, selenium and Vitamin E. Protein quality, energy levels and nutrient availability are also important considerations. Controlling all elements of a young horse's diet, including hay and roughage, is critical during this development period.

Different management needs: The needs of growing horses are also influenced by a number of other factors including genetics, management practices and environment. Whether a foal is raised on pasture or in confinement, by itself or in a group, these needs, along with management goals of accelerated, average or slow growth, should be considered. The optimum nutrition program provides the horse owner with the flexibility to tailor the feeding program to meet the specific needs of an individual growing horse. A well-thought-out nutrition, health and management program is essential during this development period.

Reproduced with permission of Purina Mills, Inc. ©1996 Purina Mills, Inc.

greater than 6 (see Chapter 8). Miniatures living in extremely cold weather or in heavy training and performance programs require more calories but not necessarily more protein.

Ca:P ratios should range from 1.1:1 to 5:1, provided the total amount of phosphorous is adequate. Diets containing more phosphorous than calcium are dangerous and are not recommended. Alfalfa hay (and other legume hays) have 7 times more calcium and twice as much protein as oat, timothy or grass hays.

All horses are grazing animals with small, simple stomachs, and they are unable to assimilate feeds as efficiently as do cattle and other ruminants. Given the opportunity, miniatures will graze all day long, with only short breaks for rest and water drinking. They prefer to stay full on a continual basis, and eating only twice daily is a radical departure from the feeding habits of horses in the wild state. Given adequate pasture conditions, miniatures will become overweight (BCS of 7 to 9) during the fall, in preparation for the elevated body heat requirements and anticipated feeding deprivations of winter.

Nutritional requirements are based upon the amount of stress a miniature is experiencing. Stress may be caused by one or more of the following: growth, overcrowding, boredom, loneliness, breeding, pregnancy, lactation, temperament, age, poor management, work load, excitement, fatigue, parasites, bad teeth or poor nutrition. TDN, protein levels, Ca:P ratio and vitamin and mineral intake must always be carefully monitored. Each horse should be considered and observed individually to ensure its nutritionally balanced state within a herd environment. Groups should be pastured together according to their psychological, physical and nutritional needs.

Nutritional elements may be separated into six basic categories, each having a different purpose within the horse's body: water, energy (carbohydrates, fats, and sometimes protein), fiber, protein, vitamins and minerals.

Water: Quality, Quantity, Availability and Temperature

The most important element in miniature horse rations is water. Although a horse can lose all of its body fat and 50% of its body protein, the loss of only 12% of its total body water can result in death (J. L. Naviaux 1985).

Unlike full-sized horses, miniatures often drink inadequate quantities of water, even when it is continually available. The common practice of placing water and feed sources at opposite ends of a pasture (thereby forcing animals to get more exercise) is a dangerous practice in miniature horse management. Given a choice between walking long distances to obtain water and going without, miniatures will usually postpone drinking as long as possible. A disastrous side effect of decreased intake of water while eating can be **fecoliths** (very dry and excessively large accumulations of feces in the colon) and impaction colics. In large pastures of miniature horses, several clean, temperate water sources should always be available, and feeding areas should be adjacent to at least one water source.

Miniature horses should be stimulated to drink as much water as possible in their stalls, their paddocks and their pastures by implementing one or more of the following suggestions. *Exception: Never give a hot, sweaty horse free-choice water until at least 30 minutes after it has fully cooled down.* To encourage sufficient consumption, water temperature in the winter may be heated to 40°F to 45°F (5°C to 7°C). Ice should be regularly cracked off and removed.

Joanne Abramson

Figure 6.3 Goose Downs Savannah *and her foal* Pacific Jetstream *drink from a water trough of height suitable for both miniatures. The trough is shallow enough for easy access by the foal, yet tall enough to discourage the water play and pawing of taller animals. Breeder of mare: Gordon and Pamela Gooby. Breeder of foal: Joanne Abramson.*

Although full-sized horses on winter pastures may eat enough snow to maintain their water requirements, miniatures are at high risk for colic without warmed and readily available water. Conversely, during the summer months, water containers should be in shaded areas where the water temperature will not rise above 75°F (24°C). Water troughs should be cleaned out at least once weekly, and there should never be any strange taste or odor that might render the water unpalatable to the horses. Small rodents and birds sometimes drown in watering containers, requiring complete replacement of the water after removal of the carcass. Larger water sources may be stocked with catfish, mosquito fish and/or bullfrogs to control mosquito populations, stagnation and algae overgrowths that could affect water quality.

During lengthy periods of exercise (for example, a trail drive or parade), frequent small offerings of palatable, cool water should be made. Miniatures being hauled in trailers for long distances should have water provided at least once every 2 hours.

All automatic waterers should be checked daily to verify that they are in good working condition and that no distasteful debris (such as rust or manure) is present. The shallow water containers necessary for small foals often encourage playing and pawing by the older animals. Manure and mud from the feet then contaminate the water, and only the thirstiest and least particular of horses will drink from the container. The tallest container that is still accessible to the shortest miniature in the pasture should be chosen (see Figure 6.3).

Some materials (such as a few types of plastic or rubber compounds, or rusty metal) are unsuitable for miniature horse watering troughs because they have a distasteful flavor that affects the water. Miniatures are extremely sensitive to new or objectionable tastes or smells in their water. Their senses of smell and taste are far more acute than those of humans. When traveling to shows in different geographical areas, miniature horses will often refuse to drink the local water or water that is offered in an unfamiliar, brightly colored or strangely shaped container. Limited water consumption, coupled with the stress of showing, often results in digestive upsets, constipation and impaction colics.

Free-choice trace mineral salt blocks should always be available throughout the year. Salt intake stimulates water consumption, and the combination of salt and water in adequate quantities is essential in order to maintain the correct **electrolyte balance** (sodium, potassium, chloride and bicarbonate) within the body tissues. Electrolytes play an important role in muscle and nerve function, metabolism, acid-base, and fluid balance in the body. Horses with a light workload can obtain adequate amounts of electrolytes from green pasture and good-quality hay. Loss of electrolytes in sweat is a major cause of electrolyte imbalances in the blood. Electrolytes are also secreted in saliva but reabsorbed after feeding (Kohnke 1992). Due to a horse's highly productive salivary and sweat glands, there is a greater demand for both salt and water than is observed in most other species of mammals.

A healthy miniature horse consumes 4 to 8 gallons of water daily. This quantity of water is required for a great number of physiological tasks. Water is essential for proper digestion and normal peristalsis, serving to liquefy and lubricate as the digestive system moves food from the mouth to the rectum. It provides the salivary glands and the sweat glands with the necessary moisture to function normally. Water also is required for the body's internal chemical reactions. It makes up most of the blood, which serves to oxygenate the body's tissues, carries nutrients to the cells and carries waste products away. Water acts as a lubricant in the body's joints and tissues. In addition, water is essential for the horse's internal cooling system, which very efficiently regulates body heat. Water consumption should be the first area investigated when attempting to evaluate health problems in a particular miniature horse feeding and management program.

Energy

Energy is provided by carbohydrates, fats and, sometimes, protein. Digestible energy (DE) may be computed by multiplying TDN (in pounds) by 2.2 to obtain DE in mega calories (Mcal) per day. The major source of equine feeds is plant material, with carbohydrates comprising about 75% of all dry matter in plants. The most digestible portion of plants includes the sugars and starches, which are easily converted within the horse's digestive tract, to usable calories. Energy nutrients are required to keep the body warm in cold weather and to power the movements of every muscle. Basic muscular functions, such as intestinal peristalsis, beating of the heart and breathing, as well as all physical activity, are fueled by the carbohydrates, fats and, sometimes, the protein being consumed. Inactive, non-producing and mature miniature horses being fed at least one-half alfalfa (or other legume hays) need not receive any supplemental concentrates to adequately meet their carbohydrate, fat and protein requirements, provided they have a BCS of 5 or higher. The DE required can easily be exceeded if green pasture or grains are added to the ration. DE should be increased only in the cases of extremely cold weather, growth, lactation, rigorous exercise, or recovery from a BCS of 3 or less. A diet of 100% alfalfa usually provides surplus protein, which is rapidly converted to an additional source of energy.

Many show horse owners and trainers feel that fat supplementation can be advantageous for increasing the sheen of the coat and the overall "bloom." Various vegetable oils and rice bran are often included as supplements to increase the dietary fat content. A small amount of fat in the diet is necessary to act as a carrier for the fat-soluble vitamins A, D, E and K. However, this amount is adequately provided by normal hays, grains, or pastures. Fats provide $2\frac{1}{4}$ times as much energy by weight as carbohydrates. Rice bran and wheat bran are low in calcium and high in phosphorous, so can be dangerous if overfed. Some companies now manufacture rice bran with an added calcium supplement, but because bran inhibits calcium absorption, large quantities of any bran product in the miniature horse's daily diet (particularly that of young, growing horses) are not recommended (Briggs 1998). Mature miniatures can tolerate high-fat diets if they are not overweight, and there is evidence that fat supplementation may be helpful for increasing the endurance of heavily used performance horses (Ensminger 1990).

Fiber

The less digestible portion of plants is fiber, which contains both cellulose and lignin (the woodiest portion). Fiber in large amounts is essential to maintain normal gut motility and healthy teeth. Roughages, such as long-stemmed hays, provide a high percentage of fiber and also are critical for maintaining body heat in cold weather. Long-stemmed hays provide twice as much body heat as grains and other concentrated feeds. Fiber helps combat the effects of dehydration by retaining water and electrolytes in the digestive mass of the large intestine, acting as a valuable reserve of fluid. Although fiber is very difficult to digest, it is made more nutritionally available to the horse by cellulose-digesting bacterial action in the cecum and colon, a process that produces heat and warmth within the body (Kohnke 1992).

Protein

While carbohydrates and fats supply energy and body warmth, proteins supply the materials from which body tissue is made. Excess proteins may eventually be utilized as energy, but the primary function of these amino acids is to grow or replace muscle, bone, internal organs, hair, hooves, skin, blood and all other tissues in the body.

When feeds are chemically analyzed, crude protein values are higher than digestible protein values. Feed tags for various processed concentrates list crude protein only. Digestible protein usually ranges from 60% to 80% of the crude protein found in most types of feed. If a feed is high in roughage (fiber), as most hays are, the digestible protein is only about 60% of the crude protein. For example, oat hay, with a crude protein of about 8%, has a digestible protein of only 4.8%. Oat hay and other grass and cereal hays are an inadequate protein source for foals, for young, growing stock and for lactating mares. Alfalfa hay has a digestible protein of more than 10%. Both alfalfa hay and alfalfa meal may be fed free choice without any danger of causing colic. The digestible protein for grains and other mixed concentrates is about 80% of the crude protein value. For example, an equine concentrate formulation labeled 10% crude protein has a digestible protein level of about 8%. Products such as soybean meal, with digestible protein levels above 36%, are often used to elevate the protein found in concentrated equine grain mixes. Feeds that are unusually high in protein are needed for growth and milk production. Extremely high protein levels are also required in recovery from emaciation or parasite infestation. Most miniatures having a BCS of under 4 will have a decreased appetite, which is one of the earliest signs of protein deprivation. All feeds offered to debilitated animals must be extremely palatable.

While excess protein in the diet is more expensive for the owner, it causes no deleterious side effects except that the horse's urine develops a strong ammonia odor because of the higher nitrogen content (Ensminger 1990). Contrary to popular myth, high-protein diets, such as straight alfalfa hay, do not cause any kidney damage (J. L. Naviaux 1985; Ensminger 1990). It is unfortunate that because of the strong odor and the increased amount of urine produced, horsemen have traditionally been suspicious of alfalfa hay. In addition to alfalfa or other legume hays and meals, the highest-quality, most digestible protein sources for miniature horses are dried powdered milk and soybean meal. It is essential that lactating mares and growing foals have high-quality protein in their daily rations and that the quantity be double that required for ordinary maintenance (Kohnke 1992).

Vitamins

Unlike protein, excess quantities of certain vitamins can cause many problems. Feeding vitamin supplements in excess of the daily requirements is not recommended by equine nutritionists (Ensminger 1990; Kohnke 1992). Vitamins A and D, as well as E and K are fat-soluble vitamins that may all be stored in the body for later use. Vitamin C and all of the B-complex vitamins are water soluble and must be supplied in the horse's ration on a daily basis. Some vitamins and amino acids may be synthesized by the horse, but most of the research in this area has been done only on rats.

Green pasture and leafy legume hay less than 9 months old are both excellent sources of vitamin A. Horses pastured outside and being fed alfalfa or other legume hays do not require any additional grain or concentrate supplements to meet their vitamin requirements. The presence of adequate protein aids in the conversion of carotene to vitamin A. However, the presence of internal parasites seriously reduces the body's ability to absorb vitamin A (Ensminger 1990).

Minerals

Grain supplementation can be dangerous if horses are being fed only grass or cereal hays, such as timothy, oat or native grasses. Alfalfa has a Ca:P ratio of 7:1, while oat hay has a Ca:P ratio of only 1:1. As previously emphasized, there must always be more calcium than phosphorous in the diet. Most grains and concentrates have a Ca:P ratio of 1:3 to 1:10, which, when combined with grass hays, results in excess phosphorous and inadequate calcium levels. Ca:P imbalances such as this may result in serious muscle and bone disease, whereas excess calcium is not known to cause any problems (J. L. Naviaux 1985). Proper utilization of both calcium and phosphorous are dependent upon sufficient vitamin D, which must be provided by adequate exposure to sunlight or through the ration.

The trace minerals, such as iron, selenium, iodine, magnesium, copper, manganese, sulfur and zinc, are usually needed in only small amounts. Most high-quality feeds provide adequate quantities of these essential minerals. Salt (sodium chloride), as stated previously, is one of the most important mineral sources, as are calcium and phosphorous. When soils are deficient in a particular mineral, the hays and grains grown on them also will be deficient. Local farm advisors should be contacted for information about soil deficiencies specific to a given locale. Worldwide, many soils are deficient in selenium. Trace mineral salt blocks may be purchased with or without selenium, according to the farm advisor's recommendation.

Signs and Correction of Malnutrition

The three most common causes of poor condition in horses are parasite infestation, teeth problems and inadequate quantities or poor quality of feeds (Kohnke in Rose & Hodgson 1993). The usual signs of malnutrition are decreased appetite, potbellies, emaciation (BCS under 3), lack of muscle and muscle tone, weakness, lethargy and shaggy, extra-long coats. Extremely thin animals, suffering from generalized malnutrition (protein and/or caloric deprivation) may usually be rehabilitated. Visible signs of malnutrition also may include intermittent diarrhea (soiled tail), coughing and a stubborn mucopurulent nasal discharge. Once recognized, protein and calorie deprivation may be treated as follows:

- Worm with ivermectin.

- Have an equine dental technician or an equine veterinarian check the teeth and float or treat, as required. This examination should include checking for mouth and tongue wounds that may have been caused by sharp tooth points or foxtails.

- Feed a high-protein, palatable diet, such as alfalfa hay and alfalfa meal with molasses, which will automatically increase the energy content (fats and carbohydrates) of the diet as well. Commercially manufactured concentrates may be added, but their crude protein content should be higher than 16%.

- Separate the horse from other animals of normal body weight.

- Feed at least three times daily.

- Ensure that clean water and a trace mineral salt block are always available.

- Introduce major changes in diet gradually over a 5- to 9-day period.

- Never feed hay that is moldy or dusty or that contains foxtails or barley barbs.

- Provide thin miniatures with shelter from winter weather or shade protection from summer heat.

- If diarrhea persists, give psyllium at least once weekly for possible retention of sand in the digestive tract.

- If nasal discharge persists, consult with an equine veterinarian for possible examination and antibiotic therapy.

Unfortunately, there are few warning signals when a miniature is not obtaining an adequate supply of a single nutrient. Such deficiencies are usually not identified until too late for corrective treatment.

Show Conditioning

Provided the show horse's diet is well planned, adequate exercise is an equally important aspect of show conditioning. Whether a miniature is to be shown at halter or in performance events, its muscle tone, athletic ability, coat quality and enthusiasm will be critically appraised and compared by the judges. Show conditioning requires that the horse be maintained in a state of vibrant good health for many months prior to being shown. Successful trainers have various methods for ensuring that miniatures being shown by them are always presented at their best. Many beautiful horses are now being exhibited by amateur owners and trainers who have learned the nutritional requirements, and grooming and exercise techniques required to produce champions.

The show horse's body must be in hard condition, with ample muscle over the neck, back and rump. Without proper nutrition and abundant exercise, this conditioning cannot be accomplished. The animal's health must radiate from within and cannot be achieved by grooming sprays and shampoos, only augmented by them. Because of the current preference for extreme refinement, many underweight miniature horses are being shown. Refinement is a genetic quality that must be selectively bred for. It is not the result of cruelly excessive exercise, inadequate nutrition or insufficient calories or protein.

Consequences of Obesity

Obesity in miniature horses (BCS greater than 7) is extremely common and is best prevented rather than corrected. Rapid weight reduction may initiate the onset of hyperlipemia (see Chapter 9), which is often fatal. Any severely overweight miniature must be put on a very gradually implemented weight (energy)-reduction ration while still maintaining adequate protein, vitamins and minerals. Non-producing mares and geldings require fewer calories and only maintenance levels of protein and other nutrients. It is usually preferable to separate these "easy keepers" from young, growing stock and from lactating and late-term pregnant mares. Obesity results in many dangerous health problems, some of which are life threatening. Fat that builds up around key organs such as the heart, kidneys, and gonads prevents them from functioning normally and can lead to terminal heart disease, laminitis, kidney failure and infertility. Arthritis can develop and will worsen with age. With obesity, there is more strain on legs, feet and joints, and an increased risk of developmental bone disease and possible stress injuries to the limbs.

Many miniatures exhibit **hypothyroidism** (abnormally low thyroid function values). These animals have insatiable appetites and often develop thick crests on the neck. If fed as much as they want, they can go from a BCS of 5 to 9 in less than a month. They founder very easily and the mares are difficult to settle. If they do settle and carry a foal to term, they often have difficult deliveries. The advice of an equine veterinarian familiar with miniature horses should be sought if hypothyroidism is suspected. It may be beneficial to obtain a blood sample and have a thyroid panel (and other studies) evaluated before proceeding further.

CHAPTER 7

The Normal Miniature Horse

W ITH MINIATURE HORSES, recognizing anything that is abnormal requires a working familiarity with what is considered normal. This mandates daily observations of miniature horses in the herd, with comparative and written records documenting each individual's normal appearance, behavior, peculiarities and vital signs.

Vital Signs

Vital signs include temperature, pulse (heart rate) and respiration rate. Vital signs of each healthy horse should be taken and recorded at least once yearly, so that should that individual become ill or injured, there will already be a record of normal baseline values for comparison. The normal vital signs of healthy full-sized horses have been well established and vary only slightly from those of miniature horses.

Normal Adult Vital Signs (Resting)

▲ Temperature: 99°F to 101°F (37.2°C to 38.3°C).

▲ Heart rate (or pulse): 32 to 44 beats per minute (bpm).

▲ Respiration rate: 12 to 25 breaths per minute.

▲ Capillary Refill: 1.5 seconds or less.

Temperature

The usual body temperature ranges from 99°F to 101°F (37.2°C to 38.3°C) (Madigan 1997). On a hot day or after a heavy workout, the normal temperature can rise above 102°F (39°C). Body temperature that exceeds 103°F (39.5°C) when the horse is at rest indicates an infection of some kind is present. However, newborn foals' temperatures are higher than those of adults (see Chapter 10). The purchase of a sturdy rectal thermometer is essential for miniature horse owners. Easily read and made of thicker glass than is used in a human rectal thermometer, the recommended type has a ring of glass at the end. This should be fitted with a 6- to 9-inch (15- to 23-cm) wire or smooth plastic cord (more easily cleaned than string) attached at one end to the glass ring and at the other end to an alligator clip (a small metal clip-type fastener commonly used in electronics) (see Figure 7.1). Before beginning, shake the thermometer down to about 85°F (29.5°C) and lubricate with Vaseline® or lubricating jelly. Gently insert full length, clipping cord to tail hair, and leave in place for 3 minutes. Used in this manner, the

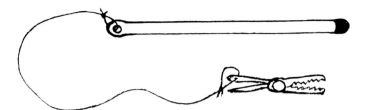

Figure 7.1 *Suggested type of equine rectal thermometer, fitted with wire or smooth plastic cord and alligator tail clip.*

thermometer cannot disappear into the rectum and can safely be left while the handler attends to other matters. Digital thermometers are now available that provide results in a minute or less.

Heart Rate

The normal heart rate (or pulse) for a horse at rest is from 32 to 44 beats per minute (bpm). If the heart rate rises above 80 bpm at rest, the horse is undergoing some type of stress, such as pain, decreased blood volume, or endotoxemia. Irregular beats are common and are not usually indicative of any abnormality. The pulse is taken by placing the fingers directly over an artery and then counting each throb, or beat, that can be felt. With the aid of an accurate watch with a second hand, it is easiest to count the beats felt in only 15 seconds and then multiply that total by 4 to arrive at the heart rate per 60 seconds. Heart rate also may be determined by using a stethoscope, placed directly over the beating heart or any artery. There are two easily felt arteries on horses that enable even novices to feel the pulse: the facial artery, under the jawbone, and the brachial artery, at the connection of the front leg to the chest (see Figure 7.2). It is important to evaluate both the speed and the strength of the pulse. If the adult horse is in extreme pain, the pulse will usually rise to above 100 bpm. If the animal is close to death, the pulse will be very weak, thready or even absent.

Respiration

The respiration rate of a normal adult miniature horse at rest ranges from 12 to 25 breaths per minute, which is slightly faster than the 8 to 16 breaths per minute of a resting full-size horse. Exercise causes a natural increase in the respiration rate, but it should never rise above a sustained rate of 60 breaths per minute in healthy, resting adult horses. Each inhalation is counted as a separate breath; the exhalations are not counted. Using an accurate watch with a second hand facilitates counting each inhalation during a 15-second period; the number of inhalations is then multiplied by 4 to arrive at the respiration rate per 60 seconds. A normal foal's respiration rate can be higher than that of an adult horse (see Chapter 10). Both the character and frequency of respirations should be noted. Standing back from the horse's side a good distance enables the owner to observe whether the horse is forcing its breathing with excessive heaving of abdominal or chest wall muscles. The inhalations and exhalations should be effortless and noiseless, with no wheezing, squeaking or coughing. A stethoscope, if available, permits more accurate evaluation of normal or abnormal breathing sounds.

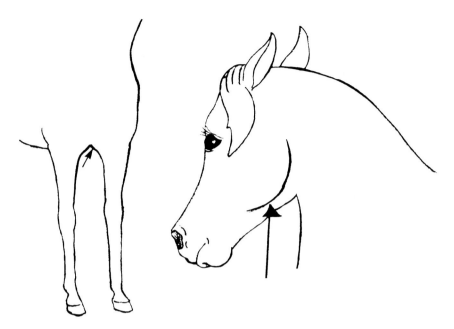

Figure 7.2 *Locations of facial artery and brachial artery for taking pulse (heart rate) of horse.*

Capillary Refill Time

In addition to the vital signs of temperature, pulse and respiration, capillary refill time and mucous membrane coloration should be noted on both foals and adults. Capillary refill time is evaluated by lifting the upper lip of the horse and pressing firmly with the forefinger or thumb on the exposed gum about an inch above a corner incisor tooth. Lifting the finger will reveal a white area on the gum caused by temporary restriction of the capillaries in the area. The pink color should return within 1.5 seconds or less. If the area stays white for longer than 2 seconds, the horse may be in a state of shock from some disease process. The capillary refill time should be counted and recorded several times if there is any suspicion that it is abnormal. The color of the gums also should be noted. Normal mucous membranes (the gums, inside of the vulva, underside of the eyelid) should be light pink, not white, brick-colored or purple, each of which may indicate various (possibly serious) health problems. Many pintos and appaloosas have both dark- and light-pigmented gums, lips, conjunctival and vaginal areas, which is a normal condition in those particular individuals and should be noted on their permanent record cards.

Determining Dehydration

Miniatures should never be dehydrated. The level of dehydration is determined by gently pinching about an inch of skin on the side of the neck, pulling it up and then releasing it. If the fold of skin remains elevated and does not immediately bounce back, flatten out and conform to the neck surface, the horse is dehydrated.

Figure 7.3 *Healthy foals spend their time nursing, running and sleeping. It is not uncommon to see a burst of activity, such as* La Vista Rowdy Remark *is displaying, followed by a nap. Breeder/owner: Susan Hopmans.*

Gut Sounds

Normal, healthy horses have bright eyes and excellent appetites. Any disinterest in food should be immediately investigated. The color, consistency, and volume of their urine and feces should be normal, with no mucous nor difficulty during passage. In the absence of observable manure passage, the horse should be evaluated with a stethoscope for audible gut sounds (caused by normal intestinal peristalsis). The stethoscope should be applied to at least two sites on each side of the horse. Normal gut sounds are extremely noisy, with many gurgles and rumblings, as well as the frequent and audible passage of gas. When there is any intestinal blockage, audible gut sounds generally disappear.

There should be no abdominal pain (evidenced by rolling, stretching out hind legs, kicking at belly or looking back at flank), visible injuries or lameness. Should a miniature horse exhibit any signs of pain or injury, such as standing with its head and ears down, or refusing its feed, its vital signs should be taken immediately in the manner previously described.

In addition to the vital signs, the horse should be observed for capillary refill time, mucous membrane coloration, dehydration and gut sounds. Abnormalities should be written down and may then be relayed to the veterinarian, if one is consulted. Obtaining this baseline information can be very helpful and does not require any medical equipment other than a thermometer.

First Aid Kit

The miniature horse owner should assemble and keep readily available a basic first aid kit for use in case of emergency or prior to the arrival of a veterinarian. Certain veterinary procedures must be carried out long before the summoned veterinarian may be able to arrive.

Pam Olsen / PRO PHOTO

Figure 7.4 *This mare is alert and bright-eyed, and has a healthy coat. Her head has been clipped, but her body and ears are untrimmed.*

Delivering a malpositioned foal or preventing blood loss from a serious injury are only two procedures that must usually be handled by the owner because of the crucially limited amount of time allowed for correction. The list of first aid supplies should be expanded after consultation with the farm's veterinarian and other experienced miniature horse breeders, but suggested items include the following:

- veterinarian's phone number
- clean towels
- flashlight
- Ace bandages
- adhesive tape
- gauze bandages
- tail wrap (self-adhesive and stretchy)
- sterile disposable syringes (5 cc to 20 cc) and needles (1 to 1.5 inch [2.5 to 3.8 cm], 18 to 21 gauge)
- sterile absorbent cotton

- disposable latex gloves, including 1 pair each of sterile surgical gloves and sterile shoulder-length gloves

- thermometer

- stethoscope

- clippers (with #10 and #30 blades)

- hoof pick and hoof knife

- stainless steel scissors

- scalpel and forceps

- nitrofurazone spray and salve; antibiotic ointments

- ophthalmic (eye) ointment (a neomycin-polymyxin-bacitracin combination, *without* any steroids, is both safe and effective.)

- alcohol

- mild liquid soap

- fly repellent

- Betadine® and Nolvasan®

- a large stainless steel bucket with a cover.

The bucket may be used as an excellent storage container for the entire first aid kit's components. After each use, the bucket should be washed and disinfected with Nolvasan® solution, all used items replaced, and the bucket covered and stored in a protected, yet convenient location. Any instruments used, such as scissors and forceps, may be washed in soap and water, boiled for 10 minutes (or cold-sterilized in Nolvasan® solution for 10 hours), dried and returned to the kit.

Miniature horse owners can become proficient at giving their own injections, with the assistance and dosage guidance of their equine veterinarians. Because the cost of veterinary care for the larger miniature breeder can be considerable, depending on the number of horses owned, most equine veterinarians make every attempt to educate and assist their miniature horse clientele to avoid any unnecessary expenses.

Understanding Laboratory Tests

With the advent of computerized diagnostic aids, the use of clinical laboratory testing has become as much of an advantage in veterinary medicine as it is in human medicine. A wide variety of laboratory tests have daily practical application, and equine reference ranges (normal values) have been well established by extensive research (Schalm 1984; B. J. Naviaux 1985). The finest of clinical laboratory services is available to veterinarians at a very reasonable cost, should their own office laboratory have limited capabilities. Veterinarians have come to recognize the great value of clinical laboratory aids in establishing accurate diagnoses or in monitoring various pathological conditions or medication regimens. The well-equipped laboratory is able to analyze almost any body fluid, including blood, feces, urine and cerebrospinal fluid. The most important of these is blood, which is analyzed as either whole blood or serum.

Hematology, Blood Chemistries and Other Tests

In studying a herd of 49 clinically healthy American Miniature Horses (AMH), all under 34 inches (86 cm) in height (35 mares and 14 stallions, ranging from 1 to 17 years of age) and all owned by one breeder in Texas, clinical biochemical values for miniature horses were compared with those already established for full-size horses (Harvey et al. 1984). The majority of miniature horse biochemical test results were within the ranges of values considered normal for full-sized horses (FSH). Exceptions were that potassium levels in AMH are statistically higher than FSH, while phosphorus levels are numerically higher. Thyroid values for AMH were in the low normal range when compared to those of FSH. AMH have more white cells than do FSH and also have fewer red blood cells. The individual red blood cells are larger, however, so are able to carry more oxygen (see Table 7.2).

Table 7.1 Comparative Ranges of Biochemical Values for 49 American Miniature Horses (AMH) and Full-Sized Horses (FSH)*

Component	Units	AMH DETERMINED VALUES			FSH STANDARD VALUES		
		Mean	SD	Minimum–Maximum	Mean	SD	Minimum–Maximum
Alkaline phosphate	IU/L	181	52.8	81–304	244	101	143–395
Aspartate amino transferase	IU/L	189	32.65	140–306	269	70	226–366
Calcium	mg/dl	11.59	.57	10.52–12.49	12.4	.58	11.2–13.6
Cholesterol	mg/dl	85.1	17.47	60–133	122	18.0	75–150
Creatinine	mg/dl	1.00	0.15	0.70–1.40	....	....	1.20–1.90
Creatine kinase (CKNAC)	IU/L	273	135.68	111–941	156	....	115–188
Gamma glutamyl transferase	IU/L	11	4.4	6–29	7.6	1.5	4.3–13.4
Glucose	mg/dl	91	12.43	68–126	95.6	8.5	75–115
Magnesium	mg/dl	1.79	.19	1.52–2.03	2.5	.31	2.2–2.8
Phosphorus	mg/dl	4.52	.94	2.97–6.14	3.5	....	2.6–4.9
Potassium	mg/dl	18.68	1.29	16.52–21.05	13.7	2.22	9.4–18.4
Sodium	mg/dl	313.64	5.1	306–321	320	8.5	303.5–336
Thyroxine (T_4)	µg/dl	1.44	0.86	0.25–3.70	190	....	0.9–2.80
Total protein	g/dl	6.6	0.59	5.2–7.9	6.1	0.07	5.2–7.9
Triglycerides	mg/dl	45.4	44.11	8.0–279.0	31.1	6.9	10.0–47.0
Triiodothyronine (T_3)	ng/dl	43.9	23.1	10.00–127.0	77.1	45.8	31.0–158.0
Urea nitrogen	mg/dl	23.7	3.82	15.2–32.5	....	....	10.0–24.0
Uric acid	mg/dl	0.62	0.13	0.40–1.00	78.7	7.1	.......–.......

* From Harvey, Hambright, & Rowe 1984

Table 7.2 Serum Hematological Values of American Miniature Horses (AMH) vs. Full-Sized Horses (FSH)

Determination	Units	AMH DETERMINED VALUES			FSH STANDARD VALUES	
		Mean	SD	Minimum–Maximum	Mean	SD
RBC count	10⁶ cells/µl	7.06	1.18	4.27–10.3	8.60	1.11
Hemoglobin	g/dl	12.6	1.85	9.0–16.0	13.3	1.60
WBC count	10³ cells/µ	9.99	2.49	6.10–18.20	8.82	1.45
Leukocyte differential Band neutrophils	% cells/µl	10.32	0.66	0–3	0.10	0.20
Segmented neutrophils	% cells/µl	37.19	8.03	22.0–54.0	47.5	6.9
Lymphocytes	% cells/µl	58.85	8.93	41.0–77.0	43.1	7.5
Eosinophils	% cells/µl	2.85	2.19	0–10.0	4.9	2.7
Monocytes	% cells/µl	0.40	0.77	0–4.0	3.7	1.9
Basophils	% cells/µl	0.49	0.88	0–4.0	0.6	0.8
PCV	%	33.83	5.03	23.7–42.7	38.4	4.7
MCV	fl	48.36	5.69	38.0–60.5	44.8	4.4
MCH	µg	18.6	2.33	14.0–22.7	15.5	1.3
MCHC	g/dl	37.34	1.35	32.7–39.7	34.5	0.8

Sixteen clinical biochemical determinations and 13 hematological measurements were performed on 49 healthy American Miniature Horses of mixed age and both sexes. Serum triiodothyronine and thyroxine values were also determined. Serum biochemical test results from American Miniature Horses compared favorably with values for full-sized horses, whereas differences in hematologic test results were noticed between American Miniature Horses and full-sized horses.

Reproduced with permission by Roger B. Harvey, D.V.M., M.S.

A computerized complete blood count (CBC) analyzes the whole blood (with an added agent to prevent clotting) for red blood cells (RBC), white blood cells (WBC), platelets, hemoglobin (Hgb) and hematocrit (Hct). The Hgb and Hct together, sometimes called the H & H, give the veterinarian information pertaining to anemia, dehydration and many other factors. Platelets play an important role in the clotting of blood after an injury. The WBCs, also called leukocytes, are the body's defense against infection, and some are capable of a process called **phagocytosis** (the digesting of foreign organisms, such as bacteria). A leukocyte differential count involves further analysis of the various sizes and types of WBCs, each of which has specific functions. By using both computers and microscopic observations, the WBC differential count is essential as a diagnostic tool. The RBCs, also called erythrocytes, carry oxygen to the body's tissues. **Anemic** horses (with low RBCs and low H & H) have very little endurance and often have difficulty taking in enough air when exercised.

Computerized tests of many types may be performed on only a few drops of serum or plasma. Whole blood is spun down in a centrifuge, forcing the heavier packed RBCs to fall to the bottom of the collection tube. The yellowish fluid remaining at the top is called serum (if the original collection tube contains no chemical additives) or plasma (if the tube contains a chemical additive at the time the blood was drawn). Various ingredients are sometimes added as preservatives or are required for specific tests. The colorful rubber corks seen on **vacutainer tubes** (glass tubes with a vacuum inside to pull the blood into the tube) identify which chemicals have been added. For example, a lavender cork indicates that **EDTA** (an anticoagulant) has been added, and that the tube is to be used primarily for CBCs.

Chemistry panels, which include the analysis of more than 30 different blood chemistries (such as sodium, potassium, protein, glucose, calcium and bilirubin), can be extremely helpful. Normal values have been established for hundreds of these possible results, enabling the veterinarian to pinpoint any abnormalities and thereby diagnose various disease processes (see Tables 7.1 and 7.2). Computerized chemistry panels are usually performed on serum or plasma, as are portions of blood typing, thyroid panels, drug levels and many other tests.

A urinalysis (UA) can be extremely informative, as can a stool analysis (fecal study). Fecal studies to determine the number of worms present (ova and parasite counts) are essential in miniature horse farm management and are discussed in Chapter 8. The analysis of peritoneal fluid can verify endotoxemia in a horse with colic. Analysis of many other body fluids and tissues can also be performed at most veterinary diagnostic laboratories. Some equine veterinarians are able to perform basic **stat** (immediate) laboratory tests at the ranch, with the use of equipment included in their mobile units.

Veterinary Terminology: Roots, Prefixes and Suffixes

Becoming familiar with the most often used veterinary terminology makes it possible to comprehend technical articles, as well as an equine veterinarian's assessment of a horse's ailment or medical status. Most medical terminology is made up of three elements: root words, prefixes and suffixes. These are used in various combinations to describe medical events, procedures and conditions.

Table 7.3 Useful Veterinary Terminology for Horse Owners

Root Word	Meaning	Root Word	Meaning
angio	vessel	lymph	water
arthr	joint	mast	breast
brady	slow	metri	womb (uterus)
bronch	windpipe (trachea)	my	muscle
cardi	heart	nephr	kidney
chol	bile (within gall bladder)	neur	nerve
cyst	bladder	pne	breathe
derm	skin	pneumo	air, lung, breathe
eryth	red	ren	kidney
enter	intestine	tachy	fast
gastr	stomach	thorac	chest
hepat	liver	ur	urine
leuko	white		

Prefix	Meaning
ap-	separation from
dys-	bad
ect-	outside
electr-	electricity
end-	inside
epi-	upon
exo-	outside
hemi-	half
hyper-	above, extreme, higher
hypo-	below, under, lower

Prefix	Meaning
intra-	inside
lamin-	laminae (sensitive laminae directly beneath hoof wall)
osteo-	bone
peri-	around
post-	after
pre-	before
poly-	much, many
py-	pus

Suffix	Meaning
-centesis	puncture
-cyte	cell
-ectomy	to cut out
-genic	producing, productive of
-gram	recorded, written
-itis	inflammation of
-logy	science of, study of

Suffix	Meaning
-osis	process or disease, abnormal increase
-pathy	disease
-penia	lack of, poverty, reduced numbers
-stasis	stoppage
-tomy	to cut
-oma	tumor

Some Examples of Combined Forms	
cardi + logy =	cardiology (study of the heart)
my + cardi =	myocardium (thick muscular heart layer)
endo + cardi + itis =	endocarditis (inflammation of inner layer of heart)
cardi + my + pathy =	cardiomyopathy (disease of muscular wall of heart)
pneumo + thorac =	pneumothorax (air leaking from punctured lung into chest cavity)
eryth + cyte =	erythrocyte (red blood cell)
leuko + penia =	leukopenia (reduced numbers of white blood cells)
arthr + itis =	arthritis (inflammation of a joint)
py + metri =	pyometra (pus in the uterus)
lamin + itis =	laminitis (inflammation of the laminae in the hoof)
osteo + arth + itis =	osteoarthritis (inflammation of both bone and joint)
my + itis =	myelitis (inflammation of muscle)

CHAPTER 8

Preventative Health Care

P REVENTATIVE HEALTH MANAGEMENT OF AN ENTIRE HERD is the key to optimum miniature horse care. There are few single-horse owners in the miniature horse industry. Like all horses, miniatures enjoy the company of their own kind, and because they are so small and inexpensive to maintain, most owners cannot resist buying at least two. This rapidly leads to parades, clinics, trail drives, shows and breeding "just one foal." Before long, the single-horse owner has acquired a small herd.

The most important horse management secret has always been the continued maintenance of vibrant good health. Vibrant good health is a direct result of excellent nutrition, a well-monitored parasite-control program, regular hoof and dental care, vaccinations, ample room for freedom and daily exercise, companions to play with, safe barns and injury-proof fences. Miniatures enjoying this high level of good health shed out earlier in the spring. They have a fat layer over their ribs and ample muscle over their necks, withers, backs and rumps. Their manes, tails and summer coats shine and glisten naturally. They do not have dried-out, split-ended manes and tails with coarse, sun-bleached areas. Their eyes are bright and clear, their nostrils are clean, their breath is fresh and their stools are well formed and frequent. They are well adjusted, frisky, curious and excited to be alive. Healthy miniatures are always hungry, and any lack of interest at feeding time should be cause for concern.

Observing Body Weight

Miniatures, more than any breed of full-sized horse, may easily become either underweight or overweight. Their small size and their undemanding dispositions (both of which permit overcrowding) may each be contributing factors to this dilemma. Miniatures are generally easy keepers, have excellent appetites and tend to be less active than larger-sized breeds. It follows that they might become overweight if they are parasite free, have adequate tooth care and are allowed to exceed their daily caloric requirements. However, a heavily parasitized or poorly nourished miniature will often appear to be fat because of its extra-long hair coat and large potbelly. Aged horses or those in a poor state of nutrition will usually grow earlier, rougher and longer winter coats than animals with ample body fat and muscle. Emaciated horses on winter pastures are easy to overlook and must be evaluated by hands-on physical examinations rather than by visual appraisals. Immature and rapidly growing young stock, as well as nursing mares, often fall into this category because of the high protein and caloric demands placed upon their systems.

Animals experiencing a continual protein deficiency will invariably develop potbellies, as well as shaggy coats that look greasy and bleached out. Their systems may have begun assimilating protein (muscle mass) from their own bodies, a condition known as **Kwashiorkor's syndrome** in humans. This type of starvation is caused by severe protein deficiency and is characterized by retarded growth, changes in skin and hair pigment, edema, mental apathy, tissue wasting, loss of subcutaneous fat, liver damage, anemia, gastrointestinal disorders (causing a decreased appetite) and dehydration (Dorland 1985). Symptomatically lethargic miniatures with diminished appetites and large potbellies may exhibit symptoms similar to the human Kwashiorkor's syndrome. Even after being frequently wormed and appropriately nourished, horses in these types of debilitating nutritional states will often take 6 months to a year to regain normal appetites, muscle mass and optimal nutritional levels (see Chapter 6).

Upon acquiring (or discovering) a miniature in this condition, it is important that the animal have its teeth checked by a veterinarian and that it also be treated for both internal and external parasites. Even very young miniature foals can have teeth problems that adversely affect their weight, and almost all thin or potbellied horses can be considered to be infested with internal parasites.

The protein content of all grain supplements should be ascertained before any such concentrates or mixed grain products are added to the ration. Most of these contain only 10% to 12% protein, which is inadequate for rehabilitating thin and potbellied miniatures. If a horse achieves its full caloric requirements from a highly palatable (but low-protein) concentrate, it will not be hungry enough to consume adequate amounts of the necessary 17% to 19% protein feeds. Fine-stemmed and leafy alfalfa hay, and alfalfa meal with molasses each contains approximately 17% to 19% protein. When implemented in a weight-gain program, these may both be safely fed free choice (without adding any lower-protein commercial supplement) and will produce excellent results (J. L. Naviaux 1985).

Foals that are weaned as early as 3 or 4 months will invariably develop potbellies. If at all possible, foals should be left with their dams until at least 5 or 6 months of age. After weaning, foals should be kept together to encourage play and social activities (see Chapters 5 and 10). Foals from multiple pastures may be put together with few problems, although there will be an initial adjustment period during which new bonds are formed. If it becomes necessary to wean foals at 3 or 4 months, extremely high-protein-content supplements may be added to their rations, such as 25% protein Calf Manna™, 26% protein lamb milk replacer (generic), or 19.5% protein Foal-Lac™ (a powdered or pelleted foal milk replacer). Any of these supplements may be used in combination with alfalfa meal as an extra ration. It takes some time for foals to develop a taste for these products, so it is wise to offer them daily at least 1 month prior to the anticipated date of separation from the mare.

Body Condition Score

In 1985, a body condition scoring system for horses was developed (Henneke 1985). The various body weights seen on horses are described using a Body Condition Score (BCS) of 1 to 9. According to this table, animals with a BCS between 4 and 6 can be considered healthy. A BCS lower than 4 or higher than 6 on this scale indicates the likelihood of metabolic or other health problems, and/or errors in nutritional or general ranch management (see Table 8.1).

Table 8.1 Body Condition Score (BCS) System   *Adapted from Henneke 1985*

Score	Condition	General Description
1	Poor	Emaciated. Spinous processes, ribs, tailhead and point of hip and point of buttocks project prominently; bone structure of withers, shoulders and neck easily noticeable; no fatty tissue can be felt.
2	Very Thin	Emaciated. Slight fat covering over the base of spinous processes; transverse processes of the lumbar vertebrae feel rounded; spinous processes, ribs, tailhead, point of hip and point of buttocks prominent; withers, shoulders, and neck structures faintly discernible.
3	Thin	Fat built up about halfway on the spinous processes; transverse processes cannot be felt; slight fat cover over ribs; spinous processes and ribs easily discernible; tailhead prominent, but individual vertebrae cannot be identified visually; point of buttocks appears rounded but easily discernible; point of hip not distinguishable; withers, shoulders and neck accentuated.
4	Moderately Thin	Slight ridge along back; faint outline of ribs discernible; tailhead prominence depends on conformation, but fat can be felt around it; point of hip not discernible; withers, shoulders and neck not obviously thin.
5	Moderate	Back is flat (no crease or ridge); ribs not visually distinguishable but can be easily felt; fat around tailhead beginning to feel spongy; withers appear rounded over spinous processes; shoulders and neck blend smoothly into body.
6	Moderate to Fleshy	May have slight crease down back; fat over ribs spongy; fat around tailhead soft; fat beginning to be deposited along the side of withers, behind shoulders and along the sides of neck.
7	Fleshy	May have crease down back; individual ribs can be felt but there is noticeable fat between ribs; fat around tailhead soft; fat deposits along withers, behind shoulders and along neck.
8	Fat	Crease down back; difficult to feel ribs; fat around tailhead very soft; area along withers filled with fat; area behind shoulder filled with fat; noticeable thickening of neck; fat deposited along inner buttocks.
9	Extremely Fat	Obvious crease down back; patchy fat appearing over ribs; bulging fat around tailhead, along withers, behind shoulders, and along neck; fat along inner buttocks may cause them to rub together; flank filled with fat.

Reprinted with permission from Equine Practice *1985 7(8):13–15.*

During cold weather, a miniature horse's basic metabolic rates increase to maintain adequate body heat. Companionship, exercise and adequate shelter are three important health considerations, but factors such as late pregnancy, lactation, old age, overcrowding, winter pasture condition or hay quality must be regularly monitored. When pastures become mature and dry, their nutritional value (especially protein and vitamins) is greatly reduced. Even fat animals on late dry or early light green and watery pasture grasses can be severely malnourished. Their caloric intake may be adequate, but they may be suffering from severe protein, vitamin or mineral deficiencies.

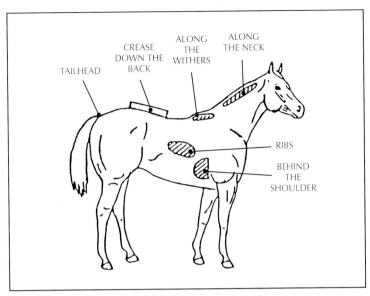

Figure 8.1 *Diagram of the body areas emphasized in body condition scoring (see Table 8.1). Reprinted with permission from* Equine Practice *1985 7(8):13–15.*

Figure 8.2 *Severely overweight mare, illustrating a BCS of 9. A beautiful chestnut splashed white overo pinto mare. This mare's obesity is compromising her health and reproductive potential.*

In early pregnancy, the total quantity of feed does not rise significantly above that needed by an idle mature horse, but a well-balanced ration in early pregnancy is very important. It is only in the last 2½ months of her pregnancy that the caloric, protein and calcium content of a healthy mare's feed should be increased. During this time, the foal attains 75% of its growth and the mare must be prepared for maximum milk production. Although mares should not be excessively fat at foaling time, many miniatures become slightly overweight during pregnancy. A BCS of 6 or 7 is acceptable, but the ideal BCS for a pregnant mare is 5. Fortunately, slightly overweight mares seem to have few problems. Underweight or undernourished mares are of greater concern.

Mature and idle miniatures can be prevented from becoming overweight by allowing them abundant exercise and by not feeding them with a group of thinner animals having greater nutritional needs. Geldings, especially, can become exceedingly overweight if they live with a group of mares and foals. Drastic caloric restriction is usually necessary in these cases, but vitamin, mineral and protein supplementation during such a weight-loss program must always be considered. It is almost impossible to exercise seriously overweight geldings enough to cause them to lose weight. **Laminitis**, or **founder** (inflammation of the laminae, or sub-surface tissues of the hoof) is a serious complication (see Chapter 9) that is sometimes associated with miniatures having a BCS above 8 or 9 (see Table 8.1).

Internal Parasite Control

Preventative health care involving the miniature horse's sensitive gastrointestinal tract is of utmost importance. Constant vigilance with a multifaceted parasite-control program is essential. This includes regularly scheduled wormings of each horse, as well as manure removal, fly control and an absence of overcrowded pastures. The potbellies so often seen on young foals and yearlings are often indicative of heavy parasite loads, which invariably cause a protein deficiency as well as other nutritional imbalances. Most important, *parasite control cannot be overemphasized in the prevention of colic*. Most equine veterinarians feel that damage to the blood vessels that supply the intestines (caused by the intermediate larval stages of bloodworms) is the number one cause of colic (Rose & Hodgson 1993).

Avermectins

Various generic and orally administered paste, liquid or pelleted anthelmintics (dewormers) are readily available to equine owners (see Table 8.4), but the advent of avermectin-based products has revolutionized modern parasite control. In contrast to most other types of dewormers, which eliminate parasites only within the gastrointestinal tract, avermectins enter the bloodstream and kill almost all internal parasites in tissues throughout the body. Highly effective parasite-control programs are now within the reach of every miniature horse owner. With the regular use of systemic dewormings, good preventative management, proper timing of administration and astute observation of each animal for individual problems, a miniature horse herd may be kept relatively free of harmful parasites. Yearly tube worming by a veterinarian is no longer necessary.

The avermectins are one of a group of complex chemical compounds called macrocyclic lactones derived from the fermentation of an organism named *Streptomyces avermitilis*. They are an antibiotic type of agent that blocks nerve transmission and paralyzes all types of parasites using the complex chemical gamma-aminobutyric acid (GABA) for the normal flow of nerve impulses. They are ineffective against tapeworms because of the absence of GABA in all flatworms. In addition to their activity on mature forms of parasites already within the gastrointestinal tract, the avermectins have systemic activity upon the many immature larval forms found elsewhere within the body's tissues. Avermectins are at least 95% effective against bots, large and small strongyles, ascarids, pinworms, stomach worms and even external parasites such as lice, ticks and sarcoptic mange mites. Most internal parasites do not carry the import of large strongyles, ascarids and bots, but there are more than 150 species now known in the horse. The avermectins have a wide range of efficacy, and almost all internal and external parasites, except tapeworms, are controlled by their regular usage. Although resistance by some parasites to various other anthelmintics has been documented, no resistance to the avermectins has yet been demonstrated. Thus, rotating with other wormers is not necessary, except for tapeworm control. Ivermectin paste (1.87%) is safe for pregnant mares at any stage in their gestation. It is also safe for foals as young as a week or so.

Large Strongyles (Bloodworms)

The mesenteric artery and its capillaries supply 90 to 95% of the intestinal tract with the nourishment and oxygen needed for active **peristalsis** (contractions that propel contents through the intestinal tract). The number one cause of colic is thought to be damage to the mesenteric arteries by immature forms of bloodworms. These larval forms spend about 150 days migrating through mesenteric blood vessels. Therefore, the importance of a systemic approach to parasite control cannot be overstated. The cost of avermectin products may be high when compared to the cost of most other paste wormers, but the cost of colic surgery and possible death is far higher.

Without frequent wormings, sleek, often overweight, healthy-appearing miniature horses (particularly those on green pasture) will almost always have many bloodworm larvae migrating through the walls of their mesenteric arteries. These larval migrations invariably cause the formation of scar tissue, **aneurysms** (abnormal blood vessel dilations) and **emboli** (blood clots). **Thromboembolic colic** is a direct result of this devastating circulatory damage. Entire sections of the intestine may be robbed of essential blood supplies, causing affected portions to die, to become necrotic and to subsequently cease normal peristalsis. Without peristalsis, food or fecal matter stops moving through the affected portion of the intestine and serious impactions can occur. Much of this circulatory damage may eventually be reversed through regeneration and formation of normal blood vessels if reinfestation can be kept at a minimum by regular wormings (Rose & Hodgson 1993).

Ascarids (Roundworms)

Ascarids are primarily a problem of young stock; their occurrence in miniatures over 5 years of age is rare. Because roundworms suck large quantities of blood, heavily parasitized foals experience grave depletions in their systemic protein and hemoglobin levels. The body attempts to correct this deficiency by consuming its own protein reserves from muscle tissue, particularly that of the neck, back and rump. In addition, the foal becomes anemic and tires easily. **Anemia** is caused by an acute shortage of the blood's oxygen-carrying component, hemoglobin. Animals suffering from severe anemia will be seen struggling for air (panting) after only minimal exercise. With ascarid infestation, nutritionally stunted, rough-coated, potbellied (protein-deficient), lethargic foals are unavoidable. A contented, healthy, parasite-free, well-nourished foal often achieves 95% of its adult height by 12 months of age. Although stunted and unthrifty yearlings will eventually reach their genetic potential in height, it may be much later in adulthood. The long-term effects of stunting in miniature horses have not been recorded, but in humans, both neurological and physical deficiencies have been documented. The quest for small size and its relationship to high prices may have compounded this problem within the miniature horse industry.

When purchasing a weanling, yearling or 2-year-old miniature, the prospective owner should observe the size of any potbelly present and the amount of muscle and fat covering the ribs, crest of the neck, rump and backbone. It is important to look for any of the following symptoms: floppy ears; bloated abdomen; lethargy (inactivity or depression); poor appetite; **ewe neck** (upside down, lack of muscling causes the neck to appear concave at the crest); narrow chest, prominent withers, backbone or hip bones and possibly diarrhea, cough or runny nose. If the miniature has a full winter coat, accurate assessments may be accomplished only by a thorough examination of the body's condition underneath the long hair. Heavily parasitized youngsters can be expected to experience rapid growth spurts after being returned to a parasite-free condition. Because the life cycle of ascarids is less than 30 days, such foals will require wormings every 21 to 30 days for at least 6 months. Frequent wormings, coupled with an extremely high-protein free-choice alfalfa hay or alfalfa meal diet (at least 17% to 19% protein), will be necessary before an adequate state of nutrition can be established. When considering the feeding of any grain or concentrate product, it is crucial for these nutritionally depleted foals that the protein content of everything they eat be higher than 17%, which is not the case for most commercial mixes. The disappearance of potbelly and ewe neck marks the reversal from protein deficiency to adequate health and vigor. The appetite will increase, the depression will disappear and there will be a noticeable return of normal muscle mass over the neck, back and hips.

Ascarids can also cause fatal colics. Their presence in large numbers, whether dead or alive, may completely obstruct the intestine. Mature ascarids are large and often measure more than 10 inches (25 cm) in length. For this reason, one must use caution when worming a foal that is heavily infested with ascarids. When too many roundworms die at once, intestinal impactions, as well as ruptures, have been known to occur. These impactions and ruptures are caused by the formation of a solid ball of dead worms too large to pass through the intestine. In addition, the damage roundworms cause to the liver and lungs during their migrating larval stages is extensive. About 3 weeks of an ascarid's life is spent as a larva migrating through these vital organs before it is coughed up, swallowed and becomes an adult in the gastrointestinal tract. Foals with dry, hacking coughs, an almost certain sign of roundworm infestation, should not be purchased.

Gasterophilus (Bots)

Bots are the larval stages of the various species of botflies. They suck blood and permanently attach themselves for 9 to 12 months by burying their mouthparts deep into the lining of the stomach. Bot larvae cause nutritional depletions, abdominal pain and serious mechanical damage. The female adult botfly lives for only 5 days. It lays its 500 to 1,000 small, yellowish eggs on the hairs of horses' legs, lips and, sometimes, the neck. Daily removal (or at least twice weekly) is easily accomplished with a safety razor and is an excellent preventative measure. Commercially manufactured bot egg scrapers may be purchased at most feed stores. The eggs should be removed in an area that is inaccessible to pastured horses, such as an asphalt driveway. When eggs are not removed, the horse licks the eggs, stimulating the eggs to hatch with its saliva, and the larvae then enter the horse's mouth. During this first larval stage, which lasts about a month, the larvae migrate extensively through the tissues of the mouth, tongue and throat. When horses chew on wooden barns and fences during the fall, bots should be suspected, as their migrations cause intense irritation. Wood chewing occurs in an attempt to relieve the inflammation and itching.

It is important to worm all horses for bots after the first hard frost of each fall, which will have killed most of the remaining adult botflies. Avermectin and moxidectin products are the most reliable and least traumatic drugs for bots, but there are other organophosphate boticides that can be administered via nasogastric (stomach) tube by an equine veterinarian. Owners and breeders should be cautious about equine veterinarians who have limited experience with miniature horses. Inappropriately large stomach tubes, boluses that become lodged in the throat and miscalculated therapeutic doses can all be fatal. Removal of all bot eggs at the time each horse is wormed for bots in the fall should ensure a winter of freedom from gastric bot larvae infestation.

Internal Parasite Management Practices

There are a few simple management practices that can greatly improve parasite-control programs. The key to effective parasite control is to follow a fixed schedule of treatment and to keep accurate worming records for each animal. Unfortunately, horses can quickly pick up more worms from pastures and paddocks after they have been treated. Keeping manure cleaned out of stalls and pastures and avoiding overcrowding of animals are essential. Pastures should be rotated frequently, allowing 30- to 60-day rest periods with no grazing horses, particularly in damp or wet weather. Rotating pastures is especially important with irrigated pastures that stay green all year. Hay should not be fed on the ground. Large-sized, heavy-duty, free-standing sheep feeders available at most feed stores function as excellent miniature horse feeders. Other low-sided feeders that cannot be tipped over by the horses but that allow the feeding of hay and grain at ground level (to both foals and adult stock) also are available (see Figure 9.1).

After seeking a qualified veterinarian's advice concerning the safest products to use, the miniature horse owner should start worming all foals by the time they are 1 month of age and worm on a monthly basis until they are yearlings. Many of the anthelmintics available are not safe for young foals. Furthermore, foals are often sensitive to certain types of dewormers, particularly if they are heavily infested with ascarids. Foals should always be observed carefully for at least 48 hours after they have been wormed. An equine veterinarian's advice should be sought before initiating any miniature foal's worming program.

Stallions, mares and foals over 12 months of age should be wormed at least once every 2 to 3 months. All adult horses should be wormed 1 to 2 days before being put on a new pasture and all horses being kept together should be wormed on the same day. All new horses should be wormed immediately after arrival on the ranch and kept separated from the main herd for at least 2 weeks. Outside mares to be bred should be wormed by their owners at least 2 weeks before their arrival at the breeding facility. Periodic ova and parasite studies (microscopic fecal examinations by a veterinarian) are highly beneficial in determining the effectiveness of a worming program. Most equine veterinarians recommend fecal studies at least twice yearly.

With some of the newer anthelmintics, accurate weight assessments are critical to the safe administration of the drug. **Weight tapes** (a paper tape with weight estimates on one side and inches on the other) have commonly been used to estimate horses' weights for medication and worming dosing. While these tapes may be beneficial for determining the weight of full-sized horses, equine weight tapes have recently been discovered to not be an accurate means of determining the weights of miniature horses (Abramson 1998a). The commonly used equine weight tapes often result in estimated weights that are consistently about 20% higher than the actual weights of the horse being measured (see Tables 8.2 and 8.3).

Determining Miniature Horse Weights

Adapted from Abramson 1998a

Accurate determination of a miniature horse weight is difficult for experienced and novice horse owners alike. Miniature horses come in all types of body builds. The relative body proportions change with age, condition score, breed and type of horse. The necessity of knowing a horse's accurate weight arises when trying to ascertain the dosage required for medicating or worming horses. Veterinarians often depend on either the owner's guess or a weight tape. Either, according to one preliminary study, would not be very accurate (see Tables 8.2 and 8.3). Because most medications are administered on a bodyweight basis, underdosing can lead to reduced effectiveness and overdosing can be fatal. The effectiveness of certain medications commonly given to foals, including worming medication, depends on accurate weights. Therefore, foals that are small enough to be held by a human should be weighed on a bathroom scale if a platform scale is unavailable.

The herd of horses used in a recent study of weight tapes numbered 21. The data for adults and foals have been separated in the tables for convenience. Five of the horses were 1997 foals 6 months old or under, 2 were stallions and 14 were mares (12 of these were 3 to 7 months pregnant). Two mares were 1- to 2-year-olds. All horses were weighed on a platform scale, then weight taped. The average of all adult horses 3 years and older was 246 pounds. The results were uniform in one respect: the weights of all horses were lower on the platform scale than with the weight tape. The amount the weight tape was off differed in the adult group from as little as 3 pounds to as much as 59, with an average of 41 pounds (see Table 8.2). It should be noted that all horses were in their full winter coats, not clipped.

Table 8.2 Miniature Horse (Adults) Weight Tape Measurements, Compared With Actual Weights*

Height	No. of Horses	Scale Weight Range	Weight Tape Range	Weight Difference
32–34 in. (80–85 cm)	4	264–345 lb (119–155 kg)	317–398 lb (143–179 kg)	48–56 lb (21–25 kg)
30–32 in. (75–80 cm)	4	204–243 lb (92–109 kg)	231–280 lb (104–126 kg)	3–47 lb (1–21 kg)
28–30 in. (70–75 cm)	7	188–274 lb (85–123 kg)	224–310 lb (101–139 kg)	36–59 lb (16–26 kg)
26–28 in. (65–70 cm)	1	196 lb (88 kg)	238 lb (107 kg)	42 lb (19 kg)

* Data collected by Joanne Abramson, at Pacific Pintos Miniature Horses.

All horses were weighed on a platform scale on the same day they were measured with a standard weight tape. The weight tape measurements on foals varied from 18 to 36 pounds higher, with an average of 23.8 pounds. However, the foals represented the greatest risk of overdosing with medication as the 18- to 36-pound overweights of the weight tape represented 1/4 to 1/3 of their total body weight (see Table 8.3).

Table 8.3 Miniature Horse (Foals) Weight Tape Measurements Compared With Actual Weights*

Height	No. of Horses	Scale Weight Range	Weight Tape Range	Weight Difference
28–30 in. (70–75 cm)	1	174 lb (79 kg)	211 lb (95 kg)	36 lb (16 kg)
26–28 in. (65–70 cm)	1	108 lb (48 kg)	131 lb (59 kg)	23 lb (10 kg)
24–26 in. (60–65 cm)	2	88–92 lb (39–41 kg)	114 lb (51 kg)	18–22 lb (8–10 kg)
22–24 in. (55–60 cm)	1	67 lb (30 kg)	87 lb (39 kg)	20 lb (9 kg)

* Data collected by Joanne Abramson, at Pacific Pintos Miniature Horses.

All foals were weighed on a platform scale on the same day they were measured with a standard weight tape. Miniature horses represent a unique type of horse that needs special treatment, including the use of an accurate scale instead of the more common weight tape currently in use. Miniature owners who depend on weight tapes should be warned that, especially with foals, the weight tape values often exceed actual weight. Commonly used wormers, such as Zimectrin® and Strongid®, have had a wide safety range and allow slight overdosing without causing severe reactions. Newer wormers, such as Quest™, however, require accurate weights. The 67-pound (30- kg) 4-month-old foal referenced in Table 8.3 would receive medication for a 100-pound (45-kg) horse based on the 87-pound (39-kg) weight tape reading. Instead, this horse should be getting a safer dose for a 50-pound (22.5-kg) weight based on the 67-pound (30-kg) platform scale weight.

Worming horses only once or twice a year results in animals that are at high risk for colic and animals that are not being maintained at the peak of their potential. Preventative health care requires perceptive observation of each individual on a daily basis, as well as a rigorous and accurately recorded parasite-control program.

New wormers are being advertised on a regular basis, each with its own unique and important uses, as well as specific guidelines for administration. Many miniatures have died because their owners listened to advertising claims, hearsay, and to their friends, instead of consulting with their veterinarians. It is extremely important to read all medication or dewormer labels carefully, noting specific directions, dosage by weight requirements, active ingredients, and which parasites are being controlled. Finally, when using any anthelmintics other than the avermectins and moxidectins, it is essential to rotate according to product category, not according to trade name (see Table 8.4). Unless ivermectin or moxidectin products are used exclusively, it is essential to rotate anthelmintics according to product category types at least once yearly to avoid the development of resistant strains of internal parasites.

The following table outlines the most commonly used anthelmintics and lists them under their product categories. Not included are several additional organophosphate products that should be administered only via nasogastric tube by a veterinarian.

Bots are controlled only by ivermectin, moxidectin and the organophosphates. Tapeworms are controlled only by the pyrimidines. Although very safe, piperazine controls only ascarids so is used only for young stock or in combination with other products. The benzimidazoles, macrocyclic lactones, pyrimidines and phenylguanidines are all effective against most other equine internal parasites.

Table 8.4 Product Categories of Commonly Used Anthelmintics

Product Category	Drug	Trade Name	Type of Formulation
Benzimidazoles (is the category most likely to cause development of resistant strains of worms)	Oxybendazole	Anthelcide EQ®	Paste or suspension
		Equipar®	Paste or suspension
	Oxfendazole	Benzelmin®	Powder, paste or suspension
		Equicide™	Paste
	Fenbendazole	Panacur®	Paste, granules or liquid
		Safe-Guard™	Paste
	Mebendazole	Telmin®	Paste or liquid
	Thiabendazole	Equizole®	Liquid
Macrocyclic lactones	Avermectins (Ivermectin)	Eqvalan®	Paste or liquid
		Equimectrin™	Paste
		Zimecterin®	Paste
		Rotectin I™	Paste
	Milbimycins (Moxidectin)	Quest™	Gel
Pyrimidines	Pyrantel pamoate	Strongid®	Paste or liquid
		Imathal®	Paste or liquid
		Rotectin II™	Paste
	Pyrantel tartrate	Strongid C™	Pellets
		EMC Wormer®	Pellets
Phenylguanidines	Febantel	Cutter Paste Wormer®	Paste
		Rintal®	Paste
Piperazine	Piperazine	Piperazine	Powder
Organophosphates	Dichlorvos	Cutter Dichlorvos	Granules

External Parasite Control

Control of **ectoparasites** (external parasites) begins with manure removal, regular grooming and the owner's daily observation of each animal. Manure may be composted, since the heat generated by the composting process will kill most parasites, as well as their eggs and larvae. Composted manure is a valuable commodity for miniature horse breeders who are interested in gardening, and composting also kills weed seeds.

Horn flies, face flies, gnats, ticks and mosquitoes are the most common pasture pests, while house flies, stable flies, mange mites and lice are the most common barn pests. Miniatures that are kept indoors without regular grooming are the most susceptible to infestation. Ectoparasites tend to target debilitated animals, and it is common for severely underweight miniatures (having a BCS under 4) to be heavily infested, particularly with lice or mange mites (see Figure 8.3).

Unless an owner acquires a single new animal with problems, all types of ectoparasitism should be considered a herd rather than an individual problem. Regularly groomed animals maintained in healthy, well-fed and well-observed herd conditions seem to have increased resistance to external parasite infestations. Overcrowded horses living in unsanitary conditions, with poor-quality pastures or hay and generally suffering from

Barbara Naviaux

Figure 8.3 *Severe lice infestation on a yearling filly (BCS of 1) that is also suffering from gross negligence. In addition to lice infestation, this horse has a severely undershot jaw that may have compromised her ability to properly chew food. Note typical appearance of the clumped and matted hair, which has been partially shed. This filly is extremely underweight, the feet need trimming and there also is heavy ascarid infestation. Worming with ivermectin eliminated both the worms and the lice over a 2-week period. Upon arrival, the filly was immediately bathed in a rotenone-base shampoo, then clipped, and the clipped hair was incinerated. A free-choice 19% protein diet, hoof trimming, floating of the molars, and ivermectin dewormings every month resulted in health improvements by the age of 18 months. Without corrective intervention, the underbite went from 1.5 inches to 0.5 inches (3.8 to 1.3 cm) during that time.*

neglect, will have compromised immune systems. Standing water, deep mud, and urine-soaked stalls should all be avoided. There are a number of ectoparasites that can cause **alopecia** (hair loss) and **pruritis** (itching) in miniature horses.

Lice

Lice are species specific; horse lice cannot be acquired from any other species, such as humans or chickens. Conversely, humans cannot be infected by horse lice. Lice are very small, but upon close inspection, both the eggs and the adult lice may be seen with the naked eye. Lice are most commonly located around the mane and tail, along the neck and shoulders and on the inside of the thighs, and infected animals will usually show intense pruritis. The tiny, cream-colored eggs are most easily seen by examination of the coarse mane hairs. Horses affected by lice often have a moth-eaten appearance (see Figure 8.3), with many areas of total alopecia easily observed. Occasionally, when the coat is matted, the lice can be seen when the hair mass is broken apart. Severe infestations of lice can result in anemia and are often seen in combination with other health problems (J. L. Naviaux 1985).

Lice infestation is relatively common, especially during the winter months and within herds, rather than in individual horses. There are two types of lice in equines, biting lice and sucking lice, both of which spend most of their life cycles on the host horse's body. **Biting lice** are active and can be seen moving through the hair, while **sucking lice** usually move about

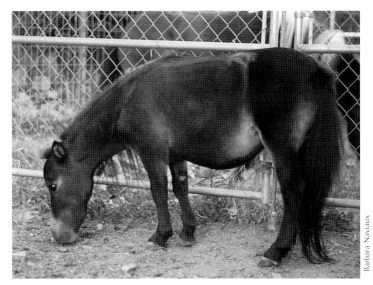

Barbara Naviaux

Figure 8.4 *Same filly as shown in Figure 8.3 after 2 months on the recuperative regimen outlined. The lice are gone and the body condition has improved to a BCS of 3, but the filly still has a potbelly, which took an additional 6 months to disappear.*

more slowly and are often found with mouthparts embedded in the skin. Eggs (or nits) are attached to the hair near the skin and hatch in approximately 2 weeks. Two weeks after hatching, the new females begin laying eggs, but die soon thereafter, and the entire life cycle is less than one month. Transmission of lice is by horse-to-horse direct contact and by contaminated grooming equipment or blankets.

Treatment of lice is best accomplished with a lindane- or rotenone-based dip or shampoo recommended by an equine veterinarian, followed or preceded by full body clipping. All discarded hair should be incinerated, although lice separated from their host are unable to live for long. After being shampooed and clipped, each horse in the herd should be wormed with ivermectin. Ivermectin will not kill or eliminate the eggs, but it enters the blood stream and effectively eliminates any lice that may still be biting or sucking blood (Rose & Hodgson 1993). Finally, all halters, blankets and grooming equipment previously in contact with lice-infested horses should be washed and treated with an appropriate insecticide.

Mange Mites

Chorioptic mange and demodectic mange occur only occasionally in miniature horses, but sarcoptic mange is a very common problem. The **sarcoptic mange mite** burrows into the skin, unlike the other two types of equine mange mites, which do not burrow. It is the most severe type of equine mange and spreads very quickly on an infested horse, as well as to other horses. Sarcoptic mange is difficult to control and tends to reoccur, especially in debilitated animals. The first signs are intense itching, followed by small papules that develop into scales, crusts and an acute dermatitis. Alopecia occurs as the mite-infested and balding skin thickens and forms thick folds, particularly on the muzzle and neck regions. Local treatment with veterinary-prescribed miticides can be augmented by the oral administration of ivermectin, but repeated treatments over a long period are often required to gain permanent control.

Ticks

Fall and winter tick infestation is fairly common in horses but seldom seems to cause the animals much discomfort, pruritis or alopecia. Ticks are usually more of a problem in low foothills or bushy areas and, unlike lice, are not species specific. The same species of ticks seem to infest horses, dogs, cats, deer and even humans. Regular grooming, accompanied by hand picking of the embedded ticks, may be the only control measure needed, although ticks in large numbers can cause severe anemia. Because ticks are a fall and winter problem, they are easily hidden within the miniature's thick winter coat. After removal, ticks should be incinerated. Good drainage and dry pastures reduce the humidity upon which ticks depend. As for lice, ticks may be chemically controlled by insecticidal sprays, dips or shampoos, the various types of which should be suggested and provided by a qualified veterinarian. Ivermectin also may be used as a control measure but is unable to affect eggs, nymphs and adult ticks that have already dropped to the ground, so reinfestation often occurs after treatment.

Ticks are known to transmit a large number of diseases. One species is known to be the intermediate vector of Lyme disease. Their saliva also causes elevated skin bumps, alopecia and localized allergic reactions, all of which may gravely affect the beauty and health of a clipped show horse's skin and hair coat, as well as its disposition.

Adult ticks may breed either on or off of their host; ticks frequently survive for long periods off their hosts and without food (as long as 5 years). Adult females lay as many as 18,000 eggs on the ground and then die. The eggs develop into larvae that climb up on grass or shrubs, where they attach themselves to a passing host. As each tick develops into maturity, it sucks blood for sustenance.

The spinose ear tick (although not as common as body ticks) causes great discomfort to infested horses, often rendering the animals ear shy and difficult to halter. This tick's larvae crawl into the horses' ears and spend as long as 7 months developing through the nymphal stage, after which they drop out of the ears and crawl to fences, barns, feed troughs and trees to molt into adults, mate and deposit new eggs. Small-animal ear mite medications may be used to control ear ticks, especially if augmented with ivermectin wormings.

Mosquitoes

In addition to causing skin welts and intense itching, mosquitoes sometimes transmit Eastern, Western and Venezuelan equine encephalomyelitis (sleeping sickness), as well as many other diseases. Some miniatures are hypersensitive to mosquito bites, which can cause severe **dermatitis** (skin inflammations). Mosquitoes breed in standing water, so watering troughs, pails, discarded tires and other small containers that tend to collect water should be emptied periodically. Mosquito fish or bullfrogs should be planted in larger ponds to eliminate as many mosquito larvae as possible.

About 3,000 species of mosquitoes have been described worldwide, with about 150 in North America. Mosquitoes are found from the salt marshes of the coastal plains to the snow pools above 16,000 feet and as low as 3,600 feet below sea level in the gold mines of India. They lay their eggs on or near standing water and the larvae (also known as wigglers) are entirely aquatic. Breaking the life cycle by eliminating all aquatic breeding sites in horse pastures remains the most effective means of control, but repellent or insecticidal sprays may also be used if mosquitoes occur in large numbers and become a serious problem.

Flies and Gnats

Many species of flies and gnats feed on the blood of horses and some, such as horse flies, have very painful bites. Horses become alarmed when approached by the larger biting flies and often injure themselves attempting to escape. When biting flies are present in large numbers, they can cause significant blood loss.

Preferring to eat the fluids excreted from the eyes and nose, face flies cause continual irritation around the eyes and are often implicated in cases of **conjunctivitis** (inflammation of the conjunctivae, sometimes called pink eye), which can easily spread from horse to horse in a given herd. Fly masks (if tolerated well and not removed by pasture mates), can provide protection to the eyes when face flies become numerous. Similarly, house flies do not feed on blood, but they also can be a constant source of irritation to horses, as well as humans, and are known to spread various diseases.

There are more than 1,000 species of black flies, buffalo flies and other biting gnats. Only female gnats suck blood, but they often cause chronic dermatitis. The gnat attacks various body parts, but many prefer the inside of horses' ears. Many blood-sucking species of flies and gnats are known to be significant vectors in the spread of certain diseases such as sleeping sickness, equine infectious anemia (swamp fever) and chronic abscesses (pigeon fever).

Effective fly control requires strict sanitation and daily removal of manure to eliminate breeding-ground opportunities. There are also various types of chemicals that may be used as residual sprays, baits, space sprays and larvicides. Some of these may be safely used for direct applications on the animals, but reports of local skin reactions and irritations are common. Many types of attractant fly traps or predator wasps offer a more organic approach to fly control. No topical fly repellent currently available for horses seems to last more than a few hours, so fly control is always best approached by prevention of large fly populations through other measures.

Ringworm

The fungal species *Trichophyton equinum* is the primary cause of ringworm in horses and is best diagnosed by an equine veterinarian. Early lesions resemble an attack of hives but then progress to alopecia and crusting in a few days. Transmission is usually by contaminated grooming equipment, saddle blankets and harnesses. Treatment requires decontamination of these items, as well as the total environment, and the horse affected is best isolated from all other animals. Iodine, chlorhexidine and other types of antifungal shampoos may be employed, but the effective and lasting management of ringworm infestation should be under the supervision of an equine veterinarian.

Rainrot

Rainrot is a common type of dermatitis, initially caused by a fungus-like organism called *dermatophilus*, and later complicated by secondary bacterial infections. Rainrot usually occurs during the springtime and is encountered more frequently in miniatures than in larger breeds of horses because of their heavier winter coats (which may be moist and muddy for long periods). In continually wet weather, when miniatures remain wet for 2 weeks or more, they often develop this type of dermatitis on their backs. Miniatures kept on irrigated pastures during the summer months may also be affected, particularly if they enjoy standing under the sprinklers. What appear to be muddy clumps of hair will peel off to reveal bleeding hot spots and raw skin. White, zigzag markings can blemish the replacement hair coat when skin scarring from this infection heals. Diluted iodine kills the *dermatophilus* organism, but it is best to consult with an equine veterinarian for the best shampoos or current therapeutic measures recommended for rainrot, as antibiotics may be required in serious cases. Keeping horses in stalls during extended rainstorms can reduce or eliminate rainrot by allowing the coat to dry. After the coat is thoroughly dry, grooming (or clipping) is helpful to remove all clumps of muddy hair that can be felt along the spine and top-line.

Hoof Care and Trimming

Prior to the formation of the AMHR registry in 1971, breeders of miniature horses paid little attention to hoof and leg structure. There was no standard of perfection and there were no miniature horse shows or breed-approved judges. Farriers (blacksmiths) were primarily engaged in the care of full-sized horses requiring shoes rather than the occasional trimming of diminutive breeds such as miniature horses. Since the focus of miniature horse breeding prior to the creation of the Standard of Perfection in 1974 was small size, the predisposition for various types of poorly conformed hooves and legs became genetically established in the foundation breeding animals.

The first miniature horse show classes in the United States were not held until 1946. Because there was no standard of perfection, the judges made all of their placements without written conformation guidelines. A large number of miniatures with disproportionately shortened legs, club feet, angular limb deformities and stiff movement achieved championships and notoriety within the breed as herd sires. In 1974, when the first Standard of Perfection was written, breeders began addressing hoof and leg problems that previously had been ignored. One of the disqualifications listed in the new standard was *dwarfism*, a single term that summarized many of the hoof and leg problems most often seen.

Because normal horses regrow a new hoof about once yearly, veterinarians and professional farriers are able to acquire at least 12 months of vital health information by examining a horse's hooves. Disease problems, such as laminitis (founder) and **thrush** (a type of sole and frog infection) may be identified by hoof examinations. Usually caused by poor management, both laminitis and thrush are almost always preventable (see Chapter 9).

Normal leg function and attractive gaits both depend upon the health, elasticity, balance and correct structure of the hoof. Each component of the hoof must interact with many others in order to circulate blood, reduce concussion and maintain moisture content. The blood-pumping mechanism of the foot is primarily at the heels and within the elastic structures found there. These softer components of the hoof function as both shock absorbers and blood circulators. Because there are no muscles in a horse's lower leg, blood circulation depends upon a complicated system of expansions and contractions of the hoof, combined with a series of venous valves going up the legs. These valves resist (or counteract) the effects of gravity by preventing deoxygenated blood from falling back to the hooves and are critical to the cycle of returning blood to the lungs for reoxygenation.

The frog, another elastic concussion-reducing structure, functions best when allowed contact with the ground. When there is no frog pressure from the ground, a deformity known as contracted heels may develop and must be corrected, very gradually, by a professional farrier.

Figure 8.5 *Overgrown and badly neglected hooves on a miniature horse mare. This mare's hooves were allowed to get so long that she was unable to walk on the sole. This forced the mare to walk on the back surface of the hoof and pastern but only at a very slow hobble. One hoof has just been trimmed and may be compared to the length of the untrimmed hoof.*

The sensitive structures of the hoof, which contain many blood vessels and nerves, are located under all horny parts of the hoof and provide blood circulation, growth potential and nerve supplies to each of those areas. The rate of growth and elasticity of the hoof is dependent upon these sensitive structures, coupled with various environmental factors such as hoof care, climate, pasture conditions and exercise. The hoof wall (being the least elastic) should contain about 25% moisture, the sole about 33% and the frog (being the most elastic) about 50% (Butler 1994). The maintenance of vital moisture in the hoof may be augmented during dry summer months by access to ponds, streams or designated muddy areas. Inadequate hoof moisture may result in chipped and cracked hoof walls and can make trimming difficult.

There are many hazards when trimming a miniature horse's feet, and most professional farriers advise a cautious approach, particularly when small foals are being corrected for certain hoof and leg faults. The overcorrection of foal hooves is one of the most common mistakes made by amateurs when attempting to trim their own animals. Slight hoof problems of young foals are frequently overcorrected, which can cause irreparable epiphyseal damage. The **epiphyses** are the cartilaginous terminal surfaces of the bones (at the joints) from which calcified bone later forms, resulting in the normal lengthening process of the leg. Each of the epiphyseal surfaces matures (becomes bone) at different ages, but most are completely calcified by 3 years of age. Only a few harden at later than 3 years. The approximate ages of epiphyseal closure in the legs of miniature horses range from less than 6 months (for joints below the lower legs), to about 3 years (for joints associated with the upper legs, shoulder and hips). After age 3, corrective trimming becomes correction for visual appeal (such as for show presentation) or to prevent the horse from injuring itself (as in the case of severe club feet) and can never be effective for permanent correction of a particular leg or hoof fault. It is important that developing foals' feet be kept sound and well balanced. Any corrective trimming of their hooves is best handled by an experienced miniature horse farrier, and overcorrection for any fault should be avoided. Miniature horse foals sometimes require trimming shortly after birth and as often as every 2 weeks thereafter. Until the foal is traveling normally and not growing too much toe or heel (has a normal pastern/hoof angle), a farrier's expertise and advice should be sought.

Many surgical and medical techniques are currently being employed in an attempt to correct angular limb deformities of young miniature foals. These are the same techniques that were originally developed for various breeds of full-sized horses, such as racing Thoroughbreds. In the larger breeds, angular limb deformities at birth are fairly common, and those that do not correct by themselves during the first few months of life are often corrected by periosteal stripping, stapling, braces, casts and/or corrective shoeing. The ethics of resorting to veterinary interventions for many of these types of angular limb deformities are questionable in the miniature horse breed because of their association with various dwarfism syndromes, most of which are genetic in nature. These veterinary techniques may be a consideration in improving the horse's mobility and comfort, but, after correction, questions arise as to whether it is ethical for these animals to be used for breeding or showing and, without a full disclosure of the animal's past veterinary care, whether it is ethical to sell these animals for either of those purposes.

Hoof care of miniature horses, like all preventative health care, depends upon an owner's critical observation of each animal at least twice daily. In this manner, injuries or unsoundnesses may be immediately recognized so that horses needing hoof care can be identified and scheduled for trimming.

In preparation for the farrier's arrival, the feet should be wiped dry with a towel and each foot thoroughly cleaned out with a hoof pick. All horses to be trimmed should be tied up and waiting, and should be well enough trained to calmly accept the farrier's work on their feet. These are simple courtesies that are greatly appreciated by even the least demanding of farriers.

Many miniature owners trim their own horses' feet, although a farrier should always be sought if any horse seems to be developing leg, hoof, gait or conformation problems. Even if the amateur hoof trimmer has made a serious study of equine anatomy, healthy hoof care and the various corrective measures, attempting to trim miniatures can be a challenging project. Furthermore, even if an owner chooses to do most of his or her own trimming, it is imperative to employ a professional farrier at least once a year for each horse.

Developing an ability to **site** (view a hoof in order to determine how to trim) a foot is an important prerequisite for all amateur trimmers. The hoof must be balanced from heel to toe and from side to side, and must be level across the bottom. Improperly balanced feet can seriously affect soundness, future adult leg conformation and the correctness of gaits.

Required tools for trimming miniatures are the hoof pick, hoof knife, hoof nippers and horseshoer's rasp. Scaled-down versions of some of these tools are available through a large variety of miniature horse and pony supplier catalogs. Each horse should be trimmed every 2 to 3 months, with variations in frequency as often as every 2 weeks (for certain foals) and as seldom as twice yearly (for certain active and mature animals whose legs are so correctly conformed that their hooves wear off evenly from exercise).

The cause of most foot and leg problems is usually the failure to properly balance the feet (Butler 1994). Faults may be hidden but can rarely be corrected by purposely trimming in an unbalanced manner. Joints and tendons will be stretched or twisted when hooves are trimmed to make them look straight, if that is not the natural leg or foot conformation of that particular horse. Conformation faults are almost always inherited. Miniature horses may inherit a predisposition to certain hoof and leg faults that can sometimes be prevented from developing if consistent and balanced trimming of their feet begins at an early age. Outside influences such as nutrition, neglect, exercise, injuries and improper trimming (or overcorrection) at a very early age occasionally cause the formation of non-genetic defects. Each of these outside influences may cause the development of conformation faults that are ultimately the result of unequal weight distribution on the epiphyseal cartilages during the early growth years.

To have an animal properly balanced overall, the slope of the shoulder and the slope of the hoof and pastern should both be about the same. Miniatures travel most comfortably and efficiently when each of these angles is from 45° to 50°. When viewed from the side in a standing position, the angles formed (from the ground) by the front of the hoof and the front of the pastern should be identical. In addition, the shoulder angle and hoof/pastern angle should also approximate the angle of the pelvis (hip bones). Alignment at both ends of the body results in a properly balanced horse.

Conscientious hoof care of miniature horses is frequently more difficult than it is for the larger equine breeds. Consulting with equine veterinarians and professional farriers who have had a great deal of experience with miniatures should be an important part of good hoof care and farm management practices.

Dental Care

Miniature horses can be born with genetic dental problems or may later develop problems associated with their teeth. Dental health problems are not limited to mature animals. Newly born foals should have their mouths examined thoroughly as a routine part of the imprinting process. The gums will reveal any malocclusion problems even before the milk teeth begin erupting (during the first week), and the foal will be getting its first lessons in submitting to later oral examinations and wormings.

As a horse gets older, its teeth continually change in size and shape. Specific configurations and markings of the teeth appear and disappear at certain ages. These changes make it possible for horses to be accurately aged by their teeth. Unfortunately, the guidelines used for aging full-sized horses cannot always be relied upon in miniatures. By the time a horse has reached the age of 5, it should have all of its permanent teeth, and all of the deciduous (baby) teeth should have been shed. As a horse ages, the incisors will become increasingly oblique (25-year-olds appear to have buck teeth).

Regular dental care is crucial to the health, well being, future development and performance ability of every horse but is the most neglected aspect of miniature horse farm management. Routine dental examinations by an equine veterinarian or by a qualified equine dental technician should be performed on each horse at least once yearly. Animals that show any signs of jaw malocclusion, poor body condition or mouth pain should be examined by a veterinarian as soon as possible.

Julia Ramos

Figure 8.6 *Three-year-old miniature mare with large, temporary tooth bumps under the lower jaw. These bumps are caused by the roots of permanent lower molars that have not yet moved up and pushed deciduous molars (molar caps) out of place.*

Dental disease can cause a variety of symptoms and signs, all of which are related to the horse's eating behavior, performance or health. If the horse is holding its head to one side while eating, spilling grain, washing its feed in the water trough or spitting out wads of partially chewed hay (quidding), it should have its teeth checked. If the horse retains persistent large lumps under the jaw or on the bridge of the nose (see Figure 8.6), or if it develops bad breath (a sure sign of bacterial invasion), its teeth should be checked.

Any miniature that is thin and rough coated, regardless of age, should always have its teeth checked. A performance animal may start tossing its head, rearing, holding its head to one side or fighting the bit because of mechanical interference from wolf teeth (first premolars) or canines. These teeth can easily be filed down or removed to alleviate the irritation they sometimes cause when a bit is in the mouth.

Sharp edges on the molars can interfere with chewing and may lacerate the sides of the tongue and cheeks. If unable to chew properly, the horse passes a large portion of its food through the intestinal tract undigested. Long strands of hay or identifiable whole grains should not be visible in a healthy miniature's manure, and dental care should be sought immediately for animals whose feed is not properly digested. Miniatures in this category are much more prone to impactions, and until their teeth problems are resolved, they are at high risk for terminal colics.

Dental problems of miniature horses can be divided into four categories:

- Individual tooth problems
- Abnormalities of wear patterns
- Dental infections
- Genetic abnormalities

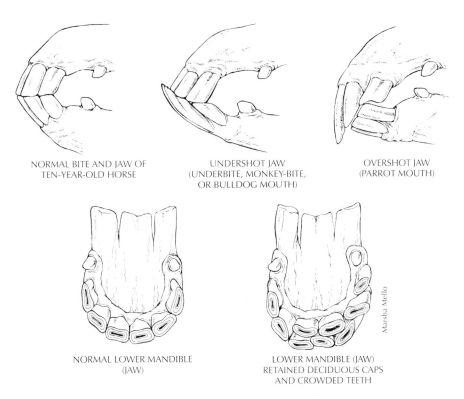

NORMAL BITE AND JAW OF
TEN-YEAR-OLD HORSE

UNDERSHOT JAW
(UNDERBITE, MONKEY-BITE,
OR BULLDOG MOUTH)

OVERSHOT JAW
(PARROT MOUTH)

NORMAL LOWER MANDIBLE
(JAW)

LOWER MANDIBLE (JAW)
RETAINED DECIDUOUS CAPS
AND CROWDED TEETH

Figure 8.7 *Normally aligned teeth and some abnormal dental conditions. Undershot jaws (resulting from abnormal lengthening of the lower jaw) are considered a characteristic of brachycephalic dwarfism and have been shown to be recessively inherited. Foals born with slightly overshot jaws (resulting from abnormal lengthening of the upper jaw) will often correct themselves by adulthood. Retained deciduous caps and crowded teeth are commonly seen dental problems of miniature horses.*

All can be interrelated and are frequently associated with one another. For example, a broken tooth may cause both an infection and an abnormality of wear on an opposing tooth.

If a miniature horse foal has a jaw malocclusion, professional dental care is best begun at an early age. Genetic abnormalities of miniature horses' teeth are common and include undershot jaws (monkey bites), overshot jaws (parrot mouths) and wry mouths (crooked mouths from side to side). These abnormalities are unacceptable for show and breeding pur- poses and although they may be corrected with orthodontistry, there are serious ethical concerns regarding their disclosure to prospective buyers (see Figure 8.7).

Studies done in Canada (Williams 1992) determined that another genetic dental problem, unique to miniature horses and ponies, is the extremely large size of their teeth in comparison to their overall height. When compared to Quarter Horses, the average size of miniature horse molars was only slightly smaller. This phenomenon results in severe overcrowding of the teeth and may require extractions. Sometimes filing between the most crowded teeth is required to temporarily alleviate the problem.

In order to diagnose dental problems early and treat them effectively, it is important to understand the functions and structure of equine dentition. Equine teeth are very long and, unlike the teeth of humans, they continue to erupt and change throughout the horse's life. Only the erupted portion of the tooth is visible, but up to 3 inches (8 cm) of fully formed

Table 8.5 Ages of Equine Tooth Eruption

Type of Tooth		Probable Age of Eruption
Deciduous	1st incisor	Birth or first week
	2nd incisor	4 to 6 weeks
	3rd incisor	6 to 9 months
	1st premolar	Birth or first 2 weeks
	2nd premolar	Birth or first 2 weeks
	3rd premolar	Birth or first 2 weeks
Permanent	1st incisor	2.5 years
	2nd incisor	3.5 years
	3rd incisor	4.5 years
	Canine, males only	4 to 5 years
	1st premolar (wolf teeth)	5 to 6 months
	2nd premolar	2.5 years
	3rd premolar	3 years
	4th premolar	4 years
	1st molar	9 to 12 months
	2nd molar	2 years
	3rd molar	3.5 to 4 years

tooth is embedded in the upper or lower jaw of each miniature horse. Table 8.5 summarizes the ages each type of tooth may be expected to erupt.

The teeth are continually worn down by side-to-side grinding as the horse chews its food. Horses being fed pellets or other processed types of diets (over a long period) will invariably develop dental problems because of the reduced silicone content (abrasive substances found in hay or pastures) of their feed, as well as the lack of grinding action required to swallow it. They will sometimes develop the dangerous behavior of eating sand to make up for this deficiency in their diet.

In normal horses the upper jaw is wider than the lower jaw. This makes it probable that sharp edges will eventually form on the outside of the upper cheek teeth and on the inside of the lower cheek teeth. Filing off these sharp points with a long-handled rasp called a dental float is referred to as **floating the teeth**. The front incisors must meet evenly for efficiency in cutting pasture grasses. The **cheek teeth** (premolars and molars) function as grinders once vegetation enters the mouth. In this manner, the grinding surfaces of the teeth are constantly being renewed, reshaped and resharpened. At any point in the mouth where the entire surface of the upper and opposing lower teeth do not meet, the non-opposing surface will grow long, sharp points, or hooks.

The **canine teeth** (tushes), which usually appear only in male horses, are large curved teeth found in the interdental space between the incisors and the premolars. After age 4 or 5, when they first erupt, it is advisable to have these filed down by a veterinarian or dental technician, especially if the horse is to be used for driving. Similarly, the **wolf teeth**, small, vestigial premolars immediately in front of the first upper cheek teeth, can cause problems for driving horses. These teeth have short roots and are often extracted if they create problems.

Another common problem in miniature horses is the improper shedding of caps, or deciduous teeth. Large bumps form under the jaw or over the bridge of the nose when molar caps are not pushed out by the adult molars. A similar problem is the unattractive appearance of a seriously crowded mouth, caused by deciduous incisors that have not been pushed out by the adult incisors (see Figure 8.7).

The most common dental disease of horses is periodontal (gum) disease. The feeding of sweet grains and processed foods with few grinding requirements for the teeth is largely responsible for the prevalence of periodontal disease. Wild mustangs, forced to exist on the harshest of forage materials, do not experience periodontal disease. With horses, as with humans, this disease syndrome begins with **gingivitis** (inflammation of the gums) and rapidly progresses, leading to pockets of pus that erode the gums so completely that the affected teeth loosen and eventually fall out. The maintenance of properly occluded molars (with no jagged edges) is essential to the prevention of periodontal disease. Gingivitis occurs in any situation where there is abnormal occlusion and a decreased amount of grinding action. Thus, regular dental examinations and subsequent procedures to maintain normal teeth and grinding action help prevent its onset (Baker in Pratt 1982).

The importance of consistently high-quality dental care for each individual in a herd cannot be overstated. Qualified professionals (equine veterinarians or certified equine dental technicians) should always be a part of a farm's preventative health management concerning the teeth and jaws. Dental health and genetic planning to avoid malocclusions are both crucial to the individual horse, as well as to the lasting future of the miniature horse industry.

Grooming

Each season of the year presents special grooming problems, even for the healthiest of miniatures in a natural herd setting. Most grooming articles recommend grooming each horse daily, although for the miniature horse owner with a large number of animals, this may be difficult. Still, grooming a miniature horse requires much less time than for a full-sized horse. Basic grooming equipment generally consists of rubber curry combs (metal curry combs may injure the skin), soft and coarse body brushes, sponges, towels, hoof picks, sweat (and water) scrapers, electric clippers and safety razors (for bot egg removal, as well as for shaving muzzles). Human hair brushes and various cat and dog grooming supplies are excellent additions to a miniature horse grooming box.

During spring, when the winter coat starts shedding out, most miniatures appreciate some human assistance with its removal. Rubber curry combs and steel, long-tined Belgian grooming combs are both excellent for removal of mats and any loose hair that has accumulated and is ready to fall out. The curry comb is used in small, gentle circles over the neck, back, sides, belly and hips, but should never be used on the head, or below the knees or hocks. An 8- by 1-inch (2- by 2.5-cm) Belgian comb used in straight line sweeps with the grain of the hair is excellent for removing mats and clumps. Scissors may be carefully used to break up the mats; one must never pull hard on any tangle or mat with the comb. Grooming should be thought of as massage therapy for the horse. It should be an opportunity for pleasure, friendship and bonding, as well as for checking body condition. Time spent grooming is an important part of good training.

Some miniatures grow excessively thick, long, unruly manes and tails. These may be thinned and made more controllable and attractive by pulling. The technique involves grasping a few hairs at a time, close to the roots and on the underside of the mane and giving them a quick jerk, which is painless to the horse and removes the hairs by the roots. Repeated pulling in this manner allows the mane to lay flatter on the neck. Tails may be similarly shaped and shortened. Tails longer than ground level are no longer in style for show purposes and are dangerous and uncomfortable for driving or pasture horses. Tails that are too heavy and too long to be easily lifted by the horse become soiled by urine and feces, cannot be easily swished for fly protection and may even interfere with or prevent pasture breeding efforts. Thinning scissors also may be used to shorten tails and thin out the undersides of an unruly mane; they are much quicker than pulling but produce less attractive results.

In summer, insect bites and skin allergies may ruin an otherwise beautiful coat. When a horse rolls in dusty areas to protect itself from insects, contact with plant stickers and thorns may cause the mane and tail to knot and tangle. Pastured animals should be groomed frequently enough to remove these knots and tangles, and the owner should constantly be aware of the condition and health of each horse's skin, coat, feet and eyes. Foxtails can cause serious problems in the mouth or eyes, and irritations of the eyes caused by flies are also common. Unless ectoparasites are a problem, or the horse is being shown, baths are rarely necessary.

As fall and winter approach, well-nourished, healthy adult miniatures are the last to start growing their winter coats, but when they do, the coats develop into a thick, velvety plush that stands out from the body and is underlaid with a downy undercoat. Baths at this time destroy the natural oils and superb insulation qualities of the miniature horse's double coat. Animals to be left outside during the winter months should not be clipped or bathed, although currying or brushing (as the winter coat begins to grow) helps to remove debris and improves the coat's ability to insulate. Healthy horses with a natural full coat usually thrive outside during the winter months and frequently stand out in the rain or snow, even when shelter is readily available. There are genetic and other variations pertaining to ultimate winter coat lengths observed in miniatures. Horses in colder climates grow longer, thicker coats, as do weanlings and yearlings. All miniatures grow longer winter coats than full-sized horses do, but an exceptionally long, shaggy, greasy coat can usually be attributed to poor condition or old age.

Ticks may become a problem in late summer and fall, and should be manually removed from the head and neck where the miniature has been unable to reach them during self grooming. **Bot eggs** (small, yellow eggs attached to the leg hairs by bot flies) should be removed at least once weekly with a safety razor or commercially manufactured bot egg remover. Currying and brushing during the early fall stimulates the healthy growth of an adequate winter coat and allows the owner to check for abrasions, scabs, lumps, and other skin problems before the heavy winter coat hides them from view.

Body Clipping

Miniatures in North America are usually body-clipped for the show season, which begins in the spring. Clipping is also done by owners in an effort to remove the horse's winter coat earlier than it would naturally be shed. Body-clipping techniques are best learned from a professional; any novice's first few clipping attempts will be easily recognizable. Some basic clipping hints follow:

- Always bathe and thoroughly dry the horse before clipping. Gritty dirt ruins clipper blades.

- Power clippers (with the motor separated form the clipper head by a long power cable) are superior to handheld clippers. The handpiece stays cool, and the clipper blades stay sharp 2 to 3 times as long.

- All clipper blades should be frequently cleaned, lubricated and sharpened.

- Use a #10 blade for the body, neck and legs. Clip against the lay of the hair to prevent blade marks. Clip with the lay of the hair to leave a longer coat and give a rough clip. Use a #30 or #40 blade for the head and ears, using a safety razor later to shave around the muzzle and eyes for a show clip.

- For the health of the miniature, it is preferable to not shave the eyelashes off. All horses need their eyelashes to protect their eyes from injury and can develop eye infections and conjunctivitis as a result of their removal.

- On sunny days, protect newly clipped areas by keeping the horse blanketed or in a stall. Sunburn can be an unexpectedly severe and debilitating problem. The burned skin will swell, thicken, wrinkle and slough off, often taking 3 to 4 months to completely heal.

Miniature horse owners who plan on showing their horses will want to become familiar with the professional techniques that are important for proper grooming. Professional trainers and groomers all have their favorite grooming and cleaning products, as well as many secrets for presenting an animal at its absolute best. Vibrant good health maintained over a long period remains the single, most important ingredient for creating a consistently successful show horse.

Sheath Cleaning

All male miniature horses should be checked at least once yearly for the healthy condition of the penis and **sheath** (a skin container for the penis). Geldings and stallions not being used for breeding usually require an annual process known as sheath cleaning. **Smegma** (a foul-smelling, waxy secretion) builds up inside the sheath, sometimes in such large quantities that it causes swelling, discomfort and even possible blockage of urine flow. Tail rubbing is a common symptom when an animal is being irritated by a dirty sheath. White or white spotted genitals accumulate smegma more rapidly and often require twice-yearly cleaning of the sheath. A blind pocket in the **glans** (head of the penis) often accumulates a large, hard ball of smegma called a bean, which needs to be gently removed from the pocket. Sheath cleaning is best accomplished as follows:

- Cross-tie the horse and have an assistant available should further restraint, such as a twitch, be necessary.

- Get two large buckets of warm water. One should contain a gentle type of degreaser soap and the other is for rinsing.

- Soak large clumps of cotton batting in both buckets.

- With a clump of wet, soapy cotton in hand (close-fitting disposable rubber gloves are suggested) enter the sheath and reach inside as far as possible, swishing and washing to remove smegma. Many repetitions of this process, with clean soapy cotton, are required.

- Partially expose the penis to remove the bean and examine the glans for possible tumorous growths.

- Finally, rinse thoroughly, using clear, warm water and wet cotton. If a hookup to warm water is available, a garden hose can be used for the final rinse and may be run up inside the sheath.

Thickened-looking, swollen, or baggy sheaths are usually caused by smegma accumulations. Sheath cleaning, because of its unappealing nature, is frequently neglected in miniature horse grooming but if ignored, causes the horse great discomfort. It should part of grooming for all male horses.

Mare Smegma

Smegma also tends to form between the two halves of a mare's udder and should be removed at least twice yearly. This area also should be cleaned prior to a new foal's first nursing. The mare's relief during this procedure is usually evidenced by her extended neck and upper lip, as the area often becomes itchy and irritated underneath the black, greasy smegma. A dry, soft rag or towel (with no soap) may be used to gently wipe out the caked debris.

Stress and Contentment

It is becoming increasingly apparent that good physical health and well being depend upon reducing stress factors and increasing the daily level of contentment. This conclusion is being medically validated for all species of mammals, including humans. The endorphins released during contentment and euphoria have been shown to protect the body from disease. Only the behavioral and psychological categories will be discussed here as the rest are discussed in other chapters.

Stress in horses can be grouped into four categories:

- Behavioral or psychological

- Mechanical, caused by injuries related to performance or facilities

- Metabolic, usually associated with nutrition and/or forced exercise

- Immunological, caused by disease and parasites (Lawrence 1995)

As with all horses, a miniature horse's state of mind and degree of satisfaction with its life and surroundings have a measurable effect on its general health. Owners and breeders have greatly altered the lifestyle of their domesticated miniature horses. Aside from the most obvious alteration, that of extremely reduced size, there are other considerations. In nature, horses originally roamed free, over thousands of acres, without any restraints such as fences, barns, halters or ropes. Wild horses continually foraged for rough grasses and shrubs, and were not fed a processed, unnatural diet twice daily. They were often forced to travel great distances to find water. Stallions were never gelded but were forced to accept their social roles on the basis of herd dominance or submission. There were untold hardships for wild horses, but they lived a natural life and had much freedom. As a consequence, most wild horses were extremely hardy.

Today's domesticated horses, including miniatures, are never free. They are controlled by the fences, rules, whims and impositions of their owners and caretakers. Behavioral problems may arise when horses rebel against these constraints. Kind treatment, coupled with a full understanding of the cause of each unwanted behavior, is necessary to maintain an animal's well being and reduce stress.

Horses are herd animals, heavily dependent upon their relationships with other animals within the herd. Single miniatures raised away from other horses consider themselves to be part of their human owner's herd. Using this knowledge, kind, thoughtful owners of a single miniature are able to easily train their horse with resistance-free methods (Dorrance 1987; Roberts 1996). Even groups of miniatures, if treated with consideration and understanding, tend to become part of their human owner's herd. They come to depend upon their owner's companionship and often suffer loneliness when separated from the owner for extended periods.

One of the most common stress factors in any horse's life can be separation anxiety. Being separated from its familiar surroundings, its herd, or from a particular herd companion often causes a miniature horse to exhibit abnormal behavior. Whinnying, pacing the fence, refusing to eat or drink and self-mutilation are only a few of the signs that a horse is experiencing separation anxiety. Boredom can also create serious problems when animals are spending much of their time in stalls or small paddocks. Behavioral anomalies such as **cribbing** or **windsucking** (the horse holds onto a fence or feeder with its teeth, arches its neck and forcibly swallows air) and **weaving** (the horse swings its head from side to side while shifting the weight back and forth from one front leg to the other) are usually a direct result of boredom, lack of freedom and exercise, or loneliness.

Eliminating stress begins with providing plenty of fresh air and ample space to run with a companion or two. The most commonly observed housing error within the miniature horse industry is overcrowding. Groups of miniatures are often left to stand, for months at a time, in small, crowded stalls or paddocks. With no room to run and play, they are usually depressed and always bored. They spend their days with nothing of interest ever happening, and although they might have the company of others, they will not thrive. Their health, vigor, behavioral attitudes and intelligence can be gravely affected by this sort of long-term confinement. Similarly, horses being shown must endure unreasonable restrictions upon their freedom and comfort. Blankets, **neck sweats** (specially designed and tightly applied wraps for the neck used in an attempt to make the neck appear slimmer), excessive training, separation from companions, restrictions of space and exercise, and a completely unnatural diet are some of the most common stresses that owners impose upon show horses.

Stress is created by the body's demand for adaptation (Lawrence 1995). Each miniature has its own tolerance level and reacts to imposed stress factors with varying degrees of acceptance. A stoic, non-reactive miniature is not necessarily free of stress. The apathy and inactivity associated with pathological states of depression may seriously compromise a horse's physical health and well being.

Playful activities, although most commonly engaged in by weanlings and yearlings, are good indicators of health and happiness. Young miniatures enjoy playing in groups and are mutually stimulated by this activity. Most play requires the establishment of social contacts and bonds prior to the play activity. Foals that have been recently moved into a new herd will stand by their mothers rather than engage in any play with strange foals.

The stable development of behavior depends upon constant stimulation of the neurological and sensory systems. Under conditions of extreme confinement, horses are restricted from adequate exercise and mental stimulation. Severe kinetic and intellectual deprivations are often associated with abnormal behavior patterns, as well as a lack of disease resistance (Fraser, Mays, & Huebner 1986). Extreme confinement for long periods can even result in retarded mental development.

Dependable indicators of contentment are mutual grooming and self-grooming. Relaxed and self-satisfied miniatures will often be seen in their pastures engaging in various grooming activities. The cessation of grooming behavior should be regarded as an early sign of sickness (Fraser et al. 1986).

Close bonds are an important aspect of associative behavior in horses, and the disruption of these bonds can cause them stress. In addition to the bond of mare and foal, other affectionate herdmate bonds are continually being broken up by sales and separations decided upon by the horse owner. Animals being removed from their offspring or from companions with whom they are strongly bonded may suffer serious depression and possible health problems. Miniatures being newly integrated into a well-established herd experience much stress and it is usually advisable to initially allow them to become well acquainted through fences.

Stallions are happiest when living with a small group of mares in pasture. A stallion forced to live apart from others is rarely content, undergoing constant frustration and depression. His disease resistance will be low and he may also develop disagreeable habits such as pawing, pacing, excessive masturbation, **coprophagia** (eating manure) or **geophagia** (eating sand, rocks or soil). Charging, rearing, striking, biting, kicking and other aggressive behaviors may be associated with a stallion's forced separation from other horses. If a stallion's isolation from other horses is necessary, his stress may be minimized by fences that allow him sight, smell and nose-to-nose contact with herd companion horses (not with other stallions). In a pasture breeding situation, mares may be separated from the herd as they approach the end of their gestation. Experienced mares are usually content at that time to gain a measure of privacy from the rest of the herd. Miniature stallions are generally very gentle with new foals, however, and if mares accidentally deliver while still in the pastures, there are usually no problems.

Avoiding stress-related factors is an important aspect of preventative health management. Every attempt should be made to increase and maintain the daily level of contentment for each animal in the herd, and individual observations should be made regularly. Extensive studies in equine sports medicine have led to important discoveries about the close relationship between endorphin production and excellence or stamina of performance. These concepts are now being accepted in human medicine, and the same theories and parameters apply to all mammals, including miniature horses.

Figure 8.8 *Healthy, fertile, active miniature horse stallion at age 20. On May 23, 1998,* Boones Little Buckeroo *celebrated an open barn 20th birthday party.* Buckeroo *was sired by* Poplar Lanes Sampson *and is out of* Johnstons Vanilla. *Breeder: Ralph C. Lawson. Owner: Ed and Marianne Eberth.*

Geriatrics

Although accurate ages of very old horses are difficult to obtain, many elderly animals have been identified. Veterinarians consider miniatures over age 20 to be geriatric horses. A 25-year-old horse is approximately equivalent to a 75-year-old human. Purina® Mills recently sponsored a search for the oldest horse in the United States and was able to find and verify the age of a pony 52 years old. Many other ponies, donkeys and horses have been proven to have lived well into their 40s. It seems to be fairly well accepted in veterinary circles that the smaller breeds (ponies and miniatures) attain older ages than those attained by the larger breeds, a correlation that is already known to be true with dogs. Breeds maturing at less than 50 pounds (22.5 kg) have a longer life span than breeds maturing over 100 pounds (45 kg).

Life span is the maximum possible length of life, while **life expectancy** is the expected number of years of life from birth. Thus, the life expectancy of both humans and horses has changed over the years, but their life spans have probably not changed. The average life span of miniature horses is considered to be about 30 years, but the average life expectancy is more realistically considered 20 years. Because miniature horses are valued more for their companionship than for the amount of work they can perform, the problems associated with old age are often negligible.

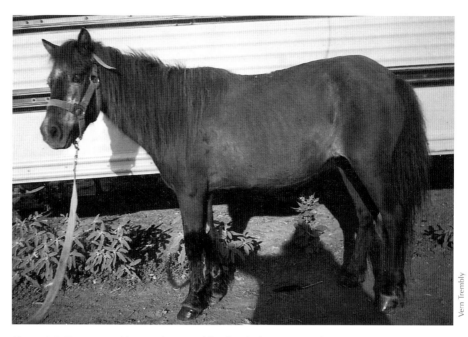

Vern Trembly

Figure 8.9 *Forty-year-old mare that raised her last foal at age 36. This miniature horse mare, Queenie, is still in good health at age 40. She has been owned by the same farm for her entire adult life and has produced foals almost every year, raising her last healthy foal at age 36. Only four of these foals were colts. Breeder: Unknown. Owner: Vern Trembly.*

Unsoundness that affects movement is one of the first visible signs of aging in miniatures. Arthritis is probably the most commonly seen ailment causing lameness. Overweight miniatures are fairly common, although excess weight can seriously aggravate the joint damage, pain, and lack of activity caused by arthritis. Older miniatures should not be allowed to become either overweight or underweight.

Other signs of aging include elongated incisors, potbellies, decreased feed efficiency, sway backs, graying faces, drooping lower lips, loss of teeth, and longer, slower-shedding coats. Inactivity, listlessness and loss of mental acuity are common. Elderly miniatures often lose their ability to maintain a constant body temperature and must be protected from extremes in heat or cold. Long-stemmed hay or pasture grasses help keep elderly miniatures warm in winter; a pound of hay produces more body heat than a pound of grain. Older animals often shiver in cold weather, but after eating hay, they will cease shivering (Ensminger 1990).

The quality, health and numbers of an old miniature horse's teeth should be closely monitored by an equine veterinarian or an equine dental technician. Frequent dewormings and routine floating of the teeth are both critical in the health care of aging horses, particularly those that might not be maintaining adequate body weight. In elderly miniatures, colic is a constant threat, as is laminitis. Sudden changes in surroundings or feeds should be avoided, and older horses should never be forced to live with younger or more aggressive animals. Commercially manufactured concentrated feeds that are specifically designed for geriatric horses can often extend the life span of well-cared-for seniors. Alfalfa meal with molasses is also an excellent supplement for thin animals not assimilating their feed properly.

Chronic obstructive pulmonary disease (COPD, or emphysema in humans; heaves in horses) sometimes becomes a problem in elderly horses. Dust, mold, and cigarette smoke greatly aggravate this condition and should all be avoided in the horse's environment. For this reason, geriatric miniatures generally do better outside in pastures, not confined to enclosed stalls. Adequate protection from inclement weather remains crucial, and easy access to shelter should always be provided. Shade in summer and shelter in winter are of equal importance.

Frequent hoof care is mandatory for all elderly miniatures but especially for those with any lameness problems. Acute problems such as laminitis, navicular disease and new injuries must always be attended to by an equine veterinarian or a well-qualified farrier. The discomfort caused by chronic problems such as arthritis and deteriorating foot conformation may be relieved by trimming and/or by correctively shoeing these animals. Oral non-steroidal anti-inflammatory drugs (NSAIDS) also may be prescribed by equine veterinarians to alleviate the inflammation and pain caused by some of these hoof and leg infirmities of old age.

Many miniatures over 20 years of age are still fertile and are often able to sire or produce healthy foals. Even if no longer fertile, aged brood mares are often excellent baby-sitters for orphaned or newly weaned foals.

Elderly miniatures can be a constant source of pride and joy to their owners. Such long-term alliances attest to the good care and affection owners bestow upon their charges. With close attention to their condition, geriatric miniatures can spend their retirement years in relatively good health and contentment. If sound and of good body weight, they should be allowed to continue with enjoyable activities such as raising foals (or baby-sitting them), driving, or being ridden by small children. With excellent preventative health management and daily observation for problems that might demand immediate attention, miniature horses can be expected to live a life of quality well into their 30s.

CHAPTER 9

Diseases

E QUINE DISEASE IS CAUSED BY ANY entity or situation that results in abnormal function or structure of any part of the horse. Diseases are manifested by a characteristic set of symptoms and signs, the etiology, pathology and prognosis of which may be known or unknown (Dorland 1985). The most common disease of miniature horses is internal parasitism, which is discussed under preventative health care (see Chapter 8). The most common cause of death is **colic**, a noninfectious combination of signs indicating extreme abdominal pain and often complicated by irreversible endotoxemia. The most commonly occurring infectious diseases include those within the respiratory disease complex, most of which are highly contagious. Of these, equine influenza, equine rhinopneumonitis and equine viral arteritis are all caused by viruses. Strangles is caused by bacteria and the dangerous complication of pneumonia is usually caused by secondary bacterial invaders as an aftermath of viral respiratory disease.

Importance of Isolation

It is imperative that horses returning from shows, newly purchased horses and mares being brought in for outside breedings be isolated as much as possible from the already established population at a particular farm. Pregnant mares should never be exposed to any newly acquired horses after their 7th month of gestation. Even young stock, stallions and geldings are able to carry herpesvirus-1 (which causes abortion during the 7th through 9th months) without showing any symptoms. Outside mares to be bred should be wormed with ivermectin about 2 weeks before their arrival at the stallion owner's farm and should be up to date on all of their vaccinations. As a further precaution and to prevent the spread of any possible disease, all horses or foals within the farm's established population should be immediately isolated should they develop any signs or symptoms of abnormal behavior or a suspected disease process of any kind. The most contagious period for many diseases is during the earliest symptoms at the onset of the disease. Therefore, even miniatures with suspected noncontagious problems should be initially isolated until further symptoms develop or until the exact cause of their illness has been verified by a veterinarian. Although sometimes not observed until symptoms become more severe, behavioral changes, such as lack of appetite, will often alert the owner to the possibility of impending disease in time for effective isolation measures.

Infectious Diseases of the Equine Respiratory Complex

Of the diseases caused by infectious agents, the various respiratory diseases are those most commonly seen. Whether viral or bacterial, they are all highly contagious, and respiratory-tract diseases initially caused by a virus can easily be complicated with secondary bacterial invaders. Transmission is usually caused by direct contact, by clothing and/or equipment, or by airborne respiratory secretions. Some respiratory-tract infections are now known to be carried from ranch to ranch, as well as to other horse-populated locations, by the hands, clothing and poorly disinfected equipment of humans. The efficacy of vaccination programs for any of the diseases within the equine respiratory disease complex remains open to question (Rose & Hodgson 1993).

Strangles (Equine Distemper)

Strangles is characterized by a high fever, a thick nasal discharge and the formation of a sizable abscess in the lymph nodes beneath the lower jaw. It primarily affects young horses, many of which seem to develop a long-term immunity after contracting their first case of strangles. The causative bacterium, *Streptococcus equi*, can be isolated both from the nasal discharge and from the pus of a draining abscess. The abscess sometimes ruptures and drains on its own but should be surgically incised by a veterinarian to facilitate removal of all pus, establish continuing drainage and administer appropriate disinfectant and antibiotic therapy. After veterinary instruction, follow-up treatments and cleanings may usually be handled by the owner. Vaccination for strangles does not prevent the disease, but it does appear to reduce the severity of the clinical signs and length of recovery time. Outbreaks often occur in the late summer and fall and are thought to be spread by flies as they travel among horses with actively draining abscesses and later, on to healthy animals. Draining abscesses will contaminate water troughs, thereby infecting healthy horses that may have access to the same water. Isolation of all infected animals and frequent application of fly repellents are suggested.

Equine Influenza (Flu)

Another of the serious respiratory diseases of horses is equine influenza, which occurs worldwide wherever horses are being shipped or are congregated in large and fluctuating numbers. Outbreaks are common after horse shows and sales but can develop at boarding and training stables. Farms can prevent outbreaks by quarantining new horses before introducing them into the established population and by implementing vaccination programs. Like strangles, flu is primarily a respiratory disease of the young; older horses sometimes seem to develop an immunity. Secondary complications, such as bacterial pneumonia (which can be life threatening) and a persistent or deep bronchitis and cough are common in poorly cared for convalescing horses and in animals that were in poor condition prior to exposure. The first symptoms of influenza are usually a lack of appetite and a rapidly rising fever. Within a day or two, a watery discharge appears from the eyes and nose, which sometimes develops into a thicker white or yellow discharge. The fever may persist for as long as 10 days, and the horse becomes weak and depressed, usually developing rapid breathing and a dry cough. Affected animals should be kept warm and as comfortable as possible in clean, well-ventilated stalls. All exercise should be discontinued immediately (Fraser et al. 1986). Fresh water (warmed, if necessary) should always be kept available, and all feeds offered should be extremely palatable. Isolation is critical to the prevention of an outbreak in a large, closely confined population. Diagnosis and treatment by an equine veterinarian is advisable, since antibiotic therapy may possibly prevent the later development of pneumonia and/or **cardiomyopathy** (heart muscle damage).

Equine Rhinopneumonitis (Viral Abortion Caused by Herpesvirus-1)

Equine herpesvirus-1 (EHV-1) is the disease of horses sometimes called "rhino." Although it often begins as a respiratory disease, EHV-1's primary danger is that of causing abortion in pregnant mares.

Rhinopneumonitis begins with less severe respiratory signs than does influenza or strangles (sometimes none), but infection of pregnant mares in their last trimester usually results in diseased foals that are aborted or that die soon after birth. Miniature horse broodmares should not be exposed to new or outside horses after the 7th month of gestation. Even apparently healthy young stock and other nonpregnant horses are capable of passing the disease on to **gravid** (pregnant) mares. EHV-1 aborting mares sometimes show no respiratory symptoms and abort suddenly, without udder development, and with little or no warning (see Chapter 10). If the aborted fetus shows no visible abnormalities that otherwise may have been responsible for its death, it can be taken to the nearest diagnostic veterinary laboratory for confirmation of EHV-1 presence in the fetal tissues. The fetus should be transported in a well-sealed, leak-free container as soon as possible after it has been expelled. Aborting mares recover uneventfully and may be bred back after 30 days.

Equine Viral Arteritis

Although equine viral arteritis begins with a fever and a watery discharge from the eyes and nose, it may usually be distinguished from other respiratory diseases by swelling of the eyelids and lower legs. Viral arteritis may also cause abortions but is less often implicated than the spontaneous abortions caused by EHV-1 (Ensminger 1990). As the disease develops, nasal discharges become thicker and extremity swellings may develop, caused by internal damage to the smaller arteries. This arterial damage results in decreased circulation of the blood and restricts the normal elimination of excess body fluids via the bloodstream. Animals stressed by shipping and attending shows and sales are the most susceptible, but the disease is nonexistent in many areas. Equine viral arteritis is considered to be a venereal disease, often being transmitted by stallions that are free of symptoms, but it is also spread by nasal discharge contact between horses. An effective vaccine is available in areas where the disease is known to occur.

Non-Respiratory Infectious Diseases

Tetanus (Lockjaw)

It is imperative that all miniature horses be vaccinated for tetanus, which, if contracted, is almost always fatal. The current tetanus toxoid vaccines are highly effective and should be given annually to each horse in the herd. The causative bacterium, *Clostridium tetani*, requires **anaerobic** (without oxygen) growth conditions so is most likely to cause disease when deposited deep within a puncture wound in the muscle or on the sole of the foot that seals closed. The spores of *C. tetani* remain viable for many years in the soil and environment of all horse facilities, without losing their ability to infect animals via puncture wounds. Once successful growth is initiated, *C. tetani* secretes dangerous toxins that cause nerve damage and muscular spasticity which has resulted in the common name of the disease, lockjaw.

Both tetanus toxoid and tetanus antitoxin vaccines are available. Toxoid, used for the initial and annual immunizations (usually called "booster shots"), is one of the most highly effective equine vaccines available. Many breeders give tetanus toxoid vaccine to every pregnant mare about one month before her expected delivery date. This boosts the immunity of the mare and also serves to protect her newborn foal with antibodies passed on to the foal in the colostrum, thus eliminating the necessity of giving tetanus antitoxin to the foal after birth.

Tetanus antitoxin is used only as short-term (7 to 14 days) but immediate protection in the face of a puncture wound, abscess or other injury on an animal not previously vaccinated with tetanus toxoid. Anaphylactic shock is a common sequela to tetanus antitoxin injections, and its administration should always be supervised by an equine veterinarian. Animals that suffer slow-healing puncture wounds or deep abrasions should be given a second dose of antitoxin in 7 days but only as advised by the attending veterinarian.

Viral Encephalomyelitis (Sleeping Sickness)

Western equine encephalomyelitis (WEE), Eastern equine encephalomyelitis (EEE), and Venezuelan equine encephalomyelitis (VEE) are dependent upon the two intermediate hosts, birds and mosquitoes, in order to infect horses. Prevention of the disease is best accomplished with yearly vaccinations and effective mosquito-control programs (see Chapter 8). The vaccines for all three varieties are highly effective and need be given only for the type being encountered in the locale of residence. Because the vaccines usually are given in combination with the annual tetanus toxoid immunization, it is best to follow the recommendations of the local area's equine veterinarian as to which varieties should be included. Unprotected horses contracting the disease exceed 80% mortality and full recovery is rare.

Equine Infectious Anemia (Swamp Fever) and the Coggins Test

Equine infectious anemia (EIA) is a viral disease with worldwide distribution for which there is no effective vaccine and no treatment. In 1997, approximately 2,000 new cases of EIA were diagnosed in the United States. Horses carrying the disease may be free of obvious symptoms. The Coggins test, developed almost 30 years ago, has been consistently reliable in detecting EIA carriers. This blood (serum) test identifies carriers by testing for antibodies against EIA, thus enabling equine health authorities to prevent their interstate and worldwide travel. Horses testing positive for EIA are usually euthanized, as asymptomatic or recovered animals remain carriers of the disease. EIA-contaminated needles and syringes should be disposed of immediately. In addition to contaminated needles, the horse fly, mosquitoes, and other biting insects are vectors. Rigorous control of stable flies is recommended (see Chapter 8). Foals out of infected mares will also be born infected but may test negative after weaning. Strict isolation of carrier foals is essential, however, until after they have been weaned and have tested negative at least twice.

In addition to EIA, there are many possible causes of anemia in horses. These include chronic infections, external or internal parasites, emaciation, ingestion of various poisonous substances, and blood loss due to injuries. Iron-deficiency anemia is rare in horses, as good-quality hay and pasture grasses are both rich in iron.

Other Infectious Diseases

There are several other infectious diseases of horses, such as leptospirosis (which causes abortions), Potomac horse fever (which causes diarrhea and abortions), rabies (the horse must be bitten by a rabid animal), Lyme disease (which causes arthritis in horses and is spread by a small species of tick) and anthrax (spores of which must be ingested from soil). Although each of these diseases occurs rarely in horses, suspected cases should be immediately diagnosed and evaluated by an equine veterinarian. There are also two infectious diseases of newborn foals, septicemia and foal-heat diarrhea (see Chapter 10).

In addition to EHV-1, equine viral arteritis, leptospirosis and Potomac horse fever, there are various other infectious causes of abortion in mares. **Mycotic** (fungal) and mixed bacterial infections may enter the uterus at the time of breeding or may occur in older mares when the cervix has partially opened prior to delivery. Long-standing uterine infections sometimes cause degeneration of the placental tissue, thus depriving the developing foal of sufficient nourishment. After its death, the foal is aborted unexpectedly and is usually undersized and underdeveloped for its gestational age.

Congenital defects, twin fetuses, hormonal imbalances, certain drugs and other chemicals, traumatic injuries, scar tissue in the uterus, and nutritional deficiencies may also be implicated as noninfectious causes of equine abortion (see Chapter 10). If there is an abortion problem within a given herd, it is imperative that the farm veterinarian be summoned for consultation, as well as for examinations of both the aborted fetuses and the aborting mares.

Vaccinations

Of the many equine vaccines available, those for tetanus (lockjaw) and encephalomyelitis (sleeping sickness) are the most essential. If contracted, both diseases are usually fatal. Furthermore, both vaccines are highly effective and cause few, if any, side effects. The danger of contracting tetanus occurs worldwide and in all species of mammals, including humans. Tetanus toxoid affords long-term immunity, although yearly boosters are recommended because of the constant exposure of horses in their environment to the causative bacterium, *Clostridium tetani*.

WEE, EEE and VEE (the three varieties of sleeping sickness) are spread by mosquitoes and are not contagious from horse to horse. The farm veterinarian should be consulted as to which of these three varieties occurs within a given locale. The vaccines are highly effective and are usually provided in combination with tetanus toxoid. For example, the term "three-way vaccine" usually refers to one injection with a combination of tetanus toxoid, WEE and EEE; "four-way vaccine" usually refers to these same three but with the addition of influenza vaccine.

Vaccinations for most of the diseases within the respiratory disease complex have less merit. Most of the available vaccines afford short-term protection and should be given only under the supervision of the farm veterinarian. Effective vaccination programs for most of the respiratory diseases require injections more frequently than once per year and some should not be given to pregnant mares or to young foals.

The killed vaccines available for rhino must be given every 2 months during the latter part of a mare's pregnancy (typically at 5, 7 and 9 months), but most vaccines against EHV-1 have appeared to give sporadic protection when tested under experimental conditions.

A rabies vaccine that must be administered by a veterinarian is available if the horse is exposed to high-risk wooded areas. If rabid bats, skunks or dogs have been reported in the immediate area (consultations with the local animal control authorities and an equine veterinarian are recommended) rabies vaccination may be an appropriate consideration. Foals must be over 3 months of age, and the vaccine is generally not recommended for use in pregnant mares (L. Couper, pers. comm. 1998).

There is no effective vaccine against equine infectious anemia, and vaccinations against diseases not occurring in a particular locale are usually not recommended. An effective and easily followed (while not excessive) vaccination program should be set up by the farm veterinarian at the request of each miniature horse breeder.

Noninfectious Diseases and Their Prevention

Respiratory diseases, colic, and choke are significantly minimized by allowing horses to always eat with their heads down. Their anatomy, salivary glands and respiratory tracts are designed for pasture grazing at ground level, not for consuming feeds at higher levels. Highly elevated feeders create an abnormal situation for horses, and feeder placement is an important consideration in colic prevention. A feed container at ground level, with sides high enough to prevent tossing any portions of the feed on the ground, is ideal (see Figure 9.1).

Large sheep feeders keep the feed in a more elevated position than is ideal but still serve to keep most of it from being thrown to the ground. It is important to prevent miniature horses from ingesting excessive sand and dirt. Whether grazing, searching for fallen tidbits, chewing on fences, or pulling plants up by the roots, horses normally ingest some dirt or sand. Lots of exercise and large quantities of consumed water aid in the daily removal and regular elimination of sand, dirt and other debris.

Colic (Abdominal Pain)

Miniature horses and Shetland Ponies have a higher incidence of small colon impactions than do other breeds of horses (Ramey 1996). Impaction colics can be a severe problem in miniatures and usually begin with inadequate intake of water, poorly maintained teeth, internal parasitism, excessive accumulations of sand or hair and/or the intake of poor-quality feeds. As discussed in Chapter 8, the larval stages of bloodworms can cause serious damage to the arteries that supply blood to the intestines. If any portion of the intestine "dies" and ceases normal peristalsis, the result is usually an impaction.

Impaction colics occur more frequently in horses fed pellets, dried grasses or grass hays than in those provided with natural green grass pastures or leafy, fine-stemmed, high-quality alfalfa hays. This is probably because green pasture grasses, alfalfa and other legume hays have a more laxative effect than do dry pasture grasses, oat hay, or grass hays. Because adequate exercise is extremely important in the prevention of colic, pastured horses with lots of

Figure 9.1 Sugar Creek Celeste *and her foal,* Pacific Dual Image, *are both able to eat hay and grain out of this ground-level feeder. The feeder, with high enough sides to discourage tossing hay out onto the ground, is made of a pliable recycled plastic compound that prevents injuries. Breeder: Lynda Baerthlein Marzec. Owner: Joanne Abramson.*

space to roam and adequate amounts of fresh green grass are less susceptible to impaction colic. However, the tendency for miniature horses to become obese when on free-choice feeds of any kind must be constantly monitored.

Extreme weather conditions, which sometimes discourage the miniature horse from drinking enough water (see Chapter 6) may also cause sluggish movement of the intestinal contents, resulting in the possible formation of an impaction. Adequate water consumption of miniature horses must always be encouraged by constant availability of clean water, by temperature modification in both hot and cold weather, and by continually available trace mineral salt blocks.

Mutual grooming activities during the spring hair shed often lead to the accidental ingestion of large quantities of hair. In addition, foals are often seen purposely eating the abdominal hair or manes and tails of their dams. Excess body, mane, or tail hair ingestion can be prevented by the following measures:

- Providing ample pasture
- Regular grooming to remove dead hair
- Exercising horses to prevent boredom
- Providing long-stemmed feeds to supply adequate roughage and chewing activity
- Clipping abdominal hair and hair surrounding udder of foaling mares
- Avoiding overcrowding of horses in small areas

Symptoms of Colic

Signs of colic include activities such as rolling, looking back at flank, kicking at belly, casting against a fence or barn, stretching out, sweating, or getting up and down repeatedly.

In sand colic cases there is sometimes intermittent diarrhea, even though the horse may have an impaction further up in the gastrointestinal tract. Although miniature horses may not immediately show signs of extreme abdominal pain, they will always refuse to eat, even in the earliest stages of colic (Marcella 1992). Care must be sought immediately from a veterinarian familiar with the sometimes unique assessment and treatment variations of miniatures, which often differ from those of full-sized horses. Early detection of colic and early treatment by an experienced miniature horse veterinarian are both crucial to recovery.

After assessment of vital signs, mucous membrane coloration, status of dehydration and capillary refill time, the intestinal activity should be evaluated with a stethoscope in at least two locations on each side of the horse. In the absence of observable manure passage and audible gut sounds (lack of gut motility), the horse should be treated aggressively for an impaction. Impactions and the subsequent complication of **endotoxemia** (bacterial toxins being released into the bloodstream) are the number one cause of death in miniature horses.

Sand Colic, Enteroliths and Ulcers

Sand colic is a common problem in miniatures resulting from the excessive ingestion of sandy soils, combined with the breakdown of the animal's normal sand-elimination processes. Large amounts of retained sand can build up over time and will often cause impactions, and the extra weight of sand in the affected portion of the intestine may lead to an intestinal **torsion** (twist). Even very small amounts of sand can irritate the gastrointestinal tract and cause the intestines to secrete water, resulting in intermittent diarrhea (Ramey 1996). The problem may then be compounded, as this condition sometimes results in **geophagia** (the purposeful eating of dirt, sand, rocks and other debris) because of the intestinal discomfort being experienced. Foals, who tend to ingest more debris and dirt than do adults, are particularly susceptible to sand colic.

Testing For Sand

The amount of sand in a miniature's intestinal tract may be assessed by the following method: Select a few freshly passed fecal balls from the top of a pile, ones not already contaminated by contact with any sandy soil. Place in a resealable plastic bag. Add some water, seal the top of the bag, crush the fecal balls inside with fingers, and shake vigorously. After waiting a few minutes, observe how much sand drops to the bottom of the bag when the mixture settles and the lighter manure floats to the top.

The fecal elimination of some sand is an expected daily event for all normal horses. However, if the amount of sand appears unusually large or if the pasture soil is extremely sandy, a preventative treatment regimen with psyllium is highly recommended.

The addition of psyllium to the diet (for about 5 days each month) has been shown to be highly effective in helping sand to be eliminated before it accumulates in excessive quantities. Another treatment regimen suggests a weekly or bi-weekly dose to help prevent the buildup of sand. The suggested amount of psyllium per feeding is 2 tablespoons (30 ml) per horse. However, psyllium slows absorption of glucose and lowers cholesterol, features that

Barbara Naviaux

Figure 9.2 *This unusually large enterolith was surgically removed from an 8-year-old, 32-inch (81-cm) miniature horse in June 1998. Weighing 2 pounds 9 ounces (1148 grams) and measuring 5 by 4 inches (14 by 10 cm), it was the largest enterolith the attending veterinarians had ever recovered from a miniature horse at the Veterinary Medical Teaching Hospital at the University of California, Davis. The horse had experienced intermittent episodes of colic for 3 years, but diagnostic radiographs were not taken until admission to the veterinary hospital.*

may not be beneficial if psyllium is overfed. Psyllium should not be fed continuously. If fed continuously, the bacteria in the horse's large intestine may begin to digest the psyllium, which decreases its effectiveness (Ramey 1996).

Psyllium is a natural product, the outer shell of the seed *Plantago ovata*, native to India. The flavored pelleted form of psyllium may be fed by itself, but the horses must be gradually acclimated to its use. The powdered form may be mixed with alfalfa meal and molasses or with sweetened grains. The successful passage of psyllium is obvious as it covers the fecal balls in a gelatinous coating. Even if psyllium has been added to the horse's feed as an aid in eliminating intestinal sand, the exact cause of any suspected abdominal discomfort should be investigated and verified.

In addition to sand accumulations, chronic, low-grade abdominal discomfort may also be caused by **enteroliths** (intestinal stones), by foreign bodies or by ulcers. Although acute symptoms may not develop until later, chronic symptoms may include intermittent diarrhea, failure to thrive, and sporadic disinterest in food. Enteroliths requiring surgery have become alarmingly more common at equine veterinary school hospitals during the last few years. Small enteroliths are sometimes passed by the horse during normal defecation. Larger enteroliths may be identified in abdominal radiographs, but their elimination always requires surgery should they be causing a complete intestinal blockage.

Geophagia is often seen in miniatures with minor or intermittent abdominal pain caused by sand, hair, foreign bodies, enteroliths, internal parasites and gastric ulcers. Ulcers are common in foals, particularly if they have been given any non-steroidal anti-inflammatory drugs (NSAIDS), (see Chapter 8) or if they have been weaned too early.

Treatment of Colic

One of the most frequently used diagnostic tools available to veterinarians for full-sized horse colics is rectal palpation. However, rectal examinations are not usually recommended in miniatures unless the examiner has extremely small arms and hands. Without the advantage of being able to use this valuable diagnostic aid, and because miniatures often fail to exhibit obvious indications of extreme abdominal pain, impactions are often undertreated. Minimal treatment should consist of mineral oil given via stomach tube; a gently administered warm, soapy enema; and an intramuscular injection of the chosen antispasmodic (to prevent intestinal cramping) and analgesic NSAIDs (to prevent pain). These are the three basic treatment requirements for all miniature horse impaction colics in order to possibly avoid the last-resort option of surgery. Although highly successful abdominal surgeries are now a reality, they are extremely expensive. For this reason, colic surgery is not a consideration for many miniature horse owners. There are many types of NSAIDs available, as well as other types of sedatives and analgesics. Several laxatives and lubricants besides mineral oil are also available and may be easily combined with the nasogastric administration of oil or may be administered separately. Liquified psyllium is an effective addition, particularly if sand impaction is suspected. The physical passage of a stomach tube sometimes facilitates the elimination of excess gastric fluids and gases, either of which cause extreme discomfort to a horse because of its inability to vomit or belch.

Because horses in abdominal pain generally refuse to drink, intravenous (IV) fluids are often necessary. Large volumes of IV fluids are effective in softening many impacted masses (Rose & Hodgson 1993). Rehydration of the intestinal tract through the circulatory system (blood) is sometimes crucial to the elimination of dry intestinal blockages. Antibiotics are required for any impaction that persists for more than a few hours (invariably causing endotoxemia). An IV heparin lock is sometimes left in place by the veterinarian so that the prescribed medications and fluids may be later administered by the owner.

Acute abdominal pain resulting from any intestinal blockage, whether it is being caused by sand, other foreign bodies, impacted fecal masses, a torsion or enteroliths, always results in the formation and accumulation of gas, which would normally be passed rapidly through a healthy intestine. The blockage then leads to a condition called **gas colic**. Gas colics rarely occur by themselves and are almost always preceded by impactions or other entities causing cessation of peristalsis.

Immovable and unresolved intestinal blockages always result in endotoxemia, which produces a state of shock and can quickly lead to death. Endotoxemia requires the IV administration of antibiotics and fluids. The cause of the impaction is not nearly as important as the immediate elimination of the blockage, although the probable cause of any particular impaction colic should be investigated later in order to avoid its reoccurrence in the future. Walking a horse with colic to prevent it from rolling does not prevent twisting of the intestine (Ramey 1996). If there is already a twist or fold in any part of the intestine, surgery will be the only option for correction.

Laminitis (Founder)

In recent years, it has been determined that laminitis is a nonvascular **necrosis** (death and degeneration) of the sensitive laminae in the hoof (Rose & Hodgson 1993). Laminitis always causes extreme pain and must be treated immediately and aggressively by a veterinarian if there is to be any hope for recovery. Because the front legs must support 50% more weight than the hind legs, hoof pain usually appears to be more excruciating in the front feet. The immovable "weight over hind legs" stance of a foundered horse is characteristic. Laminitis is much more common in ponies and miniature horses than it is in any of the larger equine breeds. This is probably due to the frequent occurrence of obesity in small equids, which may often be linked with the condition of hypothryoidism. The tendency of healthy miniature horses to overeat, if given the opportunity, must always be carefully monitored.

Possible conditions leading to founder include overeating of grain or green pasture grasses, overwhelming gram-negative bacterial infections (such as endotoxemia, uterine infections or pneumonia), obesity, hormonal abnormalities, ingestion of cold water after rigorous exercise, exposure to certain drugs and excessive concussion (on a hard surface) to the feet. Prevention of laminitis is crucial and is vastly more successful than treatment after symptoms of hoof pain have developed.

Because of the extreme pain caused by acute laminitis, affected horses have increased respiratory rates and may possibly tremble when asked to move. If frequently lying down, they sometimes become unable to rise to a standing position. There is usually a throbbing digital pulse (at the back of the pasterns) and the hoof wall often feels hot to the touch. Acute laminitis is a medical emergency and treatment by an equine veterinarian should be initiated immediately to prevent rotation of the **coffin bone**, a bone located within the hoof (Markel in Siegal 1996). After the coffin bone has rotated more than 10°, soundness and recovery sufficient for the performance of any athletic events are unlikely.

Horses with chronic reoccurring laminitis will exhibit a turned-up hoof toe ("dished" appearance) as well as visible rings across the front surface of the hoof wall. Corrective trimming can sometimes help the affected horse to be sound enough for breeding or for an inactive and relatively pain-free retirement, but the prognosis for founder is always guarded. Once a horse develops any degree of laminitis, its feet will probably never return to normal, but in miniature horses not being used for showing or performance events, this can sometimes be tolerated. The damaged hoof wall takes a full year to replace itself and grow out, necessitating the absolute prevention of any conditions that might again result in laminitis during that year. Once foundered, the horse is much more likely to experience repeat attacks, which invariably result in further coffin bone rotation and increased disability from pain.

Hyperlipemia Syndrome

The **hyperlipidemia/hyperlipemia syndrome** (elevated fats in the blood and liver) is a newly recognized, noninfectious disease process of horses. Hyperlipidemia refers to the less serious and often reversible beginning stages of the disease, during which the serum triglyceride level remains under 500 mg/dl. Hyperlipemia is characterized by blood serum triglyceride levels that exceed 500 mg/dl (the normal range should be under 75 mg/dl) and also includes **hepatic lipidosis** (fatty liver) (Rose & Hodgson 1993). Scientific studies have documented that miniature horses, ponies and miniature donkeys are more often affected than full-sized breeds of horses (Mogg & Palmer 1995). The disease is usually secondary to a primary health problem or disease (such as colic or an upper respiratory tract-infection) and begins with a history reporting an overweight animal that has not eaten for 2 or 3 days. The initial cause of reduced calorie intake can be any illness or condition that causes the horse to eat a radically decreased amount of feed. Possible primary problems that may lead to hyperlipemia are colic, respiratory disease, lengthy shows, sudden separation from a companion or foal, painful teeth, long trips without adequate feed and water, a rapidly implemented weight-reduction program and excessive forced exercise (Reid & Cowan 1998). Pregnant mares are particularly susceptible. Hepatic lipidosis and elevated serum triglyceride levels are the two events that appear to be triggered by the negative energy balance resulting from a lengthy fast.

The prognosis for horses with serum triglyceride levels above 1,200 mg/dl is grave, and the disease is thought to have less than a 20% survival rate if untreated. Early detection and treatment by an equine veterinarian experienced with miniature horses is essential. The initial cause for going off feed must be immediately ascertained, treated and eliminated. Intravenous glucose and other nutrient fluids should be given in an attempt to reverse the body's response to its perceived starvation. Other treatment depends upon the primary and underlying cause, but hyperlipemia should always be considered if a miniature horse, pony or miniature donkey begins to go off its feed and starts to act depressed (Marcella 1992). Although treatment for the primary disease is imperative, supportive nourishment (via nasogastric tube or IV feedings) is considered to be the most important factor in the treatment of hyperlipemia (Moore, Abood, & Hinchcliff 1994).

Poisonous Plants

Well-fed horses generally avoid poisonous plants that may be growing within their environment. Most poisonous plants have a very bitter taste and/or are spiny. When pastures are overgrazed and poisonous plants are present, hungry horses may consume unpalatable plants that they would otherwise avoid. Poisonous plant ingestion is much less likely when horses are well fed and parasite free. However, if poisonous plants are accidentally mixed in with the baled hay, cubes or pellets being fed, horses are more likely to ingest them by mistake. Poor-quality, weedy hays are sometimes converted into cubes and pellets, and neither the buyer or the horse will be able to identify the presence of any possible toxic elements (Fowler in Siegal 1996). A common type of insect poisoning occurs when blister beetles are baled into hay and later ingested by a horse.

Accidental ingestion of small pieces of ornamental poisonous plants are common in horses fed grass clippings. *Grass clippings should never be fed to miniature horses under any circumstances.* Aside from the extreme danger of causing colic, grass clippings often contain small pieces of highly poisonous, ornamental landscape plants such as avocado leaves, oleander, yew, azalea or rhododendron. When eagerly eating grass clippings, miniatures are unable to avoid consuming any foreign materials or poisonous plants that may be present in small pieces. Aside from poisonous plant leaves, grass clippings often contain chopped cigarettes and cigarette package wrappings, as well as bits of plastic, metal and broken glass.

Potentially poisonous plants include more than 200 species. Not all parts of each type of plant may be poisonous. For example, mistletoe berries are poisonous, but the leaves are not. Ingestion by pregnant mares of tall fescue infested with a specific type of fungus can cause various reproductive problems ending with the loss of many foals. Miniature horse breeders should learn to recognize poisonous plants, whether they may be native varieties grow-ing in their pastures or ornamental landscape plants commonly grown in their neighborhoods.

Poisoning by rodenticides may also occur. Highly palatable baited grains containing various agents to poison rats and mice should always be kept in locations that are inaccessible to any inquisitive and persistent miniature.

Each plant or other poisonous agent varies as to its active ingredients and exact cause of toxicity. Many plants are toxic only if horses consume large quantities of them over a period of time; very few are deadly in small amounts. Diagnosis and treatment should always be handled by an equine veterinarian.

The most dangerous poisonous plants for horses, listed in alphabetical order, are avo-cado leaves, azalea, black laurel or mountain laurel, black walnut, bracken fern, castor bean, death camas, fiddleneck, foxglove, hemlock, horsetail, larkspur, locoweed, lupine, milkweed, mistletoe berries, oak leaves and acorns, oleander, ragwort (tansy ragwort), red maple, star thistle (yellow star thistle), St. John's-wort, tobacco and yew. Emergency treatment by the veterinarian, should any poisoning be suspected, includes immediate stabilization of the vital signs, prevention of any additional exposure or absorption, and the administration of specific medications and antidotes (Rumbeiha & Oehme 1991).

Snake Bites

Because miniature horses are so small, the amount of venom injected into their systems during a snake bite is far more lethal than it would be in a full-sized horse. Horses are most commonly bitten on the head during grazing activity in deeper grasses, where they may encoun-ter and surprise sleeping snakes. As a rule, snakes usually bite horses only in self-defense.

Venomous snakes belong to two broad categories, elapines and viperines. Elapine snakes include cobras, mambas and coral snakes. Viperines include pit vipers such as rattlesnakes and cottonmouths and the true vipers such as adders and European adders (Fraser et al. 1986). If a horse is bitten, the dead snake, if available, should be presented with the patient so that the veterinarian may ascertain its size and variety.

The initial veterinary treatment should always include antivenin, if available. An excel-lent antivenin is available for all North American pit vipers, although antivenin for the elapine snakes is more difficult to obtain. Antivenin must be administered as soon as possible after the bite and is of little value after 24 hours.

The primary causes of death in miniature horses bitten by venomous snakes are mas-sive head and neck swellings, which may easily occlude breathing efforts. An emergency **tracheotomy** (surgically cutting into the trachea, usually to insert a tube to allow breathing) must be performed in order for the horse to obtain adequate oxygen. Wound infections and the sloughing of large areas of skin and muscle tissue are both likely to occur if a miniature recovers from the initial shock and swelling caused by a snake bite. Both guinea fowl and wild pigs are known to help control large snake populations.

Injuries and Lameness

The severity of the injury must be initially assessed by the owner in order to determine the need for veterinary services, which may require suturing, IV antibiotics or treatment for shock. The first consideration for any serious injury is the immediate control of blood loss by using direct pressure, if necessary, until the veterinarian (who should be called immediately) arrives. Large towels, clean gauze or rags, or even the hand may be used if a wound has severed vital arteries or veins. Constant pressure must be applied without stopping to check the wound or wipe it off. The platelets needed to coagulate blood must be left intact. The wound will resume rapid bleeding immediately if the clotting blood is disturbed.

Most injuries of horses can be attributed to poor ranch management and dangerous surroundings. Hazards such as overcrowded paddocks, protruding nails, sharp corners, poorly maintained (or barb wire) fences, low overhangs or broken glass must be avoided. Horses, when alarmed, tend to run into fences and buildings. Most injuries occur suddenly and unexpectedly, and the owner will be repeatedly challenged as to their cause and avoidance.

Traumatic injuries to the eye are common. A miniature that is squinting (squeezing its eyelid closed), is exhibiting eye pain. Eye pain can be caused by infection and/or by injury. **Corneal ulcers** (erosion, scratches or cuts to the cornea) are generally caused by injury and must be assessed and treated immediately by a veterinarian. Inflammation of an eye resulting from a corneal ulcer includes **conjunctivitis** (redness and swelling of the mucous membranes on the underside of the eyelid) and excruciating pain. Severe "melting" ulcers of the eye can develop if infected by any bacterial or fungal elements. During this process, the ulcer gets steadily larger as the corneal surface erodes, or "melts" away. *Never treat corneal ulcers with any ophthalmic ointment containing steroids, as this often causes fungal infections and the development of a melting ulcer.* Causes of eye injury range from foxtails (which must be removed) to trauma, but the most common cause of corneal laceration in riding horses is that of being hit with a whip or riding crop. No horse should ever be struck about the head or eyes with a whip or any other object.

Obvious scarring that creates blindness or that prevents showing is common, but eye damage from infection or injury can be so serious that surgical removal of the entire eye is required. Serious puncture wounds of the eye can occur when miniatures graze in pastures thick with star thistle, which is a poisonous plant to horses. Mowing star thistle at least twice yearly helps, but the best means for eradication is the use of sheep or cattle in the fields. Star thistle is not poisonous to either of these animals, they relish its taste, and they will completely eradicate it within 6 months. In addition, any low branches of trees that may have developed sharp points should be regularly eliminated by pruning.

All traumatic injuries, whether to the eye or to any other part of the body, eventually cause inflammation. Inflammation results in swelling, heat, pain and redness, each of which plays an important part in the healing process. Swelling and pain both encourage immobility of the injured area. The heat and redness are caused by an increase of blood supply to the affected area, which is directly responsible for any healing that occurs.

Leg and body injuries may range in severity from minor scrapes and abrasions to large jagged-edged wounds, rope burns, deep puncture wounds or fractures. The treatment and repair efforts required for each type of wound vary. Horses tend to form **proud flesh** (excess granulation tissue) that must be prevented or surgically removed for normal healing to take place. The development of proud flesh is a common complication of wounds within the lower leg region.

Fractures in miniature horses are more often repairable than they are in riding horses because of the breed's lighter weight and less excitable nature. Miniatures are usually tolerant of the necessary restraints, slings and casts required during the lengthy healing process of a fracture.

Causes of lameness in miniature horses include traumatically induced injuries, as well as trimming the hoof too closely, stone bruises, thrush, abscesses, hairline fractures, tendinitis, arthritis, laminitis (founder), **osteochondritis dissecans (OCD)** a cartilage disorder, and **patellar luxation** a rare congenital displacement of the knee cap. The many types of lameness so often seen in overly worked or prematurely trained and raced full-sized horses are not so often seen in miniature horses. Miniature owners are much less likely to be the cause of their horse's lameness by subjecting it to excess exercise at too young an age.

Examining horses for lameness requires a knowledge of anatomy and gait analysis. With any single front-leg lameness, head bobbing occurs, especially at the trot. The head rises when the lame foreleg bears weight and drops when the sound foreleg bears weight. For hind-leg lameness, the croup generally rises on the lame leg side and it drops lower on the sound leg side. Short, mincing "walking-on-eggs" steps indicate tenderness in at least two legs at once, such as is seen in founder. Patellar luxation causes the affected hind leg to periodically lock into a straightened backward and extended position. As the horse walks about on three legs, unpredictable release of the patellar ligament will cause a sudden jerk forward of the extended leg.

OCD can occur in any joint of the body but usually involves the upper leg or shoulder. It can sometimes be corrected with surgery, but the suspected cause of its development should be first investigated. Some clinicians feel that OCD is of genetic origin, while others feel it is due to mineral imbalances and/or forced and overly accelerated growth rates. Still others are concerned about the possible early and injudicious use of NSAIDs or steroids. If the OCD is not severe, the expense of radiographs, and/or corrective surgery may be considered prohibitive.

When allowed to become serious, **thrush** (fungal infection of the frog) can cause lameness. Easily diagnosed by its black, mealy appearance and foul odor, thrush erodes the sides of the frog and causes degeneration of both the frog and the adjacent tissues of the sole. Thrush is caused by poor management, during which horses are constantly forced to stand in moisture or filth. Kopertox or iodine should be applied daily after removal of damaged frog material, and the horse should be moved to dry, clean quarters.

Stone bruises can be expected to heal within a week, unless an abscess has developed. Abscesses should be diagnosed with hoof testers and then opened up and drained by an equine veterinarian. Hairline fractures and sprains should be immobilized until healed. Arthritis and tendinitis are common reasons for lameness, particularly in aged miniatures, or in miniatures with dwarfism characteristics.

Miniatures are rarely shod, except for occasional correction or training purposes. The very thin hoof wall requires extreme accuracy when nailing a shoe, to avoid penetrating the sensitive laminae. Miniatures that are trimmed too short (usually in an attempt to reduce their height measurement for a show) often develop tenderness or lameness in the overly shortened heels.

CHAPTER 10

Reproduction

EQUINE VETERINARIANS WHOSE PRACTICES INCLUDE several miniature horse breeding farms can expect that as much as 75% of their work will be related to reproduction (Judd 1994). Most of the well-documented veterinary information published on equine reproduction has been obtained on full-sized horses being managed on huge breeding farms, such as those for thoroughbred race horses. Many of these farms employ full-time veterinarians to oversee their entire breeding programs, as the resulting foals commonly sell for hundreds of thousands of dollars as yearlings. In this scenario, each mare's production of an early and yearly foal is of crucial financial importance to its owner. There are various means by which the normal cycles of mares may be altered and endless means by which infertility or sterility may be addressed and temporarily cured. Unfortunately, the subject of reproduction and related problems in miniature horses is lacking in scientific investigation, and many of the management techniques and veterinary procedures that are well accepted for full-sized horses do not apply to miniatures. Show-type full-sized horses are usually selected first for their performance ability, and second for their reproductive efficiency (Ensminger 1990), while show-type miniature horses are primarily selected for their breeding potential and excellence of conformation and pedigree.

Normal reproductive activity in full-sized horses, particularly on thoroughbred breeding farms, has been radically altered by human intervention. Because foals become yearlings on January 1 of the year after their birth, and because most breeds aim for tall, mature-looking yearlings, there is a decided advantage for full-sized breed mares to foal in January or February. Even foals that arrive as late as December will be considered yearlings on January 1 at a chronological age of less than 1 month. In order to obtain early foals, full-sized horse breeders and their veterinarians use a multitude of psychological, environmental, physiological, and medical tactics to alter the normal reproductive activity of both stallions and mares. In miniature horses, the reverse is true. A foal delivered in the middle or latter part of the year will have the show and sales advantage of being much shorter when it becomes a yearling on the following January 1. The incentive for obtaining early foals is considerably diminished in the miniature horse breed.

Without artificial conditions, mares and stallions experience winter depression of their reproductive cycles. During this time mares do not usually cycle and stallions often have a notable decrease in libido. Environmental and psychological management of full-sized horses, such as artificial lighting in stalls and daily teasing, often results in mares that start cycling in January or February and stallions that have adequate libido during those months. Hormonal management of these mares may include drugs such as

Regu-Mate™ (altrenogest, an oral progestin), Equimate™ (an injectable prostaglandin), and Cystorelin® (an injectable gonadotropic-releasing hormone). All of these artificial and medical interventions are used in conjunction with frequent rectal palpations to accurately assess the condition of the ovaries, ovarian follicles and erupting corpus luteum (the ovarian body that secretes progesterone after ovulation). The natural and most fertile breeding season of miniature horses (May through September) need not be altered by artificial lights and hormone treatments. Foals delivered in the spring, summer and fall are ideal for most miniature horse breeding farm owners, and within this time frame inclement weather during the foaling season may also be avoided.

The conception and live foal delivery rate of miniature horses appears to be lower than that of full-sized horses and ponies, which might possibly be attributed to their extremely small size and the higher incidence of abortions. **Division B mares** (over 34 inches [86 cm], up to and including 38 inches [97 cm]) appear to have fewer conception and foaling difficulties than do **Division A mares** (34 inches [86 cm] and under) (Campbell 1992; Friedman 1996).

With the exception of stallions standing at stud to several **outside mares** (mares not owned by the stallion's owner), many miniature horse breeding farms use **pasture breeding** (one stallion is placed with a group of mares for the year), rather than **hand breeding** (breedings that are controlled and supervised by human attendants). Neither the AMHA or the AMHR registry allows **artificial insemination** (AI), the process whereby semen is collected and deposited in the mare by an AI technician or veterinarian. The American Miniature Horse registries and The Jockey Club (which registers Thoroughbreds) are the only horse registries that do not allow AI procedures to be employed in order to obtain registered foals.

In pasture breeding situations, there is a rule enforced by both registries that no stallion in the pasture may be replaced by a different stallion without a mandatory 45-day waiting period between the removal of the first stallion and the introduction of the second stallion. This restriction is carefully monitored by the use of stallion breeding reports required at the end of each year by both AMHA and AMHR. It is critically important that accurate written records be maintained on a daily basis to document witnessed matings, as well as any changes, omissions or additions of stallions and mares that may have been made during the year.

When living in pasture situations with other horses, as the mares reach the end of their pregnancies, they are generally isolated from the rest of the herd so that the delivery of their foals takes place in a more easily observed and safely protected environment. The presence (although not necessarily intervention and assistance) of a knowledgeable human attendant during the birthing process is highly recommended. Miniature foals can easily die because of simple and completely avoidable events such as failure of the amniotic sac to break over the foal's nose, resulting in its subsequent suffocation.

Mares

The onset of puberty in the miniature mare is approximately 18 months but ranges from 8 to 24 months. The recommended age for first breeding of a mare is during the spring or summer of her 3rd year. The **estrus cycle** (heat cycle) of miniature mares is similar to that of full-sized mares, with the exception that many miniatures are known to cycle and conceive during the winter months when other mares exhibit **anestrus** (lack of estrus cycles).

Figure 10.1 *Miniature stallion,* Rehs Patriarch, *teasing a mare,* Tor's Pandora, *during a receptive estrus cycle. Behaviors to be noted in the stallion are loud screaming, squealing and nickering, tail flagging, foot stamping and dancing, extended and arched neck as he reaches out to mare, and sexual readiness. Behaviors to be noted in the mare are squatting, urinating, winking of the vulva, tail flagging, squealing, and backing into the stallion if he fails to advance towards her hindquarters.*

Mares that are in heat generally indicate their willingness to copulate when **teased** (introduced to an interested stallion). The teasing process causes a receptive mare to squat, urinate, open and close her vulva (called "winking"), flag her tail, squeal and nicker (see Figure 10.1).

The length of each mare's receptive period to the stallion varies widely, but the normal range should be between 5 and 8 days and the estrus cycle itself should be approximately 21 days in length. This means that it is usually about 16 days from the end of one heat to the 1st day of the next one. The average mare ovulates 1 to 2 days before the end of her receptive period. The miniature mare will have her most fertile estrus cycles during the late spring and early summer months. If a mare is to be hand bred, and only once, the 3rd or 4th day of her heat cycle is advised. If two hand breedings are preferred, she may be bred on the 2nd day and the 4th day. If she is still receptive on the 6th or 7th day, she should be covered one additional time. When a mare is correctly bred, live sperm should already be present in both of her **fallopian tubes** (tubes leading from the ovaries to the uterus) when she ovulates. Once released from the ovary, the **ovum** (egg) lives only 2 to 4 hours, and the ovum is fertilized in the fallopian tube, not in the uterus. Fortunately, active, normal sperm live within the healthy female reproductive tract for 48 to 72 hours. Actual implantation of the placenta (with its attached and developing embryo) into the **endometrium** (inner lining of uterus) often takes as long as 30 days after fertilization of the ovum takes place.

Pasture breeding usually results in a higher conception rate than hand breeding. This seems to be especially true within the miniature horse breed. In pasture breeding situations, an experienced stallion will cover the mare repeatedly during her most fertile period and will then appear to lose interest on the last 2 days of her cycle (after she has ovulated). It is important to not give the stallion too many mares (10 to 20, at the most) and to not change the members of his group. Stallions will often reject new mares being added (with surprisingly vicious attacks) and serious injuries may occur. If a new mare is to be incorporated (even one with which the stallion is familiar) she should be kept separated by a fence until coming in heat. If she is successfully hand bred the first time, she may then be added to the herd for the remainder of her estrus cycle. Even the most aggressive of stallions will usually accept the new mare's added presence from then on.

Pregnancy may be verified by careful rectal palpation, by ultrasound or by estrone sulfate/progesterone blood tests. Frequent rectal and vaginal examinations to determine ovarian follicle presence and development, pregnancy status, and the state of uterine health (such as cultures or biopsies) are not recommended in miniatures unless the examiner has extremely small arms and hands and the mares are not too small. Under most circumstances, the weekly two to three veterinary rectal palpations, which are standard on large horse breeding farms, should not be a consideration for miniature horse breeding farms.

In miniature horse mares, however, none of these tests can be relied upon to be 100% accurate, and there have been many false-positive, false-negative and inconclusive results. Some miniature horse breeding farms rely upon a well-managed teasing regimen, if using hand breeding. Mares that do not cycle after they have been bred are assumed to be pregnant. Even pasture-bred mares may be watched for subsequent estrus cycles by starting daily observations on the 14th day after the latest breeding date that may have been witnessed and recorded. If the mare has not recycled by the 20th day after her last breeding date, she is probably pregnant.

Occasional miniature mares will exhibit false heat cycles during pregnancy, especially when they are fond of a particular stallion. Some pregnant mares in their last trimester may also exhibit unusual sexual behavior, such as mounting other mares, or squealing and urinating when teased by the pasture stallion or other mares. Although there are exceptions, the well-oriented and experienced pasture breeding stallion will usually refuse to copulate with either of these types of mares. Their odor informs him that they are not in a true estrus cycle and that they are already pregnant. He will generally tease them to make absolutely sure but will hesitate to mount them.

The normal length of **gestation** (pregnancy) ranges from 320 to 335 days, slightly shorter than the 340-day average expected for most full-sized breeds (Judd 1994; Friedman 1997). This is roughly 10 to 11 months, but fully developed, fully haired, healthy, completely normal miniature horse foals are often delivered as early as 10 months' gestation, particularly when out of the shortest or most obese mares. The normal length of gestation for most mares can be mentally calculated by starting from the 2nd to last day of breeding, (the probable date of conception, rather than the last day of breeding, before which the mare had already ovulated). Figure back 1 month and simply add 10 days. Example: The mare was bred August 5, 7, and 9, and appeared to be out of heat on August 10. From August 7, go back one month to July 7 and add 10 days. This calculates her due date to be about July 17, plus or minus a few days. A foaling date based on a 340-day gestation is provided in Table 10.1.

It is imperative to observe all pregnant mares for the increasing size of their **mammary glands** (udder development), for behavioral changes and for the loosening of their hindquarter musculature. Daily checks during the last few weeks will familiarize and alert the owner to any gradual (or sudden) changes. Miniature mares often fail to **wax over** (form visible, hardened droplets of dried colostrum on the ends of their nipples). Mares that do wax over, or

Table 10.1 Mare Foaling Guide, Based on 340-Day Gestation   *LBD = last breeding date*

LBD	Foal Date	LBD	Foal Date	LBD	Foal Date	LBD	Foal Date
Jan. 1	Dec. 7	Feb. 3	Jan. 9	Mar. 2	Feb. 5	Apr. 2	Mar. 8
4	10	6	12	5	8	5	11
7	13	9	15	8	11	8	14
10	16	12	18	11	14	11	17
13	19	15	21	14	17	14	20
16	22	18	24	17	20	17	23
19	25	21	27	21	24	20	26
22	28	24	30	24	27	23	29
25	31	27	Feb. 2	27	Mar. 2	26	Apr. 1
28	Jan. 3			30	5	29	4
31	6						
May 2	Apr. 7	June 4	May 10	July 1	June 6	Aug. 3	July 9
5	10	7	13	4	9	6	12
8	13	10	16	7	12	9	15
11	16	13	19	10	15	12	18
14	19	16	22	13	18	15	21
17	22	19	25	16	21	18	24
20	25	22	28	19	22	21	27
23	28	25	31	22	27	24	30
26	May 1	28	June 3	25	30	27	Aug. 2
29	4			28	July 3	30	5
June 1	7			31	6		
Sept. 2	Aug. 8	Oct. 1	Sept. 7	Nov. 3	Oct. 10	Dec. 3	Nov. 9
5	11	4	10	6	13	6	12
8	14	7	13	9	16	9	15
11	17	10	16	12	19	12	18
14	20	13	19	15	22	15	21
17	23	16	22	18	25	18	24
20	26	19	25	21	28	21	27
23	29	22	28	24	31	24	30
26	Sept. 1	25	Oct. 1	27	Nov. 3	27	Dec. 3
29	4	28	4	30	6	30	6
		31	7				

drip milk, however, usually deliver their foals within 24 hours. Additionally, if the udder becomes suddenly larger and noticeably more firm (especially if the nipples flatten out and appear to disappear because of the extreme distention), the mare should deliver within 24 hours. The terms *bagging up* and *making a bag* are often used to describe this process. Although nonvisual udder palpation skills may be developed, checking for udder changes and milk production must sometimes be performed from a kneeling position, and for this reason is often more challenging in miniatures than in full-sized horse mares.

The mare's hormone levels during pregnancy control the events to be expected after ovulation, when the corpus luteum begins secreting progesterone. From the 5th through 11th months of gestation, progesterone levels remain high in order to maintain uterine tone, as well as the pregnancy itself. Forty-eight hours before parturition, relaxin levels rise, causing noticeable relaxation of the musculature in the pelvic area and observable elongation and puffiness of the vulva. During the **first stage of labor**, the mare often exhibits "uneasy" behaviors, such as pawing, sweating, refusing to eat and getting up and down frequently. This is caused by a decided increase in her adrenal cortical hormone levels and by the resulting dilation of the cervix. The **second stage of labor**, during which oxytocin levels rise and estrogen levels decrease, initiates uterine contractions and the birth of the foal. The **third stage of labor**, while oxytocin levels remain high, results in the passing of the placenta.

An equine veterinarian's injection of oxytocin is sometimes advisable if the mare retains her placenta for more than 2 hours after the foal's birth. A large knot may be tied in the hanging afterbirth in order to get it up off of the ground, to prevent its entanglement in the mare's hind legs, and to add some weight to its "pulling out" effect. The hanging afterbirth (if it is being retained) must never be forcefully tugged or pulled in an attempt to remove it from the uterus. Extremely gentle extraction pressure may sometimes be indicated, however. Every time the foal nurses, oxytocin will be secreted within the mare's system, and this is the vital hormone that aids in the passage of the placenta by stimulating uterine contractions. Placentas should always be examined for their healthy and entirely complete appearance. A properly formed and fully complete placenta appears quite similar in shape to a pair of pants.

Foaling

If the mare is to deliver her foal inside a box stall, she should gradually be familiarized to being enclosed within it (without any companionship) for several hours at a time. The stall should be adequate in size (preferably at least 10 by 10 feet [3 by 3 m]) and should provide the mare with a view to the outside, without her having to raise her front legs off the ground. Adequate lighting and feed, heat (if in a frigid climate), a constant water and trace mineral salt block supply, and a smooth (injury-proof) interior are all essential to the mare's safety and contentment (see Chapter 5 and Figure 5.1). Exercise is essential in order for miniatures to remain colic free. No mare should be in a stall for more than 12 hours daily. Even after the foal has been delivered, exercise and room to run are crucial to the health of both the mare and her new foal.

The preferred bedding for a foaling stall is clean, mold-free and grain-free straw, not shavings. Shavings often irritate the eyes of foals (which frequently lie down) and are also a source of bacterial contamination to the mare and her new foal. Shavings tend to adhere and advance up or into any moistened surface (for example, the foal's umbilicus and eyes, or the mare's afterbirth, her hind legs and her vulva). Their rough edges cling to the wet hairs and act in a manner similar to that of the advancing, penetrating movement of foxtails being drawn into body cavities by their barbs.

There are various foaling monitoring systems available to miniature horse owners, and most breeders using them have found them to be irreplaceable. Although there are usually a few "false alarms" before actual labor begins, innumerable foals and mares have been saved by the regular use of such devices. Foaling monitoring systems may be augmented by closed-circuit television systems, which provide the breeder (in a comfortable bedroom or a kitchen, for example) with a continuous view of the mare and her activities in the foaling stall.

Normal Deliveries

The entire foaling process should take less than 2 hours (frequently it takes as little as 15 minutes) and veterinary assistance should be sought immediately should there appear to be any problem. No more than 15 minutes should elapse between obvious abdominal contractions and the first appearance of the bulging **amniotic sac** (a filmy, water-filled "bubble") and no more than an additional 15 minutes should elapse between the bulging of the amnion and the first visible limb of the foal.

Unlike many full-sized horses, miniature mares are often comforted by the presence of their owners, particularly if the owners are gentle and the mares have been regularly and affectionately handled. While observing from a distance, however, it is best to allow the mare to deliver her foal without interference. Normal presentation includes one foreleg first (front of hoof up, sole of hoof towards the ground, when the mare is in a standing position), then the second foreleg (same position), and finally the nose. The slightly offset position of the front legs creates a narrower shoulder width and facilitates passage of the shoulders through the pelvis. If the foal is not excessively large and is in a normal position, its forelegs and head will noticeably advance each time the mare's uterus and abdominal muscles contract. As the head is presented, it is desirable to break the amniotic sac if it is still covering the nose of the foal. The sac should never be broken over the nose if the foal's head is still receding back into the vagina during the mare's rest period in the absence of a contraction. The placenta should still be attached (providing the foal with oxygen), but if the foal inhales while still in the birth canal, it may inhale amniotic fluid. This can result in choking and suffocation, or the later development of inhalation pneumonia.

If a successful delivery is accomplished, whether naturally or with assistance, the foal should be allowed to lie on the ground undisturbed (except for breaking the amniotic sac away from its nose and making sure that it is breathing). The umbilical cord should be left attached until the mare rises and causes it to break naturally. If the umbilical cord is still attached to the placenta and the placenta is still attached to the inside of the uterus, the foal may be able to benefit from the additional oxygen and blood supply provided (Beeman 1995).

Just prior to or shortly after delivery, the mare's udder and nipples should be gently washed with a very mild soap or a dilute Nolvasan® solution. Any smegma that might have accumulated between the two halves should also be gently removed at this time (see Chapter 8). Following this procedure, the udder should always be thoroughly rinsed with clear lukewarm water to render it completely "odorless" (not tainted with the smells of foreign materials) for the soon-to-be-delivered foal. After the birth of the foal, it is advisable that a squirt or two of colostrum be wiped upon the newly cleaned udder and nipples. Perfumed soaps and/or Bag Balm® should always be avoided prior to foaling, as they may easily disrupt the foal's first suckling attempts (which are guided primarily by the smell of its dam's udder and milk secretions).

Colostrum is the first thick, sticky milk after foaling, which contains all of the antibodies needed for protection of the foal from disease. Equine placentas do not allow the passage of any antibodies to the developing foal while it is still in the uterus. All of the foal's antibody protection must be acquired from the colostrum. For this reason it is essential that every neonate ingest an adequate quantity of colostrum during the first 3 or 4 hours (while its gastrointestinal tract still allows the maximum amount of antibody absorption).

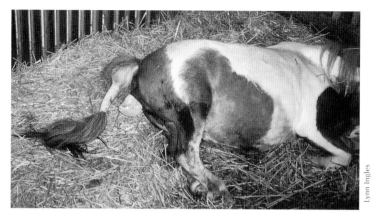

Lynn Ingles

Figure 10.2 *First appearance of the amniotic sac, or bubble. The foal's hoof is already visible within the transparent sac. Note that the tail wrap on this mare has slipped below its correct position.*

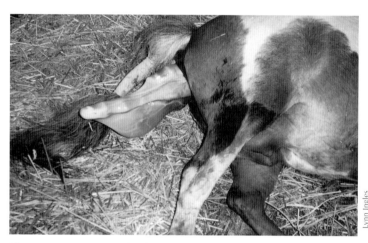

Lynn Ingles

Figure 10.3 *Five minutes after the first appearance of the amniotic sac, both hooves (one further back than the other), as well as the head are visible. This mare has remained lying down during the delivery, but some mares will stand, pace about and try to deliver the foal while in a standing position.*

Lynn Ingles

Figure 10.4 *Ten minutes after the first appearance of the amniotic sac, the foal is delivered, and the mare stands up, breaking the umbilical cord. The breeder has torn the amniotic sac away from the foal's head and nostrils in order to facilitate breathing.*

Barbara Naviaux

Figure 10.5 *Healthy foal with strong suckling reflex obtaining colostrum within 4 hours after birth.* Sugar Creek Strawberry Parfait, *affectionately nurses her foal* Rodabi-J Molokai Maid, *who is less than 4 hours old. Breeder of mare: Lynda Baerthlein Marzec. Owner of mare: Sue Borden. Breeder/owner of foal: Barbara Naviaux.*

Some miniature mares foal out in their pastures, with other mares and the stallion present, and with no human assistance. This is not usually planned, but it still occurs. If such a birth takes place during mild weather and the foal is not malpositioned, is able to get out of the sac and is not allowed to become either too cold or too hot, the results may be surprisingly successful. When discovering such a foal, it is advisable to bring it in with the mare to a more protected environment.

As for foals delivered within the safety of a stall, the neonate's umbilical stump should be disinfected and it should be **imprinted** (a now popular handling and training technique for newly born foals). The foal should be observed for a possible **meconium** (first manure of the foal) impaction. In addition, the mare should be under close observation for a few days and her bonding process with the foal should be encouraged (without the interference of other mares, who sometimes wish to "steal" the foal).

Currently 0.5% Nolvasan® solution is preferred for the disinfection of the foal's umbilical stump, and a plastic film cannister is an ideal container for its application. The miniature foal may easily be turned upside down in one's arms, with the film can half full of Nolvasan® solution pressed tightly over the umbilical stump. The Nolvasan® solution (diluted to 0.5%: one part Nolvasan® to four parts water) should be applied several times within the first few days in an attempt to dry up the umbilical stump and prevent the entry of any harmful bacteria.

Normal Parameters and Vital Signs of Foals

The normal gestational age of a newborn miniature horse foal is 325 days, plus or minus 20 days. Because this is often shorter than for full-sized horses, miniature foals should not be considered "premature" on the basis of gestational age alone. It is therefore important to observe each miniature horse foal for all of the other parameters associated with healthy neonatal viability and vitality. The foal's suckling reflex should be present within 20 minutes after foaling, and it should rise by itself to a standing position within 2 hours and nurse within 4 hours (Hayes 1993).

For the first 4 days, the normal foal's body temperature will be from 99°F to 101.5°F (37.2°C to 38.6°C). One to 5 minutes after foaling, the heart rate will usually exceed 60 beats per minute (bpm), and after 1 hour, it will range from 60 bpm to 80 bpm. During the first week of the foal's life, the normal heart rate will range from 80 bpm to 120 bpm. Heart murmurs are common in foals and should not be considered abnormal (Rose & Hodgson 1993). Immediately after foaling, the respiration rate may be slow and irregular but within 30 minutes it should rise to as much as 80 breaths per minute, without being abnormal. During the next 12-hour period, the respiration rate of normal foals generally ranges from 30 to 40 breaths per minute (Gerros 1996; Madigan 1997).

At birth, the foal will usually have limp extremities, which gain some purposeful movement and flexion capability after 1 to 2 minutes. The head will often be elevated but will be wobbly, and the ears plastered back by amniotic fluid rather than erect. The eyes will be squinting (with possible conjunctivitis) and the lashes may be rolled in under the eyelids, a condition called **entropion**. This causes the eye lashes to irritate and sometimes scratch the cornea. Manual opening of the lids and reversal of this corneal irritation is advisable and may serve to prevent the development of a more permanent type of entropion, which must be corrected surgically. The foal should urinate within 9 hours after birth, although colts may urinate sooner than fillies. The meconium should be passed within 24 hours, at which time the feces will become yellow, indicating the foal's intake of milk and its passage. There will be no blink response present until 2 weeks of age, as the foal's eyesight is very poor until then.

Impactions of the meconium are fairly common in newborn foals. This manure is black and pasty in consistency, and meconium impactions are usually within 12 inches of the anus. The rectal tissue of foals is extremely fragile and is easily perforated by roughly administered

---

Normal Parameters of a Newborn Foal   *From Madigan 1997*

 ▲   *Time to suck: 2–20 minutes. Reflex stimulated by placing a finger in the mouth.*
 ▲   *Sternal recumbency (resting on the breastbone): 1–2 minutes.*
 ▲   *Time to stand: average 60 minutes. Longer than 2 hours is considered abnormal.*
 ▲   *Time to nurse from mare: 2 hours average. Longer than 3–4 hours is considered abnormal.*

Foal Vital Signs

 ▲   *Temperature: 99°F to 101.5°F (37.2°C to 38.6°C) A.M. non-stressed value.*
 ▲   *Heart Rate:*
       1–5 minutes post-foaling: over 60 beats per minute.
       6–60 minutes: 80–130 beats per minute.
       Day 1–5: 80–120 beats per minute.
 ▲   *Respiration:*
       Immediately post-foaling: slow and irregular.
       First 30 minutes: 60–80 breaths per minute.
       1–12 hours: 30–40 breaths per minute.

enemas, sharp objects and even overly harsh digital inspections. However, an enema is often needed by such foals, although great care should be exercised during the procedure. Since a deep enema is usually not required, the use of a standard human Fleet™ enema is recommended. The tip is small, very smooth, and not too long, and the solution is both mild and effective. Fleet™ enemas are available over the counter at any drug store or supermarket.

Table 10.2 Foal Weights at Birth Compared with Foal Heights at Birth*

Birth weights of 28 foals and birth heights of 30 foals were recorded in this study (Abramson 1998b).

Criteria Number of Foals	Weight 28	Height 30
Minimum	19 lb 8.5 kg	17.5 in. 44.4 cm.
Maximum	30 lb 13.5 kg	23 in. 59.7 cm.
Average	23.11 lb 10.4 kg	19.83 in. 50.3 cm

Data collected by Marsha Kenley at Bended Knee Miniature Horse Farm 1991–1997.

Research collected at one miniature horse farm over a 7-year period from 1991 through 1997 showed that newborn foals weighed between 19 and 30 pounds (8.5 and 13.5 kg) at birth, with an average of 23 pounds (10.4 kg) (see Table 10.2). Birth weight was not found to correlate with the final height of the horse (i.e., one 30-pound [13.5-kg] foal was only 23.5 inches [59.7 cm] tall at a year old). Foal weight more likely correlated with the condition and height of the mare at foaling and the gestational age of the foal at birth (premature, term, or post-mature), as well as other genetic factors. Foals were weighed by the breeder standing on a scale while holding the horse, weighing the breeder alone and subtracting the difference.*

Foal Diarrhea Foals often develop diarrhea during the mare's **foaling heat** (the first heat cycle that occurs 7 to 12 days after foaling), but if it is mild, no treatment is required. If the diarrhea becomes extremely watery, or if the foal begins acting depressed and loses its appetite, broad-spectrum antibiotics may be indicated. It is currently thought that foaling-heat diarrhea may be initiated by strongyle (bloodworm) infestation and that its occurrence can be minimized and often prevented by worming the mare with ivermectin 1 month prior to her foal's birth. Worming with ivermectin is entirely safe during pregnancy, and neither the mare's or the impending foal's health should ever be jeopardized by not keeping the mare parasite free throughout her entire gestation.

By examining the udder of the mare, the foal's appetite and milk intake can be easily monitored. After the first few days, a healthy foal will typically keep the mare's udder fairly well drained, indicated by wet nipples and a certain degree of flaccidity. Hard, tightly filled bags with dry, distended nipples are a clear sign that the foal is not eating well. Should the foal lose its appetite, veterinary care should be sought and antibiotics may be prescribed.

Tribrissen™ (trimethoprim and sulfadiazine) is an excellent drug for the treatment of foal diarrhea; both a palatable paste and tablets are available for oral administration through any equine veterinarian, on a prescription basis. The tablets are easily dissolved in water and may be given orally with a 10-cc plastic syringe after they are in solution. A small amount of corn syrup, molasses or sugar can be added to eliminate the bitter flavor.

Foal Septicemia **Septicemia** is the word used to describe various potentially life-threatening bacterial infections which become so severe that the causative bacteria may be found (cultured) within the blood-stream. **Navel ill** (infections acquired through the umbilicus), **joint ill** (infections that localize within the joints), and **pneumonia** (lung infections) may all fall within the septicemia category. These types of generalized bacterial infections affecting miniature horse neonates are common and can rapidly become deadly if not treated promptly. The veterinarian must be summoned immediately should any newly delivered foal appear weak, unable to nurse, or compromised in any way. Almost all septicemias are caused by a failure of passive transfer of immunity through the colostrum (Rose & Hodson 1993).

Immunoglobulins (which function as antibodies) are not transferred to the foal while it is in the uterus. All disease and infection protection must be acquired by the foal's ingestion of antibody-laden colostrum during the first few hours after birth. If the mare has been dripping milk for several days prior to delivery, her milk's immunoglobulin components may have been depleted. Or if the foal fails to obtain adequate amounts of colostrum during the first few hours after birth, the intestinal lining may have become impervious to adequate antibody absorption. The veterinarian may want to test the mare's colostrum or the foal's blood for adequate immunoglobulin levels. Blood cultures should be obtained if septicemia is suspected.

Occasionally foals will attempt to suckle walls and feeders but cannot seem to locate the mare's udder and nipples. Such neonates have sometimes been called "**dummy foals.**" These foals may be showing symptoms of **neonatal maladjustment syndrome** (a term that describes a group of noninfectious conditions resulting in a foal's inability to survive without medical intervention). As many as 50% of dummy foals show symptoms of septicemia (Madigan 1997), a leading cause of death in foals, and must be seen and treated immediately by an equine veterinarian. The owner will be requested to milk out the mare's colostrum (at least 4 ounces) and have it ready for nasogastric administration to the foal by the attending veterinarian. All antibodies carried by the mare, even if her vaccinations have been brought up to date 1 month prior to foaling, must be transferred to the foal in the mare's first milk. It is extremely important that all foals consume colostrum within the first 3 to 6 hours after birth. After 6 to 8 hours, the foal's gastrointestinal tract becomes progressively less able to absorb the vital antibodies contained in the colostrum. The earlier the foal nurses, the more antibodies it absorbs and the more protected from disease it becomes (Gerros 1996; Madigan 1997).

Foals suspected of having developed navel ill will have the same symptoms as any of the septicemic conditions; failure to suckle, generalized weakness and compromised vital signs should be evaluated by the veterinarian. Blood cultures, antibiotics, **intravenous** (IV) fluids and colostrum administered by nasogastric intubation are all essential for recovery.

Foals affected by joint ill will develop lameness and noticeable enlargement of the joints. Infected synovial fluid may be extracted with a syringe and cultured by the veterinarian. The majority of foals with joint ill expire or must be euthanized.

Pneumonia is a common cause of death in neonates. Foals developing pneumonia, often accompanied by septicemia, must be treated immediately with antibiotics. Blood and/or nasal secretions are cultured to determine the causative bacteria and the most effective antibiotics. By listening to the lungs with a stethoscope an equine veterinarian will be able to assess the foal's lung condition.

Dystocias

Dystocias (difficult births) are fairly common and require the immediate attention of the owner, and, if possible, the farm veterinarian (Marcella 1992). If the foal's delivery position appears to be abnormal, or if there is any delay in the mare's progress, the veterinarian should be telephoned immediately and the owner must then proceed to determine the problem without any professional assistance. There is very little time to save the life of the foal in such cases, and it is rarely possible for any veterinarian to arrive in time. Sleeve-length sterile latex gloves are highly recommended, although well-scrubbed bare hands (with no rings and with very short fingernails) have saved the lives of many miniature horse foals. After breaking open the amniotic sac, if visible, the owner should reach inside and try to determine the location and orientation of any portion of the foal that is accessible. It is essential that the searching for and maneuvering of the foal and its limbs be done *inside* of the amniotic sac. The foal may require having its head or front legs repositioned in order for it to pass through the pelvis, and it may have to be pushed back into the mare in order to accomplish any useful repositioning. If the foal's forelegs are within reach, a gentle pulling *down* (towards the mare's hind hooves) during the mare's contractions may help to accelerate the birth. It is imperative to never pull straight back on a partially delivered foal, whether the mare is standing up or lying down.

If the owner is unable to reposition and deliver the foal, the farm veterinarian's arrival becomes crucial. The foal may no longer be alive, and the veterinarian's decisions and expertise will be necessary to save the life and future productivity of the mare. Walking the mare may help to delay her contractions, but this can be an extremely tense period should the veterinarian's arrival be delayed. The options of repositioning the foal, pulling it out with the aid of instruments or chains, **fetotomy** (dismembering the foal), or cesarean section are all decisions to be made by the veterinarian but become difficult choices for any caring owner.

Mares that have endured lengthy dystocias are often debilitated by **obturator nerve damage** (causing paralysis of the hind legs due to the crushing of pelvic nerves). Such mares will often be unable to stand, as the hind legs will uncontrollably spread apart when they attempt to rise. It is critical to get these mares up and standing as soon as possible. Tying their hind legs together at the hocks or pasterns is sometimes required, and for several days human assistance may be necessary for them to remain in a standing position. Bracing them up in a breeding stock or a very narrow stall may also be helpful, but it is absolutely essential that such mares be forced to remain in a standing position for as long as possible each day. After such life-threatening and traumatic experiences, mares should always receive intravenous (IV) fluids; intramuscular (IM), intrauterine, and sometimes oral antibiotics; effective antispasmodics and analgesics; and round-the-clock nursing care, as prescribed. If the veterinarian installs an IV heparin lock and provides adequate instruction, much of the aftercare can be handled by the owner.

Figure 10.6 *The health and vigor of miniature horse foals necessitate high-protein, high-calorie nutrition in combination with daily exercise.* Roys Toys Snippets Valentina *and her foal* La Vista Remarkable DWB *enjoy a run in their large pasture. Breeder of mare: Roy and Kay Pate. Breeder/owner of foal: Susan Hopmans.*

Post-Foaling

For the first few days after foaling, neonates must ingest a certain amount of their mother's manure. The normal bacterial flora needed to initiate healthy peristalsis and digestion are found within the mare's feces. If stalls are kept so meticulously clean that the foal is prevented from eating manure, there is a veterinary product available in a palatable paste form that contains the bacteria required for the foal's normal digestive processes to be initiated. Foals may occasionally choke on a large fecal ball, which will be easily detected by the green slime and bubbles that begin to be sneezed, coughed, and discharged from their noses. The owner may attempt to find the offending fecal ball within the esophagus (by feeling up and down the neck on the outside). Once found, it is sometimes possible to massage the fecal ball from the outside into much smaller pieces and to thereby dislodge it. Sometimes a veterinarian may have to be summoned so that the fecal ball can be mechanically pushed down into the foal's stomach with the use of a nasaogastric tube.

Miniature mares, with new foals at their sides, often exhibit **behavioral anestrus** (mare will actually be cycling but will show no overt signs of being in heat). This appears to be due to the mare's extreme emotional attachment to her foal and her fear that the stallion might cause it harm (Judd 1994). The behavioral anestrus mare will kick, strike, dash about, and angrily lay her ears back as she attempts to "protect" her foal from the stallion. Most miniature horse stallions are extremely gentle and considerate of new foals, however, and the fears of such mares are usually unfounded. A mare in this category may often be convinced to become receptive during a heat cycle by placing her just across a strong fence from the stallion with which she has already had an established relationship. If she is fond of the stallion, and he has been accessible (across the fence) since the mare has foaled, she may become receptive and will begin showing her estrus cycles. The mare can then be led out to the stallion, leaving her foal within view, but separated by the fence.

Foal Heat

Only one breeding, on the 3rd or 4th day, is recommended during the mare's **foaling heat** (7 to 12 days after foaling) to minimize possible uterine infections. A mare should never be bred during her foaling heat if there has been any difficulty with the birth, if she has retained her placenta for more than 2 hours, if there is any vaginal discharge or if there has been any vaginal bruising or injury. The absence of additional estrus cycles after the foaling heat and while still nursing a foal is a common phenomenon in miniature mares and may justify an attempt to get such mares rebred and back in foal immediately following foaling.

Infertility

There are many causes of infertility in the mare, but uterine infections are frequently implicated. Low-grade uterine infections can cause early abortions and are usually the cause of mares not settling after repeated breedings throughout several normal-appearing heat cycles. When a mare aborts what appears to be a completely normal foal, the cause may be a low-grade uterine infection. Such infections may be caused by bacteria, fungi or a combination of both bacterial and fungal elements. Low-grade infections may cause placental insufficiency. The foal is then deprived of its needed nutrient and oxygen supplies, and subsequently dies. The foal's death signals hormonal changes within the mare's system, which will result in expulsion of the dead foal after approximately 3 days (Campbell 1992).

Systemic and uterine treatments by a veterinarian are usually necessary before the mare can be expected to conceive and hold a future pregnancy. This is especially true if the mare's low-grade uterine infection has advanced to **endometritis** (severe uterine inflammation) or **pyometra** (pus in the uterus). Uterine cultures and biopsies require one arm and hand within the rectum at the same time that a vaginal speculum is placed within the vagina. The culturette or surgical instrument must be inserted through the cervix and into the uterus, with the help of the fingers pressing upon the walls of the rectum and uterus to gain apposition and the required pressure to obtain the sample. Because the miniature horse veterinarian is often handicapped by an inability to do rectal or vaginal examinations, it is sometimes necessary to diagnose such conditions by an examination of the aborted foal, vaginal discharges, the mare's vital signs and the use of blood tests. If direct treatments within the uterus are not an option, systemic antibiotics may have to suffice. All mares with uterine infections, even if they seem to be low grade, should be rested through a few estrus cycles (with teasing, but without breeding) in order to allow for complete healing after treatment.

There are many other possible causes of abortion in miniature mares, but none occurs as frequently as do uterine infections. Other infectious diseases causing abortion, such as herpesvirus-1 (rhinopneumonitis), and equine viral arteritis have been discussed in Chapter 9. Contagious equine metritis has been discussed by equine veterinarians within the full-sized horse industry, but cases in miniature horses have not yet been documented.

Noninfectious causes of abortion in miniature mares include foals with congenital anomalies, such as severe dwarfism. Foals inheriting a high number of dwarfism-characteristic genes are not usually viable. Dwarfism appears to be **polygenic** (caused by various different genes, not

Figure 10.7 *Miniature horse foal with some dwarfism characteristics, aborted at approximately 6 months' gestation.*

by a single gene) in its mode of inheritance, and the degree of severity is probably determined by the heterozygosity, homozygosity, number and assortment of genes inherited (see Chapter 11). Severely challenged dwarf foals (as well as foals inheriting other types of lethal genes) may die and be aborted at any stage of the mare's gestation from conception to full term (see Figure 10.7).

Other noninfectious causes of infertility or abortion in miniature horse mares include the following possibilities:

- Older mares with scar tissue of the uterine lining (placental attachments are impossible over scarred areas)

- Twinning (one twin must usually die in order for the other to obtain adequate nourishment and oxygen during pregnancy)

- Nutritional deficiencies or emaciation of the mare, including parasitism

- Trauma, unexpected injuries or other stress to the mare during pregnancy

- Abnormal genital tract anatomy

- Cervix sealed closed because of scar tissue

- Dwarfism of the mare

- Cystic ovaries (which may sometimes be successfully treated with chorionic gonadotropin injections)

- Impregnation with a fetus carrying any lethal genes

Foals 6 to 18 Months: The Critical Period

Most miniature mares take excellent care of their foal, providing it with loving care and discipline, lots of high-protein milk and protection from other horses. It is important that the new foal be handled as much as possible during the first few months to familiarize it with the humans who will later be training and enjoying it.

If a mare is to be bred back during the first or second post-foaling estrus cycle, her

Gail Boatman-Eads

Figure 10.8 *Gentle handling by children is an important phase of a new foal's training. MWF Muchos Best Kept Secret is relaxed as it enjoys the attention of 5-year-old Lance Eads. Breeder/ owner: Gail Boatman-Eads.*

pregnancy while lactating should not cause her any additional stress until her nursing foal is about 6 months of age. Most miniature horse foals are weaned at 5 or 6 months of age, but if weaned as early as 3 or 4 months, there may be noticeable nutritional deficiencies, which are easily identified by the foal's potbelly, decreased appetite and lethargic attitude. It is essential that the newly weaned foal be provided with high-protein (16% to 19%), palatable, free-choice feeds to prevent symptoms of protein starvation (see Chapter 6). At least a month before the foal is to be weaned, it must become accustomed to eating these high-protein feeds in large quantities.

If not weaned too early and if kept parasite free and well nourished, foals should attain most of their adult height by the age of 12 months. They will fill out, gain weight and thicken in appearance during their 12- through 18-month period. This type of rapid building of bone, muscle and fat takes an enormous quantity of protein, calories and other nutrients. Contrary to popular opinion, feeding young miniatures large quantities of high-quality, high-protein feeds does not result in "hay bellies" or potbellies. Potbellies in growing foals are usually the direct result of protein deficiency and are almost always caused by weaning too early, lack of high-quality feeds and/or heavy parasitism.

Weaning

The weaning process is a delicate one and for the first few weeks it must be made as stress free as possible for both the mare and the foal. Because excess calories and grain both tend to increase milk production, the mare should be restricted from any grain supplements for a few days prior to the expected date of weaning. The foal should also be fully accustomed to eating a high-quality, high-protein concentrate (in addition to its usual legume hay).

Complete separation (being out of sight and hearing of each other) is extremely

Figure 10.9 *Unlike adult miniatures, healthy suckling and weanling foals spend a great deal of time lying down. Pacific Matador's bright eyes, erect ears and alert appearance indicate his excellent state of health. Breeder/owner: Joanne Abramson*

stressful for both the mare and the foal and should be avoided, if possible. The least stressful means by which a foal may be weaned requires only a strong wire fence (*never barb wire*) between the foal and its dam. Such a fence allows them each a constant view of one another, as well as continued smell and touch contact, but (provided the foal is unable to get its head through) does not allow the foal to suckle. Bag Balm® may be applied to the mare's udder if its swelling appears to be causing her a great deal of discomfort. The internal pressure is necessary for the mare to dry up, so she should not be milked out. Foals must be kept separated from their dams for several months. Many mares will allow their foals to begin nursing again, even after several months have passed, and their milk supply may even return. A yearling horse still suckling its dam (often, to the surprise of its owner) is not an uncommon event in the miniature horse world. These yearlings will rob the mare of her colostrum, which is vitally needed by her soon-to-be delivered new foal. An additional reason for keeping yearlings separated from pregnant mares arises because of the mare's possible exposure to rhinopneumonitis from foals.

Teasing and Breeding Record Charts

If one is planning hand breeding only, a rigorous teasing schedule is imperative. All **open mares** (not pregnant) should be teased at least every other day, 30 days or more before the chosen breeding season begins. Each mare's cycle and individual characteristics should be carefully recorded. A teasing, breeding and foaling record chart keeps each mare's statistics accurately recorded. Individual miniature mares tend to repeat the same behaviors, estrus cycle peculiarities and foaling patterns each year. The ease with which they conceive, their length of gestation, as well as the duration and ease of their labor will also be very similar each year. Many foaling disasters can be avoided if the owner has kept meticulously accurate records on each mare and has referred to them frequently in subsequent years.

Mares that have recently foaled should be teased daily beginning on the 3rd or 4th day after foaling. The length of this heat period should be verified by daily teasing, even if there are no immediate plans to breed the mare. At 14 days from the end of this cycle, the mare should be teased daily until showing visible signs of estrus. It is usually safe to breed during this 30- to 35-day post-foaling heat cycle, and the resulting conception rates are good. If there is a suspicion that the mare might not be a good candidate for breeding at this time, or if there seems to be any difficulty is getting her **settled** (pregnant), a miniature horse veterinarian's advice should be sought. Symptoms that might necessitate a veterinary examination include the following and should be recorded on the mare's reproduction chart:

- Prolonged or continual estrus

- Anestrus during normal breeding season

- Poor condition (a body condition score [BCS] of less than 4) or poor appetite

- Abnormal vaginal discharge

- Recently had a foal born weak, severely down on its pasterns, or dead

- Depression, illness, high fever or lethargy after birth of foal

- Absent or decreased supply of milk

- Refusal to accept newborn foal

- Retained placenta for more than 2 hours

- Vaginal bruises or lacerations due to difficult birthing process

Many breeders require a veterinary pre-breeding examination and a negative uterine culture before accepting outside mares for breeding. These precautions are for the protection of other mares, as well as for the stallion, and are an excellent preventative measure against infections. Cultures must be obtained by a qualified veterinarian during the estrus cycle of a miniature mare, when her cervix is open and pliable (Judd 1994). If the sample is obtained on the 1st day of her heat cycle, it can be **cultured** (checked for bacterial growth on a nutrient media plate that has been placed in an incubator) in time for breeding on the 3rd or 4th day of that cycle, if it proves to be negative. If the mare is too small (or the veterinarian's hand and arm are too large), obtaining uterine cultures may be an impossibility. In this case, alternate arrangements must be agreed upon between the stallion owner and the outside mare owner prior to booking the mare for stud service.

It is important that a teasing, breeding and foaling record chart be maintained by the stallion owner on all outside mares, as well. Annual stallion reports must be filed with both AMHA and AMHR, and it sometimes happens that stallion owners unintentionally omit records of outside mares being bred to a particular stallion. Outside mare owners are generally given a receipt (provided by each of the registries) that verifies the dates bred, and the name and registration number of the stallion they were bred to. Mares with dwarfism characteristics (see Chapter 11), or with poor genital conformation (such as a tipped vulva or a deformed or excessively narrow pelvis) should not be considered for breeding. The possibility that such a mare might produce a foal with similar (or more severe) characteristics exists, and the defective conformation of the foal may incorrectly be blamed on the stallion.

Demands of Pregnancy and Lactation

The demands of early pregnancy are low. If the miniature mare was in good condition (BCS of 5 to 7) at the time of breeding, increases in her caloric and protein intake need not be of concern until her 8th or 9th month of gestation. After the 9th month, protein, calcium, and caloric levels should be somewhat increased. Obesity in miniature horse mares at full term should be avoided, as it may cause premature deliveries, prolonged labors, and oversized foals, and can result in decreased milk production (Harper 1991). However, subjecting any pregnant miniature mare to a sudden weight-reduction diet should be avoided because of the dangers associated with the possible triggering of hyperlipemia syndrome (see Chapter 9). It is during the last 2 months of gestation, and even more so during lactation, that the producing mare's increased nutritional requirements should be addressed. Lactating mares should never be allowed to suddenly lose body condition. As soon as it is noted that any lactating mare is beginning to lose weight, her daily intake of feed should be increased in both calorie and protein content. This may necessitate additional alfalfa hay, alfalfa meal with molasses, or a grain supplement with at least a 16% to 18% crude protein content (see Chapter 6). Even though the nursing foal may be getting enough milk, the lactating mare can easily become severely emaciated and nutritionally depleted.

Stallions

The miniature horse colt can breed as young as 12 to 18 months of age, but this is not usually recommended. Allowing a colt to live with mares of possible breeding age (such as his dam, or a weanling filly) can result in surprise conceptions that cannot be included on the year-end stallion reports, since colts of that age are not permitted to be listed as "stallions." Stallion reports are required by both AMHA and AMHR at the end of every year, and any foals born in the following year that were not included on those stallion reports cannot be registered. Colts as young as 8 months of age have been known to get their own mothers in foal.

Before fertility testing of a young stallion, he should generally be at least 2 years of age. Yearling colts may be capable of copulation and ejaculation, but they may not yet be fertile. Both of the stallion's testicles must have been fully descended for at least 3 months in order for him to be reliably fertile. Miniature horses' testicles are sometimes retained within the body cavity for a longer period than is acceptable for full-sized horses. Most veterinarians will advise the castration of any full-sized colt that has reached the age of 1 year and has not yet dropped his testicles. This has proven to be too early for miniatures, as it is fairly common for miniature horse colts to retain one or both testicles until the age of 2 and to then drop them and be fully fertile for the remainder of their lives. However, if any colt is still a **cryptorchid** (with one or both testicles having failed to descend into the scrotum) as he enters the breeding season of his 3rd year, he should be gelded. Both testicles must be descended for show purposes as a mature stallion, and in AMHA this must be verified by a veterinarian prior to entry in any show. The **bilateral** cryptorchid (two testicles retained) is sterile, but if one testicle has descended (**unilateral** cryptorchid), the individual will be fertile. Such a stallion will therefore be capable of passing this genetically defective trait on to his progeny. Whether unilateral or bilateral, the cryptorchid will display all behaviors (including copulation) of a normal stallion but will be unsuitable for showing as a "gelding" (or for use as child's pet) without the surgical removal of *both* of his testicles.

If there is any doubt about a stallion's fertility, it may be advisable to have an equine veterinarian collect the stallion's full ejaculate with an artificial vagina and perform a complete semen analysis. Total volume, motility, viability and morphology can all be accurately assessed in this manner. If an artificial vagina is not available, microscopic spot checks may also be performed by collecting seminal fluids during the stallion's dismount following a natural breeding. A recent study was conducted to determine normal parameters of semen quality, testicular size, and to establish normal criteria for evaluating and predicting potential fertility in the American Miniature Horse stallion (Metcalf, Ley, & Love 1997). Although some variations from full-sized horses were identified, sperm motility, morphology and concentrations were all comparable to those established for other breeds. If a young miniature horse stallion's fertility is marginal, it is best to wait until the following year before depending upon him to settle any mares.

A fully mature and fertile stallion of about 5 to 7 years of age can safely cover 30 to 40 problem-free mares in one season (if he is judiciously hand bred) and the conception rate should be at least 70%. Stallions used for pasture breeding should not be expected to get all of their mares in foal unless the herd is limited to less than 20 mares. With many stallions, a decreased sperm count will be noted if they are used too heavily. Excessive masturbation may also lead to the same problem, and stallions living alone and being hand bred rather than pasture bred will often masturbate excessively (usually at night and when not being observed by their owners).

The ability of a stallion to sire foals of consistently superior type and similar to his own is dependent upon his **prepotency**. Prepotency of a particular stallion is rarely an accident. Carefully planned pedigrees, usually with a noticeable degree of inbreeding, are required. Prepotency depends upon a higher than usual incidence of homozygosity as well as dominant genes for desirable traits (see Chapter 11).

The primary consideration when purchasing or keeping a young stallion has little to do with his fertility. Although stallions in their late 20s sometimes become sterile, most healthy yearling and 2-year-old fully developed miniature horse colts will eventually be fertile. The most important issue is whether the colt is a fine enough specimen to be kept as a breeding stallion. Future stallion prospects should have superior bloodlines, quality conformation and exceptional breed type (see Chapter 4). To ensure breed improvement, at least 75% of the colts being produced in the horse industry should become well-loved and well-used geldings.

Breeding Ethics and Goals

The ethics, goals and enthusiasm of all miniature horse breeders should be focused upon breed improvement. This endeavor requires a great deal of self-education and dedication but can be the most rewarding and most exciting project of one's life. Serious breed improvement is customarily tested and verified by show wins, so it is essential that all judges be well trained and experienced within the miniature horse breed, not only as full-sized horse breed judges. However, the many high-quality animals having never been shown should not be discounted by buyers of miniature horses. Bloodlines, prepotency, superior conformation and the known high quality of many progeny may all contribute to the value and worth of a particular individual.

Financial returns invariably follow the production of superior quality horses, and the ethical, goal-oriented breeder will find such rewards to be an additional inspiration towards further improvement of the breed. Accurate pedigrees are a large part of ethical breeding, and the recent emphasis on blood typing, deoxyribonucleic acid (DNA) testing and permanent identification of individual horses makes pedigree documentation increasingly valid (see Chapter 11).

The regular maintenance of excellent written (or computerized) records on each horse owned can serve to guide the breeder as to which matings result in the production of the most outstanding foals, with the highest show potential and greatest monetary value. Random matings, guided by availability rather than by genetic planning, rarely result in consistently high-quality foals.

The health, vigor and contentment of each miniature horse in the herd should be an additional concern for an ethical, goal-oriented breeder. Without vibrant good health, excellent farm management, and effective but considerate training programs, even the highest-quality miniatures will fall short of their potential.

Co-Ownership or Leasing Opportunities

There are many advantages to co-ownership or leasing of certain miniature horses. Co-ownership allows the price of an expensive animal to be shared between two or more parties. This is especially advantageous for stallion owners. Stallions that are part of a **syndicate** (an organization of several persons who co-own a horse and are allowed a specified number of breedings) are usually very highly priced, and such syndications make it financially possible for the stallion to be widely utilized, as well as affordably publicized.

Persons selling expensive foals have the option of co-ownership as a means of reducing the initial cost to a new owner. Half-interest may be retained by the breeder, while the new owner may take the foal home and perhaps show it. All mutually agreed upon arrangements (such as show expenses or future breedings) should be discussed and fully understood by both parties and should be clearly stipulated in a signed contract.

The leasing of miniature horses can also be extremely beneficial to both parties. Valuable mares are sometimes leased to provide both the original owner and the lessee with specified advantages (both AMHA and AMHR leasing forms are available from the registries, upon request). For example, the mare may be open, with the lessee planning to breed her to an outstanding stallion. After foaling, the mare is rebred to the lessee's stallion, and returned (in foal) after her first foal has been weaned. In this manner, the lessee has acquired a foal by the stallion of his or her choice, out of an outcross and highly desirable mare, while the original owner has acquired an expected foal by a highly desirable outcross stallion. If the leasing forms are properly managed, each foal may be registered with the farm prefix of its owner (or lessee) at the time of service. Neither the owner or the lessee has spent any money (except for mare care) and both have benefitted immensely.

If maintaining an "amateur" showing status is of importance to a particular owner, leasing may be used as a protection in that regard. Amateurs cannot accept any financial remuneration or other benefits from the training and/or showing of horses not self-owned. This usually prevents amateurs from training or showing horses for a friend, unless they are extremely careful to not accept any favors, gifts, services and/or other remuneration of any kind. If the horse to be shown is leased by an amateur, it is technically "owned" by the person, and its training and showing cannot affect that person's legal amateur status.

Mare, gelding, stallion and foal contracts are all available, a few of which have been suggested and drafted by attorneys with horsemanship knowledge and expertise. Such contracts must be individualized in order to be appropriate for specific situations, and the concerns of all parties involved must be stated clearly.

CHAPTER 11

Genetics

M ANY MINIATURE HORSE BREEDERS ARE INTERESTED in the genetics of various characteristics, but they are hesitant about attempting to learn the basics of genetics. There are no mysteries about basic genetics, and no advanced knowledge of science is necessary to grasp the principles involved and understand 15 to 20 key terms. A working knowledge of elementary genetics can make the difference between the owner who breeds haphazardly and one who plans each mating with the genetic expertise necessary to produce champions. The knowledgeable use of genetic planning in a breeding program separates the professionals from the amateurs.

Basic Genetic Terminology

Within the nucleus of each **somatic cell** (body cell) of every miniature horse's body, there are 32 sets of matched **chromosomes** (rod-shaped structures that contain genetic information). One of each of these matching pairs is acquired from the sire and one is acquired from the dam for a total of 64 chromosomes. The genetic information contained within these chromosomes is referred to as the **genes**, very large, complex molecules of deoxyribonucleic acid (DNA). An estimated 50,000 to 100,000 genes that control development, growth and metabolism are found on the chromosomes. Chromosomes can be seen with a microscope but not in enough detail to visually observe the base sequences of DNA molecules that comprise the individual genes (Bowling in Evans 1992). Because the chromosomes appear in matched pairs, the genes that determine an individual's specific characteristics, such as color, also occur in matched pairs. Those matched pairs, called **alleles**, each occur at specific sites called **loci** (singular: **locus**) along the paired chromosomes. Each gene is responsible for determining one or more traits; most individual traits are the result of interactions among several genes and their **modifiers** (genes that alter or change the basic genes they interact with, sometimes referred to as **polygenes**). The genetic make-up of an individual, not all of which is visible to the eye, is called the **genotype**. The visible exterior each individual shows is called the **phenotype**. For example, an animal's actual and observable color and pattern are referred to as its **color phenotype**.

A **karyotype** is a photograph of an individual's chromosomes, as seen through an electron microscope. A standard species karyotype for the domestic horse was established in 1989. Four banding techniques are used in karyotyping to define the unique identity of each chromosome. The chromosomes are then separated, arranged numerically and photographically in such a way that each chromosome is shown paired with its own matching partner. In this manner, abnormalities may be visually identified by geneticists. A normal full-sized horse karyotype is illustrated in Figure 11.1.

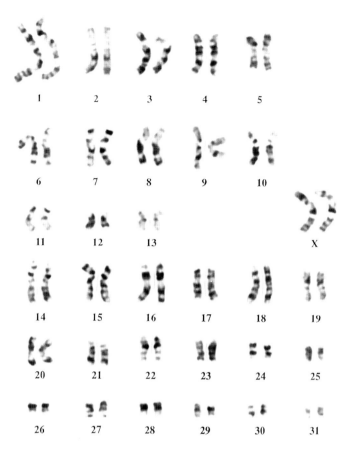

Figure 11.1 *Karyotype of a normal full-sized horse. G-banded karyotype of lymphocyte chromosomes of a female horse. Pairs are ordered according to descending size in three groups: the sex chromosomes on the third line at the right edge; meta- or submetacentric autosomal pairs numbered 1 to 13 on lines one to three; and acrocentric autosomal pairs numbered 14 to 31 on lines four to six. Karyotype supplied courtesy of A. T. Bowling and L. V. Millon, Veterinary Genetics Laboratory, School of Veterinary Medicine, University of California, Davis.*

Karyotyping is a valuable diagnostic tool often employed to detect the underlying causes of defective genotypes that may have resulted in a particular congenital anomaly. For example, karyotyping has been used in human genetics to identify the chromosomal abnormality that is characteristic of **Down's syndrome** (trisomy of chromosome 21).

Possibilities for each trait include **dominant** alleles (capable of expression when only one dominant allele is carried) and **recessive** alleles (can be expressed only when two recessive alleles for the same characteristic are carried). If the horse phenotypically (visibly) shows a recessive trait, it is known that this individual carries genes only for that recessive characteristic and none for the dominant allele. The horse thus possesses a **homozygous** genotype, meaning that both alleles for that trait are the same. If the animal phenotypically shows a dominant trait, it may be either homozygous dominant or **heterozygous**. This means that the animal may be hiding an allele that cannot be seen but that can still be passed on to its progeny, referred to as a recessive allele for that same characteristic. The terms *dominant* and *recessive* describe the relationship between alleles of one gene, not the relationship between different genes. This point must be clearly understood by anyone interested in predicting genetic traits (Bowling 1996). Without a working familiarity with the terms *dominant, recessive, homozygous* and *heterozygous*, there can be no application of genetic principles within any breeding program.

For simplicity, geneticists symbolize alleles by uppercase and lowercase letters (always in italics). The dominant allele at any given locus is always expressed in capital letters and italics (*A*), and the matching recessive allele at that corresponding locus is usually expressed in lowercase letters and italics (*a*). The reader of genetic publications will note that the use of these symbols often is not consistent among geneticists. The symbols used in this book are those used by Bowling (1996). Unfortunately, research geneticists themselves are still attempting to establish uniform nomenclature, so changes may be expected in the future. The study of genetics is a constant process of questioning and discovering new questions from the answers (Bowling 1996). The science of horse breeding involves the creative and educated juggling of homozygosity (to increase prepotency for desirable traits) and heterozygosity (to maintain health and vigor). If a breeder hopes to develop a herd of miniature horses that is prepotent for desirable conformation, colors and size limits, such an endeavor should be considered a lifelong challenge and a never-ending educational experience.

Because the presence of only one dominant allele often determines the phenotype of an individual, geneticists may take a shortcut in notation and eliminate writing the second allele. For example, all gray horses must have the genotype of *Gg* or *GG*. It does not matter what the second *G* is, for the gray horse may be either homozygous or heterozygous for its pattern genotype. As long as the horse has even one *G*, it will be gray and not any other color. Thus, geneticists sometimes write the genotype of a gray horse as *G-*, meaning a gray horse that either carries or does not carry a hidden recessive gene for non-gray. This knowledge about grays also tells us that *G* is epistatic to other pattern/color genes. **Epistasis** refers to the interaction of genes at different loci, as a result of which one hereditary characteristic is masked by the superimposition of another upon it. In simpler terms, any color foal that carries even one *G* allele will always turn gray or white in adulthood.

Some genes exhibit **incomplete dominance**, or **codominance** (neither allele completely overrides the effect of its partner and both may be expressed at the same time on the same individual). This phenomenon may be illustrated by understanding the effect of **dilution** (lightening in color) on palomino, buckskin, cremello or perlino inheritance. One C^{cr} allele equals "medium effect" in which red is diluted (creating a palomino) and black is not (creating a buckskin). Two $C^{cr}C^{cr}$ alleles equal "maximum effect" in which both black and red are almost fully diluted, the skin is pink and the eye color is always blue (cremello or perlino). Two *CC* alleles equal "no effect," in which neither black or red is diluted and the horse remains black, red, bay, etc. Codominant inheritance of alleles can be used as an efficient and powerful tool for parentage testing (Bowling 1996).

Some genes are **linked** with others, which means that they are located on the same chromosome even though they are not alleles of one other. Genes that are linked are usually inherited together. An example of this phenomenon is the linkage of the albumin blood-typing marker (AL^B) with the tobiano pinto gene. Although these are very different characteristics, because both appear on the same chromosome, an important test for determining homozygosity in tobianos has been developed using the principles of this discovery (see Chapter 12).

Punnett Squares

It is not necessary to understand the complicated science of molecular genetics in order to predict the outcome of various mating combinations. It is necessary only to become familiar with the science of Mendelian genetics (Gardner 1968; Harper & Bell 1991). All breeders should become fluent with the usage of **Punnett squares**, diagrams used for predicting outcomes of breeding two individuals of defined genotype (see Tables 11.1, 11.2 and 11.3). And every serious student of genetics should also know the principles for calculating percentages of linebreeding or inbreeding within a given pedigree (see Table 11.4).

Table 11.1 Cross Between Two Heterozygous Tobiano Pintos

Alleles Contributed by *TOto* Mare	Alleles Contributed by *TOto* Stallion	
	TO	*to*
TO	*TOTO* homozygous tobiano (25%)	*TOto* heterozygous tobiano (25%)
to	*Toto* heterozygous tobiano (25%)	*toto* homozygous for non-tobiano (in this case, solid color) (25%)

The Punnett square in Table 11.1 illustrates a cross between two heterozygous tobiano pintos. Both appear to be tobiano pintos, but each carries a recessive gene for solid-color (non-tobiano). By separating the alleles involved (two from each parent), it is possible to calculate the color patterns of offspring to be expected. The sum of the four percentages results in 25% homozygous tobianos, 50% heterozygous tobianos (a total of 75% phenotypic tobianos) and 25% solid colors (non-tobianos). This is more conveniently stated by geneticists as a ratio of 3:1, which is the ratio to be expected whenever two heterozygotes for any dominantly inherited characteristic are mated with one another.

Table 11.2 Cross Between Heterozygous Tobiano and Solid-Color

Alleles Contributed by *toto* Mare	Alleles Contributed by *TOto* Stallion	
	TO	*to*
to	*TOto* heterozygous tobiano (25%)	*toto* homozygous for solid color (25%)
to	*TOto* heterozygous tobiano (25%)	*toto* homozygous for solid color (25%)

The Punnett square in Table 11.2 illustrates a cross between a heterozygous tobiano pinto stallion and a solid-color mare (homozygous for not being tobiano). By separating the alleles involved (two from each parent), it is possible to calculate the color patterns of offspring to be expected. The sum of the four percentages results in 50% heterozygous tobianos and 50% homozygous recessive for solid color, or a phenotypic ratio of 1:1. Note that it is not possible to obtain a homozygous tobiano from this cross. This is the ratio to be expected whenever crossing a tobiano heterozygote with a solid color.

Table 11.3 *Dihybrid Cross Between Silver Dapple Pintos*

Alleles Contributed by *TOto Zz* Mare	Alleles Contributed by *TOto Zz* Stallion			
(Phenotype: Silver dapple tobiano pinto)	(Phenotype: Silver dapple tobiano pinto)			
	TO Z	*TO z*	*to Z*	*to z*
TO Z	*TOTO ZZ* (6.25%) (silver tobiano)	*TOTO Zz* (6.25%) (silver tobiano)	*TOto ZZ* (6.25%) (silver tobiano)	*TOto Zz* (6.25%) (silver tobiano)
TO z	*TOTO Zz* (6.25%) (silver tobiano)	*TOTO zz* (6.25%) (non-silver tobiano)	*TOto Zz* (6.25%) (silver tobiano)	*TOto zz* (6.25%) (non-silver tobiano)
to Z	*TOto ZZ* (6.25%) (silver tobiano)	*TOto Zz* (6.25%) (silver tobiano)	*toto ZZ* (6.25%) (solid silver)	*toto Zz* (6.25%) (solid silver)
to z	*TOto Zz* (6.25%) (silver tobiano)	*TOto zz* (6.25%) (non-silver tobiano)	*toto Zz* (6.25%) (solid color silver)	*toto zz* (6.25%) (solid color, non-silver)

The Punnett square in Table 11.3 illustrates a more complicated cross between two silver dapple pintos, each of them heterozygous for tobiano and heterozygous for silver. By separating each allelic contribution involved (four combinations from each parent), it is possible to calculate the color patterns of offspring to be expected. The sum of the 16 percentages illustrated results in 56.25% silver tobianos, 18.75% solid-color silvers, 18.75% non-silver tobianos, and 6.25% non-silver solid colors. Of the total, 75% will be tobianos and 25% of those tobianos will be homozygous. The four possible phenotypes will occur in a ratio of 9:3:3:1, which is the ratio to be expected whenever considering the mating of two horses that are heterozygous for each of two different characteristics. This Punnett square illustrates what geneticists call a **dihybrid cross.**

Percentages of Blood in a Pedigree
Table 11.4 Calculating Percentages of Blood in a Pedigree

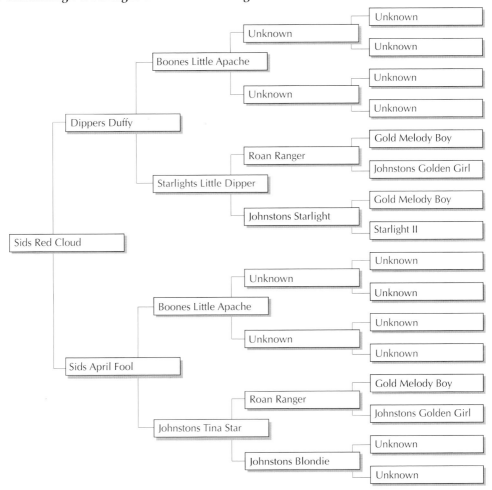

Table 11.4 shows the pedigree of a linebred show stallion *Sids Red Cloud*, owned by George and Debbie Christianson. The fraction of Red Cloud's genes most likely to come from each of his ancestors can be calculated. The first generation in this pedigree includes Red Cloud's sire and dam = 50% each; the second generation, his 4 grandparents = 25% each; the third generation, his 8 great-grandparents = 12.5% each; and the fourth generation, his 16 great-great-grandparents = 6.25% each (because only the known ancestors can be recorded, the pedigree is missing the total number of ancestors usually possible in a four-generation pedigree). Calculating the percentage of blood is accomplished as follows: Fourth-generation individual, *Johnstons Golden Girl*, appears twice, so 2 X 6.25% = 12.5% *Johnstons Golden Girl.* Another fourth-generation individual, *Gold Melody Boy,* appears three times, so 3 X 6.25% = 18.75 percent *Gold Melody Boy.* Third-generation individual, *Roan Ranger,* appears two times, so 2 X 12.5% = 25% *Roan Ranger.* Second-generation individual, *Boones Little Apache,* appears two times, so 2 X 25% = 50% *Boones Little Apache.* With this type of well-planned pedigree, *Sids Red Cloud* is likely to be very prepotent (homozygous) for the characteristics he shows in his phenotype.

Inbreeding and Hybrid Vigor Balances

For the serious breeder, detailed records cannot be overemphasized. Pedigrees that incorporate many generations of known ancestors are vitally important. One of the values of an accurate pedigree is the information contained that can be used to improve the breed. It is critical that breeders know as much as possible about their mares and stallions, and well-documented pedigrees should be a part of every breeding farm's records. The parents, grand-parents, and great-grandparents of cornerstone individuals should also be photographically represented, and additional records should include written notations pertaining to good points, bad points, coat color, conformation, height, temperament, veterinary care, reproduction charts and show wins.

It is important to buy foundation stock from serious breeders who are willing to pass on some of their knowledge. Such breeders will have probably been planning and selectively breeding their miniature horses for many years and will usually be willing to help plan their clientele's management practices and future matings with similar expertise and attention to detail. These experienced breeders have often discovered that inbreeding and linebreeding are valuable tools. **Inbreeding** is the mating of very close relatives, such as father to daughter, full brother to full sister and mother to son. **Linebreeding** describes a breeding program based on multiple pedigree crosses to a single exceptional animal and is a more conservative type of inbreeding. The consistently high-quality miniatures being produced within some herds might not have been accomplished without at least occasional use of linebreeding and inbreeding to set the type they have become noted for (Verhaege 1979).

Both linebreeding and inbreeding are surrounded by an aura of distrust and fear in the miniature horse industry, particularly by those who are inexperienced in the general science of animal breeding within other species. Unfortunately, dwarfism characteristics can some-times become a problem in highly inbred herds. However, few outstanding accomplishments in purebred animal breeding have ever been made without the intelligent use of considerable inbreeding and linebreeding.

Many studies of laboratory, domestic, and zoo animals have documented reduced survival and fecundity of inbred young. Inbreeding depression is thus a major concern in the manage-ment of a relatively small population such as is found within the miniature horse industry. The cost of inbreeding can sometimes outweigh its benefits and is of considerable relevance to the subject of inbreeding and hybrid vigor balances (Ralls, Ballou, & Templeton 1987).

It is conceded by even the staunchest of its proponents that inbreeding presents two great hazards. The first is that it intensifies the inheritance of weaknesses and other unwanted characteristics. The second hazard is that inbreeding sometimes results in a loss of **hybrid vigor** (fertility, fecundity, foal viability, disease resistance, disposition and size all may be impacted by overuse of poorly planned inbreeding). It is for these reasons that inbreeding has acquired its generally bad name, especially for the breeder who is not willing to cull the breeding herd radically nor to keep meticulously complete records. The fact remains, however, that many champions of notoriety, who are also excellent, well-known producers, boast pedigrees with some individuals appearing as many as six times in five generations. Clearly, the subject of in-breeding has its subtleties and is best approached cautiously, as well as with a great deal of study. The two objections raised above, unwanted genetic defects and loss of hybrid vigor, are both valid. Yet neither drawback tells the complete story, for if it did, the many highly successful breeders who have built their entire programs around intensive inbreeding could not exist.

All characteristics, the good as well as the bad, are concentrated by inbreeding. During the first three generations of close inbreeding, it is necessary to cull rigorously in order to eliminate all weaknesses. The AMHA and AMHR Standards of Perfection should be utilized on a regular basis in order to determine the phenotypic goals being sought. Horses kept for future breeding must be absolutely free of any unwanted defects, particularly if they show any undesirable recessive characteristics in the phenotype. Dealing with dominantly inherited defects is infinitely simplified in comparison to dealing with recessively inherited defects. An animal inheriting even one dominantly inherited allele for a defect will visibly show this defect in its phenotype and can be eliminated from a breeding program based on observation only. However, a carrier of just one allele for any recessively inherited defect will not visibly show it in the phenotype and will still be able to pass the defective gene on to 50% of its progeny. If visibly showing any recessive characteristic, the individual would be homozygous for that characteristic and would pass it on to 100% of its progeny. Recessively inherited characteristics are passed on as follows: If a homozygote is bred to a noncarrier of the characteristic, 100% will inherit a single copy of the gene for that characteristic, but none will show it in their phenotype. If a homozygote is bred to a heterozygous recessive carrier of the characteristic (one that does not visibly show it) 50% will be carriers of the unwanted defect without showing it in their phenotype (heterozygotes), and 50% will actually have the defect (homozygotes). The breeding of two animals that both show a recessively inherited and defective characteristic in their phenotype will result in 100% homozygotes (defective horses) and can have disastrous consequences relative to the future of an entire breeding program.

After the first three generations of careful inbreeding and culling, the strength of a herd's original miniatures will be established and will almost invariably be a great improvement on them in overall quality. Thus a homozygous gene pool has been established for desired characteristics (prepotency) and carriers of unwanted genes have been effectively eliminated. In other words, defects that might ordinarily be carried unobserved (recessively) are quickly made obvious as homozygosity within the herd increases.

By discontinuing close inbreeding after about three generations, the dangers of running down the vitality of the herd are avoided. However, at this point it is not advisable to make a complete **outcross** (mating of unrelated animals of the same breed) and an attempt should be made to keep within the basic family tree that goes back to some of the original matings. A breeder can systematically establish at least two, preferably three, family lines that can safely be crossed with one another. It is ideal if the original horses have been carefully selected for their own excellence, as well as for their documentable lineage.

After four or five generations of breeding, as has been outlined, there should be enough less closely related horses so that, without making any outcrosses to a totally unrelated animal, close inbreeding can be discontinued and its occasional hazards of degeneration avoided. Then, by choosing only the best for each particular mating, quality should steadily improve within the herd. Miniature horses produced by these schematics will be of uniformly high quality and will be amazingly prepotent for their visible characteristics. They will carry few unseen and perhaps undesirable recessive genes. This is the inherent and indisputable fact upon which all successful inbreeding programs are based.

To carry on an effective inbreeding or linebreeding program (while still retaining full hybrid vigor), at least two distinct family lines should be established in the manner described. If overall health or stamina seems to degenerate, an outcross may become necessary. Outcrosses between unrelated horses have two consequences: Vigor (and sometimes size) is enormously increased, and an explosion in the diversity of characteristics is inevitable. Although increased vigor is the main objective of such outcrosses, the possible side effect of an increase in the height of offspring can be devastating to a miniature horse breeder. Furthermore, since the ultimate goal should be uniform excellence in both phenotype and genotype, a wide diversity of other (sometimes unknown) characteristics can be damaging to a breeder's future gene pool. Outcrosses must be made with extreme care and only when absolutely necessary, for all of the accomplishments of one's past efforts are at stake should the chosen individual be genetically inferior.

Stallions should be chosen very carefully. The selection of a herd sire prospect who has been carefully inbred and has a known pedigree of at least three generations is the most promising choice. He will be consistently prepotent for the visible characteristics he shows in his phenotype and his own homozygosity will ensure that his genotype approximates his phenotype. It is unlikely that such a stallion will carry many undesirable recessives. It is important that one choose this individual for his actual characteristics and lineage, rather than for his long list of impressive show wins. Top conditioning, training and show presentation methods often disguise a miniature with one or more serious defects. The purchase of one exceptional stallion is much more feasible than the purchase of 10 exceptional mares, since a cornerstone stallion can be bred to 10 less expensive mares, and all of his daughters (without defects) may later be bred back to their own sire. The resulting progeny should exceed their sire in overall quality.

Even with less than show-quality miniatures, it is entirely possible to begin a breeding program that results in the production of top show-quality foals. Patience, astute observation, research, heavy culling and excellent records are mandatory. By starting with the most expensive miniatures available, almost anyone's successful breeding program can be greatly accelerated. Yet, starting with only reasonably good stock (from well-established lineage) can also lead to success. Even slight imperfections should not be duplicated in both the stallions and the mares they are to be mated with. Horses should be chosen that are particularly good in head, legs, and body type, with color being a secondary consideration. Too often, color is the major point of concern for novices. The most flashy appaloosa or pinto can never be a consistent show winner without a beautiful head, fluid gait and correct conformation.

Many inbreeding successes have made synergistic and economical use of close friendships, where both breeders involved have benefitted by trading stud services, foals and advice. Breeders need not own all of the horses that might be required to build a successful inbreeding program, but both breeders involved must be committed to investigative genetic research and self-education. They must also be dedicated to keeping meticulous herd and individual records and must never allow themselves the luxury of keeping for breeding purposes animals that fall short of their genetic goals. There are far too many stallions and mares in the miniature horse industry that should never be used as breeding animals.

In order to use inbreeding in a breeding program a breeder must thoroughly know the genetics of the animals they are inbreeding. Knowing most of their individual characteristics and those of their ancestors can make it possible for inbreeding to be an enormous boost to any breeding program.

Historically, the use of well-planned inbreeding has often enabled breeders to establish a recognizable *look* within the horses being bred in their herd. Homozygosity within a herd's gene pool has even resulted in a particular farm's being credited with distinctive characteristics that may be unique to that bloodline such as Arabian heads.

Miniature horses produced by the deliberate and delicate balancing of inbreeding, careful selection and the retention of hybrid vigor should be uniformly superior in all ways. Breeding, showing and winning with one's own inbred or linebred strain of horses can be challenging, but the many rewards will invariably outweigh the disappointments.

DNA Testing and Blood Typing

The Serology Laboratory at the University of California, Davis (UCD) was formed in the 1950s to provide parentage testing services for the cattle industry and to undertake research on cattle immunogenetics. Both the Jockey Club (Thoroughbred registry) and the American Shetland Pony Club (ASPC) recognized the need for similar services within the horse industry and funded much of the early research to develop blood typing tests for horses. As other laboratories later began similar efforts, the great need for establishing universally understood nomenclature and standardized laboratory testing methods became of interest. By 1987, worldwide expertise was being developed.

In genetics the Mendelian law of dominance excludes a foal as a mating product when it possesses a factor not present in at least one of the parents. The Mendelian law of segregation excludes a parent that fails to share a genetic marker with a foal assigned to it (Bowling 1996). The presence or absence of specific genetic markers can be ascertained by either blood typing or DNA testing.

Although full standardization of DNA technology and laboratory methodology is not yet finalized, miniature horses may now be identified genetically by blood typing (which was fully standardized in 1991), or by microsatellite DNA marker genotype-testing of either blood or hair root samples. Current automated and computerized procedures are accurate, powerful and cost effective, and worldwide cooperation between laboratories is being gradually accomplished under the auspices of the International Society of Animal Genetics.

Blood typing refers to various objective blood tests that assay the presence or absence of traits known to be inherited and not influenced by environmental variables such as age, nutrition or disease status. Two basic technical procedures (serology and electrophoresis) are used to identify the traits (variants or markers). This testing is similar to the procedures used to identify ABO and Rh factors in human blood types. Red cells, white cells or serum may be used, depending upon the tests being conducted. Blood-typing tests have been developed for a large variety of species, but only a few laboratories throughout the world have the capability to test species other than humans. These laboratories attempt to maintain contact with each other to assure relative uniformity of techniques and nomenclature. UCD has blood-typing and/or DNA-testing contracts with more than 50 breed registries, including the American Miniature Horse Association.

The mechanical side of the DNA-testing or blood-typing process is highly efficient in the case of those equine registries that communicate with the laboratories electronically. In these cases, the laboratories can let the computers do the work of finding records and putting cases together, and results can be rapidly transferred back to the registries.

Blood typing and DNA testing are not related to one another, and the results cannot be used interchangeably. If a miniature horse stallion has already been blood typed, he must still be DNA tested if the owner wishes to verify paternity on one of his foals by DNA. DNA testing can be done on hair root samples that are pulled from the mane and submitted by the owner, and blood samples need not be drawn by a veterinarian. Thus, the DNA-testing procedure is much more cost effective for the breeder than blood typing, particularly when large numbers of miniatures are being tested from a single herd. Although the markers used for blood typing and DNA testing are not the same, DNA testing can still be performed on frozen blood samples already in storage at UCD, on fresh blood samples or on many other body tissues and fluids. For the above reasons, it was advised by the 1991 AMHA Genetics Committee that mandatory blood typing be delayed until DNA testing was adequately developed for it to be made available to the breeders through the registry. Many miniature horse breeders are still in the process of switching over from blood typing to DNA-based testing procedures. These owners' expenses have been considerable because of the repeated testing required on some individuals.

DNA testing has indisputable scientific merit, as well as great popular appeal, and DNA-based tests for parentage verification will probably fully replace conventional blood testing in the future. It would thus be wise for all miniature horse breeders to use DNA testing rather than blood typing. There are many DNA techniques and markers that could be used in the equine breeding industry, but UCD is presently using **microsatellites** (also known as STRs or SLRs). Microsatellites are favored by most of the other animal-testing laboratories, as well.

Having a miniature horse blood typed or DNA tested begins with a request to AMHA for a test kit. The name of the horse and the type of test desired must be specified. Each kit is sent for a single, specific animal and must not be used for a different horse than the one for which the kit has been requested. The test kits include full directions for collection, handling and mailing of samples.

Congenital Anomalies

There are many **congenital anomalies** (abnormalities that are detectable at or before birth) that occur in all species of mammals, including humans and horses. Some are nutritional or environmental in nature, while others are known to have genetic causes. Little research has been published on congenital anomalies in the equids, but there are vast quantities of published research on other mammalian species (such as cattle) and on humans. Traditionally, however, most controlled genetic research has been carried out on species with much shorter gestations and larger size "litters" than occur within the equine, cattle or human species. Most notably, these include bacterial and fungal species such as *Escherichia* and *Neurospora*, as well as fruit flies, rats and mice. Some elegant studies involving a laboratory variety of dwarf mouse (Murine Snell Dwarfs) have shown that a lack of growth hormone, prolactin and thyroid stimulating hormone (TSH) are characteristic in all of the dwarfed individuals. The alleles concerned with the production of these three hormones are linked with the Snell dwarf allele (*dw*), and it was shown that both sets of alleles appear on mouse chromosome 16 (Jansson, Downs, Beamer, & Frohman 1986; Camper, Saunders, Katz, & Reeves 1990).

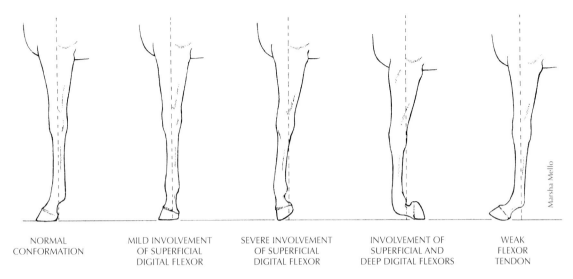

| NORMAL CONFORMATION | MILD INVOLVEMENT OF SUPERFICIAL DIGITAL FLEXOR | SEVERE INVOLVEMENT OF SUPERFICIAL DIGITAL FLEXOR | INVOLVEMENT OF SUPERFICIAL AND DEEP DIGITAL FLEXORS | WEAK FLEXOR TENDON |

Figure 11.2 *Normal leg conformation compared to dwarfism characteristics.*

Dwarfism

Congenital anomalies most often encountered in the miniature horse industry include those associated with unusually short stature and often referred to as dwarfism characteristics. In all breeds of horses, there are rare (although well documented) congenital anomalies that do not seem to be associated with short stature (Bowling 1996). In the miniature horse breed, however, these are of relatively little importance when compared to the devastating emotional and economic losses incurred because of **diastrophic dwarfism**. The word *diastrophism* refers to the process of rending and twisting of the earth's crust, which is analogous to the debilitating shortening and twisting of skeletal components observed in diastrophic dwarfism.

It has been scientifically documented that individuals exhibiting unusually short stature occur in virtually all species of mammals. Dwarfism refers to the condition of an individual who is conspicuously smaller than others of its kind. For diagnostic purposes, there are three broad classifications of short stature, as follows:

■ Short stature secondary to a chronic disease state such as chronic renal failure, rickets or hypothyroidism. Short stature of this first type is a consequence of failure to thrive, rather than a primary growth disorder.

■ Short stature as the only major feature. These would include all unusually small horses under the height of 12 hands or so (48 inches [122 cm]), as well as the human race of African Pygmies, for example.

■ Short stature as part of a short stature syndrome. This is the classification that is of primary concern within the miniature horse industry. In this category, an accurate diagnosis of dwarfism may sometimes be made on the basis of associated phenotypic features, blood studies, karyotyping and/or radiographic (x-ray) findings.

Chondrodystrophies (abnormal development of cartilage) and the various **dysmorphic syndromes** (congenital malformations) are all included in the group. Within this classification, **achondroplasia** (markedly and abnormally shortened limbs) is the most commonly observed skeletal dysplasia and is always considered to be a part of the overall syndrome called dwarfism (McKusick, Eldridge, Hostetler, & Egeland 1964; Kelly 1984).

In February of 1989, the AMHA Board of Directors voted to refuse registrations on any miniature horse that exhibited two or more serious dwarfism characteristics. Since that time, all registration application photographs are scrutinized by AMHA for dwarfism characteristics. If there is any suspicion about the presence of two or more characteristics of diastrophic dwarfism, the application is denied pending further verification by a veterinarian, should the applicant wish to appeal AMHA's decision. After much research and development prior to 1989, the author, as chairman of the Genetics Committee compiled and submitted to AMHA an outline of visible dwarfism characteristics. Since that time, adaptations of this list of characteristics have been used as the AMHA's guideline for making the above-described preliminary determinations:

Some Common Phenotypic Characteristics of Dwarfism in the Miniature Horse Breed:

- **Achondroplasia** (legs do not grow in length). Normal bone growth does not occur and often develops unevenly at the epiphyseal surfaces (joints), causing **varus** and **valgus** deformities (crooked legs). (Note that most of the illustrations exhibit varying degrees of achondroplasia).

- Dwarf foals are sometimes born with contracted tendons, club feet or buck knees that cannot be straightened out at birth (see Figure 11.2). Joint enlargements and joint deviations are common, often becoming progressively serious with age. Extreme cow hocks and splayed hind legs associated with a full-length fibula (see Figures 11.7, 11.12, 11.13, and 11.15), extremely short gaskins and severe sickle hocks, all with varying degrees of visible joint looseness and/or joint weakness also are common. Premature arthritic processes occur, resulting in progressive ambulatory disabilities.

- Some types of dwarfs have an undershot jaw (bulldog mouth or monkey bite (see Figure 11.10). If an undershot jaw is present, the molars also may be out of alignment, requiring that the teeth be floated much more frequently than for a normal-mouthed horse. Corrective orthodontics for an undershot jaw cannot correct the highly placed nostrils that always accompany this type of malocclusion.

- **Brachycephalic dwarfs** have a large bulging forehead with extreme dish (concave) face and turned-up nose, overly large and protruding eyes (sometimes placed at uneven angles) and nostrils placed too high up on face (see Figure 11.14). A second type of dwarf has a more normally shaped head and eye and a longer neck, but the head and body are still oversized when compared to the length of its legs (see Figures 11.7 and 11.15). This second type of dwarf does not usually have an undershot jaw.

- Head obviously longer than neck. The distance from the base of the ears to the withers should always be at least 1.1 times the distance from the tip of the nose to the base of the ears. In some diastrophic dwarfs, the neck is so short that the head appears to come directly out of the shoulders.

- Girth depth greater than leg length. Disproportionately oversized entrails and genitals, which are often accompanied by potbellies.

- **Scoliosis, kyphosis** and/or **lordosis** (vertebral deviations) are common (Ryan, Modransky, Welker, Moon, & Saunders 1992) (see Figure 11.11).

- Often unable to rear or stand on hind legs. Some types have an odd "tilting backward" gait, with shoulder markedly higher than croup.

- Sometimes associated with the various dwarfism syndromes are less obvious characteristics such as mental retardation, heart and other internal organ defects, sterility, shortened life span, arthritis, and inactivity or depression (both of which are probably due to pain).

Figure 11.4 Brachycephalic syndrome dwarf, 15 inches (36 cm) at 1 week of age. This foal exhibits a bulbous forehead, an undershot jaw and abnormally shortened legs and neck. The foal died of unknown causes at 1 month of age. Figure 11.6 shows a full sibling to this foal. Both parents had normal conformation. Heights of parents were 32 inches and 34 inches (81 cm and 86 cm).

Figure 11.3 Brachycephalic syndrome dwarf, 22 inches (56 cm) at 6 months of age. This foal exhibits a bulbous forehead, highly placed nostrils, an undershot jaw, abnormally shortened neck and legs, and flexural limb deformities. Both parents were stocky but had fairly normal conformation. Heights of parents were 27.5 inches and 32.5 inches (68.5 cm and 82.5 cm).

Figure 11.5 Brachycephalic syndrome dwarf, 14 inches (35.5 cm) at 1 day of age. The foal exhibits severe weakness in the pasterns and abnormally shortened neck and legs. The owner went to considerable expense having a veterinarian apply braces and casts on the legs. The foal died of unknown causes at 6 months of age. Both parents had normal conformation. Heights of parents were 32 inches and 34 inches (81 cm and 86 cm).

Figure 11.6 *Brachycephalic syndrome dwarf, 18 inches (46 cm) at 4 months of age. This is the same foal as shown in Figure 11.5, but at a later age and after the leg casts had been removed. The foal exhibits a bulbous forehead, an underbite and abnormally shortened legs and neck. The foal died of unknown causes at 6 months of age. Figure 11.4 shows a full sibling to this foal. Both parents had normal conformation. Heights of parents were 32 inches and 34 inches (81 cm and 86 cm).*

Figure 11.8 *Brachycephalic syndrome dwarf, 14 inches (35.5 cm) at birth. This foal exhibits a bulbous forehead, severe underbite, flexural limb deformities and abnormally shortened legs. Both parents were show-type animals and their conformation was excellent. Heights of parents were 31 inches and 32.5 inches (79 cm and 82.5 cm).*

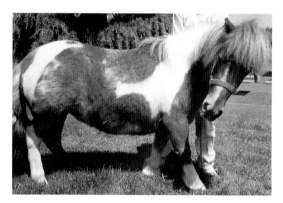

Figure 11.7 *Achondroplastic dwarf, 26 inches (66 cm) at 2 years of age. This horse exhibits extremely shortened limbs, but has a more normally shaped head and neck than that which accompanies brachycephaly. It does not have an underbite. Its hind legs are extremely splayed (cow hocked) because of the full-length fibulas, which could be observed radiographically (in x-rays). Both parents had fairly normal conformation and leg length. Heights of parents were 30 inches and 32 inches (76 cm and 81 cm).*

Figure 11.9 *Another variety of achondroplastic dwarf, 16 inches (41 cm) at birth. This foal exhibits a bulbous forehead, severe underbite, abnormally shortened legs and neck, and weak pasterns. Both parents were show-type individuals and their conformation was excellent. Heights of parents were 30 inches and 34 inches (76 cm and 86 cm).*

Figure 11.10 *Achondroplastic dwarf, 16 inches (41 cm) at birth. Severe underbite is shown on the same foal as is illustrated in Figure 11.9. Both parents had normal bites, were show-type individuals and had excellent conformation. Heights of parents were 30 inches and 34 inches (76 cm and 86 cm).*

Figure 11.12 *Diastrophic dwarf foal, at 3 months of age. The primary features exhibited by this foal are the full-length fibulas in both hind legs. These were confirmed radiographically (in x-rays). Normal horses have markedly shortened vestigial fibulas. The foal's full-length fibulas are improperly articulated with the knee and hock joints, causing the extremely splayed hind legs (cow hocks). This is a congenital condition that has been shown to be part of an achondroplastic dwarfism syndrome. It is recessive in its mode of inheritance. Both parents were of normal hind-leg conformation and were show animals. Heights of parents were 29 inches and 33.5 inches (74 cm and 85 cm).*

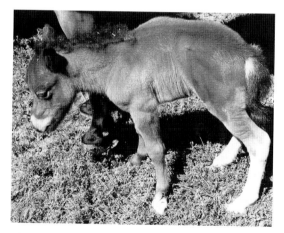

Figure 11.11 *Kyphoscoliosis dwarf syndrome foal, 18 inches (46 cm) at birth. This foal exhibits severe kyphoscoliosis and lordosis (abnormal curvatures and prematurely calcified areas of the spinal column). The neck, head and length of leg are fairly normal in appearance and the bite was even. Both parents were show-type individuals with normal spinal columns and excellent conformation. Heights of the parents were 30 inches and 33 inches (76 cm and 84 cm).*

Figure 11.13 *Diastrophic dwarf foal at 3 months of age. This is the same animal as seen in Figure 11.12, showing severely splayed hind legs caused by a full-length fibula. These were confirmed radiographically and are known to be part of one of the dwarfism syndromes seen in miniature horses. Both parents were of normal conformation. Heights of parents were 29 inches and 33.5 inches (74 cm and 85 cm).*

Dwarfism Gene Research

More than 200 variations of dwarfism characteristics have been cataloged and well-described in humans alone (McKusick 1984). Most of these human dwarfism characteristics have been proven to be genetic in nature (Kelly 1984). As with humans, most occurring within the miniature horse breed can be identified on individuals that exhibit several characteristics at the same time and appear to be a part of various recognizable syndromes. In the dwarfed miniatures, most of these characteristics are recessively inherited (both the sire and the dam appeared to have normal conformation). Many of the scientifically identified dwarfism characteristics have been researched individually (Speed 1958; Hermans 1970; Bowling 1997).

Characteristics such as a full-length ulna or fibula (which causes severely splayed legs and achondroplasia) have been proven to be recessive in Shetland Ponies (Hermans 1970). It has also been shown that lateral patellar luxation (locking of stifle joint) is recessively transmitted (Hermans, Kersjes, vanderMey, & Dik 1987). It is an unfortunate fact that most genetic diseases of concern to animal breeders are inherited as recessive genes (Bowling 1996). The inbreeding method that may be used for eliminating deleterious recessive genes within a given gene pool has already been discussed. However, it should be re-emphasized that inbreeding is one manner in which unwanted recessive genes may be exposed, in order to more rapidly facilitate removal of carrier individuals from a particular breeding herd.

In 1991, AMHA Genetics Committee member and Sonoma State University biologist Galen Clothier, Ph.D. (pers. comm. 1991), wrote the following comments pertaining to dwarfism in miniature horses:

> There is a large number of different types of dwarfism. Some causes are genetic, some are glandular (especially associated with the hypothalamus, pituitary and thyroid), some are teratogen-induced developmental arrests and many are of unknown (idiopathic) causes. To further complicate the picture, traits of dwarfism are exhibited in continuous spectrum from very slight and insignificant to acute and profoundly debilitating. Some characteristics, considered by many to be dwarf in nature, are also exhibited by non-dwarf animals and vice versa. Perhaps, as more is known about the horse genome, specific dwarfism genes or markers for such genes will be identified.

The smallest miniature horse mares and stallions are more likely to produce foals with dwarfism characteristics (Campbell 1993). This aspect has been very difficult to research further due to the reluctance of owners to reveal the incidence of dwarf foals. In one small retrospective study of breeding records 6 dwarf foals were born in 3 years to 20 mares. No close inbreeding had been done. Two were born early (295 and 297 days) and were dead. Criteria used to identify a dwarf included malaligned jaw, exacerbated "domed" cranial cavity, congenital limb deformities in two or more limbs (flexural deformities), proportionately short legs to body and a proportionately short stubby neck to a large head (Campbell 1993).

Because of the understandable reluctance of miniature horse breeders to discuss the occurrence of dwarf characteristic foals in their herds, a consent form was developed by the

1991 AMHA Genetics Committee. The intent of this form was to guarantee anonymity to the breeders and/or owners of any dwarf miniatures that might be donated for research purposes to the UCD Veterinary Genetics Laboratory. It was hoped that by guaranteeing such anonymity, more scientific and statistical information pertaining to dwarfism characteristics and syndromes could be gathered by Dr. Bowling (who headed the dwarfism research project). As a result of this consent form (and with the generous cooperation of UCD's Veterinary School and teaching staff) a few individuals were obtained that could be evaluated, and clinical workups (including radiographs) of miniature horses exhibiting various dwarfism characteristics were made possible.

Report on Dwarfism Genes in Miniature Horses (Bowling 1993)

Within a domestic animal species, size may be one of the prominent characteristics used to differentiate breeds. One conspicuous example of extremes is the oft-cited comparison of Miniature Horses with Shires, which commonly would demonstrate at least a twofold difference in height, drawing upon randomly selected representatives from either breed. Dog breeds could also be given as dramatic examples of height differences within a species. Since Shires and Miniature Horses breed true for their height extremes, their distinctive size traits can be assumed to have a genetic basis. From our understanding of size traits in other species and the origin of horse breeds, the differences are probably based on several to many genes. Any breed with an historically narrow pedigree definition may have relatively few genes that are involved in the production of the distinctive type, but a broadly based breed may have a more heterogeneous collection of genes that provide the standard phenotype.

Genes involved with reduction of size have no a priori [theoretical] association with health problems. However, in some cases genes that cause a plethora of congenital abnormalities compromising health may be accompanied by size reduction. Such genes would be expected to be homologous [similar] to genes relatively well documented in humans and mice. We may be able to apply the research findings in these species toward recognizing the presence (or absence) of dwarfing genes associated with undesirable effects in Miniature Horses. The identification of genes and the development of objective carrier tests could allow concerned breeders to avoid paring animals with genes that could result in the production of unhealthy foals.

Examples of gene types that affect human adult stature include a variety of mutations in the growth hormone gene. Affected persons may have fewer related health problems and the administration of growth hormone may allow the person to attain normal height. Other genes that may cause growth retardation include mutations affecting multiple systems, including bony abnormalities seriously compromising gait; mental retardation; and effects to internal organs including heart, liver, kidneys or gut. It is possible that some genes could cause the desirable small size in single dose but have drastic effects in a homozygous condition. Chromosomal abnormalities of either autosomes or sex chromosomes may also affect size. None of the latter kinds of mutations would be desirable as agents effecting the distinctive small size of Miniature Horses.

Breeders concerned with the future of the Miniature Horse understand the importance of investigating the question of dwarfism genes that may have associated health problems and the following proposal is submitted as a preliminary document for discussion of the types of research avenues that could be pursued.

Figure 11.14 *Basic features of a brachycephalic-type dwarf foal. The bulging forehead, highly placed nostrils, underbite, abnormally shortened legs and neck, enlarged joints and thick girth are all typical.*

Figure 11.15 *Basic features of one type of achondroplasia seen in miniature horses. The splayed (severely cowhocked) hind legs and extremely shortened gaskins (with skin wrinkling) are caused by the full-length, improperly articulated fibulas, as well as by the lack of normal long bone growth. This example also illustrates club feet, in addition to the abnormally shortened legs. Note that in this type of dwarfism, the head and neck appear to be normal and there is no underbite.*

Dwarfism Gene Report

At the AMHA Annual meeting of November 1993, Dr. Ann T. Bowling's progress report was presented by the Genetics Committee Chairman. During 1992 and 1993, the major focus of the UCD genetic studies of miniature horses was on dwarfism. This was partially financed by a $5,000 grant from AMHA, which was approved by the Board of Directors in 1991. Bowling's research included two approaches:

■ An extensive literature review to identify growth-associated candidate genes, based on information available from other species.

■ Clinical studies of diastrophically affected miniature horses. Miniature horses suffering only from achondroplasia (with no associated deformities of the legs other than severe shortening of the limbs, and with no other characteristics of dwarfism) were not considered nor included in the study.

It was hoped that by indentifying genes well known within other species that progress could be made in developing a DNA-based diagnostic test that would allow breeders the option to avoid production of horses whose health was compromised due to complications of dwarfism. Information about the genetics of some of these genes in horses is almost completely lacking. However, some published studies in humans and mice verified that there are several genes associated with small stature in those species. These include various collagen genes, insulin-like growth factor (IGF) (Caetano & Bowling 1998), growth hormone (GH), growth hormone releasing factor (GRF), and growth hormone receptor (GHR). Basic research was begun in an attempt to characterize these genes in miniature horses being affected by diastrophic dwarfism.

Important progress was made when one breeder supplied radiographs from a miniature horse dwarf foal with markedly crooked legs. Fibular malformations obvious in the foal were absent in both of the parents. An ulnar and fibular abnormality in Dutch Shetland Ponies that compromised gait, and that was always associated with unusually short stature appeared to be identical (Hermans 1970; Bowling 1996; Philipsson, Brendour, Dalin, & Wallin 1998). Genetic studies of the Shetland leg abnormality showed that it was inherited as a simple autosomal recessive disease. The defect is associated with full-length fibulas (and sometimes ulnas) with improper articulation, causing extreme cow hocks and marked ambulatory disabilities.

Other miniature horse dwarf contributions were evaluated (with non-invasive chromosome studies) in order to rule in or out sex chromosome deficiencies and autosomal trisomies known to be associated with small stature and multiple skeletal abnormalities in other species (Sponenberg & Bowling 1985). Some of these studies have included photographs of the affected individuals, as well as the sire, dam and siblings, when available. They have also included measurements, gait analysis, radiographs, and collection of blood and hair root samples for hormone and DNA analysis.

Without grants, meaningful research cannot be continued or initiated. The industries that will benefit most generally support their own research. Responsibility for raising funds for such research grants in the miniature horse industry logically falls upon the registries, but qualified researchers must first propose and fully outline the desired research projects (or be requested to do so). After approval, AMHA and AMHR could then donate grant money and encourage donations (tax deductible) from their members.

Equine genetics has always been of interest to breeders, and it is only with cooperation between geneticists and miniature horse breeders that new breakthroughs will occur in the future. Further dwarfism research has been severely restricted because of the total absence of dwarfism-dedicated research funds since 1992. The Veterinary Genetics Laboratory at UCD has been unable to generate the needed funds that would be required to proceed further. The initial grant, awarded in 1991 by the AMHA, has long since been exhausted. Interested benefactors (miniature horse breeders, as well as the miniature horse registries) are needed if any meaningful dwarfism research project is to be continued at UCD. Currently, dwarfism research in the United States (on the West Coast) is limited to the work of only three persons conducting studies at their own personal expense: Ann Bowling, Nancy Rivenburgh and the author.

Outline of 1993 Program for Dwarfism Research

- *Identification of distinctive phenotypes*
  - *Age-associated measurements and photographs*
  - *Dentition observations*
  - *Radiological workup*
  - *Hematological and biochemical workup*
  - *Serum/plasma assays of growth hormone, pituitary hormones, thyroid hormone, mucopolysaccharides, etc.*
  - *Gait analysis*
  - *Cardiology, and studies of other internal organ systems*
  - *Comparison with identified syndromes associated with size reduction in other species*
- *Genetic data*
  - *Recording of coat color and pattern*
  - *Blood typing of offspring, parents, full-siblings*
  - *Storage of DNA, serum and hemolysates for future testing of additional systems*
  - *Karyotype analysis*
  - *Analysis of possible linkage association of phenotype with genetic markers that could be used in breeding program management*

Genetic Selection Priorities

Within the miniature horse breed there has been a traditional emphasis upon the two characteristics of flashy coat colors and short stature. Consequently, there have been many poorly conformed animals that were considered highly desirable (and very expensive) only because of their outstanding color, or very short stature. Most present-day breeders that are consistently winning at horse shows have recently adjusted their genetic selection priorities. Conformation and breed type are foremost, with color and extremely short stature only secondary considerations. This trend follows that of some of the full-sized breeds of horses.

As increasing knowledge is shared by geneticists with breeders, practical uses of genetic principles have become important aspects of horsemanship. Even in the color breeds such as Palominos, Paints, or Appaloosas, conformational excellence is of crucial importance for consistent show wins. Although color breeding can be very exciting, breeding for color should always be considered secondary to breeding for high-quality, genetically sound individuals. An individual breeder's genetic selection priorities may ultimately determine future success in the miniature horse industry, as well as the show ring.

CHAPTER 12

Coat Colors and Patterns

MINIATURE HORSES ARE A UNIQUE BREED and the genetic parameters established for full-sized equids rarely fit them. Nowhere is that dichotomy more evident than in coat color genetics and identification. The wide diversity of coat colors and patterns seen so commonly in miniature horses (silver dapples, chocolate silvers, silver bays, silver chestnuts, buckskins, palominos, cremellos, pintaloosas and appaloosas), are virtually unknown among most of the larger breeds.

There are still many unidentified genetic factors that influence and determine coat color, patterns and markings in horses, despite new information currently being researched, debated and confirmed by equine geneticists. In most coat color discussions being published, descriptive adjectives are usually augmented by the use of actual genotype notation. A basic understanding of genetics is necessary to make intelligent use of the wealth of information now available and to effectively plan a breeding program (see Chapter 11). It can be difficult for a horse breeder to remain current with the latest genetic information.

Both color genes and pattern genes interact to produce the ultimate color of every horse. Some genes affect only the **point** (mane, tail, ear tips and lower legs) color of an individual, while others affect only the main body color. There are basically only two pigment colors in horses, black and red. Some genes affect only one of those two colors. The many shades and combinations seen are merely the black pigment, called **eumelanin**, and/or the red pigment, called **pheomelanin**, being affected by a multitude of color- and pattern-alteration genes. These **alteration genes** function by distributing, diluting, intensifying, spotting (various patterns) and roaning, etc.

The characteristic of dappling has not yet been genetically researched and identified, but sometimes occurs phenotypically in combination with both the silver allele, Z (silver dapple) and the gray allele, G ([dapple] gray). In the miniature horse breed, many silver dapples are incorrectly registered as (dapple) grays. Dappling may also be seen in combination with other colors and patterns such as buckskin, bay and palomino. Visible dappling is often absent on silver-gened miniatures and the single characteristic of dappling cannot be used to identify horses within either the gray or silver series of colors.

The American Miniature Horse Standard of Perfection specifies the coat color, pattern, and eye color requirements of miniature horses as follows: "**Any color, eye color and/or marking pattern is equally acceptable.**" This standard has very important differences when compared with the other breeds. An excellent example is the pintaloosa miniature, which shows both pinto and appaloosa patterns in its phenotype. This coloration is accepted in miniature horses and should not be penalized at the shows. Similarly, blue or amber eye color (one, both, or flecked with blue) should not be penalized, even though some American Horse Show Association (AHSA) breeds may disallow them.

Because the miniature horse color classes are judged primarily on color and pattern alone (100% color in AMHR; and 80% color, 20% conformation in AMHA) judges must observe esoteric qualities such as presentation, overall condition of the coat, and brilliance of color and pattern. At this point, a judge's personal opinion as to correctness of color or pattern may or may not be used, but there is no need to adhere to any other breed's color standards in order to make final placements. The miniature horse color classes are divided into Multicolor (appaloosa, pintaloosa, and pinto only) and Solid Color (all other colors). Horses with stockings or blazes, as well as bays, palominos, silver dapples and other brightly colored two-toned individuals compete in the Solid Color classes, unless they have pinto and/or appaloosa markings.

In addition to the body color of a horse, there are white markings that frequently occur on the head, **facial markings** (see Figure 12.1), or on the legs, **leg markings** (see Figure 12.2). White markings are frequently used as a means of identification, since they do not usually change with age. The underlying skin of a white marking is pink, and roaning may occur at the junction of the marking and the body color. Prior to the use of DNA testing, these markings were used by the horse registries as a means of visually verifying an individual horse's identity. Even today, a horse's markings are an important aspect of horse registration. However, not all horses have white markings and the genotype controlling white markings is not clearly understood.

Significant activity has been taking place concerning genetic marker programs (blood typing or DNA testing) for miniature horses. Certain coat color crosses are genetically impossible (e.g., two solid colors cannot produce an appaloosa or a tobiano pinto. Two chestnuts cannot produce a bay or a black). Many full-sized horse breed registries are now requiring blood typing or DNA testing in cases where the foal's color does not meet the established criteria. Unfortunately, all genetic marker programs now in effect rely heavily upon accurate coat color descriptions. It follows that because miniature horses exhibit so many colors and patterns that are seldom seen or recognized in other breeds, there is a compelling need for the development and understanding of consistent nomenclature.

Of primary importance is the fact that the silver allele (Z) is extremely rare in any American breeds other than Shetland Ponies and miniature horses. For this reason, very little has been researched and published by equine geneticists about its visual appearance, its mode of inheritance and the far-reaching impact it has had on the miniature horse breed. Previously thought to have been a new equine color, supposedly arising from a mutation during the 1800s, the discovery in 1994 of a 26,000-year-old frozen horse dispels that original theory. This specimen, similar in type and size to a small Icelandic horse, was so well preserved by freezing that its hair was intact and its silver bay coat color was clearly visible (deRibeaux 1994).

Tests Available for Identifying Color Genotypes

The requirements for obtaining homozygous tobiano, red factor, or lethal white overo testing kits may be procured from the University of California, Davis, Veterinary Genetics Laboratory (see Sources).

Tobiano Blood Testing

Two of the genes used for blood-typing information (AL^B and GC) are linked with the tobiano pinto gene (TO). By using this information about a particular individual, homozygous tobianos may be identified. **Homozygous tobianos** produce 100% tobiano pintos, even when bred to solid-color mates.

Owners of tobiano miniatures who are interested in knowing whether their horses are homozygous for the tobiano spotting gene need to accumulate several kinds of information. The horses being tested must fit certain parameters before being considered for homozygous tobiano testing. Initially, it is necessary that both parents be tobiano pintos. If the horse has already sired or produced foals, none of its offspring may be solid color. All progeny, even from solid-color mates, must be tobianos, and at least five tobiano foals from solid-color mates is the minimum test mating advised. If present, secondary body spotting (ink spots, paw prints) may also help to visually identify homozygotes, but ink spots are not a requirement for tobiano homozygosity.

Red Factor DNA-Based Test

A red factor test is available to determine whether a particular horse is homozygous for black (*EE*) or whether it carries a recessive allele for red (*Ee*). This information is of equal interest to breeders who wish to produce 100% blacks in their breeding programs. Coupled with the tobiano test outlined previously, it is now possible to select a stallion who sires almost 100% black, bay, brown or buckskin tobiano pintos. If the stallion is homozygous for both tobiano and black, he cannot sire any reds or any solid colors. Even if homozygous for black, however, he can still sire grays, silvers, and silver dapples if bred to gray or silver mares. Both the silver gene (*Z-*) and the gray gene (*G-*) are epistatic to black.

The silver gene can dilute the black pigment on a bay such that it might be incorrectly registered as chestnut. This test could determine which horses might more correctly be labeled as silver bays, rather than chestnuts. The red factor test used for color registration clarification is of interest to owners of miniature horses as well as Shetlands and Icelandics in which the silver gene is common.

Unlike the tobiano test, the red factor test is DNA based and can be performed with hair root samples from the mane or tail. This test may also be used to differentiate perlinos from cremellos when the phenotype alone is not sufficient for identification.

Lethal White Overo DNA-Based Test

A DNA-based test using hair root samples to identify carriers of the lethal white overo (*LWO*) gene is now available. Frame overos carrying only one gene for the frame overo pattern are designated *NO* (one allele for not being overo, and one allele for being overo), while lethal white overos are designated *OO*, because they are homozygous for the *O* allele. If developing to full term, these foals are usually born solid white and always die within 3 days of birth. An affected foal may also die while still in the uterus as an undeveloped fetus. Genetic studies based on the new DNA diagnostic test for the *LWO* gene confirm the proposal that the lethal foal problem is due to an offspring having two copies of a gene that in single copy usually produces the color pattern known as frame overo (Metallinos, Bowling, & Rine 1998). Miniatures with an *NO* genotype (with only a single copy of the *LWO* gene) are healthy animals, exhibiting the attractive frame overo pattern. With the use of this testing procedure, lethal white overo foals can be avoided by not breeding two carriers of the *O* allele together (*NO X NO* = 25% lethal white foals).

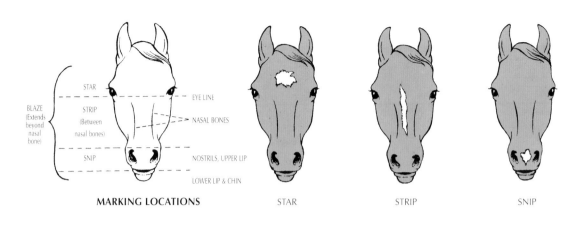

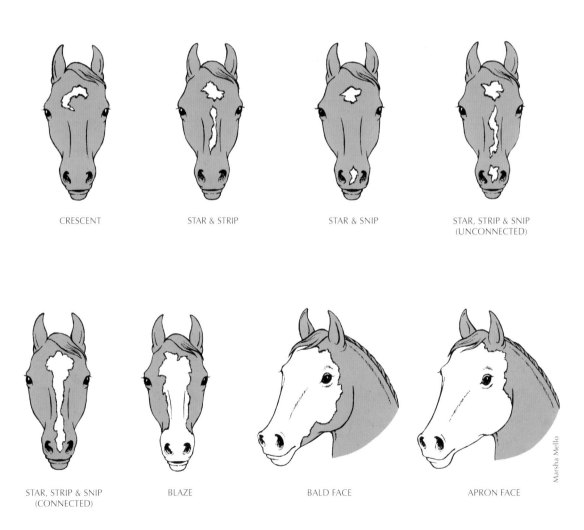

Figure 12.1 *Facial Markings*

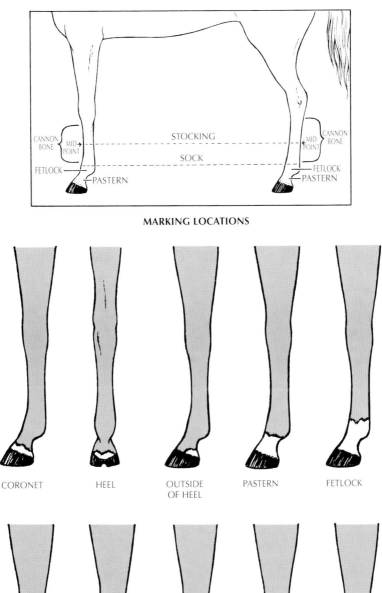

MARKING LOCATIONS

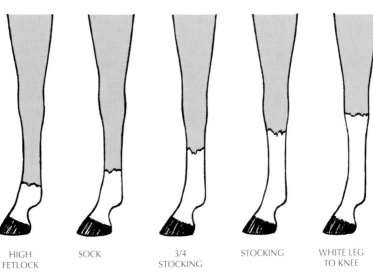

CORONET   HEEL   OUTSIDE OF HEEL   PASTERN   FETLOCK

HIGH FETLOCK   SOCK   3/4 STOCKING   STOCKING   WHITE LEG TO KNEE

Figure 12.2 Leg Markings

Paint or Pinto

Spotted horses and ponies have been known since recorded history, with their images having been found in the cave art of our earliest ancestors. Prior to the establishment of the American Paint Horse Association (APHA) in 1962, a non-appaloosa spotted horse could have been called the English term *paint*, or the Spanish term *pinto*, which translates *paint*. Although the terms were originally synonymous and were used according to culture and geographic location, paint and pinto have vastly different meanings today and are no longer synonymous.

The American Paint Horse breed is now based upon the bloodlines of horses registered by the American Paint Horse Association (APHA), American Paint Stock Horse Association (APSHA), the American Paint Quarter Horse Association (APQHA), the American Quarter Horse Association (AQHA), the Jockey Club of New York (Jockey Club) or any two of these registries combined. This means that all **Paint Horses**, by modern definition, must have some documented and provable Quarter Horse or Thoroughbred blood in their pedigrees. Thus, the American Paint is a modern stock-type breed of full-sized horse with pinto markings and does not include miniature horses.

In contrast, the **Pinto Horse** Association (PtHA) registers any breed of horse, including miniature, that meets the minimum color requirements established by that registry. There is no ancestral or conformational requirement for pintos within this registry, but there are stringent color and pattern requirements. Therefore, APHA-registered Paints may be registered as pintos in the PtHA, but PtHA-registered Pintos with no Quarter Horse or Thoroughbred background may not be registered as Paints in the APHA.

The Paint Registry and the Pinto Registry are not associated and operate under the guidance of separate governing bodies. They have different rules and registration requirements and very different Standards of Perfection, both for color patterns and for conformation. The Paint has both breed and color requirements, while the Pinto has only color requirements. Following those guidelines, paint miniature horses do not exist and cannot be designated as a registered color in any of the miniature horse registries.

Tobiano, Overo or Tovero

The pinto-marked miniature horse ranges from almost total color with minimal white markings to almost total white with minimal color markings (see Figure 12.3). Occasional horses with the tobiano or overo allele are so dark as to not have any body spots. These individuals will sometimes show a roan spot, pink spotting on the genitals or possibly white feet or legs. Although these minimally marked horses may be genetically tobiano or overo, they are often missed because they lack body spots. They usually do not meet the minimal standards established by the registries for pinto markings, so must be registered as solid-colors. However, they will produce tobiano or overo offspring as reliably as an obviously marked pinto.

Some of the genes that are still considered to be unreliable and unpredictable in their mode of inheritance include those that influence the amount of white spotting seen in pintos, as well as the extent of white markings seen on horses (not necessarily pinto) on the lower legs and face (Bowling 1996). Minimally marked pintos can produce loud-colored offspring

TOBIANO

OVERO

Barbara Naviaux

Figure 12.3 *Comparison between some of the possible variations in tobiano and overo patterns. Both patterns range from almost fully white individuals to almost fully dark ones and neither pattern can be said to have more white in it than the other.*

and loud-colored pintos can produce minimally marked pintos, as well as solid colors. If both parents are heterozygous for their pinto alleles, they are capable of producing 25% solid colors that do not carry a pinto gene (see Chapter 11).

The dark portion of pinto markings may range from cremello to very pale silver dapple, red or black and encompass all of the hues known to the horse world. There are two major pattern forms, tobiano and overo. In general terms, a **tobiano** has the white sections spreading from over its back and downwards while the **overo** has the white sections spreading from under its belly and upwards. In addition, the edges of the overo's pattern are often ragged or roaned in appearance in contrast to those of the tobiano, which are usually more clearly defined. The tobiano pattern is more common in miniatures, but occasional overos of all types occur and some miniature breeders are breeding specifically for the overo pattern.

Overo may be further divided into frame, sabino and splashed white categories. All of these spotting patterns are present at birth and remain fairly stable throughout life. Overo breeders should be aware of the lethal factor involved when breeding frame (overo) to frame. Foal losses may occur due to the genetic abnormality called lethal white foal syndrome (ileo-colonic aganglionosis). In the Paint Horse breed, it has been shown that frames bred to frames will produce about 25% overo homozygotes, which will be lethal white foals with this congenital defect (Bowling 1994; Metallinos, Bowling, & White 1998). Frame overos can now be tested for the presence of a single overo (O) gene, so that homozygous (OO) foals can be avoided by not breeding two O carriers together.

Dr. Bowling of the Veterinary Genetics Laboratory at the University of California, Davis had suspected that overo must be inherited as a dominant gene, for if it were recessive, all phenotypic overos would necessarily be homozygous recessive. Because it was known that overo homozygotes were lethal whites that died within 3 days of birth, there was an obvious error requiring further research. It is now known that frame overo is passed on as a dominant gene. The results of Dr. Bowling's research on overo pintos (1994) reflect her documentation of computer records from the Paint Horse Association registry. She studied a total of 697 overo foals, all sired by 13 overo stallions and all out of solid-color mares. Those results scientifically fit the model of frame overo being inherited as an autosomal dominant gene. Dr. Bowling's study showed that APHA-registered Paint Horse frame overos sire at least 50% overos out of solid-color mares. This was scientific proof that the frame overo gene was dominant over its allele for non-overo. There is still dispute over the new overo genetics, and for good reason. Large numbers of cropout foals continue to be produced. **Cropouts** are simply overo foals with neither a sire or a dam that appears to be overo marked. The *Rowdy* line in miniature horses is behind many genetically unexplainable events resulting in the production of well-marked frame overo cropouts occurring from what appear to be two solid-color parents (Naviaux 1997).

Bowling uses *TO* for the tobiano locus and *O* for the overo locus, and both Sponenberg (1996) and Bowling (1996) agree that each is inherited as a dominant gene. Thus, the genotype of all tobianos is either *TOTO* (homozygous) or *TOto* (heterozygous), while the basic genotype of frame overos would be simply *NO* (where *N* designates a non-overo allele) since homozygotes (*OO*) would not be viable. Again, all horses with the homozygous genotype, *TOTO*, will produce 100% tobiano pintos, even when bred to solid-color mates. A *TOTO* horse cannot occur unless both sire and dam are tobiano pintos. Paint horse breeders have observed that it is sometimes possible to identify homozygous tobiano individuals by their unique, oddly located small body spots, often referred to as ink spots or paw prints. Some animals with a small number of ink spots are not homozygotes, however, and *TOTO* homozygotes will not necessarily show inkspot markings. Scientific verification of homozygosity for tobiano spotting requires blood testing, as previously discussed or progeny records.

Blue eyes are of a consuming interest to current overo enthusiasts and occur frequently in combination with any of the pinto patterns. Many of the cropout overos originating from otherwise solid-color parentage have a parent with at least one blue eye (Naviaux 1997). Blue eyes or dark eyes flecked with blue areas are particularly prevalent when any white markings extend over the face or eyelids. However, blue eyes may also occur in individuals with no white markings, as well as with all other patterns and solid colors. Cremellos and perlinos always have blue eyes. In many cases, neither parent of a blue-eyed foal has blue eyes, so it is not a simple dominant trait (Bowling 1996). The inheritance of blue eyes is one of many unanswered questions in equine genetics.

Some of the overo types of pintos may be inherited at different loci than those for frame overo, yet are still registered as overos. Because more than one type of spotting is being registered as overo, it follows that not all homozygous overo combinations would be lethal whites. As further proof of these exceptions, some APHA Paint stallions who are the products of two overo parents have already been shown to sire a much higher percentage of overo foals (when bred to solid-color mates), suggesting they are heterozygotes at two unlinked loci.

When tobiano is crossed with overo, four possibilities arise: tobiano, overo, solid, or **tovero** (a mix of both patterns). Tovero horses appear to have two different dominant white spotting genes. Toveros can produce four types of patterns, even when bred to solid-color mates: tobiano, overo, solid and tovero (Bowling 1996).

The minimum percentages of colored foals that can be expected when breeding animals carrying the three independent (unlinked) dominant white spotting genes (tobiano, overo and appaloosa) have been calculated (Bowling 1996). **Tovero pintaloosas** (a combination of tobiano, overo and appaloosa patterns) will sire or produce about 87.5% spotted foals when bred to solid-color mates. Toveros (tobiano and overo) will sire or produce about 75% spotted foals when bred to solid-color mates. Both overos and tobianos will sire or produce about 50% spotted foals when bred to solid-color mates. Minimal marked tobianos, with so little white that they have been registered as solid colors, will still sire or produce 50% tobianos when bred to solid-color mates. The identification of such minimal tobiano markings may include roan (rather than white) body spots, white sections on manes or tails, pink spotting of genitals and one or more high white stockings.

Bay Pinto or Tri-Color Pinto

Bay describes not only a particular body color but also a particular point color and thus designates both a pattern and a specific combination of colors. All non-pinto **bay horses** have black manes, tails, ear tips and lower legs. The body color of bays may vary from **sandy bay** (light red) to **blood bay** (bright red), **mahogany bay** or **black bay** (very dark brownish red to almost black), with various increments in between those shades. Thus, a bay pinto is automatically a tri-colored individual, as both red and black must be showing on the above described specific areas of the body and points where they are not spotted with white. For registration purposes, all horses meeting this description should simply be called bay pinto because tri-color pintos also occur in other shades such as buckskin pinto and bay roan pinto. Buckskin and bay roan pintos should also be registered with their actual color, rather than by the less descriptive term *tri-color.*

Silver Dapple, (Dapple) Gray or Silver White

Miniature horses having **silver (Z-)** genotypes occur in a wide array of beautiful colors and patterns, which are usually not registered correctly. Breeders and scientific researchers cannot rely upon the colors listed in the stud books nor on the blood-typing and DNA-testing forms. Until registries understand and accept these colors and patterns for what they actually are, accurate miniature horse coat color identification, (as recorded on the registration certificate) will remain a frustrating impossibility. Because a silver-gened foal's coloration and its final adult coloration bear little resemblance to one another, photographs and descriptions of newborn foals may lead to incorrect conclusions for registry purposes. For example, silver dapples never develop their dapples until they are at least 1 year of age, and they are often born red or tan, not shedding out to silver (with dapples) until they are yearlings. It is probable that an accurate assessment of these horses' coat colors cannot be decided upon until the horse matures and is in a natural unclipped summer coat. Even then, however, registries often refuse to register the silver-gened miniature with its correct color designation, as many of these colors are not yet listed as options on the official registration application blanks. The descriptions (phenotypes) of some of these adult phase silver-gened colors are as follows:

- **Silver dapple:** Many dapples, light silver to almost black body, silver to white mane and tail, black skin and eyes (see Figure 12.35).
- **Silver bay:** No dapples, red body, chocolate legs, silver to white mane and tail, gray undercoat, black skin and eyes (see Figure 12.25).
- **Silver chestnut:** Only occasional (seasonal) dapples, red or gold body (some look like palominos), flaxen legs and underbelly, flaxen to white mane and tail, black skin and eyes (see Figure 12.29).
- **Silver white:** White body, mane and tail; black skin and eyes (see Figure 12.45).
- **Chocolate silver:** Few, if any, (seasonal) dapples, cocoa-colored body, flaxen to white mane and tail, black skin and eyes (see Figure 12.32).

Note: Blue eyes may occur with any of the above described silver-gened colors but are always associated with the addition of pinto alleles.

Table 12.1 Phenotypically Silver Miniature Horses

Silver-Gened Colors	Body Color	Mane and Tail	Skin and Eye Color
Silver Dapple	Light silver to near black Many dapples	Silver to white	Black
Silver Bay	Red, chocolate legs Gray undercoat No dapples	Silver to white	Black
Silver Chestnut	Red or golden Seasonal or no dapples	Flaxen to white	Black
Silver White	White	White	Black
Chocolate Silver	Chocolate or cocoa color Occasional dapples	Flaxen to white	Black

Only miniature horses with black, dark brown or dark red manes and tails seem to be fully exempt from the silver gene, or Z allele. In the miniature horse breed, any time a light mane and tail are seen, it is quite possibly due to the presence of this frequently occurring dilution gene (pinto and/or appaloosa white are exceptions). As most miniature breeders are aware, many genetic silver dapples are being registered as dapple grays or duns. Similarly, many chocolate silvers and silver bays are registered as chestnuts with flaxen manes and tails. The actual characteristic of dappling does not in itself adequately distinguish this silver series of colors from the dappling so often seen on non-silver-gened grays, palominos, buckskins and other colors. Because visible dappling does not occur on several shades of silver (dapple), the word *dapple* has been dropped from most of the silver-gened (Z) color descriptions. Considering the undisputed prevalence of these striking colors in the miniature horse breed, it is hoped that these colors will soon be added to the possible options listed on the registration applications and that the many coat color inaccuracies will be corrected.

It is not difficult to describe the important differences between gray and silver (dapple). The **gray (G-)** is always born any other color or pattern except for gray; for example, bay, black, brown, sorrel, palomino, dun, etc. As the foal ages, white hairs become noticeable around the eyes, indicating that as the horse matures, it will start turning gray all over. This occurs with the appearance of ever-increasing numbers of white hairs being interspersed among the darker base-colored hairs. With each year's hair shed in the spring, the horse will be a little lighter than it was in its previous year, until it finally turns almost white. The speed with which it turns white varies considerably, some horses whitening within less than a year and some not whitening completely until old age. The presence or absence of dappling also varies between individual gray horses, at different ages, and at different times of the year.

The Silver Gene

In contrast to grays (G-), **adult silver-gened miniatures (Z-)** remain the same color throughout their entire lives. They are generally a lighter shade when in their long winter coats but always shed out in the summer to their former coat color.

In 1953, a new silver white variation was identified. **Silver whites** appear to be white but always have black skin and dark brown or black eyes. This color pattern can result only when silver dapple occurs in combination with gray in one individual's genotype. When this happens, the combined genes seem to have a synergistic effect on one another. Thus, silver whites, having a genotype of *G-Z-*, are sometimes born white or very lightly colored, becoming white much earlier in age than a gray not carrying a *Z* allele. Although not yet scientifically documented, silver white coloration may account for many of the whites that have been said to occur in the miniature horse breed. Silver white coloration was first described more than 40 years ago in the *The Journal of Heredity* (Castle & Smith 1953).

As previously emphasized, silver-gened foals *never* have any dappling, and there are many adults within the silver group that show no dappling. Until the foal is at least 1 year of age, no dappling may be visible. Furthermore, visible dappling is never necessary to determine that a particular horse is being affected by the *Z* allele. Registrations of silver dapples are often refused because of a foal's lack of dappling pattern and are sent back to the owners classified as duns, rather than the correct silver (dapple) classification. The requirements for dun coloration are a dorsal stripe, zebra markings on the legs and darker points than the base color of body. This error is made because many of the silver-gene colors have visible dorsal stripes that are not related to the dun pattern. The **silver shades** range from very pale silver to chocolate, gold, bright red, and dark steel gray (almost black, from a distance). These colors are typically framed by lighter manes and tails, and always have black skin and eyes. The lightest examples of silver chestnuts often appear to be (and may be incorrectly registered as) palominos, but these individuals do not carry the necessary cremello allele (*C^cr*) required for traditional palomino breeding. Breeding two silver chestnuts together (or breeding a palomino or buckskin to a silver chestnut) will never result in a cremello foal.

The current system of designating color and pattern for registration (which indicates all miniature horse coat colors in the Stud Books) was set up prior to the latest genetic discoveries concerning coat colors. Currently, breeders who wish to register their silver foals have only one option, silver dapple, which is inadequate to accurately describe the many silver colors. The system of registering horses according to the presence or absence of dapples is a serious error. Considering the rarity of dapples occurring on non-silver-gened miniature horses, it would be advisable to eliminate the color designation "dapple." Furthermore, the following colors should be added to the registration application:

- Silver Bay
- Silver Chestnut
- Silver White
- Chocolate Silver
- Perlino, which must have blue eyes.

Additionally the following changes need to be made:

- Grulla: Add "dorsal stripes, zebra markings on the legs and darker points."
- Dun colors: Add "dorsal stripes, zebra markings on the legs and darker points."
- White: Delete the reference to "albino" and the words "white eyes." Albino horses, which have pink eyes, have not been documented in the miniature horse breed.
- Cremello: Eliminate the wording "lightest dun," and add that "cremellos always have blue eyes."

Among pinto and appaloosa enthusiasts, the use of gray breeding stock is considered to be one of the crosses that will kill color markings. Gray pinto and gray appaloosa foals can be disappointing because both lose their dark-haired markings as they age. Although they retain their skin pattern, showing both pink and black skin as before, those areas that were dark at birth will eventually be covered with white hair.

In contrast to the grays, silver dapples are a superb choice for appaloosa or pinto breeding because there is no fading of their dark markings as they age. A silver dapple can be thought of as a solid black that is being masked by the *Z* allele (which is located at a different locus from that of gray). *Z*, like *G*, is inherited as an epistatic dominant, and all miniatures within the silver dapple group have the genotype of either *ZZ* or *Zz*. **Silver foals** are born various shades of pale gray, gold, tan, silvery black, chestnut, etc. Their manes and tails are often at least partially dark at birth. During the first facial shed of hair, at about 3 months old, the probable adult body color starts becoming apparent. The mane and tail become increasingly lighter, if not already completely white. There are no white hairs around the eyes as there always are on a gray. The undercoat of the 6-month-old silver-gened foal is often a smoky gray color, which becomes readily apparent if the foal is body clipped.

A solid black horse, influenced genetically by *Z*, will become a **silver dapple**, a horse that appears to be dapple gray with a light mane and tail. Because a bay horse has a red body with black points, the *Z* allele, influencing primarily the black, causes the horse to have a much diluted and lightened mane, tail and legs but has a limited effect on the red-colored body. Thus, the **silver bay** is a red horse with silver to white mane and tail, smoky gray undercoat (when clipped they look grayish) and chocolate legs, ear tips and muzzle (diluted from the original black). This particular phase of silver coloration is the one that causes the most unpredictable progeny when incorrectly registered as a chestnut with flaxen mane and tail, but the chocolate-colored legs (if the horse does not have four high white stockings) and often a few darker-colored hairs in the light mane and tail may be relied upon for positive identification.

The following example illustrates one of the problems caused by incorrect coat color registrations. Two heterozygous silver bays, both incorrectly registered as chestnuts with flaxen manes and tails, are bred together (*Zz* X *Zz*). The resulting foal easily may be bay with a red body and black points. In fact, 25% of the time when these two individuals are mated together, they will have bay offspring with the homozygous recessive genotype of *zz*. Within the full-sized horse breeds, if one attempts to register a bay foal out of a chestnut X chestnut mating, the parentage assignment will be questioned and genetic marker testing (blood typing or DNA testing) may be requested by the registry. A bay foal that results from the breeding of two chestnuts is considered to be a genetically unexpected event.

Gray or Roan

The **roan pattern (RN)** is distinguished by a mixture of colored and white hairs that, unlike that of a gray, stays constant throughout the horse's life except for seasonal changes as hair is shed and replaced. The white hairs occur only on the body and do not affect the points. For this reason, roans usually have darker manes, tails, lower legs and heads than their base body color. Grays and roans are easily differentiated because gray horses get whiter each year and usually have lighter heads than their base body color. At certain stages in their lives, red roans and rose grays are extremely difficult to differentiate. However, roans do not have any dappling, and their heads, legs, manes and tails are invariably much darker in appearance than their base color. Black roans and seal brown roans are correctly called **blue roans**, meaning that they have black points and the body color is a mixture of black, brown and white hairs. Chestnut or sorrel roans are correctly called **red roans** because their body color and darker point color is reddish when viewed from a distance.

The locus for the dominantly inherited roaning pattern is *RN*. Although Geurts (1977) has convincingly identified some healthy homozygous roans, in the past it was recommended that breeders refrain from breeding roan to roan because of suspected lethal gene problems. To date, however, lethal homozygous roan is not a scientifically proven hypothesis. Furthermore, the roaning often associated with various appaloosa and many pinto patterns is not caused by the *RN* allele. *RN*-gened horses are surprisingly rare in miniatures; however, a few excellent examples do exist. Unfortunately, many non-roans (often genetic appaloosas) have been incorrectly registered as roans simply because they have sufficient areas of white body hairs to look suspicious.

The three loci thus responsible for the entire array of colors and patterns caused by gray, roan and silver dapple are *G*, *RN* and *Z*, and they differ widely from one another, both in genotype as well as in phenotype.

Roan or Grulla

Unlike the roan patterns, **grulla horses** must have the primitive wild-type markings found within the dun series of colors. These include a dorsal stripe (line-back), withers stripe and zebra leg markings. Grullas are a type of dun having black or diluted black points. Some of the lightest shades of grulla have blue eyes or other shades of dilute eye color. Amber, hazel and even gray eyes are common within the dun and grulla series of colors. In contrast, roans usually have dark brown or black eye color. Blue roan may be very difficult to distinguish from the darkest shades of grulla, when viewed from a distance. However, roans are the result of the intermingling of white, black and brown body hairs, while grullas are the result of one fairly uniform-colored body hair, without any interspersed white hairs.

Buckskin, Palomino, Cremello or White

All genetically white horses have the genotype *Ww*, and all non-white horses have the genotype *ww* because there is a lethal gene involved with all dominant homozygotes and the *WW* fetus is not viable. There are very few, if any, actual *Ww* whites within the miniature horse breed. The large numbers of grays, silver whites and cremellos that regularly occur probably account for most of the white and albino miniature horses presently registered. **Ww whites** have pink skin and brown eyes (rarely blue). C^cC^c **cremellos** and **perlinos** have tannish pink skin and blue eyes, while **G- grays** and **G-Z- silver whites** have black skin and dark brown or black eyes.

In the miniature breed there are many cremellos and perlinos that are so light in appearance that they may be mistaken for *Ww* white, but this is due to an entirely different set of genes. The blue-eyed whites that occur from breeding palominos or buckskins together are actually cremellos or perlinos and are the result of a homozygous C^cC^c genotype.

It is sometimes difficult to tell perlinos from cremellos, but **perlinos** usually have faintly visible bluish or tannish points. The DNA-based red factor test may be used to differentiate perlino from cremello. The C^{cr} dilution gene, when in the heterozygous state, dilutes pheomelanin (red) markedly more than it dilutes eumelanin (black). In this manner, a CC^{cr} genotype is very influential in determining buckskin and palomino coloration. The nature of this interesting gene when paired with a C (fully pigmented) allele is that it allows the mane and tail to remain black while it dilutes the red body color to various lighter shades of yellow or tan. If the horse's base color is sorrel or chestnut with a self-colored or flaxen mane and tail, the CC^{cr} genotype results in a palomino, diluting the mane and tail as well as the body, because the mane and tail are not black. The C^{cr} allele does not exist in many other breeds of horses, but it is a common allele among miniature horses.

Because the cremello dilution genes are inherited as an incomplete dominant or codominant, cremellos may occur unexpectedly within a herd when two non-cremello heterozygotes that carry the C^{cr} allele, such as buckskin, are bred together (CC^{cr} X CC^{cr} = 25% $C^{cr}C^{cr}$ cremello). Even a solid black miniature may carry the C^{cr} allele without showing it in its phenotype because a single dose of this dilution allele does not affect black pigment. The occurrence of a totally unexpected cremello from the mating of two solid blacks or dark browns thus becomes a surprising possibility. As previously stated, such cremellos are no doubt one explanation for the whites that are said to occur from non-white parentage. Their genotype would be $C^{cr}C^{cr}ww$, not Ww, as it would be for a genetic white. Perlinos and cremellos always have blue eyes and pink skin, while palominos will usually have dark eyes and dark skin. Ivory- or cream-colored horses with black skin and brown eyes are palominos, not cremellos, but palomino foals sometimes take a few weeks after birth to develop their black skin pigmentation.

Table 12.2 Phenotypically White Miniature Horses

Example	Coat Color	Genotype	Skin	Eye	Color Pedigree
Cremello	Ivory or cream-colored body and points	$C^{cr}C^{cr}ee$	Tannish pink	Blue	Palomino X Palomino = 25% cremello
Perlino	Ivory or cream-colored body; pale, but slightly darker points	$C^{cr}C^{cr}E\text{-}$	Tannish pink	Blue	Buckskin X Buckskin = less than 25% perlinos
Gray	Any color other than gray when born, gradually turning white	$G\text{-}$	Black	Brown or Black	Gray X any color = at least 50% gray
Silver White	White	$G\text{-}Z\text{-}$	Black	Brown or Black	Gray X silver dapple = 25% silver white
White	White	Ww	Pink	Brown (Rarely blue)	White X any other color = 50% white

Cremello or Dun

Often very difficult to visually distinguish between one another, a single copy of the cremello dilution allele (C^v) is genetically quite different from the dun dilution allele (*D*). The most obvious of these differences is that dun is inherited as a simple dominant. Thus, all horses carrying the dun gene will show it in their phenotype. The second major difference is that the *D* allele dilutes both pheomelanin and eumelanin on the body but does not dilute them on the points. Horses being affected by the **dun allele** usually have darker points, a dorsal stripe and zebra markings on the legs. Generally speaking, a buckskin or palomino, being affected by only the C^v allele, will not have these primitive sorts of markings. Finally, homozygosity for the *D* allele (*DD*) does not cause any increase in dilution effect from that of heterozygosity (*Dd*) (Bowling 1996). However, it is possible for any given horse to have the combination genotype of CC^vD-Z-, thus exhibiting a wide variety of visible dilution, color and pattern effects. When silver dapple and dun are combined, the result is a dun animal with a lighter mane and tail, not a typical dun with dark points. The *D* allele is seen in some of the stock horse breeds, in various breeds of ponies, in donkeys and mules and in miniature horses, but its effects may also be observed in Fjord horses and in some of the ancient wild types of horses, such as Tarpans and Przewalskis. Many silver dapples are incorrectly registered as duns. However, these miniature horses are generally lacking the dark mane and tail and zebra markings of a correctly marked dun. This error is made because many silver-gened miniatures have dorsal stripes (not associated with the dun allele). Without the zebra markings across the front of their hocks and behind their front knees, these horses are not genetically qualified as duns.

Sorrel, Chestnut, or Red

As stated previously, eumelanin (black) and pheomelanin (red) are the only two actual hair pigments that occur in coat color genetics of horses. For miniature horse registration purposes, however, the sorrel and chestnut color descriptions noted on the AMHA and AMHR registration forms must be used as a guide. These read as follows:

- **Sorrel:** Reddish or copper-red coat; mane and tail usually same color, may be flaxen.
- **Chestnut:** Dark mahogany red or dark reddish brown; mane and tail usually same color, may be flaxen.

As previously mentioned, red (chestnut or sorrel) miniature horses with flaxen manes and tails are usually silver chestnuts.

For the purposes of discussing how these colors are inherited, however, both sorrel and chestnut are generally combined into a single category that is simply described as red. Some breed registries do not allow the term *sorrel* to be used in naming the color of a horse. For example, there is no such thing as a sorrel Arabian or Thoroughbred horse. All reds without black manes and tails in those breeds are considered chestnuts. In a general sense, the word *sorrel* implies a western derivation, while the word *chestnut* connotes more of an English derivation.

Black, Bay, Chestnut or Sorrel

There are two very important loci that have not yet been discussed, agouti *(A)* and extension *(E)*. The alleles at these two loci are responsible for the production of the basic chestnut, bay or black-colored animal. Alleles at the **agouti locus *(A)*** control the distribution of eumelanin. In a homozygous recessive state *(aa)*, eumelanin is allowed over the entire body, and the horse thus becomes a uniform black or brown. If the *A* allele is present, only the point color is affected, for *A* restricts any eumelanin to the points only, and the horse thus becomes a bay, buckskin or other black/brown pointed horse.

The **extension locus *(E)*** allows or does not allow black or red points. One of the alleles at the *E* locus allows full extension of black or brown pigments to the entire coat. It is thus responsible for creating the solid-black horse called *dominant black*. Another allele at the *E* locus allows pheomelanic points and restricts eumelanin from entering the hair, thus producing chestnut. The phenotypic effects caused by interactions of the many alleles at the *A* and *E* loci influence all of the colors: black, brown, bay, and red (chestnut or sorrel).

There are many other genes that could be considered and that greatly alter such features as those for seal brown, black fading tendencies or lighter point colors. It is often difficult to tell a very dark bay, brown or liver chestnut from a solid black. In actuality, there are very few blacks within any breed of horse, including miniatures. Most will have obvious brownish-appearing areas in the flanks, and many will fade out to darker shades of seal brown during summer. When continually exposed to sunlight, the manes and tails of many blacks will appear reddish.

Appaloosa or Pintaloosa

Even though there are many types of appaloosa colors and patterns, well-marked appaloosas are the easiest for a novice to visually identify. However, the genetics of appaloosa coloration is exceedingly complicated, probably being controlled by a single dominant appaloosa gene and many modifiers. These modifiers determine such features as blanket size, number of spots within the blanket, size and number of spots present on leopards, varnishing, roaning and so on. Many of these modifiers are inherited quantitatively and have been assigned numbers to indicate the degree with which they will affect the final phenotype. Appaloosa genetics has changed radically from that of the past. Because of these changes, information published prior to 1990 cannot be relied upon and is largely inaccurate (Sponenberg, Carr, Simak, & Schwink 1990; Bowling 1996; Sponenberg 1996).

There have been rare, yet supposedly well documented, occurrences of appaloosa cropouts from non-appaloosa parentage. These could possibly be mutations, but are otherwise genetically unexplainable events, since appaloosas must have at least one parent with appaloosa characteristics in order to have any true and inheritable appaloosa characteristics and markings.

Although the appaloosa breed must adhere to the full-sized appaloosa horse registry's Standard of Perfection, appaloosa patterns occur in many other breeds of horses, ponies and mules. Appaloosa is a relatively rare pattern in miniature horses, but its numbers are increasing

SPOTTED BLANKET
DARK, WHITE WITH DARK SPOTS
OVER LOIN AND HIPS

LEOPARD
WHITE, DARK SPOTS
OVER ENTIRE BODY

WHITE BLANKET OR FROST
DARK, WHITE
OVER LOIN AND HIPS

SNOWFLAKE
DARK, WHITE SPOTS
OVER ENTIRE BODY

VARNISHED ROAN OR MARBLED
VARNISHED DARK ROAN
WITH MINIMAL SPOTS

SNOWFLAKE BLANKET
DARK, WHITE SPOTS
OVER LOIN AND HIPS

Barbara Naviaux

Figure 12.4 Variations of appaloosa patterns. Appaloosa coloration is controlled by a single dominant gene affected by many modifiers. Appaloosa foals can occur only when at least one of the parents shows appaloosa characteristics. Appaloosa coloration is extremely varied and this illustration represents only a small number of possible patterns. These categories are representative of the accepted full-sized horse Appaloosa breed characteristic guidelines developed by the Animal Science Department at Montana State University (Miller 1964). The number of categories is multiplied for miniatures because of the permissible addition of pinto patterns that create pintaloosas.

rapidly because of so many breeders' fascination with appaloosa and pintaloosa coloration.

Pintaloosas represent the combination of one or more types of pinto pattern with one or more types of appaloosa pattern. For example, a **tobiano pintaloosa** carries both tobiano and appaloosa, an **overo pintaloosa** carries both overo and appaloosa and a **tovero pintaloosa** carries the three independent (unlinked) dominant white spotting genes of tobiano, overo and appaloosa. Bowling (1996) has calculated that 87.5% of the foals sired or produced by a horse carrying three different dominant white spotting genes will be colored, 75% of the foals sired or produced by a horse carrying two different dominant white spotting genes will be colored, and 50% of an appaloosa's foals will be colored when bred to solid-color mates. It is an exciting bonus to many miniature owners that the wild-patterned pintaloosas may be correctly included in the industry's appaloosa and pinto breeding programs, and some of the most important foundation sires in the breed are pintaloosas.

Appaloosa horses typically have certain characteristics that distinguish them entirely from any of the colors and patterns previously discussed. The white sclera of the eye (smaller irises than in other breeds); mottled skin surrounding the eyes, nose, lips and genitals; striped hooves; and sometimes a very sparse mane and "rat tail" are all characteristics sometimes seen on even the least colorful of appaloosas. Because an **appaloosa foal** is often born without any bright appaloosa markings, one must rely on some of these secondary characteristics either developing or being present at birth to determine whether the foal will develop appaloosa coloration later on in life, sometimes as late as 4 or 5 years of age. Testosterone is also thought to have some effect on coloration, and geneticists seem fairly certain that some of the modifier genes associated with the appaloosa patterns are sex influenced. This may explain the higher incidence of brightly colored male, rather than female, appaloosa horses.

The **Noriker**, an Austrian breed of draft horse, frequently occurs as a leopard-patterned appaloosa. Evidence in this breed indicates that blankets and the leopard pattern may be different extremes of the same pattern. In the Noriker, homozygotes *(LpLp)* are the few-spot leopard pattern (which appears almost entirely white) and heterozygotes *(Lplp)*, as an incomplete dominant inherited quantitatively, are the brightly spotted leopard patterns. Another interesting feature of this breed is that the Norikers always have full, flowing manes and tails, thus leading to the fact that sparse manes and rat tails are features not actually linked with appaloosa coloration. This phenomenon seems to be true within the miniature horse breed, and many beautifully marked appaloosa miniatures often have full manes and tails.

Typical appaloosa color patterns generally fall into one or more well described categories. The dark portion may be any color or combination of colors and patterns that occurs in miniature horses, including pinto, silver (dapple), roan, bay, tan, black, etc. There may be large areas of white background, and the spots may be of a similar or darker color than those of the main base colors, or the spots may be white, overlaid and scattered over a dark portion. In pintaloosas, pinto markings may obliterate some of the appaloosa spotting, but all normal appaloosa markings will generally show within other areas.

A common phenomenon on horses exhibiting appaloosa (leopard complex) patterns is concentration of pigment, which results in some dark areas, and dilution of pigment in other areas, which results in light areas. This frequently occurring phenomenon is often observable on the same horse concurrently. Melanin concentrations will be much darker than the base body color (Sponenberg et al. 1990; Sponenberg 1996). For example, a pale silver dapple spotted blanket appaloosa may have a white blanket with black spots.

The minimal expression of the leopard complex is the mottled skin pattern. **Mottling** occurs as small dots on the skin of the anus, genitalia, mouth and eyelids. On pink skin the dots are pigmented, and on pigmented skin the dots are pink or white. The maximum expression of the leopard complex is the few spot appaloosa (which appears almost entirely white), usually considered to be homozygous for its *LpLp* genotype, even though occasional few spots have been shown to be heterozygotes *(Lplp)* (Sponenberg et al.1990; Sponenberg 1996).

In miniature horses, the term *near leopard* is sometimes used. When a foal is born as a white horse with dark spots and the pattern does not change as it matures, the horse is called a **leopard appaloosa**. However, when a white or white-blanketed dark-spotted foal is born with darker legs and neck that later become white with dark spots, the horse is called a **near leopard**. Near leopards often retain dark areas on their lower legs but otherwise appear to be leopards.

Progress in Coat Color Genetics

Equine coat color genetics made two giant leaps forward in the summer of 1996 with the publication of two new books: Ann T. Bowling's *Horse Genetics*, with more than 60 of the 200 pages devoted specifically to coat color, and D. Phillip Sponenberg's *Equine Color Genetics* (see Sources). As a direct result of these two formidable geneticists' findings on many issues concerning equine coat color identification and inheritance, major updates in genetic theory and nomenclature have become necessary. The excitement generated by Bowling's and Sponenberg's new books has been widespread, although multiple unknowns and controversies concerning equine coat color inheritance are yet to be resolved. However, research aimed at answering some of the questions can lead only to a much expanded understanding of how coat color is inherited, described and ultimately planned for within miniature horse breeding programs. Equine coat color genetics is still an evolving science with the tantalizing promise of many surprises yet to come.

Caroline Fyffe

Figure 12.5 Silver bay frame overo pinto *mare, with blue eyes,* Deer Haven Peaches N Cream, *sired by a solid silver bay stallion,* Capricorn Star Studded, *with irregular snip, and out of a black mare,* Deer Haven Noonstar, *with one blue eye. Note the distinct frame overo markings, which have jagged edges and seem to originate from the underside. Peaches' dorsal aspect is entirely colored. Breeder/owner: Marjorie Vliet.*

Figure 12.6 Silver bay frame overo pinto *mare, with blue eyes,* Deer Haven Peaches N Cream *(same horse as shown in Figure 12.5), showing the left neck surface shortly after partial winter clipping. A smoky gray undercoat beneath the bright red top coat is typical of silver bays, as are the lack of dapples, chocolate legs and silvery mane and tail. This mare has tested positive for one copy of the dominant frame overo gene (O). Using the new overo nomenclature, her genotype is written NO. Breeder/owner: Marjorie Vliet.*

Barbara Naviaux

Figure 12.7 Chestnut frame overo pinto stallion, NFC Rowdys Standing Ovation, *sired by* Rowdy, *a solid bay with blaze, and out of a solid chestnut mare. Standing Ovation is one of several cropout overo miniatures that trace their ancestry back to* Rowdy. *Breeder: Bob and Sandy Erwin. Owner: Jack Burchill.*

©Amy Toner

Figure 12.8 Chestnut frame overo pinto stallion, La Vista Remarkable's Remarkable, *a son of the solid bay with large star,* NFC Remarkable Rowdy, *and out of a solid chestnut mare. Breeder/owner: Susan Hopmans.*

Susan Hopmans

Figure 12.9 Chestnut frame overo pinto colt, La Vista Rowdy Remark, *sired by the frame overo,* La Vista Remarkable's Remarkable *(Figure 12.8) and out of a black mare with irregular blaze, white socks, one blue eye and a small body spot. Breeder/Owner: Susan Hopmans.*

Susan Hopmans

Figure 12.10 Black frame overo pinto colt with blue eyes, LTD's Medicine Cat *(left)*, and **red frame overo pinto** colt with blue eyes, LTD's Nacho Macho Man *(right)*. The black frame is sired by a solid black with one blue eye and is out of a black frame overo with two blue eyes. The red frame is sired by LTD's Medicine Man, *a black frame, and is out of a solid red mare with two blue eyes. The lighter gray color on Medicine Cat has become jet black in adulthood. Breeder/owner: Lisa Davis.*

Figure 12.11 Black frame medicine hat overo pinto with blue eyes, LTD's Medicine Cat, *the same colt as shown in Figure 12.10 as a weanling. Note the unusual gray coloration on the right lower foreleg and the deepened black markings. Breeder/owner: Lisa Davis.*

Figure 12.12 Black frame medicine hat overo pinto with blue eyes, LTD's Magic Man. *This stallion is sired by a black tobiano with no white markings crossing over his back. Magic Man's dam,* Samples Wendy, *is solid white with blue eyes. Wendy is the result of breeding a frame overo to a non-overo daughter of a frame overo. Breeder/owner: Lisa Davis.*

Figure 12.13 Silver chestnut splashed white overo pinto stallion, with blue eyes and an apron face, Flabys Medicine Man *as a yearling. Breeder: Gerald and Joan Flaby. Owner: Henry H. Horrox.*

Figure 12.14 Minimally marked black overo pinto *filly with blue eyes,* Bended Knee Spring Eclipse. *The sire is a black tovero with one blue eye,* Bended Knee Partial Eclipse, *and the dam is a black tovero with blue eyes,* Willie Lee's Pixie. *Originally registered as a solid black, these belly spots were not discovered until the foal was body clipped. Breeder: Wayne and Marsha Kenley. Owner: Joanne Abramson.*

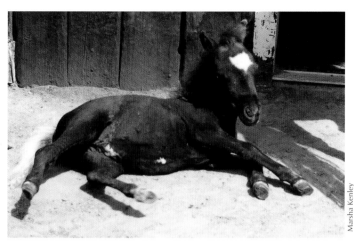

Marsha Kenley

Cloe Rehdantz

Figure 12.15 Minimally marked bay tobiano pinto *stallion,* Bond Rollback. *This stallion is registered as a solid bay because he shows no white spotting large enough to qualify for registration as a pinto. He was sired by a solid bay and his dam was a red tobiano. Rollback has consistently sired tobianos out of solid-color mares. Because the tobiano pinto gene is inherited as a dominant, this would be an impossibility were he genetically a solid color. Note the tiny white pinto marking on upper lip. Breeder: C. M. Bond. Owner: Lindalee M. Akin.*

Cloe Rehdantz

Figure 12.16 Minimally marked black tobiano pinto *stallion,* Rehs Royal Gem, *with a roan spot over withers. Royal Gem is registered as a solid black. This stallion sires about 50% tobiano pintos out of solid-color mares and is genetically a tobiano pinto (TOto). The only body spot is entirely roan (not solid white), so Royal Gem cannot be registered as a pinto. Breeder/owner: Cloe Rehdantz.*

Pam Olsen/PRO PHOTO

Figure 12.17 Chestnut tobiano pinto
mare, Bended Knee Indian Lace, *blood-tested homozygous for the tobiano allele. Note ink spots (or paw prints) on back and girth area. Indian Lace will produce 100% tobiano pintos, even if bred to solid-color non-pintos. Both sire and dam are tobianos, a genetic requirement for all homozygous tobianos. Breeder: Wayne and Marsha Kenley. Owner: Joanne Abramson.*

Figure 12.18 Black tobiano pinto
stallion, Scott Creek High Roller. *Note the black roan smudge near withers, an unusual but permanent marking. Progeny records indicate that High Roller's genotype is* Toto Ee. *Breeder: Larry and Joanne Ross. Owner: Kim Sterchi.*

©Amy Toner

Figure 12.19 Bay tobiano pinto
stallion, Stiehls Apache Splash, *blood-tested homozygous for the tobiano allele. Even though this stallion has four white legs (masking his black points), the black forelock and tail verify that Apache Splash is a bay, not a chestnut. All bay pintos (sometimes incorrectly called tri-colors) must have black points except where spotted with white markings. Breeder: Gerald and Joan Flaby. Owner: Joe and Sandy Wesner.*

Sandy Wesner

Jim Børtvedt

Figure 12.20 Minimally marked dark liver chestnut tobiano pinto *stallion*, Flabys Supreme. *Supreme has very minimal white pinto markings, including a partially white tail, but sires well-marked pintos out of solid-color mares. Supreme has also sired three overos out of solid-color mares. Breeder: Gerald and Joan Flaby. Owner: Nancy Rivenburgh.*

Jim Børtvedt

Figure 12.21 Sorrel tobiano pinto *colt*, Rivenburghs Supreme in Technicolor. *Although this colt is sired by Flabys Supreme (the minimally marked tobiano shown in Figure 12.20) and is out of a solid color mare, Technicolor has a much larger area of white than his sire. This phenomenon is common in pinto breeding. Breeder/owner: Nancy Rivenburgh.*

Figure 12.22 Sorrel tobiano pinto *colt with blue eyes, Rodabi-J Paiute Pogonip. Pogonip is sired by a brown-eyed tobiano with very little white and is out of a solid sorrel mare with very small blue eye flecks. This colt has inherited blue eyes and much more white than either of his parents. Although almost a medicine hat, Pogonip is tobiano, not overo. Breeder: Barbara Naviaux. Owner: Carole Resor.*

LiLa Foucher

Figure 12.23 Chocolate silver tobiano pinto gelding, Rivenburgh Farms Hank the Cowboy. *Note that the color is not brown or chestnut pinto, as this gelding carries the silver (Z) allele and has a white mane and tail. Breeder/ owner: Nancy Rivenburgh.*

Jim Børtvedt

Figure 12.24 Bay tobiano pinto stallion, Rodabi-J Shot in the Dark. *This stallion's sire was a red tobiano and his dam was a silver dapple tobiano, both having light manes and tails. Shot in the Dark's bay coloration with black mane and tail had to come from his dam, whose silver dapple genotype is masking her base color of black. Breeder: Barbara Naviaux. Owner: Pat Meier.*

Barbara Naviaux

Kim Sterchi

Figure 12.25 Silver bay *stallion,* Pheasant Dreams Stretch. *Note the chocolate-colored legs and silvery mane and tail, both of which clearly distinguish this color from a chestnut with flaxen mane and tail. Breeder: Jo Hastings. Owner: Allan Toner.*

Barbara Naviaux

Figure 12.26 Silver bay *daughter of stallion in Figure 12.25,* Sierras Amberlita. *This illustrates the typical coat color appearance of a 4-month-old silver bay. If the reddish body hair is parted, the undercoat appears smoky gray. When born, Amberlita's dark lower legs were silver, the tail was fringed in white and the mane was brownish gray, not white. Breeder: Kim Sterchi. Owner: Dixie Baker.*

Barbara Naviaux

Figure 12.27 Silver dapple *yearling colt,* Half Measures Silver Legacy, *after being body clipped. Note the vividly striped hooves that often accompany each of the silver dapple patterns. This colt has no appaloosa background, and the striped hooves are genetically due to the Z allele only. Breeder/owner: Dennis Haney.*

Figure 12.28 Silver chestnut tobiano pinto *stallion,* Rehs Patriarch. *Patriarch is registered as a sorrel pinto. Because Patriarch has sired several silver dapples and silver bays when bred to black pointed bays and solid blacks (neither of which can carry the silver allele), he has proven to be genetically a silver chestnut. Although often mistaken for a palomino, Patriarch does not carry the cremello allele that is a genetic requirement for palominos. Breeder: Cloe Rehdantz. Owner: Barbara Naviaux.*

Figure 12.29 Silver chestnut *filly,* Rodabi-J Strawberry Delight. *Note the flaxen legs (not white socks), mane, and tail. Delight's mane was red at birth. This filly's silver allele is well hidden because she has no areas on her body or points that would ordinarily be black. The silver allele works primarily by diluting black, not red. Breeder: Barbara Naviaux. Owner: Ron and Gina Fritzke.*

Barbara Naviaux

Figures 12.30 and 12.31 show the progression of one shade of silver dapple, as a foal that was originally born red ages into adulthood.

Figure 12.30 Silver dapple filly, Unicorn Lotsa Spirit, *sired by a silver chestnut stallion and out of a solid black mare (who cannot carry the silver gene). Born a bright red chestnut, Spirit is shown here still in the red phase, just prior to body clipping. Breeder/ owner: Cheryl Berner.*

Barbara Naviaux

Figure 12.31 Silver dapple filly, Unicorn Lotsa Spirit, *same filly as shown in Figure 12.30, but now body clipped. Breeder/ owner: Cheryl Berner.*

Cheryl Berner

Figure 12.32 Chocolate silver *mare*, Creme D'Mocha, *with 1-month-old chocolate silver filly*, Rodabi-J Cafe Au Lait *(foal will darken with age). Note that the foal's mane is not yet white. Mocha is a uniform cocoa color, except for the white mane and tail, and rarely shows any dappling pattern. Breeder of mare: Unknown. Owner of mare: Barbara Naviaux. Breeder of foal: Barbara Naviaux. Owner of foal: Fran Nicolai.*

Barbara Naviaux

Barbara Naviaux

Figure 12.33 Chocolate silver *filly*, Rodabi-J Cafe Au Lait, *same as shown in Figure 12.32, but at age 4 months. The mane and tail are now white, but the body color has not yet darkened to the final adult shade. Breeder: Barbara Naviaux. Owner: Fran Nicolai.*

Figures 12.34 and 12.35 show the progression of another shade of silver dapple, as a foal that was originally born silvery gray ages into adulthood.

Figure 12.34 Silver dapple tobiano pinto, Rodabi-J Crystal Vision, *just a few hours old. Because Crystal's dam is a black and cannot carry the silver (dapple) or tobiano pinto alleles, Crystal's coloration had to come from her silver chestnut tobiano sire. Breeder: Barbara Naviaux. Owner: Julia Ramos.*

Barbara Naviaux

Julia Ramos

Figure 12.35 Silver dapple tobiano pinto, Rodabi-J Crystal Vision, *as a 3-year-old. This is the same filly as shown in Figure 12.34. Crystal Vision's color and pattern exemplify silver dapple ideals. Breeder: Barbara Naviaux. Owner: Julia Ramos.*

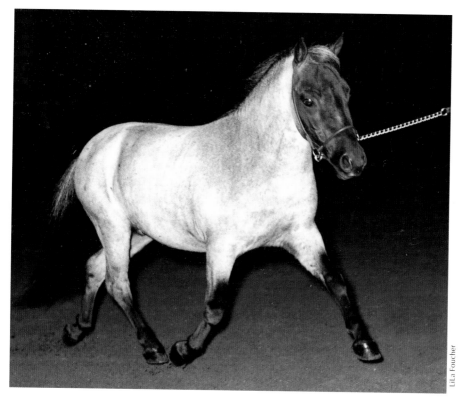

Figure 12.36 Blue roan (black roan) stallion, Komokos War Dance. *Note the black points, which are very pronounced and unlike those of a gray or a silver dapple. All roans have darker point color and, unlike the grullas (which have single-colored body hairs) have body color caused by a mixture of white hairs with other darker-colored hairs. Breeder: Joel Bridges. Owner: Jim and Valerie Bell.*

Figure 12.37 Blue roan *colt, Tomahawks Shadow Dancer, at about 1 month of age, and partially clipped. Shadow Dancer is sired by the blue roan in Figure 12.36. Note that the legs and tail have not yet turned black. Breeder/owner: Nancy Turner.*

Nancy Turner

Figure 12.38 Silver bay roan *mare,* Komokos Shoshonee Maiden, *dam of the blue roan,* Komokos War Dance, *shown in Figure 12.36. Shoshonee Maiden's color, although very unusual, may be easily identified because of her light mane and tail, chocolate muzzle and lower legs and her overall roan pattern. Breeder: Joel Bridges. Owner: Nancy Turner.*

Nancy Turner

Wade Burns

Figure 12.39 Gray *stallion,* Lucky Four Strike Me Silver. *Note that the head is basically the same color as the neck, which is fairly typical for grays but not for blue roans. Strike me Silver is in the process of turning white, after being born black. Breeder/owner: Wade Burns.*

Lynn Ingles

Figure 12.40 Gray (born black) tobiano pinto *colt,* Inglemist Photo Flash, *sired by a gray stallion. Note the white hairs on upper eyelids and muzzle, which are the first indication that this colt is actually a genetic gray and will eventually lose the definition of the black pinto markings at maturity. Breeder/owner: Lynn Ingles.*

Figure 12.41 Gray tobiano pinto, Inglemist Photo Flash, *same colt as shown in Figure 12.40, in the process of turning white after being born a black pinto. Breeder/owner: Lynn Ingles.*

Lynn Ingles

Figures 12.42, 12.43 and 12.44 show the progression of chestnut to rose-gray to white on a gray miniature horse born red.

Lynn Ingles

Figure 12.42 Gray (born red) *foal,* Inglemist Dominique Sunshane, *at 3 months of age, showing first facial shed. Breeder/owner: Lynn Ingles.*

Figure 12.43 Gray, now rose-gray (born red) *foal at 4 months,* Inglemist Dominique Sunshane, *same foal as shown in Figure 12.42. Breeder/ owner: Lynn Ingles.*

Lynn Ingles

Lynn Ingles

Figure 12.44 Gray (born red) *colt as a yearling,* Inglemist Dominique Sunshane, *same horse as shown in Figures 12.42 and 12.43. Breeder/ owner: Lynn Ingles.*

Marjorie Vliet

Figure 12.45 Silver white *mare,* Thunderhead's Stardust, *with her newly born black filly,* Deer Haven Sparkle, *sired by a black tobiano. Sparkle has remained black in adulthood because she did not inherit the Z, G, or TO alleles from either of her parents. Silver whites, first described more than 40 years ago, are the phenotype that results when the individual carries both a silver allele (Z) and a gray allele (G). Unlike traditional grays (which are born any darker coat color than white) silver whites are sometimes born white (see Table 12.1). Note the mare's black skin and dark eyes. Breeder/owner: Marjorie Vliet.*

Figure 12.46 Buckskin dun *stallion,* Rodabi-J Vanishing Point. *Note the much darker points, the dark withers and the zebra markings on hock. A dun's mane, tail and lower legs are usually darker than its overall body color. Although not visible in this photograph, the darker-colored dorsal stripe (line-back) that begins at the forelock and runs down the back to the end of the tail vertebrae is also typical of duns. This phenomenon causes Vanishing Point's forelock, mane, line-back and tail all to be black. Zebra markings and a dorsal line-back are requirements for all duns. Breeder: Barbara Naviaux. Owner: David Ochs.*

Barbara Naviaux

Figure 12.47 Unnamed color and pattern, *shown on* Gold Hill Ice Angel, *a mature mare. This is the phenotype resulting when the dun gene is combined with the silver (dapple) gene. Unlike a typical dun, the mane and tail are lighter than the body color because of the silver gene, but Ice Angel has the typical dun characteristics of a dorsal stripe (line-back) with zebra markings (far right) on her legs. Progeny records indicate that the genotype is probably ZzDd. Breeder/owner: Lindalee M. Akin.*

 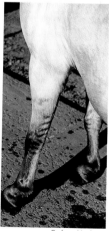

Barbara Naviaux

Figure 12.48
Buckskin *stallion,* Just
Bronco. *Buckskins
(not buckskin duns)
have a single copy of
the cremello dilution
gene, which results in
the dilution of only
red, not black. This
phenomenon allows a
base-colored bay
horse to retain its
black points, even
though the red body
is diluted to a much
lighter shade of beige.
Breeder: Marguerite
Coxe. Owner: Kim
Sterchi.*

Figure 12.49 Buckskin *filly,* Samis Just Bananas Premadonna, *sired by* Shadow
Oaks Top Banana *(a buckskin), and out of a chestnut mare. Note that the legs
are not yet black, which is typical of buckskin foals. Breeder: Sami and Ron
Scheuring. Owner: Carmen Jacobsen.*

Figure 12.50 Buckskin stallion, Longview Royal T, showing the frost overlay on mane and tail that sometimes occurs with this color. These frost markings are rarely observed because the manes and tails of buckskins legally may be color-enhanced to jet black for show purposes. Breeder: Thomas R. Phillips. Owner: Lynn Ingles.

Lynn Ingles

Figure 12.51 Buckskin stallion, Boones Little Buckeroo 2nd. This stallion was sired by the buckskin, Boones Little Buckeroo, and is out of a dark bay mare. Like most other buckskins, Buckeroo 2nd carries a single copy of the cremello allele. Breeder: Lowell and Marie Boone. Owner: Barbara and Nolan Norman, Ray and Betty Jean Kaliski.

©Amy Toner

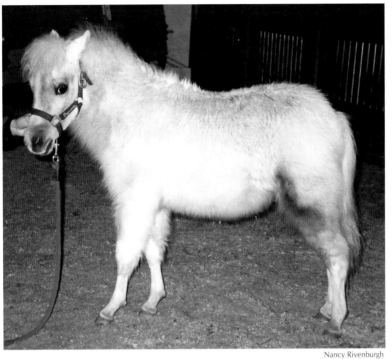

Figure 12.52 Palomino tobiano pinto colt, Rivenburghs Goin Bananas, at age 9 months and in winter coat. Both of this colt's parents were black pintos. Because a single cremello dilution gene does not affect black coat color and because red is recessive to black, it was known that each parent could carry the needed (but hidden) dilution factors, without showing them in their actual coat color. One of Bananas' parents had to contribute a cremello gene and both had to contribute a red gene to the final genotype. Breeder/owner: Nancy Rivenburgh.

Nancy Rivenburgh

Jim Bortvedt

Figure 12.53 Palomino tobiano pinto colt, Rivenburghs Goin Bananas, same horse as shown in Figure 12.48, but at 18 months. In this photograph, Bananas is body clipped and all of the pinto markings are now clearly visible. Breeder/owner: Nancy Rivenburgh.

Julia Ramos

Figure 12.54 Cremello mare, Winter Creeks Golden Jubilee. *This mare is not an albino or a white. Jubilee shows the effect of a double dose of the cremello gene, one inherited from the dam (a palomino) and another one inherited from the sire (a dark brown). With tannish pink skin, blue eyes and creamy white hair coat, Jubilee is an excellent example of cremello coloration. Breeder/owner: Julia Ramos.*

Nikki Vartikian

Figure 12.55 Dark brown stallion, HNF's Quapau, *sire of cremello filly in Figure 12.54. Quapau carries a hidden cremello gene and has sired both palominos and buckskins out of non-cremello carrier mares. Because the cremello gene (C^{cr}) does not affect black when only a single copy is present, blacks and browns can carry the allele without showing it. Breeder: Jo Hastings. Owner: Vel Branscum.*

Figure 12.56 Perlino foal, Inglemist My Golden Toy. *Note the slightly darker mane and tail, and the blue eyes. Golden Toy is the result of breeding a palomino to a buckskin. Perlinos or cremellos can be expected about 25% of the time when palominos and/or buckskins are bred to each other. Perlinos are base-colored bays, being affected by a double dose of the cremello gene. Breeder/owner: Lynn Ingles.*

Lynn Ingles

Figure 12.57 Chestnut (Sorrel or Red) *stallion, Sids Rebel, a solid red with a dark (self-colored) mane and tail. The dark points indicate that this stallion does not carry the silver (dapple) gene. His genotype is eezz, not EeZz. Breeder: Sid and Norma Rodehorst. Owner: Wade Burns and Jon Woodring.*

Wade Burns

LiLa Foucher

Figure 12.58 Seal brown *stallion, Sierra's Stetson. Black-pigmented horses (E-) can be black, brown, bay, buckskin, black roan (blue roan), or grulla. Brown horses fall between black and bay in the darkness of their body color, but the points must be black. Note Stetson's black points. If an almost black horse has lighter points, it is a liver chestnut, having an ee genotype. Breeder/owner: Kim Sterchi.*

Figure 12.59 Blood bay colt, Rodabi-J Cafe Francais, *shortly after birth. Note the silver-colored lower legs, muzzle and tail, which will all shed out to black by age 3 months. The sire is a silver chestnut and the dam is a chocolate silver (masking black). Both sire and dam have flaxen manes and tails. This is an example of two miniatures incorrectly registered as chestnuts producing a bay (with black mane and tail), a phenomenon that cannot occur in most full-sized breeds of horses. Breeder/owner: Barbara Naviaux.*

Barbara Naviaux

Figure 12.60 Blood bay mare, Rodabi-J Spindrift Bay, *shown unbathed and in her natural summer coat and color. Note that the points of a bay are black in adulthood. Breeder: Barbara Naviaux. Owner: Ron and Gina Fritzke.*

Barbara Naviaux

Figure 12.61 Mahogany bay *yearling filly, Rodabi-J Garnet Bay, shortly after being clipped. The dark red top coat has all been clipped off and the horse now appears to be brown. Breeder: Barbara Naviaux. Owner: Julia Ramos.*

Figure 12.62 Black *filly at birth, Rodabi-J Ima Raven, illustrating the typical grayish coloration of a foal that will later turn black. Raven's sire is a black tobiano and her dam is a red tobiano. Both parents are heterozygous for tobiano pinto, so 25% of their foals can be expected to be solid colors. Breeder/owner: Barbara Naviaux.*

Barbara Naviaux

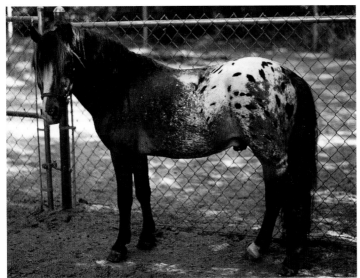

Figure 12.63 Bay spotted blanket appaloosa, Rodabi-J Tattoo, at age 23. This stallion has unknown background. Although he has been bred primarily to solid colors and pintos, Tattoo has sired 100% appaloosas, so he is probably homozygous for his appaloosa genotype. Breeder: Unknown. Owner: Barbara Naviaux.

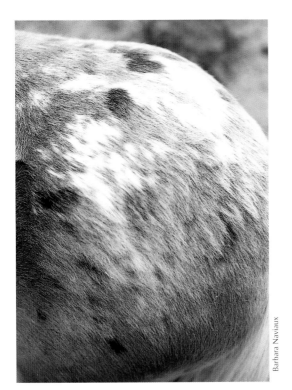

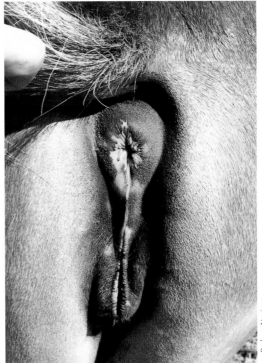

Figure 12.64 Chocolate silver spotted blanket appaloosa mare (hindquarters), Rodabi-J Tattoo's Last Tango, sired by Rodabi-J Tattoo, shown in Figure 12.63. Tango's dam is a silver bay. The overlaid and much darker spots (melanin concentrations) are typical of this particular appaloosa pattern and coloration. Breeder/owner: Barbara Naviaux.

Figure 12.65 Bay appaloosa mare, Rodabi-J Micro Dot, showing genital spotting. Micro Dot was born solid bay with only one small, pink rectal spot and striped hooves, but with no other appaloosa markings or characteristics. In this photograph, taken at 1 year, the genital mottling has noticeably increased. At maturity, this mare shows heavy skin mottling and pronounced roaning, with snowflake spotting over entire neck, back, sides and hindquarters. Micro Dot's sire is Rodabi-J Tattoo, shown in Figure 12.63. Breeder/owner: Barbara Naviaux.

Figure 12.66 Black appaloosa stallion, Toyland Little Sombrero, sired by a black leopard and out of a solid black dam with appaloosa parentage. Sombrero's get include a high percentage of appaloosa foals out of solid-color mares. Breeder: Laurie Stevens. Owner: Cloe Rehdantz.

Figure 12.67 Silver bay appaloosa stallion, Harris Polka Dot, at age 9, during a dark-color phase of this stallion's adulthood. Polka Dot's coloration at ages 5 through 8, and again, at ages 10 through 13, is much whiter (with very few red markings). This stallion's progeny have been 100% appaloosa. Breeder: D. L. Rawlinson. Owners: Jim Curry and Barbara Naviaux.

Jim Børtvedt

Figure 12.68 Minimally marked chestnut pintaloosa *(both pinto and appaloosa markings) mare, Rivenburghs Mariah. This mare is registered as a red roan. She does not carry the* RN *allele, however, and Mariah's roan pattern is due only to the appaloosa genotype. Note the mottled lips and self-colored head, which would be much darker than her body color if she were a roan. Breeder/ owner: Nancy Rivenburgh.*

K. C. Montgomery

Figure 12.69 Bay tobiano pintaloosa *(both tobiano pinto and appaloosa markings) filly,* Tomahawks Sparkling Image, *sired by* Brewers Orion Image, *a pintaloosa son of* Orion Light Van't Huttenest *(also a pintaloosa). Breeder/ owner: Nancy Turner.*

Figure 12.70 Black overo pintaloosa (both overo pinto and appaloosa markings) colt, Haligonian Halation. *Note the apron face and overo markings under chest, neck and underbelly. Breeder/ owner: Harriett Rubins.*

Harriett Rubins

Pete West

Figure 12.71 Silver bay tovero pintaloosa (tobiano, overo, and appaloosa markings) stallion with blue eyes, Rodabi-J Aztec Ariston. *Before clipping, Ariston's markings appeared to be dark red, but because of being a typical silver bay, the undercoat was light gray. The darker liver spots (melanin concentrations) are typical of all silver-gened appaloosas. Breeder/owner: Barbara Naviaux.*

Figure 12.72 Silver bay tovero pintaloosa, Rodabi-J Aztec Ariston *(same horse as in Figure 12.71), but as a 2-year-old, and in a natural summer coat. Ariston's sire is a dark-eyed, non-overo silver chestnut tobiano and the dam is a silver dapple appaloosa with blaze face and one blue eye. Breeder/owner: Barbara Naviaux.*

Barbara Naviaux

Jane Macon

Figure 12.73 Chestnut leopard appaloosa *stallion,* Carousel Custom Design. *Custom Design was born with the same pattern and coloration as shown in adulthood, which is a requirement for leopard appaloosas. Custom Design is shown here with a 1996 chestnut leopard appaloosa son,* Orion Pleasure, *out of a Brewers Orion Illusion daughter. Breeder of stallion: Carole Ann Ford. Breeder of foal: Vincente Fernandez. Owner of both: Vincente Fernandez.*

Figure 12.74 Buckskin dun spotted blanket appaloosa *stallion,* McArthurs Imperial Gold Dust. *Gold Dust is sired by a buckskin dun stallion and is out of a blue roan appaloosa mare. Breeder: Jackie McArthur. Owner: Kim Sterchi and Jim and Valerie Bell.*

LiLa Foucher

Figure 12.75 Silver white appaloosa mare, Jandt's Ecstacy, who has lost any visible appaloosa hair markings because of the gray allele. Ecstacy has retained all of the appaloosa skin mottling and has produced appaloosa foals sired by non-appaloosa stallions. Silver whites carry both the silver dapple gene and the gray gene and are sometimes white at birth. Breeder: Joseph Jandt. Owner: Mona Stone.

Figure 12.76 Gray appaloosa stallion, Goodins Popcorn Ball, showing genital area. Although losing all dark-haired body spotting because of the gray allele, Popcorn Ball has retained all of the black appaloosa skin mottling. Breeder: James and Sarah Goodin. Owner: Betty Epplin.

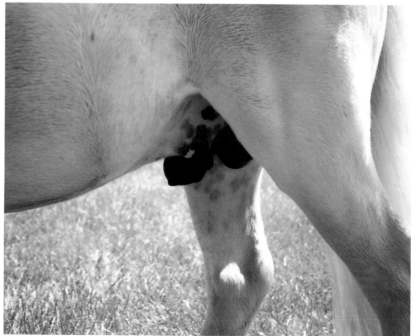

Figure 12.77 Sorrel spotted blanket appaloosa colt, Celebrations Reno Royale, *sired by a solid sorrel and out of a black mare with appaloosa characteristics but with no obvious appaloosa pattern. Breeder: Phil and Shari Washburn. Owner: Carmen and Sue Millhorn.*

Shari Washburn

©Amy Toner

Figure 12.78 Sorrel spotted blanket appaloosa stallion, Celebrations Reno Royale, *same horse as in Figure 12.77 but as an adult. Note that this stallion's white areas are quite similar to those he was born with, but the appearance of melanin concentration spots over the rump is now evident. The dark mane and tail indicate that Reno Royale does not carry a Z allele. Breeder: Phil and Shari Washburn. Owner: Carmen and Sue Millhorn.*

Nancy Turner

Figure 12.79 Black near leopard appaloosa *mare,* Mini Dreams Suchadoll Babee, *as a yearling. This filly was born a black appaloosa with hip blanket only. The percentage of white has been steadily increasing since birth, which indicates that Babee is a near leopard. Breeder: Louis T. Fontes. Owner: Nancy Turner.*

Caroline Fyfie

Figure 12.80 Black near leopard *mare,* Mini Dreams Suchadoll Babee, *as a 4-year-old (same horse as shown in Figure 12.79). Note the decreasing amount of black on this mare's neck, head and legs. Also note that the tail has turned from black to white. Breeder: Louis and Virginia Fontes. Owner: Nancy Turner.*

CHAPTER 13

Marketing

O NLY A SMALL PERCENTAGE OF THE BREEDERS in the miniature horse industry make most of the sales. Of the more than 15,000 miniature horses registered each year in the United States, it is estimated that at least 10,000 are being supplied to the local (mostly pet) markets within the general vicinity of each selling farm. Few small- and mid-sized breeders sell many horses outside of their own geographical vicinity. Widespread, consistent advertising coupled with frequent wins at the shows are two of the most common strategies many breeders use to increase sales. Some ranches with many highly satisfied customers throughout a large area, however, are able to depend almost solely upon their excellent reputations. Success in the marketing phase of miniature horse production can be attained by observing and implementing the techniques being used by the industry's most successful breeders and sellers.

Miniature horses are usually kept for one of two primary reasons: first, a business with the aim of financial gain; second, a hobby with the aim of pleasure and companionship. Unless an owner never acquires more horses than he or she wishes to own (by purchasing or breeding), selling a horse eventually becomes necessary. Many modern horse farms are sophisticated businesses, with computerized pedigree, reproduction, health, management, tax and sales records. In the United States, tax regulations recently have been revised for horse ranch operations, but the first and most important qualification, according to the Internal Revenue Service (IRS), is whether the owner considers the horse operation to be a hobby or a business. Proof of business intent is sometimes difficult to document; taxpayers usually have no more than 7 years in which to demonstrate a profit. It is important that ranch owners consult with experienced horse business accountants or attorneys who are familiar with current tax laws. Under the IRS code, a horse business must be operated with "the actual and honest objective of making a profit" (Craigo 1998). In determining whether a horse operation is a business or a hobby, the IRS considers some of the following factors (Ensminger 1990):

- Accurate record-keeping, business-like activity and conduct by the horseman
- Expertise of horseman and employees
- Time and effort invested
- The expectation that assets will appreciate
- Prior business successes
- The operation's history of income and losses
- Pattern of profits (occasional or consistent)

- Financial status of the horseman (Is the business possibly used only as a tax shelter?)
- Elements of recreation or pleasure

In addition to having a business plan, the successful marketing of miniature horses requires maintaining healthy horses. Consistent production of sleek (with natural summer coats, or body clipped), well-nourished, well-trained animals is required. In the process of **fitting** (conditioning) show or sale horses, a miniature's finish must remain firm and hard, the action superb, and the soundness unquestioned. Horses must be brought gradually into condition. The cost of producing miniature horses may be lowered by limiting the number of ranch employees, utilizing permanent pastures, keeping horses free of parasites, vaccinating regularly, providing balanced rations, and increasing fertility levels in both stallions and mares (Ensminger 1990). Cost containment should be a consideration but should never result in the sacrifice of quality horse care. Well-kept (vaccinated, wormed, trimmed) horses normally sell for a higher price than those from poorly managed farms or hobby breeders, and educated buyers prefer to support well-managed operations.

Ethics

In all aspects of marketing, it is crucial for buyers to be so completely satisfied with their new purchase that they not only become repeat customers but also become the selling breeder's ranch emissaries. A satisfied buyer's recommendations to friends and acquaintances are that customer's gifts to an ethical miniature horse breeder. Cultivating appreciative clientele depends upon honest, professional, ethical management of every horse sale. Breeders committed to such principles follow certain essential guidelines of operation:

- They maintain clean, well-managed facilities that are not overcrowded.
- They offer contented, healthy horses that are accurately represented.
- They keep meticulous written (or computerized) records on each horse, not just on those being sold.
- They demonstrate a polite, caring attitude, always welcoming visitors to the ranch and expressing eagerness to meet and help new miniature horse enthusiasts, even those who are not buying.
- They offer friendly foals that have been handled frequently and affectionately.
- They freely offer information on health care, management and the breed.
- They keep necessary paperwork current, including registrations, stallion reports, pedigrees, veterinary records, etc.
- They ask potential buyers about their ranches and future plans for involvement with miniature horses.
- They try to determine the type of horse that best suits a prospective customer's needs.
- They answer all inquiries promptly and courteously.
- They price their horses realistically and are willing to work with buyers with limited finances.

- They encourage potential buyers to visit shows, sales, and other ranches to compare quality and prices.
- They offer friendship and clientele support long after the initial sale.

Keeping Accurate Records

An essential requirement for any breeder seeking to develop a successful marketing program is keeping accurate records. Foals must be registered before 6 months of age, and adults must be registered as permanent (with their adult height recorded) at 3 years of age (in AMHR) or at 5 years of age (in AMHA). DNA testing or blood typing is required of certain horses and foals in AMHA; specifics are available from the registry. Annual stallion reports are required by each registry; foals sired by stallions not reported in the previous year cannot be registered. There are significant penalties for any late registrations or transfer of ownership applications.

In AMHA, current photographs are required with all registrations and transfers of ownership. The manner in which photographs are taken and the poses required are strictly monitored and are described with the forms provided. If taken incorrectly, photographs are returned and new photographs are requested. For the registration of new foals, it is usually best to take photographs within the first few weeks. Markings become less distinct as the foal ages and its hair increases in length. It is frequently necessary to update a horse's registered color as a foal before it is old enough to register permanently, since certain markings and colors change radically from weanling age to adulthood at 3 years old (see Chapter 12). In AMHR, drawings illustrating the foal's markings must be submitted. When the markings are extensive, these drawings can be rendered more accurately if copied from good-quality photographs.

Height Prediction

The American Miniature Horse breed is a height-based breed with the adult height required to not exceed specific protocols, depending on the registry. Predicting the mature height of young miniature horses can be challenging, and breeders have experimented with many methods. Some breeders even specialize in specific adult heights. For example, some owners want taller horses for pulling carts; others may want only the smaller horses. There is great interest in knowing what size a foal will be as an adult. The most commonly used four methods are described.

Method One Measuring the length of the cannon bone is probably the easiest and most accurate method. It involves measuring a newborn foal from the cannon bone down to the coronary band (see Figure 13.1), multiplying by 4, and adding 2 inches (5.08 cm). Example: 7-inch (17.78-cm) cannon bone x 4 = 28 inches (71.12 cm) + 2 = 30 inches (76.2 cm) predicted mature height.

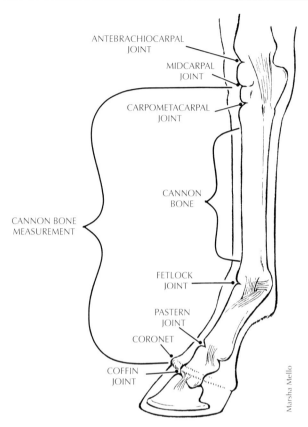

ANTEBRACHIOCARPAL
JOINT

MIDCARPAL
JOINT

CARPOMETACARPAL
JOINT

CANNON
BONE

CANNON BONE
MEASUREMENT

FETLOCK
JOINT

PASTERN
JOINT

CORONET

COFFIN
JOINT

Marsha Mello

Figure 13.1 *Proper cannon bone measurement parameters*

Table 13.1 Comparison of Foal Heights and Cannon Bone Length on 30 Miniature Horse Foals*

Adapted from Abramson 1998b

Criteria Number of Foals	Height 30	Cannon Bone Length 30
Minimum	17.5 in. (44.45 cm)	6 in. (15.24 cm)
Maximum	23 in. (58.42 cm)	8.5 (21.59 cm)
Average	19.83 in. (50.37 cm)	7.23 (18.36 cm)

Data collected by Marsha Kenley at Bended Knee Miniature Horse Farm 1991–1997.

Initial heights were taken on foaling day (using the standard AMHA method for measuring) and varied from 17.5 to 23 inches (44.45 to 58.42 cm) with an average of 19.83 inches (50.37 cm). Initial height was not found to always correlate with the final height (e.g., one 20-inch [50.8-cm] foal was only 25 inches [63.5 cm] as a yearling). The initial height may correlate more with genetic or foaling (premature, term or post-mature) factors other than the final, mature height. The cannon bone was measured from the upper epiphyseal surface of the front cannon bone, straight down the leg to the coronary band (see Figure 13.1). In this study cannon bone length proved to be the most accurate method of determining the mature height of the foal. Foals that had an initial cannon bone measurement of 6 to 7 inches (15.24 to 17.78 cm) were 28 inches (71.12 cm) or less as yearlings.

Method Two Another method involves measuring the height at the withers of the 3-day-old foal. The standard AMHA/AMHR method for measuring was used (see Figure 13.2). When the foal is exactly 12 weeks old, the height at the withers is measured again. The difference between these two measurements is added to the total 12-week-old height in order to predict the adult height. Example: A foal at 3 days measures 20 inches (50.8 cm), and at 12 weeks it measures 26 inches (66.04 cm). 26 inches - 20 inches = 6 inches (66.04 cm - 50.8 cm =15.24 cm). 26 inches + 6 inches = 32 inches (66.04 cm + 15.24 cm = 81.28 cm) predicted adult height. In 1989, 1990 and 1991, records on 14 miniature horses were calculated using this method. The total foal crop for each of those 3 years was included, and the list includes both AMHA- and AMHR-registered horses. The results are tabulated in Table 13.2.

Table 13.2 Results of One Farm's Method of Predicting Miniature Horse Adult Height*

Heights					
Sire's	Dam's	Foal's at 3 Days	Foal's at 12 Weeks	Predicted Adult	Mature at 5 Years
32.25 in. 81.91 cm	32.5 in. 82.55 cm	20 in. 50.8 cm	26 in. 66.04 cm	32 in. 81.28 cm	33 in. 83.82 cm
32.25 in. 81.91 cm	31 in. 78.74 cm	19 in. 48.26 cm	25 in. 63.5 cm	31 in. 78.74 cm	30.5 in. 77.47 cm
32.25 in. 81.91 cm	33 in. 83.83 cm	22 in. 55.88 cm	28 in. 71.12 cm	34 in. 86.36 cm	34 in. 86.36 cm
32.25 in. 81.91 cm	32.5 in. 82.55 cm	20 in. 50.8 cm	25.25 in 64.14 cm	30.5 in 77.47 cm	31 in. 78.74 cm
33.50 in. 85.09 cm	31 in. 78.74 cm	22 in. 55.88 cm	26.5 in. 67.31 cm	31 in. 78.74 cm	32 in. 81.28 cm
32.25 in. 81.91 cm	38 in. 96.52 cm	21.5 in. 54.61 cm	28 in. 71.12 cm	34.5 in. 87.63 cm	34 in. 86.36 cm
33.50 in. 85.09 cm	37 in. 93.98 cm	22 in. 55.88 cm	27.5 in. 69.85 cm	33 in. 83.82 cm	33 in. 83.82 cm
32.25 in. 81.91 cm	33 in. 83.82 cm	22 in. 55.88 cm	27 in. 68.58 cm	32 in. 81.28 cm	32 in. 81.28 cm
32.25 in. 81.91 cm	35 in. 88.90 cm	22 in. 45.72 cm	26 in. 66.04 cm	34 in. 86.36 cm	33.5 in. 85.09 cm
32.25 in. 81.91 cm	31 in. 78.74 cm	18 in. 49.53 cm	25 in. 63.5 cm	30.5 in. 77.47 cm	31.5 in. 80.01 cm
32.25 in. 81.91 cm	32.5 in. 82.55 cm	21 in. 53.34 cm	26.6 in. 67.31 cm	32 in. 81.28 cm	32.5 in. 82.55 cm
32.25 in. 81.91 cm	32 in. 81.28 cm	20 in. 50.8 cm	27 in. 68.58 cm	34 in. 86.36 cm	35 in. 88.9 cm
32.25 in. 81.91 cm	32.25 in. 95.25cm	24 in. 60.96 cm	30 in. 76.2 cm	36 in. 91.44 cm	36 in. 91.44 cm
32.25 in. 81.91 cm	32.25 in. 96.52 cm	20 in. 50.8 cm	27 in. 68.58 cm	34 in. 86.36 cm	34 in. 87.63 cm

Data collected at Rodabi-J Ranch 1989–1991.

Foals were measured at 3 days and again at 12 weeks. The difference between these two measurements was added to the 12-week height in order to calculate a predicted adult height.

LAST HAIRS
OF MANE

Figure 13.2 How to measure a miniature horse: The height of a miniature horse is the vertical distance from the last hairs of the mane to the ground when the animal is standing squarely on a level area.

Method Three   Another method of predicting adult height calculates heights at maturity on the basis of heights at younger ages. These calculations assume that miniature horses at certain ages achieve predictable percentages of their adult height. The chart using these predictions is shown in Table 13.3 and was formulated in Canada (Williams 1992).

Table 13.3 Height at Maturity Calculated by Age of Foal in Months

	Height at Maturity							
Age in Months	28"	29"	30"	31"	32"	33"	34"	36"
Birth	18.20	18.85	19.50	20.15	20.80	21.45	21.95	23.40
1	19.60	20.30	21.00	21.70	22.40	23.10	23.80	25.20
2	21,56	22.33	23.10	23.87	24.64	25.41	26.18	27.72
3	22.40	23.20	24.00	24.80	25.60	26.40	27.20	28.80
4	22.96	23.78	24.60	25.42	26.24	27.06	27.88	29.52
5	23.52	24.36	25.20	26.04	26.88	27.72	28.56	30.24
6	23.80	24.65	25.50	26.35	27.20	28.05	28.90	30.60
7	24.08	24.94	25.80	26.66	27.52	28.38	29.24	30.96
8	24.36	25.23	26.10	26.97	27.84	28.71	29.58	31.32
9	24.64	25.52	26.40	27.28	28.16	29.04	29.92	31.68
12	25.20	26.10	27.00	27.90	28.80	29.70	30.60	32.40
15	25.75	26.28	27.60	28.52	29.44	30.36	31.28	33.12
18	26.32	27.26	28.20	29.14	30.08	31.02	31.96	33.84
21	26.74	27.70	28.65	29.61	30.56	31.52	32.47	34.48
24	27.15	28.13	29.10	30.07	31.04	32.07	32.98	34.92
30	27.58	28.57	29.55	30.54	31.52	32.51	33.49	35.46
36	28.00	29.00	30.00	31.00	32.00	33.00	34.00	36.00

This chart was shown to be 90% accurate, with a $\frac{1}{2}$-in. (1.27-cm) plus or minus factor.

Method Four In 1990, a group of 300 mature horses from four major sales was studied for height data (Jenny 1990). Statistically, these data produced a normal curve, indicating that the data were meaningful (see Table 13.4). Although the heights of the 300 study horses were measured accurately at each sale, the heights of their sires and dams were only assumed to be correct and were recorded as printed on the sale horses' registration papers. Some interesting conclusions for predicting horse height were then made, as follows:

- Only 1% of the time will the foal mature more than 4 inches (10.16 cm) taller than the average of the sire's and dam's heights.

- Only 1% of the time will the foal mature less than 4 inches (10.16 cm) shorter than the average of the sire's and dam's heights.

- Breedings with an average parents' height of 32 inches (81.28 cm) will result in a 10% chance of miniatures taller than 34 inches (86.36 cm).

- Breedings with an average parents' height of 31 inches (78.74 cm) will result in only a 1% chance of miniatures taller than 34 inches (86.36 cm).

- The results indicated that 35% to 40% of the foals will mature taller than the average of the parents' heights, and 35% to 40% of the foals will mature shorter.

Table 13.4 Heights of 300 Sale Horses Compared With Those of Their Parents*

	Number of Horses	Percentage of Horses	
4" taller	3	1	
3" taller	20	7	39% were taller than the average of both parents
2" taller	34	11	
1" taller	59	20	
0" (same height as average)	76	25	59% ±1" 82% ±2"
1" shorter	41	14	
2" shorter	36	12	36% were shorter than the average of both parents
3" shorter	28	9	
4" shorter	3	1	
Total Horses	300		

*Data collected by Ted Jenny 1990.

These data produced a normal curve, indicating that the data were meaningful.

Breeding Dates, Birth Dates and Weaning Dates

It is essential that each mare's reproduction records be regularly maintained (see Chapter 10). As mares reach the end of their pregnancies, these records can be used to predict individual idiosyncrasies, as well as the normal behavior to be expected. Buyers of pregnant mares find these records to be invaluable. Their confidence in the animal's future productivity (as well as the seller's integrity) is greatly enhanced if accurate records are readily available.

Foaling dates accompanied by clear photographs of the new foal taken in the first few weeks should be recorded and maintained by all breeders. Recording the dates foals are weaned along with worming and vaccination dates prepares the buyer with information on their future foal's needs. Advice on nutrition and additional supplements that may be required should be provided by the breeder.

Pedigrees and Prompt Registrations

Computer software for ranch management, including pedigree documentation of each horse owned, has simplified record keeping for the horse owner. Prompt registrations and accurate pedigrees are essential elements for the effective marketing of miniatures, and both can be made more readily available by the use of computer technology. Computerization of a farm's records are important if miniature horse sales at competitive prices are a priority.

Health Care, Hoof Trimming and Veterinary Records

Dates of all hoof trimmings, wormings and vaccinations for each individual should be recorded and regularly updated. Such records are crucial when selling any miniature, and the new owner should be encouraged to continue keeping detailed accounts. Many ranch veterinarians now maintain computerized records of their clients' animals that can be accessed when needed.

Advertising

The type of advertising selected depends upon the number of individuals for sale and the prices being asked for them. Some farms may spend very little on advertising, thus enabling them to sell their horses at very reasonable prices. If not carefully monitored, advertising costs, which also may include the expense of hiring trainers to compete in shows, can rapidly exceed sales income. If only a small number of horses are being marketed each year, advertising in local newspapers and magazines (such as free horse publications available at feed stores) is probably sufficient. Repeated advertising in local club newsletters and national breed magazines is more expensive but is usually essential for establishing a breeder's (or ranch stallion's) reputation.

When representing sales animals as "show-type" individuals, breeders must be cautious. There is a wide gap between horses that can win grand championships and horses that legally can be shown without being disqualified by the judge. "Show type" at a small local show is frequently not considered "show type" for a large national show.

If photographs are to be used in any advertising campaign, it is essential that they be of professional quality. Complimentary poses of well-groomed, well-nourished horses are mandatory. Potential buyers pay more attention to attractive photographs than they do to wordy advertising claims. The most effective advertisements usually have excellent photographs of fine-quality animals and minimal copy.

Buyers interested in breeding registered miniature horses and later selling their offspring need to purchase high-quality animals from reputable breeders. They also need to investigate and plan an attractive advertising campaign appropriate to the number of horses they have for sale.

Sales Contracts and Agreements

All sales contracts and sales agreements should be customized according to the seller's and buyer's stipulated preferences. Miniature foals are sometimes sold with a height guarantee, and pregnant mares are sometimes sold with a live foal guarantee. The prices for such animals may be higher than those asked for non-guaranteed animals, and such guarantees must be included in a written sales agreement. Older stallions should be certified fertile by a veterinarian after microscopic evaluation of the horse's freshly collected semen. Time payments, co-ownerships, and other special arrangements also should be specified in writing. Both buyers and sellers tend to forget verbal agreements, and it is for both of their protection that written contracts, sales agreements and clearly defined receipts are recommended.

Clientele Support After Sale

New miniature horse enthusiasts are eager to acquire accurate information about the breed, its management and proper showing techniques. Such information should be freely and enthusiastically provided by all those marketing miniature horses. Although well informed and satisfied buyers are not generally thought of as a "marketing strategy," they are essential to the overall health of the industry. Any time a buyer requests information, the seller should take the time to provide it. Clientele support may include recommending educational reading material, sharing management and grooming secrets, offering rides to club meetings and shows or helping a buyer through a mare's pregnancy and foaling. Frequent phone calls, e-mail or letters should be part of the new relationship. How is the horse doing? Is the buyer having any problems that the former owner can help with? Can the seller help the new owner with any conditioning, training or showing specifics? Has the new owner been able to locate a satisfactory farrier and veterinarian, both of whom are experienced with miniature horses?

For any novice, gentle guidance from a friendly, more experienced breeder can make the difference between enthusiastic success and possible failure with the new project. Less experienced buyers should always be treated with great care and respect, and the sale of honestly represented and reasonably priced horses is the first step toward achieving this goal. Adequate post-purchase clientele support enables everyone in the miniature horse industry to continue to expand, thrive and prosper.

Shipping and Transporting

Miniature horses may be transported in many ways, traditional and unusual. The safety of their trip should always be of primary concern, but their small size and easy-going dispositions frequently make alternative low-cost horse hauling methods satisfactory. When traveling to local shows or a short distance from the breeder to a new owner, foals and small adults may be easily transported in a car, van or truck with a camper shell (see Figure 13.3). Home-made or commercially manufactured horse boxes, which are loaded into the back of pickup trucks, may be used effectively. Specially made miniature horse trailers or even full-sized horse trailers also can be used.

Dixie Baker

Marsha Kenley

Figure 13.3 *Miniature horses can usually fit inside a pickup's camper shell. Rodabi-J Aztec Ariston travels comfortably and safely to his first show in the camper shell of a compact pickup. Breeder/owner: Barbara Naviaux.*

Figure 13.4 *The air-freight shipment of miniature horses is both safe and convenient. Bended Knee Spring Eclipse steps out of an airline-approved shipping crate. The size of the crate should allow the horse to keep its head in a normal position. A flake of straw or flat carpet remnant placed in the bottom provides a non-slip surface. Breeder: Wayne and Marsha Kenley. Owner: Joanne Abramson.*

Many buyers of their first miniature horse have no means of hauling their new purchase home, and frequently ask whether the selling price includes delivery. Most breeders find that providing safe delivery of their sales stock is appreciated by new buyers. One advantage of offering this service is that it allows the seller to view the buyer's ranch and other horses. It often becomes the basis for a valuable and lasting new friendship, and gives the buyer a positive feeling about his or her new project.

Horses being transported for longer distances may travel by air or by a professional hauling service. Foals may be rapidly and safely transported in larger-sized dog crates that are approved by most airlines as acceptable for animal air cargo. These crates are commercially available or can be custom made of plywood for a specific horse's needs. For decades, large-breed dogs such as Saint Bernards, Great Danes, and Newfoundlands have been air-freighted thousands of miles to shows and buyers. Often larger than miniature horses, these animals historically have experienced few difficulties in their air travels (see Figure 13.4). The horse seller must provide the required Coggins tests and health certificates, which vary according to local specifications. Most equine veterinarians can provide these services and paperwork, as well as complete descriptions of what is required for each proposed destination.

Reliable professional hauling services are available for all sizes of horses, including miniatures. The cost can be equivalent to or more than that of shipping by air, since air-freight costs are calculated by the weight of a horse plus its shipping crate. For larger miniatures, however, trailering is much more economical, especially if more than one horse is being shipped. These commercial carriers are generally well insured and give the horses excellent care in transit, but the lengthy travel time for cross-country hauls in a van or trailer can be very stressful to the animals.

Barbara Naviaux

Figure 13.5 *A custom-designed miniature horse trailer, capable of comfortably hauling nine miniature horses. Designed and owned by Gary Beckinger of Dream Makers Ranch, this trailer includes an ample walk-in tack room.*

Many successful miniature horse breeders make what they consider to be necessary investments in order to haul their horses to shows, sales, and purchasing clientele (see Figure 13.5). The well-appointed horse trailers and vans seen at the shows, many of which include living quarters, are expensive, but their practicality lies in the fact that it is usually preferable to haul one's own horses. Being hauled by their owners allows miniatures to experience a safer, more comfortable, less stressful trip, and is usually less expensive than hiring a professional shipper (Ambrosiano 1998).

CHAPTER 14

Shows and Show Rules

ATTENDING SHOWS IS ONE OF THE MOST EXCITING aspects of miniature horse involvement. Whether the reason for attending is to purchase a horse or to compete, shows can be a superb source of education about the breed and about the horse industry in general. Picking winners from the grandstands and comparing the results with those of the judges is an excellent way to become educated about miniature horse conformation, training and fitting techniques.

Shows provide opportunities to observe each judge's expertise and conduct, winning handler behavior, show attire, show rules, and a variety of showing techniques. The careful observer can watch what the winners are doing in each class, noting each exhibitor's body carriage, level of confidence, and manner of presenting. Are their horses in a state of vibrant good health, and are they groomed and trained to perfection? Do the handlers have their horses' full attention? What are the losers doing wrong? Why are their horses not winning?

It is helpful to subscribe to at least one of the breed registries' magazines, *Miniature Horse World*, published by the American Miniature Horse Association (AMHA); or *The Journal*, published by the American Miniature Horse Registry (AMHR) (see Sources). Additionally, an active membership in a local area's miniature horse club will provide continual announcements of the coming shows. Regular attendance at as many shows as possible, coupled with astute observation while there, will rapidly transform any novice into a seasoned miniature horse owner and potential exhibitor.

What to Expect at the First Show As an Observer

Members of any local miniature horse clubs can expect to receive **premium lists** (show specifications, class lists, announcements and entry blanks) for all of the upcoming shows. Nonmembers can obtain these by phoning the listed contact or show secretary. The premium lists contain needed information for visitors and exhibitors (such as listings for restaurants and motels, and maps), a few of the most important show rules, and announcements of any special events (such as a Saturday night exhibitors' dinner).

Observers attending a miniature horse show for the first time should request a class list, often available at no charge to the exhibitors and visiting public, at the horse show office. By following the show's class list, it is possible to become familiar with the names of the various classes, their order and the days and times they are expected to be held. The smaller shows do not usually print show catalogs, but if available, they are an excellent investment for first-time observers. It is important to listen to the show announcer carefully, since class times and the order in which they have been scheduled often are revised during the shows.

Locke Photography

Figure 14.1 *Jumping classes require much preparation, training, conditioning and athletic ability.* Sugar Creek Geronimo *is shown as he clears a 36-inch (91-cm) jump with ease. Shown and trained by Robin Hopson. Breeder: Lynda Baerthlein Marzec. Owner: Robin Hopson.*

Exhibitors, owners and trainers at shows are extremely busy preparing to show in their next event. Miniature horse exhibitors are no different in this respect from exhibitors in other specialties. Having spent many thousands of dollars to accumulate and raise their entries, and to prepare for and enter the show, exhibitors understandably are preoccupied with the meticulous preparation and flawless presentation of their horses and rarely have time to socialize.

The best way to become acquainted with exhibitors, owners and trainers at the shows is to go back into the barn areas during lunch or dinner breaks and view the stalled horses and the ranch owners' posted materials and displays. Owners or trainers who are busy grooming, bathing or otherwise readying animals for classes should not be interrupted with questions. It is always best to wait until they are sitting in front of their stalls, indicating that the exhibitors may have a little time before their horses' next class, and would probably enjoy talking with visitors and potential customers. Ranch flyers, sales lists and ribbons won at the show are usually displayed. Rosettes and trophies won generally have class descriptions printed on them, such as "Grand Champion Mare" or "First Place, Obstacle Driving."

Negative comments at the shows should be avoided. The negative or critical discussions frequently overheard at the shows are one of the worst forms of poor sportsmanship. They never serve any constructive purpose and usually cause other breeders and miniature horse owners to be cautious in their relationships with the person perpetrating them.

One of the goals of visiting a miniature horse show may be getting to know a few club members and exhibitors. Becoming acquainted with the show rules, learning about miniature horse conformation and show conditioning, and the observation of exhibitor etiquette are important as well. A primary objective of attending shows may be the purchase of a new miniature horse. Many shows present a "Parade of Sale Horses," which is usually advertised in the premium list. Sale-horse exhibition times are generally announced repeatedly over the

Figure 14.2 *All age-group halter classes require that the horse stand square and at attention. Rodabi-J Skyline Sparkler is being shown in the 2-year-old mare halter class. The judge also evaluates each entry's conformation, body condition, presentation and athletic ability at both the walk and the trot. Grand Champions and Reserve Grand Champions are then selected from the first- and second-place winners of each age-group halter class. Breeder/owner: Bill Ench and Barbara Naviaux.*

public address system. In addition, other exhibitors who have brought sale horses to the show will usually display a pedigree, a small "for sale" sign, and the asking price on the horse's stall door. Shows provide an excellent opportunity to see potential sale horses at their best, rather than ungroomed or unclipped at home in their pastures. If purchasing a horse is a possibility during the show, the visitor should come well prepared with a means of hauling it home and with sufficient funds to consummate the transaction (see Chapter 3). Bargains should be acted upon decisively, since owners who return home with their sale horses may change their minds about selling them.

What to Expect at the First Show as an Exhibitor

After receiving the premium list for a coming show, the prospective exhibitors must decide which classes they are interested in and are qualified to enter. The official rule book for the appropriate registry should be studied for any classes being considered, and the conformation of the horse should be critically compared to that specified by the Standard of Perfection, which is printed in the rule book. Becoming a member of AMHA and AMHR assures

Jim Bortvedt

Figure 14.3 *Obstacle-Driving classes include the negotiation of horses by their drivers through a series of obstacles, such as the "water and bushes" shown.* Komokos Gold Crest, *being driven by trainer Jim Curry. Breeder: Joel Bridges. Owner: Jim and Mary Coffman.*

receiving each registry's official rule book for the current year. Photocopies of the horse's registration papers (*never* the originals) are usually required when the entries are sent in. Additionally, for all AMHA-sanctioned shows, mature stallions (age 3 years and older) must have veterinary certification that both testicles are descended. AMHA (or the show management) provides the blank form required for this certification.

AMHR shows must offer a full slate of classes for miniature horses in two different height categories, Division A (34 inches [86 cm] and under) and Division B (over 34 inches [86 cm], up to and including 38 inches [97 cm]). For these reasons, there are often more classes at AMHR shows; many AMHR-sanctioned shows include classes for registered Shetlands.

AMHA show participants must measure 34 inches (86 cm) and under, and the weanling, yearling and 2-year-old halter classes are split according to their heights in each age group. Weanlings must not exceed 30 inches (76 cm), yearlings must not exceed 32 inches (81 cm), and 2-year-olds must not exceed 33 inches (84 cm). In both AMHA and AMHR, the horse's show age is determined from January 1 of its year of birth.

The number of judges who preside at shows varies; each judge has an assigned steward. Exhibitors should always follow the instructions of the stewards and judges during classes but should never attempt to carry on a conversation with any judge during the show. Ring stewards are there to assist the judges and the exhibitors in any way possible. Some shows have only one judge, while others may be separately judged by as many as six judges. If there are multiple judges, all judges and their stewards will be in the arena at the same time, which can often be confusing to a first-time exhibitor or observer. The horses are shown in their individual classes only once, with all judges evaluating them separately, and without

J Bar D Studios

Figure 14.4 *Multicolor classes are for pinto, pintaloosa and appaloosa horses only. Me He Midnight Rose, a black, suspected homozygous tobiano pinto (based on her ink spots, or paw prints), illustrates one example of the brilliant patterns and colors often seen in multicolor classes. Breeder/owner: Harry and Mary Lou Elder.*

conferring with one another. Each judge's decisions are then announced separately, with a full complement of awards presented for each set of winners. The points awarded and the final effects are the same as entering several shows separately.

Another form of multiple-judge show is practiced at the national shows, with all the judges' placings entered into a computer and numerically averaged. This results in a single winner and set of awards for each class, based upon the combined scores of all judges. The national shows for both AMHA and AMHR require specific point qualifications at local shows to enter, and each registry varies in their requirements. There are classes for conformation (halter classes) and a wide variety of performance classes at each show. There are also classes judged on the handler (showmanship classes) or on the horse's color (solid-color and multicolor classes).

Sanctioned shows must be approved by one of the two registries and must follow their rules for each class description and for the general management of the show. In this manner, the horses' wins are awarded points and year-end awards at the national level, as well as within their local club's high point and incentive programs. Many non-sanctioned events such as schooling shows, clinics, parades and other exhibitions also take place each year. Schooling shows can provide a wealth of experience and fun, and they cost very little to enter. AMHA- or AMHR-licensed judges are required at all registry-sanctioned shows, while schooling shows and clinics may obtain judges or presenters that are not certified with either registry.

Harness racing events for miniature horses have recently become popular in many areas and are often sanctioned by the International Miniature Horse Trotting and Pacing Association (IMTPA). Each horse must submit a qualifying time when entered, and the horses are entered in appropriate heats according to their submitted times.

Figure 14.5 *Miniature horse harness race trotting winner. The winning horse of this heat,* Sugar Creek Geronimo, *is shown with owner and trainer Robin Hopson at the whip. Breeder: Lynda Baerthlein Marzec. Owner: Robin Hopson.*

Halter Classes or Performance Classes

The preparation and training required for halter classes are usually less than that required for driving and other performance classes. The halter horse must be trained to stand squarely at attention (ears up and not fidgeting), with its neck up and extended, as well as to trot out willingly, with animation. Its body condition and coat quality must be nurtured by months of carefully planned nutrition and parasite control (see Chapters 6 and 8), grooming and exercise. One judge has been quoted as having said, "Horse shows are won at home" (Leland 1996b). Almost all performance classes demand the same conditioning and health parameters, but with the additional need for extensive performance training. Unless the first-time exhibitor has had previous experience with showing and training full-sized horses, it is usually safest to enter only halter, color, or costume classes at their first show, unless a professional trainer has been hired.

Showing in Conformation or Color Classes

The best way to learn how to show a halter horse is to show the horse as often as possible. In addition to the open classes, qualified exhibitors may enter the amateur classes, which do not allow entries shown by professional trainers. In AMHA, an amateur card must be applied for each year, and there are two levels of amateur ability and experience considered; in AMHR, exhibitors must be able to readily verify their amateur status. Although hiring a trainer is much less stressful (and is usually more successful), the pride and joy of showing one's own horse cannot be duplicated. Reading the AMHA and AMHR rule books, and studying other articles and showing-method handbooks (Leland 1996b) can provide valuable information to the first-time exhibitor, but for this information to be fully assimilated, practice in the show ring is essential. All well-read and well-informed exhibitors are ultimately guided

Jim Bortvedt

Figure 14.6 *Single Fine Harness, Viceroy class.* Grampa's Gambling Man *being driven by trainer Jim Curry. Viceroys are very formal in appearance and always have four wheels. Breeder: George Moore. Owner: Dennis and Jan Haney.*

by their show ring experiences. The main purpose of exhibition and judging at shows is breed improvement. Noting the top winners at several shows helps give observers, owners and breeders a better idea of what is expected for outstanding breed type, conformation and movement. This enables them to more accurately understand and visualize what the Standard of Perfection is referring to.

In addition to age-group halter classes, which are further divided into youth, amateur and open categories, there are other specialty halter classes such as the following:

- Produce of dam (two produce of either sex to be shown, dam to not be shown)
- Get of sire (three get of either sex to be shown, sire to not be shown)
- Mare and foal (must be current-year foal)
- Three by one owner (three horses owned by one person or farm)
- Best matched pair (the two horses should have similar color and markings)
- Model horse (to be judged in standing position only)
- Broodmare (the mare must be currently nursing a foal, but foal is not judged)
- Multicolor (pinto, pintaloosa, or appaloosa)
- Solid color (all other colors and patterns)

Miniature horse color classes must be adjudicated without any color standard for the judge or exhibitor to refer to. Any mane, tail and body color or combination of colors, as well as any eye color or combination of eye colors, is permissible. This situation mandates that all multicolor and solid-color entries be brightly colored or brilliantly marked, as well as expertly conditioned, presented and groomed. Multicolor entries must be pinto, pintaloosa or appaloosa, while solid-color entries include all other colors. Color patterns such as palomino, silver dapple, buckskin, and horses with blazes or stockings must be entered in the

Pam Olsen / PRO PHOTO

Figure 14.7 *Roadster classes require that the driver wear racing silks. The horse's speed at the trot is emphasized more than it is in the pleasure driving classes.* Kamelots Tuxedo *is being driven by Cyndi Eberhart. Trainer: Eileen Lindgren. Breeder: Jerry and Nadine Kesting. Owner: William J. Schueller and Cyndi Eberhart.*

solid-color classes (see Chapter 12). In AMHR, the color classes are judged 100% on their color and pattern, while in AMHA, they are judged 80% on color and pattern, and 20% on conformation.

Driving and Other Performance Classes

Performance classes include a wide variety of driving classes for all ages of exhibitors. Horses must be at least 3 years old to compete in any of the driving classes, but their initial training, such as ground driving or longeing, can begin much earlier. Animals with short necks, straight shoulders and short, stiff legs (see Chapter 4) rarely become competitive in any of the driving classes at the shows but can still be enjoyed as pleasure driving horses for trail drives and parades. Driving classes offered at sanctioned shows include Pleasure, Country Pleasure, Formal Park, Roadster, Obstacle, Multiple Hitch, President's Touch of Class, and Fine Harness Viceroy.

Because the age and experience of the driver also are considered in judging, many driving classes are further split into open, amateur and youth classes. Children who have spent their young lives being involved with miniature horses and other animals gain psychological, intellectual, physical and social advantages as a result of continually experiencing responsibility, good sportsmanship, compassion, pride of accomplishment and the ability to accept success with humility and defeat with grace. Their lives are forever enriched, and their involvement with and love of their miniature horse charges enable them to treat their fellow humans with dignity, tolerance and respect.

Pleasure driving horses may be shown in various specified height, driver age and ability divisions, and may be further divided into single pleasure driving and country pleasure driving, with no cross-entries allowed between these two classifications. All pleasure

Figure 14.8 *Youth classes often divide children into 12 and under, and 13 to 17 age groups. Melanie Mitchell is shown here after winning the 1988 Futurity with Winners Circle B's Leprechaun. After spending many years as a child caring for, training and showing miniature horses, Melanie is now a veterinarian. Breeder/owner: Nolan and Barbara Norman, Ray and B. J. Kaliski.*

driving vehicles must have a basket or a safe and suitable floor. The two most important show advantages for any pleasure driving horse are extensive training and flawless movement, and their manners must always be impeccable. The quality of performance and the horse's manners usually overlap, each affecting the other (Wilson 1995).

In roadster classes, the horses must trot at three distinct and easily differentiated gaits: slow jog trot, road gait, and fully extended drive-on trot. The horses are never asked to walk or rein back. Drivers must wear racing silks, and their vehicles are much more streamlined and closer to the horse than are those required for pleasure classes. Roadster class emphasis is placed upon quality of performance (including well-differentiated gaits) and speed at the drive-on trot.

Formal park driving emphasizes a brilliant performance with a great deal more animation and elevated leg movement than is desired for pleasure driving. Formal park driving horses cannot be cross-entered in any pleasure driving classes, and viceroys are required. The horses are judged in only two gaits, the animated walk and the park trot, and are never asked to rein back. The park trot must be extremely animated, with high-stepping action, and the horse's head and neck should be carried in a much more upright position than is desirable for other miniature horse driving classes. Very few miniatures are genetically endowed with park driving conformation or action, and must usually be extensively trained with aids to become competitive in these classes.

Devin Baldwin / PRO PHOTO

Figure 14.9 *A draft pair (multiple) hitch, with draft-style harness, pulling a miniature buckboard.* Bar Double S Chief *(left) and* Bar Double S Cheyenne *(right) driven by trainer Vern Ames. Breeder/owner: Vern and Phyllis Ames.*

Multiple hitches of any number of horses greater than one are judged at a flat-footed walk and a trot. They are also required to back up and to trot a figure eight. Their ability to work as a team is highly emphasized. Multiple-hitch classes may be offered for pairs (two horses side by side), tandems (two horses, one in front of the other), unicorns (three horses, one in front, two side by side in rear), four-in-hands and six-in-hands (or more, all lined up in pairs side by side). Many different harness and vehicle types are both encouraged and allowed. Multiple hitches are particularly sought after for parades and other special exhibitions with large audiences.

The President's Touch of Class is an elegant harness class, open to single horses or any multiple hitch. The overall impression of elegance and uniform beauty of the entire matched unit are crucial judging points. Multiple horses must perform as a single unit, but an individual horse's performance is not judged unless it detracts from the elegance of the entry.

In addition to the various driving disciplines, there are many other popular performance classes at the shows, including hunters, jumpers, liberty, costume, showmanship and classes for the physically or mentally challenged. As for driving classes, most of these performance classes are further broken down by the ages and experience of the different types of handlers.

All hunter and jumper horses must be at least 3 years of age. Sample hunter and jumper courses are suggested and illustrated in the rule books, and the courses chosen for a specific show must be posted at least 2 hours before a class is scheduled to begin. Jumpers are scored mathematically, based upon faults incurred between the starting line and finishing line. Exciting jump-offs are often held for first-place horses tying in points. For jumpers, the emphasis is on the height jumped, while for hunters, the emphasis is on style, manners and smooth

Barbara Naviaux

Figure 14.10 *A President's Touch of Class entry. Harris Polka Dot, being driven by Suzy Hooper, has been decorated in a modified full-sized horse's Arabian costume. Breeder: D. L. Rawlinson. Owners: Jim Curry and Barbara Naviaux.*

uniformity of gait. Hunters must maintain the same gait (either a trot or a canter) throughout the entire course, and their jumps must never exceed 24 inches (61 cm) for a 34-inch (86-cm) and under horse. The height of jumps may be increased to as much as 44 inches (112 cm) during the final first-place jump-offs in jumper classes.

Liberty classes are very popular and the number of entries can be large. Music is required, and entrants must supply the show management with their chosen audio tape. Suitability of the horse's movement to the chosen music must be evaluated by the judges. Liberty classes are timed, and they are judged upon the horse's natural beauty at liberty and the ease with which the handler is able to catch and rehalter the horse. Liberty classes are also scored mathematically; horses must be at least 1 year of age.

Costume classes are judged 75% on originality of costume and 25% on presentation. They may be offered as separate classes for youth, adults, or a combination of both youth and adults (judged as one entry). Always a crowd pleaser, the costume classes challenge each entrant's inventiveness, organizational skills and acting abilities.

Showmanship classes are judged upon the exhibitor's ability to turn out, handle and show a well-presented horse. Correct attire and the handler's body movements in relation to the horse and judge are highly emphasized. Only the exhibitor is judged, not the horse. Showmanship classes are divided into youth, amateur, physically or mentally challenged, Jack Benny (men over 39) and Lucille Ball (women over 39) classifications.

Obstacle classes, in both halter and driving, are offered at most shows. The chosen obstacle course must be posted not less than 2 hours prior to the class. Halter obstacle horses must be at least 2 years of age, and obstacle driving horses must be at least 3 years of age. Obstacle classes are judged on performance and way of going, with emphasis on manners throughout the entire course. The often challenging obstacles are similar to those seen in full-sized horse shows for western trail classes but should never be designed with the intent of purposely frightening the horse.

Exhibitions, Harness Racing, Parades and Other Events

Miniature horses have gained worldwide exposure, as well as popularity, in many events and exhibitions other than shows. Their unique abilities to delight and attract enormous audiences has made them a highly sought after commodity. Yearly events such as the Calgary Stampede in Canada and the Rose Bowl Parade in Pasadena are noted for their attractive, appealing miniature horse contingents. The drill teams formed by enthusiastic miniature horse-driving groups frequently find that they cannot keep abreast of the large number of performance requests they receive.

Harness racing is becoming increasingly popular, and many miniature horses and their owners seem to enjoy the high-pitched excitement of a close trotting race. Miniature horse harness racing events usually occur between races at a full-sized horse race track, which often guarantees a large and enthusiastic audience.

Local parades of all kinds welcome the participation of miniatures. Whether being led or driven, the horses always contribute an aura of petite perfection to the audience. Themes such as Christmas, Easter or "The Old West" provide many ideas for unusual and attractive costumes, decorated vehicles, and tack.

Many miniature horse owners visit their local convalescent hospitals every year with at least one tiny, gentle horse. These visits are enormously appreciated by the residents, many of whom spent the early parts of their lives riding and raising full-sized horses. Patients who rarely respond to human contact are often known to reach out and hug a visiting miniature.

Judging Conventions

Impact on Direction of Breeding for Excellence

Judges at all shows must be approved and licensed by either AMHA or AMHR, depending upon the show's sanctioning body. Apprentice judges, who must always be accompanied in the show ring by a senior judge, may confer with the senior judge only after the senior judge has turned in the class cards for each class and before the gate is opened for the next class to enter the ring. Educational judges' clinics are required of all apprentice, temporary and senior judges. Temporary judges may officiate at sanctioned shows without another judge's assistance. Senior judges are required to have judged at least six shows as temporary judges (in addition to other requirements) before qualifying for their senior judges' card.

Although not amply discussed in either association's show rule books, every judge should have memorized the Standard of Perfection, as well as most of the official rule book. Judges whose main experience has been with breeds other than miniature horses cannot be expected to officiate at a miniature show without discrepancies. An officiating judge's behavior should be beyond reproach. Conversations with exhibitors, especially with close friends, should not occur during the show. The judge's overall demeanor should be one of professionalism, with neat and appropriate attire reflecting that image.

Variations From the Standard of Perfection and Show Rules

Judging determines the genetic and management techniques most frequently used in miniature horse breeding and showing. The winners of many championships are assumed to be the finest examples of the breed, and judges are responsible for the placement of those winners in their classes. Successful breeders are compelled to pay attention to what examples are winning at the shows, even if they find a judge's decision questionable. Judges who consistently place animals that do not personify the Standard of Perfection or that fail to perform in a manner consistent with the published show rules are rarely asked back by the club that originally hired them, having failed to take their assignments seriously enough to study the standard and the show rules. Fortunately, highly respected judges within the miniature horse industry are in the majority, and both of the associations are stringently monitoring and rapidly improving accreditation programs for judges.

Sources

Official publication of the American Miniature Horse Association (AMHA):

Miniature Horse World
5601 S. Interstate 35 W.
Alvarado, Texas 76009 USA
Phone: (817) 783-5600
Fax: (817) 783-6403
Web address: http//www.minihorse.com/amha
e-mail: amha@flash.net

Official publication of the American Miniature Horse Registry (AMHR):

The Journal
81B E. Queenwood
Morton, Illinois 01550 USA
Phone: (309) 263-4044
Fax: (309) 263-5113
Web address: http//www.Shetlandminiature.com
e-mail: aspcamhr@flash.net

Measuring stick:

Sligo Stick
3604 Kimberly Lane
Fort Worth, Texas 76133 USA
(Make check payable to "Sligo Miniature Horse Farm")
Cost: $85.00 US, shipping and handling included.

Genetic testing information:

Veterinary Genetics Laboratory
1 Shield Ave.
University of California
Davis, California 95616-8744 USA

Send blood samples by UPS or Federal Express to:
Veterinary Genetics Laboratory
Old Davis Road
University of California
Davis, California 95616-8744 USA

Phone: (530) 752-2211
Fax: (530) 752-3556
Web address: http//www.vglucdavis.edu

Miniature horse supplies:

Equine Supreme Design
P.O. Box 911
Taylor, Texas 76574 USA
Phone: (512) 352-8812 or (800) 447-6053
Fax: (800) 499-5634
Web address: supreme-equine@worldnet.att.net

Dream Makers
3200 Sorrel Lane
Placerville, California 95667 USA
Phone: (530) 626-8666
Fax: (530) 626-1549
e-mail: dreammini@aol.com

Literature Cited

Abramson, J. (1997) DNA Testing and Parent Qualification. *Miniature Horse World* 14(6):48–52.

Abramson, J. (1998a) Miniature Horse Weights. *Miniature Horse World* 15(1):58–59.

Abramson, J. (1998b) Foal Weights and Heights. *Miniature Horse World* (in press).

Ambrosiano, N. (1998) The Long Haul. *Equus* 246:90–101.

American Miniature Horse Association (1998) *Official Rule Book of the American Miniature Horse Association, 11th Edition.* Alvarado, TX: American Miniature Horse Association.

American Miniature Horse Registry (1997) *The American Miniature Horse Registry Official Rulebook.* Morton, IL: American Miniature Horse Registry.

Baker, G. J., in Pratt, P.W., Editor (1982) Diseases of the Teeth and Paranasal Sinuses. *Equine Medicine and Surgery, 3rd Edition.* Goleta, CA: American Veterinary Publications, Inc.

Bedell, L. F. (1959) *The Shetland Pony.* Ames, IA: Iowa State University Press.

Beeman, G. M. (1995) Foaling: A Practical Guide to the Foaling Process. *Miniature Horse World* 11(6):131–141.

Blair, L. B. (1989) A Summary History of the American Miniature Horse. *Miniature Horse News* 3(9):12–13.

Boomhower, L. L. (1990) Early Ponies and People. *The Pony Journal* XLV(5):54–57.

Bowling, A. T. (1985) The Use and Efficacy of Horse Blood Typing Tests. *The Journal of Equine Veterinary Science* 5(4):195–199.

Bowling, A. T. (1987) Equine Linkage Group II: Phase Conservation of *TO* with *Al^B* and *Gc^S*. *Journal of Heredity* 78:248–250.

Bowling, A. T., in Evans, J. W., Editor (1992) Genetics of the Horse. *Horse Breeding and Management.* College Station, TX: Texas A & M University Press.

Bowling, A. T. (1993) California Researcher Reports on Study of Overo Inheritance. *Paint Horse Journal* 27(8):66–67.

Bowling, A. T. (1994) Dominant Inheritance of Overo Spotting in Paint Horses. *The Journal of Heredity* 85(3):222–224.

Bowling, A. T. (1996) *Horse Genetics.* Cambridge, UK: Cab International.

Bowling, A. T. (1997) Coat Color Genetics. *The Quarter Horse Journal* 49(11):48–58.

Brady, I. (1969) *America's Horses and Ponies.* Boston, MA: Houghton Mifflin Company.

Briggs, K. (1998) Cookin' Supper: Nutrition. *The Horse* XV(1):67–69.

Butler, D. (1994) Normal and Corrective Trimming of the Hoof. *Miniature Horse World* 9(4):209–251.

Cabell Self, M. (1964) *Horses of Today.* New York, NY: Duell, Sloan & Pearce.

Caetano, A. R., & Bowling, A. T. (1998) Characterization of a Microsatellite in the Promoter Region of IGF1 in Domestic Horses and Other Equids. *Genome* 41:70–73.

Campbell, M. E. (1992) Selected Aspects of Miniature Horse Reproduction: Serologic and Ultrasonographic Characteristics During Pregnancy and Clinical Observations. *Proceedings of the 1992 American Association of Equine Practitioners Convention.*

Camper, S. A., Saunders, T. L., Katz, R. W., & Reeves, R. H. (1990) The Pit-1 Transcription Factor Gene is a Candidate for the Murine Snell Dwarf Mutation. *Genomics* 8(6):586–590.

Castle, W. E. (1948) ABC of Color Inheritance in Horses. *Genetics* 33:22–35.

Castle, W. E., & Smith, F. H. (1953) Silver Dapple, a Unique Color Variety Among Shetland Ponies. *Journal of Heredity* 44:139–145.

Castle, W. E. (1960) Fashion in the Color of Shetland Ponies and its Genetic Basis. *Journal of Heredity* 51(6)247–248.

Craigo, R. W. (1998) Business or Hobby? *Equus* 246:108–115.

deRibeaux, M. B. (1994) 25,000 Year Old Frozen Horse. *Equus* 200:95.

Dorland, W. A. (1985) *Dorland's Illustrated Medical Dictionary, Twenty Sixth Edition.* Philadelphia, PA: W. B. Saunders Company.

Dorrance, T. (1987) *True Unity: Willing Communication Between Horse and Human.* Bruneau, ID: Give-It-A-Go Enterprises.

Duggan, M. (1972) *Horses: A Golden Handbook Guide.* New York, NY: Golden Press.

Edwards, E. H. (1993) *Horses: The Visual Guide to Over 100 Horse Breeds From Around the World.* New York, NY: Dorling Kindersley, Inc.

Ensminger, M. E. (1990) *Horses and Horsemanship, Sixth Edition.* Danville, IL: Interstate Publishers, Inc.

Fowler, M. E., in Siegal, M., Editor (1996) Poisonous Plants. *UC Davis, School of Veterinary Medicine Book of Horses: A Complete Medical Reference Guide for Horses and Foals.* New York, NY: HarperCollins Publishers.

Fraser, C. M., Mays, A., & Huebner, R. A., Editors (1986) *Merck Veterinary Manual.* Rathway, NJ: Merck & Company, Inc.

Friedman, R. (1996) Miniature Horses: Reproduction and Health Topics. *Northwest Miniature Horse Club Newsletter* 1(67):9–10.

Gardner, E. J. (1968) *Principles of Genetics, Third Edition.* New York, NY: John Wiley & Sons, Inc.

Gerros, T. C. (1996) *Foal Emergencies.* Corvallis, OR: Oregon State University Publications.

Geurts, R. (1977) *Hair Color in the Horse.* London, UK: J. A. Allen & Company Limited.

Griffen, J. (1966) *The Pony Book.* Garden City, NY: Doubleday & Company.

Harper, F., & Bell, B. (1991) Genetics for the Horse Breeder. *Tennessee Horse Express* (Agricultural Extension Service, University of Tennessee) 1(10):1–4.

Harper, F. (1992) Facilities for Horses—Fencing. *Tennessee Horse Express* (Agricultural Extension Service, University of Tennessee) 2(2):1–4.

Harper, F. (1991) Not Too Fat, Not Too Thin. *Modern Horse Breeding* 8(2):9–12.

Harvey, R. B., Hambright, M. B., & Rowe, L.D. (1984) Clinical Biochemical and Hematologic Values of the American Miniature Horse: Reference Values. *American Journal of Veterinary Research* 45(5):987–990.

Hatch, J., & Parnell, L. (1996) An Historical Look at AMHR. *The ASPC/AMHR Journal* 51(6):104–105.

Hatley, G. B. (1962) *Appaloosa Horses: Color Patterns, Breed Characteristics and Descriptions.* Moscow, ID: Appaloosa Horse Club, Inc.

Hawcroft, T. (1983) *The Complete Book of Horse Care.* Sydney, Australia: Lansdowne Press.

Hayes, K. E. (1993) *The Complete Book of Foaling: An Illustrated Guide for the Foaling Attendant.* New York, NY: Howell Book House, Macmillan Publishing.

Henneke, D. R. (1985) A Condition Score System for Horses. *Equine Practice* 7(8):13–15.

Hermans, W. A. (1970) A Hereditary Anomaly in Shetland Ponies. *Netherlands Journal of Veterinary Science* 3(1):55–63.

Hermans, W. A., Kersjes, A. W., vanderMey, G. J., & Dik, K. J. (1987) Investigation Into the Heredity of Congenital Lateral Patellar (Sub) Luxation in the Shetland Pony. *The Veterinary Quarterly* 9(1):1–8.

Hill, C. (1990) *Horsekeeping on a Small Acreage: Facilities Design and Management.* Pownal, VT: Garden Way Publishing.

Iron Gate Farm (1985) Freeman's Star advertisement. *Miniature Horse World* 1(6):Inside front cover.

Jansson, J. O., Downs, T. R., Beamer, W. G., & Frohman, L. A. (1986) Receptor-Associated Resistance to Growth Hormone-Releasing Factor in Dwarf "Little" Mice. *Science* 232:511–512.

Jenny, T. (1990) Miniature Horse Breeding for Height. *Western Canadian Miniature Horse Club Newsletter* January 1990:14.

Judd, R. C. (1994) A Practitioner's Approach to Reproductive Problems in Miniature Mares. *Equine Practice* 16(6):9–14.

Kainer, R. A., & McCracken, T. O. (1994) *The Coloring Atlas of Horse Anatomy*. Loveland, CO: Alpine Publications.

Kelly, T. E. (1984) *Clinical Genetics and Genetic Counseling*. Chicago, IL: Year Book Medical Publishers, Inc.

Kohnke, J. R. (1992) *Feeding and Nutrition: The Making of a Champion*. North South Wales, Australia: Birubi Pacific.

Kohnke, J. R., in Rose, R., & Hodgson, D. (1993) Clinical Nutrition. *Manual of Equine Practice*. Philadelphia, PA: W. B. Saunders Company.

Krienke, M. (1987) Pony Tracks. *Ponies Magazine* 1(8):4.

Lawrence, L. A. (1995) Reducing Stress. *Miniature Horse World* 11(3):54–63.

Leland, T. (1996a) *Look it Up!: A Comprehensive Equine Glossary*. Grants Pass, OR: Equine Graphics Publishing.

Leland, T. (1996b) *Show Your Mini!: A Complete How-To Workbook for the First-Time Exhibitor*. Grants Pass, OR: Small Horse Press Publications.

Madigan, J. E., Editor (1997) *Manual of Equine Neonatal Medicine, Third Edition*. Woodland, CA: Live Oak Publishing.

Marcella, K. L. (1992) General Care of Miniature Horses. *Equine Practice* 14(5):25–28, and 14(6):26–28.

Markel, M.D., in Siegal, M., Editor (1996) The Musculoskeletal System and Various Disorders. *UC Davis, School of Veterinary Medicine Book of Horses: A Complete Medical Reference Guide for Horses and Foals*. New York, NY: HarperCollins Publishers.

McBane, S. (1997) Falabella. *The Illustrated Encyclopedia of Horse Breeds*. London, UK: Quarto Publishing Company.

McCoy, S. (1963) Are There Any More Like These? *Pony Record* (Jan–Feb 1963).

McKusick, V. A. (1984) Mendelian Inheritance in Man—Catalogs of Autosomal Dominant, Autosomal Recessive and X-Linked Phenotypes, Sixth Edition. Baltimore, MD: Johns Hopkins University Press.

McKusick, V. A., Eldridge, R., Hostetler, J. A., & Egeland, J. A. (1964) Dwarfism of the Amish. *Seventy Seventh Session Transactions of the Association of American Physicians* LXXVII:151–168.

Metallinos, D. L., Bowling, A. T., & Rine, J. (1998) A Missense Mutation in the Endothelin-B Receptor Gene is Associated with Lethal White Foal Syndrome: An Equine Version of Hirschsprung Disease. *Mammalian Genome* 9:426–431.

Metcalf, E. S., Ley, W. B., & Love, C. C. (1997) Semen Parameters of the American Miniature Horse Stallion. *Proceedings of the 43rd Annual Convention of the American Association of Equine Practitioners* 43(1):202–203.

Miller, R. W. (1964) *Appaloosa Coat Color Inheritance*. Bozeman, MT: Animal Science Department, Montana State University Press.

Mogg, T. D., & Palmer, J. E. (1995) Hyperlipidemia, Hyperlipemia, and Hepatic Lipidosis in American Miniature Horses: 23 Cases (1990–1994). *Journal of the American Veterinary Medical Association* 207(5):604–607.

Moore, B. R., Abood, S. K., & Hinchcliff, K. W. (1994) Hyperlipemia in 9 Miniature Horses and Miniature Donkeys. *Journal of Veterinary Internal Medicine* 8(5):376–381.

Naviaux, B. J. (1985) Clinical Laboratory Aids in Equine Medicine. *Miniature Show Horse Times* 1(3):14–31.

Naviaux, B. J. (1991) Coat Color Identification—Differentiating Coat Color Variations in Miniature Horses. *Miniature Horse World* 7(5):169–183.

Naviaux, B. J. (1995) Miniatures—The Horse of a Different Color. *The ASPC/AMHR Journal* 50(4):42–61.

Naviaux, B. J. (1997) The Overo Pinto Controversy Rages. *The American Miniature Horse* 1(3):33–36.

Naviaux, J. L. (1985) *Horses in Health and Disease, Second Edition.* Philadelphia, PA: Lea & Febiger.

Nystrom, M. B. (1984) Miniature Horse Registries—Where are we Headed? *Equuleus* 2(202):21–23.

Pauley, J. (1980) History of the Miniature Horse—An Interview With Tom Field. *International Miniature Horse Registry Journal* 2(3):19–22.

Pauley, J. (1981) History of the Miniature Horse—Smith McCoy's Midget Ponies. *International Miniature Horse Registry Journal* 3(1):84–89.

Philipsson, J., Brendow, E., Dalin, G., & Wallin, L. (1998) Genetic Aspects of Diseases and Lesions in Horses. *Proceedings of the 6th World Congress on Genetics Applied to Livestock Production* 24:408–415. New South Wales, Australia.

Physick-Sheard, P. W., in Pratt, P. W., Editor (1991) Abnormalities of Cardiac Sound. *Equine Medicine and Surgery, 4th Edition.* Goleta, CA: American Veterinary Publications, Inc.

Pratt, P. W., Editor (1991) *Equine Medicine and Surgery, 4th Edition.* Goleta, CA: American Veterinary Publications, Inc.

Ralls, K., Ballou, J. D., & Templeton, A. (1988) Estimates of Lethal Equivalents and the Cost of Inbreeding in Mammals. *Conservation Biology* 2(2):185–193.

Ramey, D. W. (1996) *Colic in the Horse.* New York, NY: Howell Book House, Simon and Schuster Macmillan Company.

Reid, S. W., & Cowan, S. J. (1998) Risk Factors Associated with Hyperlipemia in the Donkey. *Miniature Donkey Talk* 1(76):44–48.

Roberts, J. (1960) Fifty Years of Shetlands. *The American Shetland Pony Journal* XV(5):2–12.

Roberts, M. (1996) *The Man Who Listens to Horses.* London, UK: Random House.

Rose, R., & Hodgson, D. (1993) *Manual of Equine Practice.* Philadelphia, PA: W. B. Saunders Company.

Rumbeiha, W. K., & Oehme, F. W. (1991) *Emergency Procedures for Equine Toxicoses.* Santa Barbara, CA: Veterinary Practice Publishing Company.

Ryan, J. A., Modransky, P. D., Welker, F. H., Moon, M. L., & Saunders, G. K. (1992) Kyphoscoliosis in Two Miniature Horses. *Equine Practice* 14(2):4–5.

Siegal, M., Editor (1996) *UC Davis, School of Veterinary Medicine Book of Horses: A Complete Medical Reference Guide for Horses and Foals.* New York, NY: HarperCollins Publishers.

Speed, J. G. (1958) A Cause of Malformation of the Limbs of Shetland Ponies With a Note on its Phylogenic Significance. *British Veterinary Journal* 114:18–22.

Sponenberg, D. P., & Bowling, A. T. (1985) Heritable Syndrome of Skeletal Defects in a Family of Australian Shepherd Dogs. *Journal of Heredity* 76:393–394.

Sponenberg, D. P., Carr, G., Simak, E., & Schwink, K. (1990) The Inheritance of the Leopard Spotting Patterns in Horses. *Journal of Heredity* 81(4):323–331.

Sponenberg, D. P. (1996) *Equine Color Genetics.* Ames, IA: Iowa State University Press.

Thorson, J. S., & Snyder, R. (1998) Your Favorite Breeds and Where They Rank. *Horse and Rider* XXXVII(1):39–41.

Verhaege, M. (1979) One Plus One = ? Or, Some Ideas on Selective Breeding of Miniature Horses. *International Miniature Horse Registry 1979 Annual Directory.*

Williams, T. R. (1992) Dental Problems in Miniature Horses. *Western Canadian Miniature Horse Club Newsletter* June 1992: 30–33.

Wilson, C. (1995) Ask the Judge. *The ASPC/AMHR Journal* 50(4):17.

Index of Horses' Names

Bold page numbers indicate photographs.

AR Sampson's Domingo Royale **25**

Bar Double S Cheyenne **237**

Bar Double S Chief **237**

Bended Knee Indian Lace **189**

Bended Knee Moqui Warrior **38**

Bended Knee Partial Eclipse 188

Bended Knee Spring Eclipse **188**, **226**

Bond Rollback **188**

Boones Little Apache 149

Boones Little Buckeroo **103**, 203

Boones Little Buckeroo 2nd **203**

Brewers Orion Illusion 213

Brewers Orion Image 211

Capricorn Star Studded 185

Carousel Custom Design **213**

Celebrations Reno Royal **215**

Charro of Arenosa 9

Chianti 9

C-Jo's Topper 9

Creme D'Mocha **195**

Deer Haven Noonstar 185

Deer Haven Peaches N Cream **185**

Deer Haven Sparkle **Front cover (right)**, **201**

Dippers Duffy 149

Flabys Medicine Man **187**

Flabys Supreme **190**

Freeman's Star 6, 13

FWF Blue Boy's Delft Blue **Back cover (left)**, **22**

Gold Hill Ice Angel **201**

Gold Melody Boy 9, 149

Goodins Popcorn Ball **214**

Goose Downs Savannah **59**

Grampas Gambling Man **234**

Grosshills Comofin **10**

Half Measures Silver Legacy **192**

Haligonian Halation **Back cover (bottom)**, **212**

Harris Polka Dot **35**, **210**, **238**

HNF's Quapau **Front cover (left)**, **205**

Hobby Horse Hill's Tiny Tim 13

Inglemist Dominique Sunshane **200**

Inglemist My Golden Toy **205**

Inglemist Photo Flash **199**

Jandts Ecstacy **214**

Johnstons Blondie 149

Johnstons Golden Girl 149

Johnstons Starlight 149

Johnstons Tina Star 149

Johnstons Vanilla 103

Just Bronco **202**

Kamelots Tuxedo **235**

Kays Calico **Back cover (top)**

Komokos Gold Crest **231**

Komokos Shoshonee Maiden **198**

Komokos War Dance **197**, 198

La Vista Remarkable's Remarkable **186**

La Vista Rowdy Remark 68, 186

La Vista Remarkable DWB **134**

Little King's Buckaroo Bonsai **Front cover (top)**

Longview Royal T **203**

LTD's Magic Man **187**

LTD's Medicine Cat **187**

LTD's Medicine Man **187**

LTD's Nacho Macho Man **187**

LTD's Red Cloud **Front cover (middle)**

Lucky Four Strike Me Silver **198**

Lute's Komo Dandy **48**

McArthurs Imperial Gold Dust **213**

Me He Midnight Rose **232**

Mini Dreams Suchadoll Babee **216**

Mini Pony Tony 13

MWF Muchos Best Kept Secret **Back cover (right)**, **137**

My Golden Toy 5, 9

NFC Remarkable Rowdy 186

NFC Rowdys Standing Ovation **186**

Orion Light Van't Huttenest 211

Orion Pleasure **213**

Pacific Dual Image **112**

Pacific Jetstream **59**

Pacific Matador **138**

Pegasus Desperado **23**

Pheasant Dreams Stretch **192**

Poplar Lanes Sampson 103

Queenie **104**

Regina 9

Rehs Patriarch **123**, **193**

Rehs Royal Gem **188**

Rivenburgh Farms Hank the Cowboy **191**

Rivenburghs Goin Bananas **204**

Rivenburghs Mariah **211**

Rivenburghs Supreme in Technicolor **190**

Roan Ranger 149

Rodabi-J Aztec Ariston **212**, **226**

Rodabi-J Cafe Au Lait **195**

Rodabi-J Cafe Francais **207**

Rodabi-J Celestial Seasonings **40**

Rodabi-J Crystal Vision **196**

Rodabi-J Elfin Echo **27**

Rodabi-J Garnet Bay **208**

Rodabi-J Ima Raven **208**

Rodabi-J Micro Dot **209**

Rodabi-J Molokai Maid **129**

Rodabi-J Paiute Pogonip **190**

Rodabi-J Shot in the Dark **191**

Rodabi-J Skyline Sparkler **230**

Rodabi-J Spindrift Bay **207**

Rodabi-J Strawberry Delight **193**

Rodabi-J Tattoo **209**

Rodabi-J Tattoo's Last Tango **209**

Rodabi-J Vanishing Point **201**

Rodabi-J Velvet Viking **40**

Rowdy 9, 172, 186

Roys Toys Snippets Valentina **134**

Samis Kassanova **20**

Samis Just Bananas Premadonna **202**

Samples Wendy 187

Scott Creek High Roller **189**

Shadow Oaks Paul Bunyan 16

Shadow Oaks Top Banana 202

Sids April Fool 149

Sids Rebel **206**

Sids Red Cloud 149

Sierras Amberlita **192**

Sierras Stetson **206**

Sligo Nikki **15**

Starlight II 149

Starlights Little Dipper 149

Stiehls Apache Splash **189**

Sugar Creek Celeste **112**

Sugar Creek Geronimo **229**, **233**

Sugar Creek Strawberry Parfait **129**

Thunderhead's Stardust **Front cover (right)**, **201**

Tinkerville Hobby 14

Tiny Tim 13

Tomahawks Shadow Dancer **197**

Tomahawks Sparkling Image **211**

Tor's Pandora **123**

Toyland Little Sombrero **210**

Unicorn Lotsa Spirit **194**

West Coasts Sudden Reignbow **Back cover (top)**

Willie Lee's Pixie 188

Winners Circle B's Leprechaun **236**

Winter Creeks Golden Jubilee **205**

Index

Bold page numbers indicate photographs; *italics* indicate illustrations

——— **A** ———

abdominal pain
    indicators of 68, 115
    causes 81, 114
    See also colic
abortion
    and dwarfism **136**
    caused by infectious disease 110, 135
    caused by mycotic (fungal) infection 110
    caused by noninfectious conditions 110, 135–136
    caused by uterine infection 110, 135
    caused by viral infection 106
abscess
    as cause of lameness 120
    associated with strangles 107
    associated with tetanus 109
    chronic 89
achondroplasia **44**, 155–156, **158, 159**. *See also* dwarfism
action
    and Standard of Perfection 35
    in driving horse **35**
    in healthy horses 218
    in show-quality horses 236
    See also conformation; movement
advertising 217, 224. *See also* marketing
aging. *See* geriatric horses
albino 176
alertness, as indicator of soundness 1, 36, **69, 138**
allele(s)
    as matched pair of chromosomes 144
    dominant 145
    hidden 145
    recessive 145
    Snell dwarf 154
    symbology for 146
    See also genetics; locus
alopecia 86, **86,** 87, 88, 89
alteration gene 165
amateur showing status, 64
    and leasing 142–143
    in show classes 64, 233, 238
American Association of Equine Practitioners (AAEP) 27
American Miniature Horse (AMH)
    as business investment 2, 19, 217–218
    as hobby or pet 2, 19, 21, 23, 25–26, 33, 55, 141, 217
    breed foundation sire(s) 6, 9
    cost of maintaining 1
    general breed characteristics 1–2
    history of 4–11
    origins of 2–4
    See also American Shetland Pony; Falabella; Miniature Shetland; Shetland Pony; Standard of Perfection
American Miniature Horse Association (AMHA)
    formation of 3, 15–17, 18
    Genetics Committee 17, 43, 156–157, 160, 161, 162
    judging and showing protocols 35, 42–45, 166, 231–239
    Miniature Horse World 13, 15, 16, 18, 26, 228
    registration protocols 9, 10, 16–17, 22, 29, 122, 156, 180, 219
    stallion reports 28, 139, 140, 218, 219
    See also disqualification; Standard of Perfection
American Miniature Horse Registry (AMHR)
    designation of miniature breed type 2
    formation of 3, 9, 12–15, 16, 17
    Journal, The 16, 26, 228
    judging and showing protocols 35, 42–45, 166, 231–239
    registration protocols 9, 10, 14, 22, 29, 122, 180, 219
    See also disqualification; Standard of Perfection
American Paint Horse Association (APHA) 170
American Paint Quarter Horse Association (APQHA) 170
American Paint Stock Horse Association (APSHA) 170
American Quarter Horse Association (AQHA) 170
American Shetland Pony
    Arenosa line 9, 13
    breed characteristics 4
    congenital abnormalities 160, 163
    height protocols 5, 32, 42
    history 4–9
    registry types 4, 42
    show classes for 42, 231
    silver dapple coloration in 5, 167
    See also American Shetland Pony Club; Miniature Shetland; Shetland Pony
American Shetland Pony Club (ASPC) 4, 5, 12, 16, 17, 153
    and parentage testing 153
    ASPC Miniature Horse Registry 17
    ASPC Pony Journal (journal) 5, 13, 16
    registration protocols 4–5
    Stud Book Society 4, 5
amniotic fluid 127, 130
amniotic sac 127, **128,** 133
anatomy, equine *33*. *See also* conformation ideals; Standard of Perfection
anemia
    caused by ascarids 80
    caused by ectoparasites 86, 88, 110
    caused by protein deficiency 76
    symptoms of 72
    See also equine infectious anemia
anestrus 122, 139
    behavioral 134
aneurysm 80
angulation **34, 35,** 36, 37, 39
anthelmintic(s)
    and efficacy of avermectins 79–80
    and parasite control 82–85
    product categories 85
    use in young foals 80, 82, 84
    See also deworming; weight tape
anthrax 110
antibody(ies)
    and detection of equine infectious anemia carriers 109
    transference to foal 127, 132
antispasmodic drugs
    for treatment of colic 115
    for use following dystocia 133
antitoxin, tetanus 108–109
antivenin, snake 118
appaloosa coat pattern 181–183

and gray breeding stock 177
and silver dapple breeding stock 177
bay **209**
black 10, **210**
buckskin dun **213**
chestnut leopard **213**
chocolate silver **209**
gray **214**
in Falabella stock 9, **10**
near leopard **216**
silver bay **210**
silver white **214**
sorrel **215**
sorrel spotted blanket **215**
See also appaloosa variations; pintaloosa
appaloosa variations 181, *182*, 183
few-spot leopard 183
genital spot **209**
leopard *182*, **210**, **213**
mottled **209**
near leopard **216**
snowflake *182*, **209**
snowflake blanket *182*
spotted blanket *182*, **209, 213, 215**
varnish roan or marbled *182*
white blanket or frost *182*
appetite
decreased, as general indicator of disease 106, 107
decreased, in foals 131, 137
decreased, in mares 139
decreased, in malnurition 61, 63, 76
decreased, in parasitism 81
healthy, as indicator of well being 52, 68
in hypothryoidsm 64
in pregnant and lactating mares 52
Arabian-type head 39, **40**
arteritis. *See* equine viral arteritis
artery 66, *67*, 80. *See also* equine viral arteritis
arthritis 74, 120
as consequence of obesity 64
associated with dwarfism 157
caused by Lyme disease 110
in aging horses 104, 105
artificial insemination (AI) 122
ascarid. *See* roundworm
Ashby, Barbara 16
athletic ability
as general breed requirement 34, 63
effects of acute laminitis on 116
in show classes **229, 230**

————— **B** —————

barn(s)
pests 85, 88
modifying for miniatures 47, 51
safety of 48, 49, 75
ventilation of 47–48
See also housing
Barrett, Audrey 13, 14
baths
and growth of winter hair coat 98
as preparation for body clipping 99
color-enhancing 29
for control of ectoparasites 87

bay coat color 173
blood **207**
mahogany **208**
pinto (tri-color) 173–174
silver 177, **185, 192, 198, 210, 212**
snowflake appaloosa **209**
spotted blanket appaloosa **209**
tobiano pintaloosa **211**
tobiano pinto **188, 189, 191**
See also multicolor show class
bedding
for foaling stall 126
moldy, and respiratory problems 48
behavioral anomalies
associated with confinement 47, 51
associated with onset of disease 102, 106
associated with stress 100–102
in mares 124, 134
in stallions 51, 102
in ungelded colts 24
birth. *See* delivery; dystocia; foaling; reproduction
biting
during mouth inspections 54
in stallions 25, 102
in ungelded coats 24
in untrained young horses 30
black coat color 146, 165, 167, 177, 179, 181
dominant black 181
in newborns **201, 208**
tobiano pinto registered as black **188**
Blair, Leon B., Ph.D. 3, 13, 15, **15**, 16, 17, 42
Blasingame, Dixie 9, 16
bleaching, to enhance mane and tail color 29
blindness
and Standard of Perfection 37
caused by infection or injury 119
blood loss
caused by biting flies 89
caused by injury 69, 110, 119
blood testing
for genetic determination 166
to assess uterine infection 135
to confirm pregnancy 24, 28, 124
See also laboratory tests
blood typing
and AMHA hardship clause 14
and genetics 17, 154, 164
for pedigree documentation 142, 166
records 219
bloodline 22, 23, 26, 27, 141, 153, 170
bloodworm (strongyle) 79, 80, 111, 131. *See also* internal parasite management
body clipping **69**, 98–99, 218
for showing 1, 21, 28, 39, 53
in treatment of ectoparasites 87, 90
of foals to reveal coloration 177
body condition score (BCS) 56, 76–79, *78*, **78**, 139
body temperature
in aging horses 104
in foals 65, 130
in normal adults 65–66
procedure for taking 65–66
thermometer for 66–67, *66*

body weight
　as reference for estimating dosages 82–84
　in aging horses 75, 104
　in foals 57
　in malnourished horses 63, 75
　in nursing mares 75
　in pregnant mares 78, 140
　obesity 64, **78**, 116
　observing 75–79
　reduction 64, 116–117, 140
　See also body condition score; malnutrition;
　　nutrition
Bond, C. M., and Lucy 14
bonding 23, 76, 97, 102, 129. *See also* imprinting
bone
　abnormalities 57, 156, *162*
　disease 62, 64
　fracture 119, 120
　growth 57, 61, 137
　structure 4, 38–39, **40,** 77
boredom
　and chewing activity 55
　and exercise 112
　as cause of stress 58, 101
bots (gasterophilus) 79, 81–82, 84
Bowling, Ann, Ph.D.
　and blood typing/DNA testing 17
　and color inheritance research 17, 172, 184
　and dwarfism research 17, 161, 162, 163, 164
　and genetic nomenclature 146
brachycephaly 43, **44,** *95,* 156, **157, 158,** *162. See also*
　　dwarfism
breed improvement
　as breeding program goal 18
　relationship of, to show wins 18, 234
breed type 23, 32, 34, 35, 141, 164, 234
breeding
　and general nutritional requirements 56
　dates, chart 125
　ethics and goals 141–142, 240
　for color and pattern 164, 165, 166, 167, 170–183
　for height 12, 33, 150, 152, 219
　foundation stock 24, 26
　pre-breeding examination 139
　programs 33, 34, 35, 151, 152–153
　See also conception; inbreeding; mating; pregnancy
breeding farms 24, 26–27
Bridges, Joel R. 14
bronchitis
　associated with equine influenza 107
　associated with poor ventilation 48
Brown, Capt. Alwin R. 14
brown coat color 179, 181
　and agouti and extension loci 181
　and red factor 167
　dark **205**
　seal **206**
　solid 9
buckskin coat color 167, 174, 175, 178, 180, **203,** 234
　effects of dilution on 146
　in foal **202**
　with frost markings **203**

——— C ———

Cabell Self, Margaret 5–6
Calgary Stampede 2, 239
cannon bone
　and proper parameters for measuring height 220, *220*
　as reference point in height prediction 219–220
capillary refill time 65, 67, 68, 113
cardiology, equine 28, 74, 164
castration 21, 54. *See also* gelding
cecum *56,* 61
cesarean section 133. *See also* dystocia
chest
　and brachial artery 66
　and respiration 66
　narrow, association with roundworms 81
chestnut coat color 14, 165, 167, 174, 175, 176, 177,
　　179, 180, 181
　dark liver **190**
　frame overo pinto **186**
　leopard appaloosa **213**
　pintaloosa **211**
　silver **193**
　silver chestnut splashed white overo **78**
　silver chestnut tobiano **193**
　solid red **206**
chewing
　activity 55, 112
　and tooth problems 94
　chew-resistant fencing 49, 51
　of wood 51, 81–82, 111
　See also mastication
children
　and fencing 49
　and geldings 23
　and stallions 24
　and training of foals **22, 137**
　and youth classes **236**
　miniatures as pets for 22
　miniatures as riding horses for **25,** 105
　value of horse ownership for 2
chocolate silver coat color 165, 175, 174, **195**
　as color designation 176
　spotted blanket appaloosa **209**
　tobiano pinto **191**
chondrodystrophy 155. *See also* dwarfism
chromosomal abnormalities
　and dwarfism 43–44, **44,** 55–157, **157–159,**
　　160–164, *162*
　and malocclusion 95, *95*
　in aborted foals 135–136
chromosomes(s) 144, 144, *145,* 146. *See also*
　　chromosomal abnormalities
chronic obstructive pulmonary disease (COPD)
　and secondary smoke 48
　associated with poorly ventilated stalls 47–48
　in aging horses 105
cigarettes
　and secondary smoke 48, 105
　in grass clippings 117
class list 228
classes, show 230
　height categories for 42, 231
　temporary disqualification from 42–43
　See also specific show classes

Classic Miniature Horse Registry 18
clippers 70, 97, 99. *See also* body clipping
Clothier, Galen, Ph.D. 161
club feet
    and hoof care 90, 91
    in dwarf foals 156, *162*
    incidence of 39
clubs, miniature horse
    and clientele support 225
    and show judges 240
    and shows 229
    benefits of membership in 21, 228
    publications, advertising in 224
    See also registries
Clydesdale, as height-identified breed 32, **38**
coat, hair
    and ectoparasites 85–90, **86, 98**
    condition of 39, 60, 63, **69,** 98, 233
    grooming of 26, 29, 97–98
    in aging horses 104
    in malnourished horses 75, 94
    in parasitism 80–89
    shedding of 97, 177
    summer 20, **20,** 21, 28, 98, 175, **207, 212,** 218
    winter 1, 20, **20,** 21, 26, 50, 98, 175, **204**
    See also body clipping
coat color
    alteration genes 165
    and Standard of Perfection 36, 37, 165
    as breeding objective 164
    clarification of 175, 177
    dilution 146
    diversity 165, 166
    identification 17, 26, 166–167, 174, 176, 184
    inheritance 17, 146, 170, 172, 173, 177, 178, 179,
        180, 181, 183, 184
    phenotype 144
    records 150, 164
    unnamed **201**
    See also coat patterns; color patterns; foal color;
        specific coat colors
coat pattern
    alteration genes 165
    and Standard of Perfection 36, 37, 165
    in appaloosas 177, 181–183, **209, 211, 213**
    in duns 180
    in grays 175
    in grullas 178
    in pintaloosas 182
    in pintos 170, *171,* 172, 173, 174, 177, **232**
    in roans 177–178, **198**
    in silver dapples 176, **192, 196**
    phenotype 144, 146
    records of 150
    unnamed **201**
    variations 1, *182*
    See also color pattern; markings; *specific* coat
        patterns
codominance, genetic 146
coffin bone 116. *See also* laminitis
Coggins test 28, 109, 226
colic 111–114
    gas 115
    impaction 111–112
    sand 113
        symptoms of 106, 112–113
        thromboembolic 80
        treatment of 113, 114, 115
colon *56, 58,* 61, 111. *See also* colic
color classes
    and Standard of Perfection 39, 165
    designation of 166, 232, 233
    multicolor **232,** 234
    solid-color 234–235
    See also coat color; coat pattern; color patterns;
        specific coat colors *and* patterns
color genotype tests 166–167
color pattern 147–148, 167, 183
    and show classes 234–235
    blaze 166, 234
    stocking 166, 234
    See also specific color patterns
color phenotype 144
colostrum 109, 124, 127, **129,** 132, 138
colt(s) 31
    as pets 23, 140
    gelding of 24 , 141
    sexual maturity in 140
    undescended testicles in 45, 140
    See also neonate(s)
companionship 48, 103, 217
    as health factor 77, 101
    for stallions, provided by older horses 25
conception
    and abortion of genetically defective foals 136
    and pasture breeding 123–124
    confirmation of 124
    rate 122, 139, 141
    surprise 140
conditioning, show 63–64, 152, 218, 225, 229, **229**
confinement
    behavioral and health effects of 51, 52, 101, 102
    of late-term pregnant mares 126
conformation 1, 31, 228, 229, *230*
    and breed type 32–35
    and equine anatomy 33
    as criterion for purchase 19, 23
    as criterion in breeding 121, 139, 141, 146, 150,
        152, 164
    evaluating for 20, 22, 28, 230
    faults 26, **40,** 93
    ideals 38–39, **40**
    leg *41, 155*
    See also show classes; Standard of Perfection
conjunctivae 67, 89
conjunctivitis 67, 89, 99, 119, 130
contentment
    and health 100
    indicators of 102
contracts and agreements 24, 29, 142, 143, 225. *See
        also* guarantees
co-ownership 29, 142, 225
coprophagia 102
Cornellier, Dick 14
costume show classes 1, 233, 237, **238**
coughing
    and evaluation of respiration 66
    caused by equine influenza 107
    caused by parasites 81
    caused by poor ventilation 48

Coxe, Charles and Marguerite 14
cremello coat color 178–180, **205**
  and blue eye color 173
  and color clarification 176
  and dilution gene 146, **202**
  and red factor test 167
cribbing 101
croup
  and gait analysis 120
  in dwarfism 157
cryptorchidism
  and Standard of Perfection 36, 37
  as cause for show disqualification 36, 37, 44–45
  bilateral 45, 140
  certificate of veterinary inspection for 44, 140
  diagnosis of 140
  monorchidism 45
  unilateral 140
  veterinary inspection for 28

————— **D** —————

dapple gray coat color 174–175, 177
  and color clarification 176, 177
dappling 165, 175
  in roans 167
  in silver-gened foals 176
Darwinian selection 3, 32
Dedear, John F. 14
deformities
  and dwarfism 155–157, *155*, **157–159**
  angular limb 90, 92
  inheritable 36, 43
dehydration
  evaluating status of 67, 68, 72
  in colic 113, 115
  in malnourished horses 76
  rehydration 115
delivery
  complications of. *See* dystocia
  first stage of 126, 127
  post-foaling care following 127, 134
  pre-delivery checks for 124–125
  presentation in 127, 133
  second stage of 126, 127, **128**
  third stage of 126, 127
  See also dystocia; neonate(s); placenta; umbilical
    cord
dental care 75, 93–97
  and digestion 94
  categories of dental problems 94
  equine dentition 95, **95**, 96, 97
  floating 96
  genetic abnormalities 95, **95**
  importance of 97
  in aging horses 104
  periodontal disease 97
  symptoms of problems 94
  See also malocclusion; teeth
deoxyribonucleic acid (DNA). *See* DNA testing
depression
  and health 101
  and inbreeding 150
  and social bonds 102
  associated with parasitism 81

dermatitis 87, 88, 89
  in dwarfs 157
  in stallions 102
  of reproductive cycles 121, 139
deworming 79–85
  and gastrointestinal health 79
  and intestinal rupture 81
  estimating dosages for 82–84
  of aging horses 104
  of foals 82–84
  records 82
  tube worming 84
  See also anthelmintics; internal parasite management
diarrhea
  caused by enteroliths 114
  caused by malnutrition 63
  caused by parasitism 81, 131
  caused by Potomac horse fever 110
  caused by sand colic 113
  in foals 110, 131–132
diastrophy 43, 155, *155*, 156, **159**, 162, 163. *See also*
    dwarfism
digestion
  and dental health 39
  and water 58–59, 60
  in foals 134
digestive tract *56*, 57, *58*
dihybrid cross 148. *See also* genetic cross
dilution 146, 165, 167, **202**, **204**
  in appaloosas 183
  in cremellos 178, 179, **202**
  in duns 180
  in grullas 178
  in perlinos 178, 179
  in silver-gened colors 175, 177, **193**
discharge
  nasal 63, 107, 108, 134
  vaginal 135, 139
disease
  importance of isolation in 106
  infectious 107–110
  noninfectious 111–117
  orthopedic, sites of *57*
  resistance 47, 102, 150
  See also preventative health management; *specific*
    diseases
disqualification
  and Standard of Perfection 36, 37, 42–45
  for showing 28, 224
  temporary 42–43
  See also cryptorchidism; dwarfism; height;
    injury(ies); unsoundness
DNA testing
  and AMHA Genetics Committee 17
  and diagnosis of diastrophic dwarfism 162–163
  and hardship registration 16–17
  and pedigree documentation 142
  for identification 153
  kits 154
dominance, genetic 145–146
  co-dominance 146
  incomplete 146
  law of 153
Dorrance, T. 30

dorsal stripe (line-back) **201**
    in duns 176, **201**
    in grullas 178
    in silver-gened colors 176
double-registration 29
Down's syndrome 145
draft hitch **237**
draft horse-type 38, **38,** 39
driving classes 1–2, 23, 28, 34, 42, 233, 235–239
    country pleasure 235
    fine harness viceroy **234,** 235
    formal park 235, 236
    multiple hitch 2, 235, 237, **237**
    obstacle **231,** 235
    pleasure 235–236
    president's touch of class 235, 237, **238**
    roadster **233,** 235, **235,** 236
    youth **236**
    See also show classes
drug(s)
    analgesic 105
    anesthetic 53
    anthelmintic 79, 81, 85
    anti-inflammatory 105
    associated with abortion 108
    dosing estimates 82
    levels, testing for 73
    tranquilizing 53
    See also weight tape
"dummy foal" 132
dun coat color
    and color clarification 176
    buckskin **201**
    characteristics 176, 178, 180
    spotted blanket appaloosa **213**
dwarfs
    as pets 26
    foal viability in 135–136
    See also dwarfism
dwarfism 8, 155–160
    achondroplastic **44,** 155–156, **158, 159**
    and abortion 135–136, **136**
    and dental abnormalities 95, *95*
    and glandular anomalies 160
    and inbreeding 150
    and lameness 120
    and limb deformities 90, *155*
    as cause for disqualification 36, 37 , 43–44
    brachycephalic 43, **44,** *95,* 156, **157, 158,** *162*
    characteristics 8, 43–44, **44,** 156–157
    diastrophic 43, 155, *155,* 156, **159,** 162, 163
    gene research 17, 154, 160–164
dysmorphic syndromes 155. *See also* dwarfism
dystocia
    associated with obesity 140
    effects of, on future reproductive health 133
    indications of 133
    repositioning of fetus in 133

——— **E** ———

ear(s)
    floppiness, as symptom of poor health 39, 81
    position, as indicator of mood 39
    position, as means of communication 39
    tick, spinose 88

Eastern equine encephalomyelitis (EEE) 109
ectoparasite(s) 85
electrolyte balance 59–60. *See also* minerals; nutrition
electrophoresis 153
Elliott, Eli 4, 5
Ely, Rayford 14, 16
emaciation
    and abortion 136
    and protein levels 61
    associated with anemia 110
    in lactating mares 140
    in malnutrition 63
    See also body condition score; malnutrition;
        nutrition
emboli 80
encephalomyelitis, viral equine (sleeping sickness) 109
endometritis 135
endorphin production
    and health 100
    and overall quality 102
    in foals 52
endotoxemia 106, 113, 115, 116
enema
    for treating colic 115
    for treating impaction in foals 130–131
energy
    digestible (DE) 55, 60–61
    needs of foals 57
    See also feed; nutrition
enterolith 114, **114,** 115
entropion 130
epistasis 146, 167, 177
equine distemper. *See* strangles
equine infectious anemia (EIA) (swamp fever) 109–110
equine influenza 106, 107–108
equine rhinopneumonitis 106, 108, 135, 138
equine terminology and usage conventions 30–31
equine viral arteritis 106, 108, 110, 135
Equuleus Miniature Horse Registry 17, 18
Equus caballus 32
estrus
    anestrus 122, 134, 139
    cycle 122–123, 134
    false heat cycle 124
    foaling heat 135
ethics
    breeding 18, 141–142
    marketing, in representing horses for sale 218–219
    of intervention in genetic deformities 92, 95
    veterinary, in pre-purchase examination 28
eumelanin 165, 179, 180, 181
euthanasia 109, 132
exercise
    and health maintenance 55, 77, **134**
    and hoof condition 91, 92, 93
    and obesity 79
    and respiration 66, 72, 80
    and show conditioning 64–65
    and water consumption 58, 59, 60
    for foals **134**
    for pregant mares 52
    for stallions 51
    hazard-free environment for 46
exhibitions 237, 239

eye(s)
    accentuation of 28
    and blindness 37, 42
    and Standard of Perfection 36, 37
    conformation ideals 39
    corneal ulceration 42, 119
    in neonates 130
    pink eye 89
    See also eye color
eye color
    amber 165, 178
    and Standard of Perfection 165
    black 174, 175, 176, 178, 179
    blue 146, 165, 173, 174, 176, 178, 179, **185, 186,
        187, 188, 190, 205, 212**
    brown 175, 178, 179
    flecked 165, 173
    gray 178
    hazel 178
    in silver-gened colors 175
eye lashes, and entropion in neonates 130

———— **F** ————

facial markings 166, *168*
    apron face *168*, **187, 212**
    bald face *168*
    blaze 166, 234–235
    snip *168*, **185**
facial shed 177
failure to thrive 50, 114, 155
Falabella
    Emilio 9
    Juan 9
    Julio Cesar 9
    Maria Angelica 9
    Maria Luisa 9
Falabella Miniature Horse Farms, Inc. 10
Falabella Ranch, Argentina 6, 9
Falabella Registry 17
Falabella (strain)
    and contributions of Criollo and Petizo breeds 9
    as separate strain from miniatures 6, 10
    black appaloosa **10**
    hardship registration of 10
    history of 9–11
fallopian tube 123
farrier 90, 91, 92, 105. *See also* hoof care
fatty liver. *See* hepatic lipidosis.
fecal studies, for detection of parasites 73, 82
feces
    in foals (meconium) 130–131
    ingestion of, by foals 134
    in normal horse 68
    See also impaction; manure
fecolith 58
feed
    alfalfa hay 57, 60, 61–62, 63, 76, 81, 111, 140
    alfalfa meal 61, 63, 76, 81, 104, 114
    bran 60–61
    concentrate formulations 61
    dried powdered milk 62
    fat supplementation 60–61
    foal supplements 76
    grain supplements 62, 76, 140

    grass hay 57, 61
    legume hay 61, 62
    oat hay 57, 61
    soybean meal 62
    timothy hay 57
    See also feeding management; nutrition
feeding management
    feeders and mangers 48, 82, 111, **112**
    pasture grazing 111
    waterers 48, 58, 59, **59**
    See also energy; fiber; malnutrition; minerals;
        nutrition; protein; vitamins; water
fencing
    materials for *48*, **48**, 49
    modifications for miniatures 49
Ferguson, Bill 12
fertility
    and nutritional requirements 56
    in dwarfs 44
    of stallions 140–141
    See also infertility
fetotomy 133
fiber 55, **56**, 58, 61. *See also* nutrition
Field, Moorman 5, 6
Field, Tom 6
filly 31
first aid kit 68–70
fitting 218
flatworms 79. *See also* internal parasite management
fly 89, 98, 107, 109
foal(s), weanling and yearling 21, 23, 24, 31, 136–138
    activity levels in 52, **68**, 101–102, **134, 138**
    facilities 52
    growth of **57**
    halter classes for 231
    heart murmurs in 28, 130
    nutritional requirements of 56, **57**, 13, **134**, 137
    predicting mature height of 22
    training of 22, 30
    weaning of 137–138
    See also neonate(s); nutrition
foal coloration
    accuracy of descriptions for 166
    and lethal white foal syndrome 167
    black frame overo pinto **187**
    black newborn **201, 208**
    black overo pintaloosa **212**
    black overo pinto **188**
    blood bay newborn **207**
    blue roan **197**
    buckskin **202**
    chestnut frame overo pinto **186**
    chestnut (progression) **200**
    chocolate silver **195**
    gray tobiano pinto **199**
    in appaloosas 182, 183
    in gray pintos and appaloosas 177
    in palominos 179
    in silver-gened foals 174, 175, 176
    palomino tobiano pinto **204**
    perlino **205**
    red frame overo pinto **187**
    silver bay **192**
    silver dapple **192, 194**

silver dapple tobiano pinto **196**
sorrel spotted blanket appaloosa **215**
sorrel tobiano pinto **190**
foaling
    attendant 52, 126
    barns 51–52
    guide, based on 340-day gestation 125
    monitoring systems for 52, 126
    pasture (unassisted) 129
    post-foaling care 127–129
    stall 51–52, 126
    See also delivery; dystocia; neonate(s)
foaling date(s)
    calculating 124
    guide, based on 340-day gestation 125
    records 138–139
foaling heat 131, 135
founder. *See* laminitis
frame overo pattern 172, 173
    and lethal white DNA test 167
    black **187**
    chestnut **186**
    red **187**
    silver bay **185**
Freeman, Alton 6, 12, 13, 14
frog
    and contracted heels 90
    and thrush 90, 120

——— **G** ———

gait analysis
    in assessing lameness 120
    in dwarfism research 163, 164
gaits, required in roadster classes 236
gaskin, and dwarfism **44**, 156, **157**
gasterophilus. *See* bots
gelding(s) 31
    as driving horse 23, **23**, 25
    as pet 23, 25
    nutritional requirements of 64
gene
    linked 146
    modifier 144, 181, *182*, 183
    pool 8, 14, 33, 151, 152
genetic cross 147, 148, 166
    dihybrid 148
    in linebreeding 150, 151
    outcross 142 , 151, 152
genetic marker 153, 164, 166
genetic selection priorities 164
genetics, coat color 12, 17, 165, 180
genetics, Mendelian
    symbols 146
    terminology 144–149
Genetics Committee of the American Miniature Horse
    Association 17, 43, 156–157, 160, 161, 162
genital spotting **209, 214**
genotype 144
    testing 153–154
geophagia 102, 113
geriatric horses
    as baby-sitters for foals 25, 105
    as pasture companions for stallions 25
    as reliable trail driving horses 25

health issues in 104–105
    longevity of 2, 103, **103, 104**
gestation
    and calculation of foaling date 124, 125
    hormone levels in 125–126
    length of 2, 224
get 31
    of sire, as show class 234
girth
    and conformation of body **34**, 36, *37*, 38, **38,** 40
    in dwarfism **157**
gnats 89
Goforth, Allen 12
Gold Seal Miniature Horse Registry Corporation 18
grade stock 3
grass clippings 117
gray coat color 146, 165, 167, 175, 176, 177, 178, 179
    born black **198**
    born red (progression) **200**
    genetic gray **199**
    in pinto and appaloosa foals 177
    tobiano pinto (progression) **199**
    See also (dapple) gray
grazing
    habits 57–58
    pastures, rotation of 82
grooming 26, 29
    and conditioning of show horses 64–65
    and control of ectoparasites 85
    for halter classes 233
    mutual and self- 102
    seasonal grooming tasks 97–98
    See also body clipping; smegma
growth, foal 57
growth hormone, and dwarfism 154
grulla coat color 178
    and color clarification 176
guarantees
    fertility 225
    height 29, 225
    live foal 29, 31, 225
    pregnancy 24
gums
    and capillary refill time 67
    and periodontal disease 97
    in neonates 93
gut
    motility 61
    sounds 68, 113

——— **H** ———

hair
    preventing ingestion of 112
    root sample 153, 154, 163, 167
    shedding 75, 97, 98, 112,
    thinning of mane and tail 98
halter
    breaking **27,** 52
    for restraint 53
    training 54
halter (breed classes)
    age-group 1, **230,** 231, 232, 233–235
    specialty categories 1, 28, 234
handling 2, 23, 24, 30, 52, 53–54, 129, *137*

hardship clause 10, **10**, 14, 16, 29. *See also* registration
harness racing 23, 232, 239
Hart, George 12, 13
Hash, Gene 5
Hatch, Jean 14
hauling. *See* transportation
hay 38, 60, 61, 62, 63, 76, 77, 81, 111, 137, 140
    and aging horses 103
    and plant and insect poisoning 117
    moldy, and respiratory problems 48
    quality of 57, 77, 85, 110
    See also feed; feeding management
head
    and conformation ideals 1, 36, 37, *37*, **38**, 39, **40**
    position, during feeding 111
    position, during height measurement 42
    position, indicating pain or injury 68
head bobbing, associated with front-leg lameness 120
heart disease
    and obesity 64
    cardiomyopathy 74, 108
heart murmur, in foals 28, 130
heart rate (pulse)
    in foals 130
    in normal adults 65, 66
    procedure for taking 66, *67*
heat. *See* estrus
heaves. *See* chronic obstructive pulmonary disease
    (COPD)
heel 39, 43, 90, 91, 92, 120
height
    AMHA protocols for 1, 16–17, 36, 42
    AMHR protocols for 1, 14, 29, 37, 42
    ASPC protocols for 4, 19
    guarantees 29
    in foals, compared with weights at birth 131
    measuring 29, 42, *222*
    predicting 22, 219–223
    See also dwarfism
hepatic lipidosis 116
herd
    dependency, and stress 101
    foundation stock for 24, 34, 142, 146, 150, 152
    records 8, 152
herpesvirus-1
    and equine rhinopneumonitis 108
    and spontaneous abortion 106, 108
Hess, H. H. 14
heterozygosity 136, 145, 146, 147, 148, 151, 172, 173,
    177, 179, 181
Hill, James 16
hobble. *See* restraint
hock
    cow *41*, **44**, 156, **158, 159,** *162*, 163
    sickle *41*, 156
homozygosity 136, 141, 145, 146, 151, 152, 153, 167,
    173, 180
hoof
    anatomy of 90–91
    and lameness **91**, 120
    conformation of 36, 37, 39, 93
    disorders of 115–116, 120
    evolution of 32
    stripes 182, **192**

hoof care
    and corrective trimming 91–92
    in aging horses 105
    records 224
    tools for 92
    trimming 91–93, **91**
housing
    barns 47, 48, 49, 51, 75, 85, 88
    modifying for miniatures 47–48
    sheds 46, **50**, 51
    stalls 47, **47**, 48, 51, 52
    ventilation of 47–48
    visibility in 47
    See also fencing
Howell, Billy M. 12, 14
Huston, Robert 12
hybrid vigor 150–153. *See also* inbreeding
hyperlipemia 64, 116–117, 140
hyperlipidemia 116
hypothyroidism 55, 64, 116, 155

——— **I** ———

ileocolonic aganglionosis 172
immunity
    and antibody absorption in neonates 109
    and stress 100
immunization. *See* vaccination
immunogenetics 153–154
immunoglobulin, in colostrum 132
impaction
    and causes of intestinal blockage 80–81, 94, 111–112
    incidence of, in miniatures and Shetlands 111
    meconium 129, 130–131
    See also colic; fecolith
infertility
    and dwarfism 136
    and obesity 64
    in mares 135–136
injury(ies)
    as cause for disqualification 43
    associated with feeders 48, **112**
    first aid supplies for 69–70
    treatment of 120–121
ink spots 167, 173, **189, 232**
internal parasite management 82–85
International American Miniature Horse Association
    (IAMHA) 16, 17
International Miniature Horse Registry (IMHR) 17
International Miniature Horse Trotters and Pacers 18
International Society of Animal Genetics 153
intravenous (IV) administration
    and heparin lock 115, 133
    in dystocia 133
    in foal septicemia 132
    in hyperlipemia 117
    in injury 119
    in intestinal blockages 114

——— **J/K** ———

Jackson, Russell 12, 13
jaw
    abnormalities associated with dwarfism 43, **44**, 156,
    157
    malocclusion **86**, 93, 95, *95*

Jockey Club 122, 153, 170
join-up training method 30
joint ill 132
Jones, Michelle 15
judges, show
    and Standard of Perfection 39, 239
    conventions 239
    responsibilities of 39, 141, 166, 231, 240
karyotype 144, **145**
    analysis 144–145
    use in diagnosis of dwarfism 155
King, Verna 17
Kinsel, Robert I., Jr. 14
knee, buck, in dwarf foals 156
knee cap, and patellar luxation 120
Kwashiorkor's syndrome 76
kyphoscoliosis, in dwarf foals 156, **159**

——— **L** ———

laboratory tests 72–73, 153–154
lactation
    and nutritional needs 61–62, 140
    preparation of udder for 127
    See also weaning
lameness 119–120
    as cause for disqualification 42–43
    in aging horses 105
    in foals 132
laminae 74, 79, 115, 116, 120
laminitis (founder) 74, 90, 115–116
    as cause of lameness 120
    as complication of obesity 79
    in aging horses 105
LaPlante, Glyndean 15
Lavelock, Betty A. 14
laxative(s)
    green pasture grass as 111
    legume hay as 111
    for treating colic 115
lead (longe) line class **25**, 31, 235
leasing 142–143
Lee, Ray 12, 13
Lee, Ruby 13
leg
    and attempts to correct conformation faults 91, 92, 93
    and dwarfism characteristics **44**, 90, *155*, 156, 157,
        157, 158, 159, 160, *162*, 163
    and obesity 64
    conformation 36, 37, 38, **40**, *41*, 92, *155*
    injuries and disorders 119–120
leg markings
    as means of identification 166, *169*
    marking locations for *169*
    zebra 176, 178, 180, **201**
See also facial markings
leptospirosis 110
lethal white overo gene 167, 172, 178
    See also white coat color
levade 3
liberty class 237, 238
libido
    and nutrition 56
    seasonal depression of 121
lice 79, 85, 86–87, **86**
life expectancy 103

life span 103
    and nutrition in aging horses 104
    in dwarfism 26
linebreeding 147, 150–153
linked gene 146
lipidosis, hepatic 116, 117
loci. *See* locus
lockjaw. *See* tetanus
locus 144, 146
    agouti 181
    and epistasis 146
    bay 181
    black 181
    chestnut 181
    extension 181
    gray 178
    overo 172, 173
    roan 178
    silver dapple 177, 178
    sorrel 181
    tobiano 172
lordosis 156, **157**
lung
    damage associated with ascarids 81
    infections associated with septicemia 132
Lyme disease 88, 110

——— **M** ———

Madaris, P. A. 14
making a bag 125
malnutrition 63, 77. *See also* nutrition
malocclusion 39, 93, 95, 97
    associated with genetic abnormalities 156
    orthodontic treatment for 95
mammary gland 124. *See also* udder
mane
    and hair root samples 154
    and lice infestation 86
mane color
    and frost overlay, in buckskin **203**
    and Standard of Perfection 39
    in chestnut **206**
    in duns **201**
    in height measurement 13, 29, 37
    in perlino foal **205**
    in silver-gened colors 175, 176, 177, **191, 192, 193,
        195, 198**
    in sorrel spotted blanket appaloosa **215**
    in unnamed color **201**
    thinning of 98
mange mite 79, 85, 87–88
manure
    ingestion of, by neonates 134
    removal of 46, 51, 79, 82, 89
    See also cophragia; meconium
mare(s)
    and difficulty in settling 139
    causes of infertility in 135–136
    confirming pregnancy in 28
    mothering capabilities of 2, 136
    purchase of 24
    See also breeding; fertility; pregnancy
marketing
    advertising 224
    clientele support 225

marketing *(continued)*
    contracts and agreements 225
    ethics 218–219
    record-keeping 219–224
    shipping and transporting 225–227
markings 39, 166, 170
    and Standard of Perfection 36, 37, 165
    frost **203**
    identifying for registration 28, **219**
    in matched pairs 234
    ink spot (paw print) 173
    wild-type 178, 180, **201**
    zebra 176, 178, 180, **201**
    See also facial markings; leg markings; *specific* coat
        patterns
mastication 56. *See also* chewing
masturbation 102, 141
mating
    hand breeding 122
    maintaining records of 122, 142
    pasture breeding 122, 123–124
    planned 144, 150
    See also breeding; teasing
McCoy, Smith 5, 6, 7, **7**
measurement cards 42
measuring devices 16, 42
meconium 129, 130–131
medicine hat pattern, in black frame **187**
mental development
    and extreme confinement 102
    and malnutrition 76
    in aging horses 104
    in dwarfism 157, 161
microsatellites 153, 154
midget ponies 2, 3, 9, 12
milk production. *See* lactation
mineral(s)
    and nutritional requirements of foals 56, **57**, 58
    deficiencies 77
    imbalances and osteochondritis dissecans 120
    in grain supplementation 62
    in overweight horses 64
    in treating malnutrition 63
    supplementation during weight loss 79
    trace 59, 112, 126
    See also nutrition
mineral oil, for treating impaction 115
Miniature Shetland (breed) 5, 13
Miniature Show Horse Registry 17
Mitchell, L. C. 14
miticide 87
Montana State University, Animal Science Department
    182
Moody, Delmer 12, 13, 14
Moorman Field 5, 6
mosquito(es)
    and dermatitis 88
    and equine encephalomyelitis 88, 109, 110
    and equine infectious anemia 109
    control of 59, 88
mottling
    in appaloosas 182, 183, **209, 214**
    in pintaloosas **211**

mouth
    and digestion 55, **56**
    and gasterophilus 81
    inspection of 28, 54, 63
movement
    and Standard of Perfection 37
    as criterion for breeding 23, 32
    in show-quality horses 34, 236, 237
    See also action; gait
mucous membrane(s) 67. *See also* capillary refill time
multicolor show class 166, 232, **232**
    specialty halter classes in 234
multiple hitch show classes 2, 235, 237, **237**
Murphy, James K. 14
muscle
    and amino acids 61
    and mineral imbalances 62
    building, in young foals **57**, 137
    functioning, and electrolytes 60
    in anemia associated with parasitism 80, 81
    in healthy horses 75
    in show conditioning 64
    movement, and energy 60
    tissue, in malnutrition 63, 76
    tissue, in snake bite 118
muzzle
    and conformation 36, **40**
    and sarcoptic mange 87
    shaving of 97, 99
mycotic (fungal) infection, and abortion 110

——— **N** ———

navel ill 132
navicular disease 105
neonatal maladjustment syndrome 124
neonate(s)
    and ingestion of mother's manure 134
    diarrhea in 131–132
    entropion in 130
    maladjustment syndrome in 132
    meconium impaction in 130–131
    normal parameters for 129–131
    passage of meconium 129, 130–131
    septicemia in 132–133
    suckling reflex in 127, **129**, 130
    urination in 130
    vital signs for 129–131
Newell, Patrick 9
nipple
    pre-delivery care of 127
    waxing over of 124–125
    See also lactation; udder
noninfectious disease 111–117
non-steroidal anti-inflammatory drugs (NSAIDS)
    and association with osteochondritis dissecans 120
    as cause of gastric ulcers in foals 114
    for treatment of colic 115
    for treatment of hoof and leg disorders in aging
        horses 105
Noriker (breed), and leopard pattern 183
nursing. *See* lactation
nutrition
    and calcium/phosphorous ratio (Ca:P) 55, 57, 62
    and crude protein 55, 56, 61

and dental health 96
and show conditioning 63–64, 233
and stress 58, 62, 76
and total digestible nutrients (TDN) 55, 60
in aging horses 104
in foals 56, *57*, 13, **134,** 137
in geldings 23, 64
in lactating and pregnant mares 61–62, 78, 140
in management of obesity 64, 116–117, 140
in nonproducing mares 64
in stallions 56
See also malnutrition
nutritional components
energy 60–61
fiber 61
minerals 62
protein 61–62
vitamins 62
water 58–60
Nystrom, D. J., and Marilyn 18
Nystrom Lithocraft Corporation 18

——— **O** ———

obesity
and free-choice rations 112
health consequences of 64, **78,** 116
in pregnant or lactating mares 124, 140
See also body condition score; nutrition
obstacle classes **231,** 238–239
obturator nerve damage 133. *See also* dystocia
offspring 31
calculation of color patterns in 147
separation from, and stress 102
orthodontistry
for genetic defects 95, 156
for undershot jaws 39, 95, **95**
osteochondritis dissecans (OCD) 120
outcross 142 , 151, 152
outside mare
breeding of 122
pre-breeding examination 139
record-keeping for breeding of 139
worming of 82
overo coat pattern 170–173
and lethal white DNA test 167
black **188**
black frame **187**
black frame medicine hat **187**
black overo pintaloosa **212**
blue eye color in 173, **185, 187, 188, 190**
chestnut frame **186**
cropouts 172
pintaloosa **212**
red frame **187**
silver bay frame **185**
silver chestnut splashed white **187**
variations 170, *171,* 172, 173

——— **P** ———

Paint Registry 170
Palmer, Charles F. 15
palomino coat color 178–179
tobiano pinto **204**
palpation 115, 124
parentage verification 154

pasture(s) 50–51
pests 85
providing shelter in 50
rotation of 82
stallion 51
patellar luxation 120, 160
paw print (ink spot) 167, 173, **189, 232**
pedigree(s)
and dwarfism gene 161
and ethical breeding 142
as criterion for purchasing 19, 26, 32, 121
calculating percentages of bloodlines in 147, 149
documenting 12, 18, 150, 217, 218, 224
in AMHA Stud Books 17
in history of early miniatures 4, 5, 8
of Falabella-bred miniatures 10
relationship of, to prepotency 141, 152
performance classes
costume 1, 233, **238**
fine harness 1, **234,** 235
hunter 1, 237–238
jumper 1, 237–238
liberty 238
obstacle 1, **231,** 238–239
showmanship 232, 237, 238
periodontal disease 97. *See also* dental care
periosteal stripping 92
peristalsis 55, 60, 68, 80, 115, 134
perlino coat color 176, 178
and red factor test 167
foal **205**
pet-quality stock 26, 33
phagocytosis 72
phenotype 144
pheomelanin 165, 179, 180
photographs
and dwarfism research 163, 164
and pedigree documentation 150
and record-keeping 223
and registration requirements 156, 174, 219
as requirement for transfer of ownership 219
for use in advertising 224
pigment
colors 165
concentration 183
dilution 146
pintaloosa coat pattern 165, 166, 181, 182, *182,* 183
bay tobiano **211**
black overo **212**
chestnut **211**
silver bay tovero **212**
See also overo; tobiano; tovero patterns
pinto coat pattern 147, 148, 165, 166, 167, 170, *171*
and gray breeding stock 177, **199**
bay 173–174
bay tobiano **188, 189,** 191
black frame medicine hat overo **187**
black frame overo **187**
black overo **188**
black tobiano **188, 189,** 232
chestnut frame overo **186**
chestnut tobiano **189**
chocolate silver tobiano **191**
dark liver chestnut tobiano **190**
palomino tobiano **204**

pinto coat pattern (*continued*)
  red frame overo **187**
  silver bay frame overo **185**
  silver chestnut splashed white overo **187**
  silver chestnut tobiano **193**
  silver dapple tobiano **196**
  sorrel tobiano **190**
  variations *171*, 172
  See also overo; tobiano; tovero
Pinto Horse Association (PtHA) 170
Pinto Registry 170
pinworms 79
pit pony 5
placenta
  and oxygen supply to neonate 127
  degeneration of, and uterine infection 110
  implantation of 123
  importance of examining 126
  insufficiency of 135
  passage of 126
  retention of 135, 139
play, as indicator of health and contentment 101
pneumonia
  and septicemia 132
  as complication of equine influenza 107
  as possible cause of laminitis 116
  in neonates 133
  inhalation 127
point color 165
  accentuation of 28
  bay 173–174
  in browns **206**
  in buckskins **202**
  in chestnut **206**
  in duns 176, 180, **201**
  in grullas 178
  in perlinos 179
  in roans 178, **197**
  in silver-gened horses 177
poisoning
  plant 117–118
  protein, fallacy of 56
  rodenticide 118
polygene 144
Pony of the Americas (POA) 32
potbelly
  associated with malnutrition 75
  associated with parasitism 75, **86, 87**
  in protein-deficient foals **86, 87**, 137
  in young sale horses 81
Potomac horse fever 110
pregnancy
  conception 122, 123, 139, 140, 141
  guarantee 24, 225
  length of gestation 2, 124
  nutritional requirements of 56, 78, 140
  tests for confirming 24, 28, 124
  twinning in 110, 136
  See also breeding; fertility; infertility; reproduction
premium list 228, 229, 230
pre-purchase examination 27–29
prepotency 141, 152
preventative health management 75
  and aging horses 105
  and parasite control 79, 84

and professional dental care 97
and stress 102
pricing of sale horses 19, 21, 22, 23, 24, 25, 26, 27, 218
  and co-ownerships 142
  and financing 218
  and syndicates 142
prolactin, and dwarfism 154
proportions
  and conformation ideals *37*, 38–39, **40**, *41*
  and Standard of Perfection 36, 37
  in dwarfism 90, 156, 160
protein
  crude 55, 56, 61
  digestible 61, 62
  deprivation 61
  poisoning, fallacy of 56
  signs of deficiency 75–76
  See also feed; nutrition
proud flesh 119–120
psychological development, and feed quality 52
psyllium, for eliminating sand 63, 114
pulse
  digital, in laminitis 116
  in normal foals 130
  in normal adults 65, 66
  procedure for taking 66, **67**
puncture wound 119
Punnett square 147–148
purchasing
  and novice buyer 19, 26, 225
  intended use and price as criteria for 21–26
  pre-purchase examinations 27–29
  research, of breed and breeders 19–21
  See also contracts and agreements
pyometra 135

—— Q/R ——

Quarter Horse-type 38
quidding 94
rabies 111
racing silks, as requirement for roadster classes **235**, 236
Rader, Rick 14
radiography
  and diagnosis of dwarfism 155, **158, 159**, 161, 163
  and identification of enteroliths 114, **114**
  and investigation of osteochondritis dissecans 120
rainrot 89–90
ranch layout 46. *See also* housing; pasture
rearing
  and position of handler 53
  associated with irritation from wolf teeth 94
  associated with isolation in stallions 102
  in ungelded colts 24
recession, genetic 145, 146, 148, 151
  and color genes 167, 177, 181
  and dwarfism syndromes 160
  and malformed fibula 159
  and Shetland leg abnormality 163
records
  blood typing 153, 219
  computerized 142, 217, 218, 224
  DNA testing 153, 219
  foaling 138, 223
  for baseline values for vital signs 65
  genetic, for dwarfism research 164

hoof trimming 224
pedigree 149, 150, 224
production 24, 26, 223–224
registration papers 219, 224
stallion reports 28, 139, 140, 218, 219
teasing and breeding 122, 123, 138, 139
transfer of ownership 29, 219
vaccination 224
value of 218, 219
veterinary 224
weaning 223
worming 82, 84, 224
rectal examination
    hazards of, in miniatures 115, 122
    for diagnosis of infertility 135
    for verification of pregnancy 124
rectal thermometer 65, 66, **66**
red coat color 146, 165, 180
    and red factor DNA test 167
    chestnut **206**
    frame overo pinto **187**
    in bays 173, 177
    mahogany bay **208**
    silver dapple born chestnut (progression) **194**
refinement 26, 33, 34, 35
    and conformation ideals 38, **40**
    and show conditioning 64
    and Standard of Perfection 36
    in Classic (American type) Shetland 4
    visibility of, in summer coat **20**
Regina Winery 9
registration(s)
    and color clarification 167, 175, 176, 177
    and facial and leg markings 166
    blood typing or DNA testing for 219
    designation of coat color for 174, 180
    double 29
    hardship clause for 10, **10,** 14, 16, 29
    in AMHA 14, 29
    in AMHR 14, 29
    late 219
    number of (annually) 19
    of horses with dwarfism characteristics 43, 156
    promptness of, and computer technology 224
    transfer of ownership 219
reproduction
    and mare foaling guide 125
    management of, comparison with full-sized breeds
        121–122
    See also breeding
resistance free training 30, 101
respiration
    assessing character and frequency of 66
    during exercise 66, 72, 80
    in healthy adults 65, 66
    in newborn foals 66, 130
restraint methods 53–54. *See also* training
ringworm 89
Rivenburgh, Nancy 17, 163
roan 177–178
    bay roan pinto 174
    blue 178, **197**
    red 178
    silver bay **198**
    strawberry 13

roaning 165, 166, 170, 172, 173, 181
    in bay appaloosa **209**
    in black tobiano pinto **188, 189**
    varnished roan or marbled *182*
Roberts, Monty 30
Rose Bowl Parade, Pasadena, Calif. 239
roughage 55, 57, 61, 112
roundworm (ascarid) 80–81. *See also* internal parasite
        management
rupture, intestinal 81

—— S ——

sand
    psyllium for elimination of 63, 113–114
    testing for 113
Scheuring, Ron and Sami 9
scoliosis 156
scrotum 28, 140. *See also* cryptorchidism
selling of horses
    and ethical representation 218–219
    See also contracts and agreements; guarantees;
        pricing of sale horses
semen analysis 141
separation anxiety, and stress 101
septicemia, foal 110, 132–133
settling difficulties 139
sexual maturity
    and surprise conceptions 140
    in colts 140
    in mares 122
shade, providing 50, 58, 63, 105
sheath cleaning 99–100
Shetland Pony (native) 3–4, 9
shipping. *See* tranporting
shock
    anaphylactic, and tetanus antitoxin 109
    and capillary refill time 67
    associated with endotoxemia 115
    associated with injury 119
    associated with snake bite 118
shoeing
    and show regulations 1
    corrective 92, 105, 120
show classes
    color 232, **232,** 233, 234–235
    conformation 26, 233
    driving 1–2, 23, 28, 34, 42, **233,** 235–239
    halter 1, 28, **230,** 231, 232, 233–235
    performance 1, **229, 231,** 233, **233, 234,** 235–239,
        237, 238
show conditioning 63–64, 229, **229**
showmanship classes 232, 237, 238
shows
    attending as an observer 228–230
    exhibiting in 230–232
    national 15, 17, 42, 224, 232
    rules and regulations for 29, 42, 228, 229, 233, 240
silver bay coat color 166, **192**
    and red factor DNA test 167
    and color clarification 177
    appaloosa **210**
    as color designation 175, 176
    foal **192**
    frame overo pinto **185**

silver bay coat color *(continued)*
    roan **198**
    tovero pintaloosa **212**
silver chestnut coat color 174, 175, 176, **193**
    splashed white overo pinto **187**
    tobiano pinto **193**
silver dapple coat color 5, 17, 148, 165, 166, 167, 172,
       174–177, 180, 183, **192, 194,** 234
    chestnut red (progression) **194**
    in Shetland pony 5
    roan **198**
    tobiano pinto (progression) **196**
    yearling **192**
silver-gened coat colors 165, 167, 175–177, 180
    in foals 174
    phenotypically silver colors 175
    unnamed color and pattern **102**
    See also chocolate silver; silver bay; silver chestnut;
       silver dapple; silver white
silver white coat color 174, 175–176, 178, **201**
    appaloosa **214**
skin
    and testing for dehydration 67
    and grooming 98
    allergies 88, 98
    blemishes 36, 43, 90
    sunburn 99
    wrinkling of gaskins, in dwarfism *162*
    See also specific ectoparasites
skin color 146, 166, 178, 179, **209**
    in gray pintos and appaloosas 177, 181–182, 183, **214**
    in silver-gened colors 174, 175, 176, **201, 214**
sleeping sickness. *See* viral equine encephalomyelitis
smegma 99–100, 127
snake bite 118
Soat, Earl "Bud" 12
solid-color 147, 148, 167, 170, 172, 173, 177, 181, 182,
       206
    and body clipping 28
    show classes 166, 234–235
    See also color patterns
sorrel coat color 180, 181
    chestnut **206**
    spotted blanket appaloosa **215**
    tobiano pinto **190**
spermatozoa
    analysis 141
    and conception 123
    viability of, in cryptorchidism 44–45
spinose ear tick 88
Spirek, Gerald 14
spotting patterns *182*
    few-spot leopard 183
    genital spots **209, 214**
    leopard 181, *182*, 183, **213**
    mottled 182, 183, **209, 211, 214**
    near leopard 183, **216**
    snowflake *182*
    snowflake blanket *182*
    spotted blanket *182*, **209, 213, 215**
    varnished roan or marbled *182*
    white blanket or frost *182*
    See also overo; pintaloosa; pinto; tobiano; tovero
sprain 120

stall(s)
    and ventilation 47–48, **47**
    and visibility 47, **47**
    foaling 51, 126
    modifications for miniatures 47–48
stallion(s)
    and safety of young children 24
    behavioral anomalies in 51, 102
    fertility in 140–141
    grooming of 99–100
    libido in 56, 121
    pasture companions for 25
    reports 28, 139, 140, 218, 219
    See also breeding; fertility
Standard of Perfection
    as guideline for breed improvement 1, 18, 33, 34, 35
    as guideline for judging 35, 42–45
    as guideline for purchasing 19, 26, 28
    as guideline for showing 1, 18, 33, 34
    of AMHA 3, 15, 17, 19, 29, 33, 36, 38, 151, 165
    of AMHR 3, 13, 15, 19, 29, 33, 37, 38, 90, 151, 165
    See also conformation ideals; disqualification
Stetler, C. H. 14
stone bruise 120
strangles. *See* equine distemper
stress
    and behavioral anomalies 100–102
    and contentment 100–102
    and immunity 100
    and nutrition 58, 62, 76
    causative factors in 58
strongyle. *See* bloodworm
stud service 31, 122
    and inbreeding 152
stunting of growth, and ascarid infestation 80–81
suckling reflex 127, **129,** 130
sunburn 99
surgery
    for angular limb deformities 92
    for colic 80, 115
    for enteroliths 114, **114**
    for leg wounds 120
    for undescended testicles 45
    See also injury(ies)
swamp fever. *See* equine infectious anemia
syndicate 142

——— **T** ———

tail color 165, 174, 175, 176, 177, 179, 180, 183
tailhead, and body condition scoring 77, **78**
tapeworms 79, 80, 84
Taylor, Faith 14
tax regulations
    and donations for genetic research 163
    and horse operations 217–218
    and record-keeping 217
teasing
    of mares in estrus 123, **123,** 124
    of mares following uterine infections 135
    records 138–139
    to alter reproductive cycles 121
teeth 93–97
    and periodontal disease 97
    alignment of 95, **95**

eruption of 93, 95, 96
floating of 96, 104
genetic abnormalities of 95, 156
in aging horses 104
overcrowding of 95
shedding of deciduous 93, **94,** 97
wearing down of 96
See also dental care; malocclusion
temperature. *See* body temperature
tendinitis 120
terminology, equine 30–31
veterinary 73–74
testicles. *See* cryptorchidism; gelding
testing, genetic
for diagnosis of diastrophic dwarfism 162–163
for homozygous tobiano gene 166
for lethal white overo gene 167
for parentage testing 153
for red-factor gene 167
testosterone
effect of, on coloration 183
levels in gelded colts 24
tetanus (lockjaw) 108–109
antitoxin vaccine for 109
toxoid vaccine for 108–109
Thompson, Beverly 15
thrush 90, 120
thyroid levels
and dwarfism 154, 160
compared with full-sized horses 71
in hypothyroidism 64
relationship of, to activity levels 55
See also laboratory tests
thyroid stimulating hormone (TSH), and dwarfism 154
tick(s) 79, 85, 88
and Lyme disease 110
spinose ear 88
tobiano coat pattern 146, 147, 148, 170, *171,* 172, 173
bay **188, 189, 191, 211**
black **188, 189**
blood testing for 166–167
chestnut **189**
chocolate silver **191**
gray (progression) **199**
dark liver chestnut **190**
palomino (progression) **204**
silver chestnut **193**
silver dapple **196**
sorrel **190**
variations 170, *171,* 172, 173
See also overo; pinto; tovero
torsion, intestinal 113, 115
tooth bumps **94,** 97. See also teeth
tovero coat pattern 170, 173, 182
silver bay **212**
See also overo; pintaloosa; pinto
trace mineral salt block 59–60, 62, 63, 112, 126
training
arena, for foaling barn 51
by amateurs 142–143
by children **22, 137**
by seniors **27**
grooming, as form of 97
imprinting, as form of 129

resistance free methods for 30, 101
See also handling; restraint
transfer of ownership 29, 219
transporting and shipping
crating for air cargo 226, **226**
hauling services for 226
of aborted fetus for laboratory testing 108
trailering 227, **227**
tri-color pinto 173–174. *See also* bay pinto
twinning 110, 136
twitch 53–54. *See also* restraint

—— **U** ——

udder
and hair removal 112
and monitoring of foal's milk intake 131
and smegma removal 100, 127
bagging up of 125
care of, during weaning 138
development during pregnancy 124–125
pre-foaling checking and care of 51, 112, 127
ulcer
corneal 42, 119
gastric 114
umbilical cord
breaking of 127, **128**
stump, disinfecting of 129
umbilicus
and bedding for foaling stall 126
and navel ill 132
undercoat 98
in silver bays 174, 175, **185, 212**
in silver-gened foals 177, **192**
Universal Miniature Horse Registry 18
University of California, Davis
Serology Laboratory 153
Veterinary Genetics Laboratory **145,** 161, 163, 166, 172
Veterinary Medical Teaching Hospital **114**
unnamed coat color and pattern **201**
unsoundness
and Standard of Perfection 36, 37
as cause for disqualification 42–43
urinalysis 73
urination
in neonates 130
in sexually receptive mares 123
uterine culture
as requirement for outside mares 139
feasibility of, for miniatures 124, 135
uterine infection
and placental degeneration 110
assessing 135
associated with abortion 110, 116, 135

—— **V** ——

vaccination 110–111
for equine encephalomyelitis 110
for rabies 111
records 224
tetanus antitoxin 108–109
tetanus toxoid 108–109
vaginal examination
feasibility of, for miniatures 124, 135

valgus and varus deformities, in dwarfism 156
varnishing, in apaloosas 181, *182*
Venezuelan equine encephalomyelitis (VEE) 109
vertebral deviations, in dwarfism 156
veterinarian
    and advice on first aid supplies 68
    and advice on worming products 82, 84
    and checking for cryptorchidism 44
    and health certificates for shipping 226
    and laboratory services 70
    and pre-purchase examinations 27, 28, 225
    and treatment of colic 113, 115
    and treatment of hyperlipemia 117
    show 36
veterinary terminology 73–74
    See also equine terminology
vital signs
    baseline values for 65–68
    in neonates 130
    in normal adults 65
    See also body temperature; capillary refill time; gut sounds; heart rate; hydration; respiration
vitamins 56, 58, 60, 62, 64, 77, 79. *See also* nutrition

W

water
    accessibility of 58–59
    and contamination of water troughs 107
    and digestion 60
    and exercise 59, 60
    and health 52, 58, 60, 111, 112, 126
    cold, and laminitis 116
    containers and mechanisms for 48, 59, **59**
    role of, in equine nutrition 58–60, 63
    standing, as breeding ground for ectoparasites 86, 88
waxing over 124–125
weakness
    associated with equine influenza 107
    associated with foal septicemia 132
    associated with malnutrition 63
    associated with parasitism 80
    genetic, and loss of hybrid vigor 150
    joint, in dwarfism 156, **157, 158**
weaning
    age for 137, 138
    premature, and gastric ulcers 114
    records 223–224
weanling. *See* foal(s), weanling and yearling
weather
    adapatility to 1
    and foaling 122, 129
    and nutritional requirements 57, 60, 61, 63, 77, 104, 112
    providing shelter from 50, **50**, 89, 105, 112
weaving 101
weight. *See* body weight
weight tape, for estimating dosages 82–84
Welsh Pony, as height-identified breed 32
Western equine encephalomyelitis (WEE) 109
white blood cell (WBC) count 72
white coat color 178–179
    and color clarification 176
    and lethal white overo syndrome 167, 172
    phenotypically white colors 179
    See also cremello; gray; perlino; silver white
Wilson, Cheryl 13
wind-sucking 101
windbreaks 50. *See* weather
withers, as reference point for height measurement 33, 221, *222*
World Class Miniature Horse Registry 18
World Wide Miniature Horse Registry 17

Y/Z

yearling 31. *See also* foal(s), weanling and yearling
zebra markings 176, 178, 180, *201*
Zuege, Burt 12

About the Author

Barbara Naviaux holds a bachelor's degree in biology, with a minor in ethology. She is a retired clinical laboratory technician. Naviaux was the Chairperson of the American Miniature Horse Association (AMHA) Standard of Perfection Committee in 1988, during which time the currently used Standard was revised and accepted by the membership. She originated the AMHA Genetics Committee and was Chairperson from 1989 through 1992. Naviaux has written more than 100 articles pertaining to equine, feline, and canine coat color inheritance; veterinary science and animal husbandry. Her articles have been published in *AMHA Miniature Horse World, ASPC/AMHR Journal, American Miniature Horse Magazine, Miniature Show Horse Times, Contra Costa County Green Sheet* (a weekly horse column), *Shetland Sheepdog News, AKC Gazette, Cat Fanciers of America Yearbooks, Cat Fancy Magazine, die Edelkatze, Cat Tab, Cat World, Harper's Illustrated Handbook of Cats,* and *Cat Fanciers of America News.*

Naviaux, who purchased her first miniature horse mare in 1979, currently owns a small breeding herd of 25 registered American Miniature Horses in California. Specializing in pintaloosa coloration, Naviaux's miniatures are also noted for their refinement and Arabian type.